DOCUMENTS,

CONTAINING

STATISTICS OF VIRGINIA,

ORDERED TO BE PRINTED BY THE

STATE CONVENTION

SITTING IN THE

CITY OF RICHMOND,

1850–51.

RICHMOND:
WILLIAM CULLEY, PRINTER,
1851.

STATEMENT

SHOWING THE

NUMBER OF PATENTS

ISSUED ANNUALLY

FROM THE

VIRGINIA LAND OFFICE,

FROM JAN. 1, 1840, TO OCT. 31, 1850;

AND THE

AGGREGATE AMOUNT OF ACRES OF LAND

PATENTED IN EACH YEAR,

WITHIN THE SAME PERIOD.

VIRGINIA LAND OFFICE,
RICHMOND, Nov. 23, 1850.

Sir—In conformity with a resolution adopted by the Convention on the 31st ultimo, I have the honor to transmit the subjoined statement, showing the number of Patents issued annually from this office, from the 1st day of January, 1840, to the date last above mentioned; and the aggregate amount of acres of land patented in each year, within the period designated in said resolution.

I have the honor to be, sir,
With great respect and consideration,
Your obedient servant,

S. H. PARKER,
Register Va. Land Office.

STATEMENT

Showing the number of Patents issued annually from the Virginia Land Office, from January 1st, 1840, to October 31st, 1850; and the aggregate amount of acres of land patented in each year, within the same period.

Counties.	1840.	1841.	1842.	1843.	1844.	1845.	1846.	1847.	1848.	1849.	1850.
	No. acres.	No. acres.	No. acres.	No. acres.	No. acres.	No. acres.	No. acres.	No. acres.	No. acres.	No. acres.	No. acres.
ACCOMACK		880									
ALBEMARLE	969	107	1383	749½	982¼	810½	453	524	152	193½	41½
ALLEGHANY	499	304	359½	1101	355	655¾	1584½	638	6292	10498	11663¾
AMHERST	292	73	119	141¼	280	2	14¼	4½		10	150
APPOMATTOX								363	306¾	1050	
AUGUSTA	994¾	234½	647	567¾	6¾	223	2111¾	255½	19¾	881¾	709
BARBOUR					966⅓	1300	7000	4156¾	7109¾	1537	1413¼
BATH	1349	3337½	6383	7295½	4080	4381	7647	3338½	4704¼	6943½	7296
BEDFORD	37¼		29			133½	1782				
BERKELEY	149	41			¾		195	50	259	409¾	28
BOONE										2843	7113
BOTETOURT	9230	3204¼	2493½	1644¾	738⅓	1135¼	1981¾	673	566¾	999¼	240
BRAXTON		250	100	254	2672	871	670	2181	2262	7865½	8950
BROOKE	105½	52½	64	244	58	71½	11			9	
BUCKINGHAM			250		24		45	250			
CABELL	544	2837	4220½	4832	1496	4220	6735	8785½	6837½	9002	28503½
CAMPBELL			40	221¾	9¼	125	61½		217		46
CAROLINE			55¼								
CARROLL				286	150	1554½	2404½	1368½	2308¾	593¾	2241
CHESTERFIELD										1½	
CULPEPER	85						7				
DINWIDDIE						3½	½				
DODDRIDGE							1641½	2008½	2302	5301	4806¼
ELIZABETH CITY	76¾	150									
FAIRFAX		1½		9¾	259		49½	15½			
FAUQUIER						3¼	16½			2	
FAYETTE	235	814	9496	2870	363	815	2229	984	3759¼	7167½	1114½
FLOYD	1861½	4237½	1883½	4117	663	1144¾	1017	609	2214¼	70	224½
FLUVANNA	132	1461	18½	212	7¼	137½	94	18	272	84½	228½
FRANKLIN	948	415½	168	642		554	235	27	83		493
FREDERICK	174	34	2161		73	501	59	5	15½	36¼	111¼
GILES	1469	748	939½	453	1320	44	1176¾	1732	2146	2134	2481¾
GILMER							848	6639	13912½	17968½	20383½
GLOUCESTER										1665	

Counties.	1840. No. acres	1841. No. acres	1842. No. acres.	1843. No. acres.	1844. No. acres.	1845. No. acres.	1846. No. acres.	1847. No. acres	1848. No. acres.	1849. No. acres.	1850. No. acres.
GRAYSON	4991	8538	6455	3752½	7556	5126½	6113	1026	2285	1933	2959
GREENBRIER	153½	495¾	697	810½	3198	3442½	7961¾	970	4391	2456¾	4093¾
GREENE		115	195	46	45½	210		92			
HALIFAX	123	178				8	13			11	204
HAMPSHIRE	1657	2815½	3843	2743¼	1142	4094¼	1522	1634¼	2246	1352¼	1706
HANOVER			22½			78¼			5		
HARDY	5032½	1742	2843	3833¼	4522½	3249	2726	3022½	2384¾	3614¼	2582
HARRISON	140	173½	6216¾	3733	11634½	1757	2174	812½	2226	1492¾	123½
HENRICO	11	93	85½	64½	9	131¾	9½	6	53½	63¼	331¼
HENRY			899	5	119	56	53		43	14	76½
HIGHLAND									1910	821½	2164½
JACKSON	458	2174¼	6549	708	9136	1669	4065	13373½	18463½	4932½	9129
JAMES CITY	57¾		109¼								
KANAWHA	1285	831¾	934½	2260½	3701½	1461½	1242½	1076	8109	461	1516½
KING & QUEEN		2½									
LEE	1670½	2207½	1280½	2744½	2170	5374	4922½	5089	3473½	2781¾	485
LEWIS	1541	3058	20878	7023	67660	4321¼	2502	12285½	8215	3598	6910¾
LOGAN	294	1348	3300½	2578	4449½	2585	2440	8223	8228	4081¾	16171
LOUISA				285	80¾	71		46		132	
MADISON				89		17				166	354¾
MARION			925	299	529½	861½	1045¼	2571	572¾	1043¼	481
MARSHALL	17	34	20	4737	533½	155	200½	76¾	308½	493	233
MASON	1586	229	3933½	1875	2831	562	3906	6484½	3956½	7062	2251
MECKLENBURG						198					
MERCER	452	195	613	80	60	465	300	607	365	4590	1690
MIDDLESEX					1						
MONONGALIA	162½	3623¾	3870½	856½	1239¼	1208	1944	2413½	758¾	322	216
MONROE	717½	978	1638	1437	3310	1481	4024	3529½	1966	1936	2474¾
MONTGOMERY	2048	4396	2668½	640½	462	1990	945	385	1816¼	277¼	546½
MORGAN	284½	1071	515½	639	148	473	215½	33[illegible]¾		850¼	669
NANSEMOND						577	276¼				
NEW KENT	208										
NELSON			9	5½	6[illegible]¼	15¼	35				67½
NICHOLAS	1549	5223	6014	4608½	2104	781[illegible]¾	2330	2625	7198	2548	4070
NORFOLK	2664½	536½	476	½	2¾	2363¾	640	2469¼	70½	55	12¾
NORTHUMBERLAND			98								
OHIO			56	117	12½	4019		3¾			
ORANGE	831	67	354¾		101½						
PAGE	23		360				112¾	455½	523½	57	4
PATRICK	1112	2799	870	436	385	276	1519½	2831	3050	1731½	839
PENDLETON	4370	5838¼	3955	3323	1967½	8005	4957¾	4868½	5288	6814	4511

PITTSYLVANIA		50½	76¾			20½	978½				418⅓
POCAHONTAS	4407	2596¾	1235	2869	1108½	1087	680	1543½	1470	5416¾	23518⅓
POWHATAN											13⅓
PRESTON		3139	4115	975	5450¾	3187¼	3436½	3705	5768½	1431¾	216
PRINCESS ANNE	89¾	122¼	7¼						244	506	34¼
PRINCE EDWARD							114	25			
PRINCE GEORGE		8½	45								
PRINCE WILLIAM								700			9
PULASKI		196¾	388	94½	1542	207¾	540	343½	763	612½	3807⅓
PUTNAM										1514	
RANDOLPH	1659	4539	7139½	2896	7406	10458¼	2151¼	10576	5681	10403¾	32190
RAPPAHANNOCK	308¼	316		100	2¾			90¾			
RITCHIE					4185	758	3074	3891	10068½	6422	8102
ROANOKE		320	857½	741¾	223	638	977	357	1030		367½
ROCKBRIDGE	115	586¾	143¼	125½	386	1523	1297	876	48¼	21⅛	1013¼
ROCKINGHAM	1578	4038¼	3687	564½	2440¾	957¼	3336½	5632½	1101	903¾	3130¼
RUSSELL		99	188		68						
SCOTT	68	314	2571¼	611	435	408½	1982	1196	545	1343½	427
SHENANDOAH	173¾	1302¼	81½	3¾	173	439¾		150	465	335¼	860
SMYTH	243	1211	717	334	76	585¾	3030¼	2765¾	2179¾	192	5504⅔
SPOTTSYLVANIA	44 ps.							15 ps.			
SURRY						84		51⅛			
SUSSEX	12										
TAYLOR					27	50	201¼	384¾	291½	605	268
TAZEWELL	411	2394	1024	1863	3447	3511	13 9	7130	8468	5322	8791¾
TYLER	4373	4686	10302½	10502	5330	1175	3827	3754½	2780	710	1287
WARREN	7¾				200			391	21		
WASHINGTON	933½	730¾	861	5526½	399	1076	298	122¼	156¾	1140¼	282
WAYNE				3727½	773	6938	15562½	8155	5826	9598	16582
WETZEL									2507	12836	7265
WOOD	4173	4957	12473	2416	10528	5006	2694	4372½	4019	200	6336
WYTHE	3244	393	8241	3752¾	1550	2877¼	1625½	2363½	3425	665¾	336¼
WIRT											1082
TOTAL	75036	96081¾	165653¼	112543½	187409¾	118534	145450	171371	204205⅛	193147⅛	290017⅛
No. of Patents	493	835	1190	757	972	738	988	1184	1188	1156	1350

Total No. of Patents issued from Jan 1, 1840, to Oct 31, 1850 ....10921.

S. H. PARKER, *Reg. Va. Land Office.*

STATEMENT

OF THE

NUMBER OF PERSONS PAYING TAXES

ON

LAND, SLAVES,

AND

OTHER PROPERTY.

FIRST AUDITOR'S OFFICE, Nov. 28th, 1850.

SIR:

I have handed to the Secretary of the Convention, as I was requested, by resolution of that body, passed on the 4th day of November last, to do, my reports to it as to the results of the recent assessment of land in the commonwealth, of the number of persons shown by the commissioners books of 1850, assessed with taxes on certain subjects of taxation, as to the salaries, &c., of Judges, &c., and as to the amount paid out of the treasury since the year 1800, for convict slaves. I have on hand other unfinished reports in answer to calls of the convention, which will be soon finished.

I am with great respect
your obedient serv't,

ROBERT JOHNSTON,
First Auditor.

To the Hon. John Y. Mason, President of the State Convention.

A STATEMENT showing the number of persons in each county, town and city, having a seperate commissioner of the Revenue in the Commonwealth, assessed with tax on slaves, and the number assessed with tax on other property for the year 1850, *collected from the commissioners' books, in compliance with a resolution of the Convention, passed the* 21*st of October*, 1850.

TRANS ALLEGHANY DISTRICT.

	Number of persons assessed with tax on land.	Number of persons assessed with tax on slaves.	Number of persons assessed with tax on other property.
Barbour,	1,301	37	1,346
Braxton,	658	26	650
Boone,	289	29	432
Brooke,	508	18	819
Cabell,	1,196	34	907
Carroll,	743	6	701
Doddridge,	373	10	410
Fayette,	590	36	546
Floyd,	816	83	805
Grayson,	772	112	836
Greenbrier,	1,415	277	1,498
Giles,	776	127	834
Gilmer,	590	14	487
Hancock,	435	2	697
Harrison,	1,294	133	1,649
Jackson,	935	19	460
Kanawha,	1,312	480	1,564
Lee,	1,090	149	1,357
Lewis,	1,222	73	1,425
Logan,	613	24	532
Marion,	1,209	29	1,532
Marshall,	1,168	21	1,515
Mason,	757	108	1,025
Mercer,	589	44	626
Monongalia,	1,695	59	1,806
Monroe,	1,028	189	1,491
Montgomery	705	111	901
Nicholas,	894	19	564
Ohio,	470	27	945
Preston,	1,309	28	1,543
Pocahontas,	634	69	584
Pulaski,	359	137	503
Putnam,	456	104	708

		Number of persons assessed with tax on land.	Number of persons assessed with tax on slaves.	Number of persons assessed with tax on other property.
TRANS-ATLANTIC DISTRICT.	Raleigh, - - -	191	10	302
	Randolph, - - -	1,000	58	726
	Ritchie, - - -	587	6	535
	Russell, - - -	640	149	1,505
	Scott, - - -	1,201	97	1,292
	Smyth, - - -	878	172	540
	Taylor, - - -	619	44	793
	Tazewell, - - -	1,035	183	1,249
	Tyler, - - -	704	14	823
	Washington, - - -	1,438	362	1,903
	Wayne, - - -	1,180	44	672
	Wetzel, - - -	518	5	605
	Wirt, - - -	424	13	459
	Wood, - - -	930	101	1,342
	Wyoming, - - -	144	5	222
	Wythe, - - -	1,254	246	1,279
	Wheeling, - - -	930	26	1,336
		41,874	4,169	47,281
VALLEY DISTRICT.	Alleghany, - - -	496	104	441
	Augusta, - - -	2,339	742	2,649
	Bath, - - -	486	115	430
	Berkeley, - - -	1,314	443	1,348
	Botetourt, - - -	1,234	512	1,576
	Clarke, - - -	537	188	580
	Frederick, - - -	1,596	362	1,617
	Hampshire, - - -	1,796	244	1,869
	Hardy, - - -	1,358	148	1,151
	Highland, - - -	656	93	661
	Jefferson, - - -	827	675	1,671
	Morgan, - - -	505	31	555
	Page, - - -	717	215	975
	Pendleton, - - -	857	62	876
	Roanoke, - - -	679	271	817
	Rockbridge, - - -	1,310	611	1,668
	Rockingham, - - -	2,306	404	2,577
	Shenandoah, - - -	1,710	204	2,036
	Warren, - - -	414	269	615
	Staunton, - - -	220	125	148
	Winchester, - - -	418	175	522
		22,775	5,993	24,782

PIEDMONT DISTRICT.	Number of persons assessed with tax on land.	Number of persons assessed with tax on slaves.	Number of persons assessed with tax on other property.
Albemarle, - - -	1,903	1,202	1,871
Amelia, - - -	628	466	513
Amherst, - - -	1,011	583	1,027
Appomattox, - - -	782	447	678
Bedford, - - -	1,770	954	3,131
Brunswick, - - -	895	636	833
Buckingham, - -	1,239	723	963
Campbell, - - -	1,220	795	1,271
Charlotte, - - -	845	450	619
Culpeper, - - -	968	149	427
Cumberland, - - -	596	480	546
Dinwiddie, - - -	1,158	573	760
Fauquier, - - -	1,271	1,128	1,769
Franklin, - - -	1,702	692	1,893
Fluvanna, - - -	804	482	733
Greene, - - -	449	204	450
Goochland, - - -	927	508	757
Halifax, - - -	1,968	1,168	1,820
Henry, - - -	614	272	798
Loudoun, - - -	1,851	1,007	2,529
Louisa, - - -	1,305	806	1,080
Lunenburg, - - -	794	605	749
Madison, - - -	687	447	726
Mecklenburg, - -	1,144	944	1,234
Nelson, - - -	802	517	973
Nottoway, - - -	517	405	468
Orange, - - -	767	497	732
Patrick, - - -	917	256	971
Pittsylvania, - - -	1,903	1,214	2,199
Prince Edward, - -	732	651	787
Powhatan, - -	653	421	493
Rappahannock, - -	899	454	853
Lynchburg, - - -	474	377	539
	34,195	20,513	35,197

TIDE-WATER DISTRICT.

	Number of persons assessed with tax on land.	Number of persons assessed with tax on slaves.	Number of persons assessed with tax no other property.
Alexandria, - - -	1,521	359	998
Accomack, - - -	1,618	782	1,551
Charles City, - -	436	96	334
Caroline, - - -	1,228	742	1,048
Chesterfield, - - -	1,681	906	1,258
Essex, - - - -	592	410	542
Elizabeth City, - -	307	264	296
Fairfax, - - -	1,121	497	1,031
Greenesville, - - -	492	260	323
Gloucester, - - -	735	468	595
Hanover, - - -	1,582	782	1,092
Henrico, - - -	2,466	905	1,347
Isle of Wight, - -	1,068	451	740
James City, - - -	371	152	316
King George, - - -	337	243	400
King William, - -	608	394	492
King and Queen, - -	797	532	682
Lancaster, - - -	458	290	366
Matthews, - - -	611	368	357
Middlesex, - - -	378	252	295
Nansemond, - - -	1,103	567	922
New Kent, - - -	617	316	404
Norfolk County, - -	1,286	631	1,036
Northumberland, - -	521	252	465
Northampton, - -	561	438	573
Princess Anne, - -	644	490	827
Prince George, - -	775	374	509
Prince William, - -	936	392	845
Richmond, - - -	949	243	390
Stafford, - - -	654	354	687
Southampton, - -	1,082	508	926
Spottsylvania, - -	917	566	788
Surry, - - - -	637	234	411
Sussex, - - -	847	487	625
Warwick, - - -	165	98	109
Westmoreland, - -	555	298	456
York, - - - -	392	207	310
Norfolk City, - - -	949	903	1,064
Richmond City, - -	2,060	1,699	2,041
Petersdurg, - -	1,088	762	925
Williamsburg, - -	125	109	115
Fredericksburg, - -	350	254	366
	35,620	19,425	28,857

RECAPITULATION.

Trans-Alleghany District,	41,874	4,169	47,381
Valley District, - -	21,775	5,993	24,782
Piedmont District, - -	34,195	20,513	35,197
Tide-Water District, -	35,620	19,425	28,857
Totals for the whole State,	133,464	50,100	136,117

The resolution under which this report is made, requests me "to report the number of persons paying tax on land, the number of persons paying on slaves, and the number of persons paying on all other property, so far as the same appears on the Commissioners' books of 1850. The Commissioners' books show the number of persons, of these several classes, assessed with tax in 1850, but as the revenue is not yet paid in and the delinquent and insolvent lists have not yet been returned to this office, and are not required to be so returned before the 1st day of May next, I have given the number of persons assessed with taxes.—In the table presented, persons charged with tax are counted as often as their names occur in different Commissioners' districts, but their names are counted but once in the same district as being assessed with lands, if they are so assessed, and once as assessed with slaves, if they are so assessed, and once as assessed with other property if they are so assessed.

Respectfully submitted,

RO. JOHNSTON,
First Auditor.

Auditor's Office,
November 28th, 1850.

STATEMENT

SHOWING THE

VALUE OF THE LANDS AND LOTS

IN THE SEVERAL

COUNTIES AND DISTRICTS OF VIRGINIA,

UNDER THE

ASSESSMENT OF 1850.

A STATEMENT, *shewing the value of the lands and lots in the several counties and districts of Virginia, under the assessment of* 1850,—*also, the amount that would be payable at the rate of taxation now prescribed by law, prepared in compliance with a resolution of the State Convention, adopted on the* 17*th Oct.*, 1850.

COUNTIES *In the First District.*	No. of acres of land.	Sum added to the land on account of buildings.	Total value of land and buildings.	Value of buildings on lots.	Value of lots including buildings.	Aggregate value of land and lots.	Average value of land, per acre.	Amo't that would be payable at the present rates of taxation.
Alexandria	17,603	68,350 00	593,496 50	1,228,200 00	2,349,531 00	2,943,027 50	33 71	4,337 13
Accomack	235,781	271,340 00	2,730,327 29	21,950 00	36,225 00	2,766,552 29	11 57	2,801 36
Charles City	111,142	169,688 45	861,579 59			861,579 59	7 75	861 57
Caroline	325,482	431,675 00	2,487,154 62	27,275 00	34,550 00	2,521,704 62	7 64	2,563 98
Chesterfield	295,156	1,101,007 62	3,221,536 50	147,310 00	183,808 00	3,405,344 50	10 91	3,561 26
Essex	162,784	246,455 00	1,557,947 85	29,680 00	39,590 00	1,597,537 85	9 57	1,614 74
Elizabeth City	34,878	121,955 00	538,718 20	116,270 00	155,798 00	694 516 20	15 44	798 16
Fairfax	261,006	517,127 62	2,901,301 47	36,105 00	44,623 00	2,945,924 47	11 11	3,006 77
Greensville	184,095	117,430 20	520,146 86	22,250 00	28,840 00	548,986 86	2 82	564 36
Gloucester	135,081	358,781 17	1,296,595 35	350 00	837 50	1,297,432 85	9 59	1,301 10
Hanover	289,572	482,329 88	2,331,394 89		2,280 00	2,333,674 89	8 05	2,333 30
Henrico	165,202	1,297,621 29	4,247,398 72			4,247,398 72	25 71	4,247 39
Isle of Wight	187,314	382,893 00	1,122,321 34	69,800 00	87,250 00	1,209,571 34	5 99	1,256 45
James City	91,683	109,690 00	568,557 79			568,557 79	6 20	568 55
King George	112,967	197,120 00	1,086,593 86	6,525 00	7,250 00	1,093,843 86	9 61	1,092 59
King and Queen	189,958	312,420 00	1,337,468 87			1,337,468 87	7 04	1,337 46
King William	168,649	157,125 00	1,366,702 00			1,366,702 00	8 10	1,366 70
Lancaster	81,676	164,978 00	792,171 79			792,171 79	9 69	792 17
Mathews	54,222	178 791 00	634,471 90			634,471 90	11 70	634 47
Middlesex	81,892	104,756 15	699,082 50	4,855 00	5,800 00	704,882 50	8 53	715 96
Nansemond	252,248	343,627 75	1,292,956 01	132,700 00	171,375 00	1,464,331 01	5 12	1,554 31

Norfolk county	208,782	418,455 00	1,698,655 89	21,850 00	33,950 00	1,732,605 89	8 13	1,740 15
New Kent	130,302	185,222 00	708,110 27			708,110 27	5 43	708 11
Northumberland	118,489	192,334 00	944,880 08	15,500 00	21,200 00	966,080 08	7 97	978 53
Northampton	105,106	218,989 98	1,280,557 09			1,280,557 09	11 23	1,280 55
Princess Anne	157,403	327,544 00	1,210.129 65	13,110 00	16,247 00	1,226,376 65	7 68	1,232 17
Prince George	180,100	252,877 45	1,351,200 59	310 00	915 00	1,352,115 59	7 50	1,485 04
Prince William	219,805	164.365 00	1,607,395 01	67,565 00	95,841 00	1,703,236 01	7 31	1,759 03
Richmond	119,782	189,753 20	811,286 61			811,286 61	6 77	811 28
Southampton	365,498	327.607 00	1,081,935 73	11,725 00	14,240 00	1,096,175 73	2 96	1,115 75
Spotsylvania	256,223	528,782 58	1,864,395 17			1,864,395 17	7 27	1,864 39
Surry	159,262	192,424 31	725,085 92	1,075 00	1,357 50	726,443 42	4 55	727 01
Sussex	295,330	243,004 00	905,978 50			905,978 50	3 06	905 97
Stafford	167,413	224,239 25	1,189,923 41	52,700 00	85,740 64	1,275,664 05	7 10	1,338 90
Warwick	42,947	37.840 00	309,263 64			309,263 64	7 20	309 26
Westmoreland	143,816	183,426 50	1,109,867 24	1,125 00	1,715 00	1,111.582 24	7 71	1,116 20
York	70,067	99,845 20	627,693 35	15,015 00	16,523 83	644,217 18	8 95	666 73
Fredericksburg				826,780 00	1,107,150 00	1,107,150 00		1,570 53
Norfolk				2,811,315 00	4,587,325 00	4,587,325 00		8,148 38
Petersburg				2,449,900 00	3,767,128 00	3,767.128 00		5,846 59
Portsmouth				935,450 00	1,534,560 00	1,534,560 00		2,480 08
Richmond				6,953,133 00	13,735.307 00	13,735,307 00		17,645 83
Williamsburg				145,225 00	183,335 00	183,335 00		330 04
	6.178,716	$10,921,871 60	$49,614,282 05	$16,165,048 00	$28,350,292 47	$77,964,574 52	$8 02	$91,370 30

COUNTIES *In the Second District.*	No. of acres of land.	Sum added to the land on account of buildings.	Total value of land and buildings.	Value of buildings on lots.	Value of lots including buildings.	Aggregate value of land and lots.	Average value of land, per acre.	Amo't that would be payable at present rates of taxation.
Appomattox	204 917	219,980 00	1.075.066 05	13.540 00	16.605 00	1.091,671 05	5 24	1,110 26
Albemarle	467,391	838 732 34	4,893,402 70	295,850 00	390,098 10	5 283,500 80	10 46	5,651 48
Amelia	221,215	248.775 50	1.340.550 76			1 340.550 76	6 05	1,340 55
Amherst	291,765	271,754 21	1.889,671 66	10,945 00	29,790 00	1.919,461 66	6 47	1,932 88
Bedford	482.429	442,955 00	2,927,440 06	55,950 00	78 073 00	3,005.513 06	6 06	3,044 09
Brunswick	349.328	322,585 00	1,106.149 51	20,850 00	26,500 00	1.132,649 51	3 16	1,141 15
Buckingham	363.120	331,180 00	2,053,974 12	42.985 00	49,625 00	2.103,599 12	5 65	2,153 78
Campbell	327.528	576,047 00	2,574,258 62	31,950 00	40,300 02	2.614,558 64	7 85	2,633 75
Charlotte	298,662	427,355 00	2,658,838 54			2.658,838 54	8 90	2,658 83
Culpeper	229.809	229,665 00	2.411,059 08	56,180 00	99.110 00	2.510.169 08	10 49	2,573 34
Cumberland	188.707	381,494 00	1,524,104 96	11,870 00	14,236 00	1,538,340 96	8 07	1,563 77
Dinwiddie	322,587	310.451 00	1,227,515 74			1,227,515 74	3 80	1,227 51
Fluvanna	181.545	285.533 00	1,392,820 10	23.635 00	31,316 00	1.424.136 10	7 67	1,464 25
Fauquier	405.939	820.168 00	5.967.927 00	238.475 00	307,825 00	6 275.752 00	14 70	6,509 80
Franklin	429.264	305 704 50	1,789.669 42	14,525 00	18,166 00	1.807.835 42	4 16	1,823 25
Goochland	177.332	353 348 07	2,218.768 71			2.218 768 71	12 51	2,218 76
Greene	102 759	76,720 00	684.022 35	15,800 00	23 985 00	708.007 35	6 65	722 35
Halifax	508,801	659,121 00	3,792.214 15	13,652 00	16.122 20	3,808 336 35	7 45	3,828 14
Henry	220.198	81.650 00	936 281 00	13.520 00	21,331 00	957.612 00	4 25	957 88
Loudoun	321.537	1,127,181 00	8,843.442 69	268,142 00	313,404 00	9,156 846 69	27 50	9.582 86
Louisa	318.793	422.969 31	2.627,115 39			2.627.115 39	8 24	2,627 11
Lunenburg	267.704	197.035 00	1 029.429 58	3,550 00	6.595 00	1.036.024 58	3 84	1,043 11
Madison	224.560	243.667 00	1 784 636 63	36.050 00	44.400 00	1.829,036 63	7 94	1.846 94
Mecklenburg	410,057	470.121 00	2.522.344 25	151,535 00	203.052 84	2,725.397 09	6 15	2,874 57
Nelson	303,912	360.305 00	2.034,222 09	37,920 00	43,075 00	2 077.297 09	6 69	2,119 47
Nottoway	197,518	296 597 00	1,109.291 53			1,109.291 53	5 61	1,109 29
Orange	214,029	339,480 20	2.004.703 65	43,800 00	53.080 00	2,057,783 65	9 36	2,093 72
Patrick	758.727	79 913 00	736.456 84	9.200 00	14.985 00	751,441 84	97	756 14
Pittsylvania	622 063	413 318 00	2,878,608 42	12 825 00	17.578 50	2,896,186 92	4 62	2.909 85
Powhatan	147.886	343.595 00	1,497.825 48	17,115 00	20.114 00	1,517,939 48	10 12	1.542 66
Prince Edward	218,850	374 937 00	1,841.103 42	158,447 00	230.017 75	2,071.121 17	8 41	2.299 05
Rappahannock	166,430	276,375 00	1,913,201 08	47,779 00	53 585 00	1,966 786 08	11 49	2,022 60
Danville				117.500 00	317.530 00	317.530 00		335 99
Lynchburg				978.745 00	2,019 862 00	2 019.862 00		3,299 25
	9,945,362	$12,128,712 06	$73,286,115 58	$2,742,335 00	$4,500,361 41	$77,786,476 99	$7 36	$81,018 43

COUNTIES *In the Third District.*	No. of acres of land.	Sum added to the land on account of buildings.	Total value of land and buildings.	Value of buildings on lots.	Value of lots including buildings.	Aggregate value of land and lots.	Average value of land, per acre.	Amo't that would be payable at present rates of taxation.
Alleghany	340,057	139,674 00	592 906 16	30,626 00	31.350 50	624.256 66	1 74	632 98
Augusta	602.538	1,251,587 13	8.178.948 96	97,740 00	129 902 00	8,308,850 96	13 57	8,349 72
Bath	445.788	159,585 04	765.993 64		2.050 00	768 043 64	1 71	768 02
Berkeley	195 991	511.005 00	4.047,348 50	225,000 00	360 670 00	4.408.018 50	20 65	4,638 03
Botetourt	427,875	367.266 00	2.214,188 21	74,078 00	204,106 00	2,418.294 21	5 17	2,546 83
Clarke	113 811	401.825 00	3,362.876 10	37.375 00	57,425 00	3.420,301 10	29 54	3,447 35
Frederick	270,928	637.408 75	2,082,445 37	48,075 00	65,840 00	2,148.285 37	7 68	2.091 07
Hardy	683,635	209.287 85	2,586,718 57	48,410 00	67,505 00	2,654 223 57	3 78	2,684 11
Hampshire	610,167	391.320 09	2,838 018 17	98,275 00	125,760 00	2,963,778 17	4 65	2,986 47
Highland	210.622	125,244 00	1 263.101 85	7,270 00	8,570 00	1,271,671 85	5 99	1,274 71
Jefferson	126,808	863.780 00	5,577,854 00	426 245 00	557,193 00	6,135,047 00	43 98	6,624 35
Morgan	145.783	125,925 25	615.409 77	56,030 00	71,850 00	687,259 77	4 22	720 72
Page	193.959	284,643 66	1,647,113 63	44.720 00	54,450 00	1,701,563 63	8 49	1,721 46
Pendleton	461,001	129,437 00	968.242 05	18.870 00	23,880 00	992.122 05	2 10	1.006 70
Roanoke	209,811	319,430 00	1,691.571 44	59,740 00	80,289 00	1,771.860 44	8 06	1,824 79
Rockingham	603.036	977,694 00	6,600.253 90	179,675 00	252,490 00	6,852.743 90	10 94	6,890 28
Rockbridge	445,653	472.320 00	3.135,167 00	238.351 00	332.010 00	3.467,177 00	7 03	3.525 52
Shenandoah	318,950	464.072 58	3,419.037 03	144.947 00	219,785 76	3,638,822 79	10 71	3,737 84
Warren	120,955	208,215 00	1,538,462 68	46.100 00	55,755 00	1,594,217 68	12 71	1,642 81
Staunton				278.330 00	481,881 00	481.881 00		601 48
Winchester				721,300 00	1,107,827 00	1,107,827 00		1,630 81
	6,527,368	$8,039,750 26	$53,125,657 03	$2,881,157 00	$4,290,589 26	$57,416,246 29	$8 13	$59,346 05

COUNTIES *In the Fourth District.*	No. of acres of land.	Sum added to the land on account of buildings.	Total value of land and buildings.	Value of buildings on lots.	Value of lots including buildings.	Aggregate value of land and lots.	Average value of land, per acre.	Amo't that would be payable at present rates of taxation.
Barbour	285,333	98,320 00	1,193,718 57	13,415 09	22,470 00	1,216,182 57	4 18	1,212 20
Boone	323,734	24,010 00	228,233 73			228,233 73	70	228 23
Braxton	958,652	23,173 67	482.975 22	8,375 00	12,672 00	495,647 22	50	501 85
Brooke	56,615	157,825 00	1,283.004 86	149,425 00	231,500 00	1,614,504 86	22 66	1,663 58
Cabell	443.485	125.948 98	1,118,156 63	42,475 00	64,510 00	1,182,666 63	2 52	1,181 61
Carroll	369.086	78,016 00	440,812 05	15,690 00	19,550 00	460,362 05	1 19	471 75
Doddridge	340,214	27,895 00	494,274 98	13,025 00	19,930 00	514,204 98	1 45	526 04
Fayette	530,918	59,235 00	467.592 10			467,592 10	88	467 59
Floyd	280,686	72,670 00	623.706 00	24,900 00	35,245 00	658 951 00	2 22	658 86
Giles	308.903	94.627 00	936,085 50	33,055 00	40,795 00	976,880 50	3 03	977 03
Gilmer	989,424	36,161 00	924,425 04	13,890 00	16.902 00	941.327 04	93	944 08
Grayson	463.621	89,320 00	564,828 57	3,725 00	5.700 00	570,528 57	1 21	582 15
Greenbrier	766,206	448.188 00	2,649,730 22	111,772 00	157,904 00	2,807,634 22	3 45	2,869 30
Hancock	52.455	75,339 00	753,588 53	12,825 00	21.685 00	775,273 53	14 36	788 34
Harrison	368.059	265,021 00	2,681,411 86	163 195 00	232,933 00	2.914,344 86	7 28	2,943 22
Jackson	737,905	70,945 00	1.294,628 62	24,220 00	31,385 00	1,326,013 62	1 75	1,350 85
Kanawha	1,303 696	452,780 66	2,603,082 64	148,150 00	254.620 00	2,857,702 64	1 99	2,943 49
Lee	436,570	116,419 00	1,062,051 12	12,449 00	16,910 00	1,078 961 12	2 43	1,089 20
Lewis	1,009,318	161.711 50	1,890,681 42	50,470 00	82,130 00	1,972.811 42	1 87	1,969 87
Logan	961,587	30.990 00	322,853 04	3,380 00	4,955 00	327,808 04	33	328 70
Marion	229.297	185,391 85	1,920.048 76	92,210 00	130,423 00	2,050,471 76	8 37	2.067 92
Marshall	225.289	143,400 00	1,962,872 47	72,411 00	134,625 00	2.097,497 47	8 71	2,109 98
Mason	317,338	118,881 00	1,733,761 27	49,250 00	92,125 00	1,825,886 27	5 46	1.845 71
Monroe	409,759	294.800 00	2,153.252 92	53.040 00	66,154 00	2,219,406 92	5 25	2,253 23
Mercer	380 687	15,655 00	406,932 96	5,780 00	8,070 00	415,002 96	1 06	422 72
Monongalia	277,789	231,138 50	2,194,692 17	124,100 00	196,320 00	2,391,012 17	7 90	2,380 89
Montgomery	230,315	196,525 00	1,347,128 01	76,550 00	103.065 00	1,450,193 01	5 84	1,461 08
Nicholas	1,314,587	59,673 00	785,584 06	5.740 00	7,082 75	792.666 81	59	799 57
Ohio	65,000	221,285 00	1,354.154 00	1,249,830 00	2,680,360 00	4,034,514 00	20 83	6,918 95
Pocahontas	722,914	92,517 76	947,075 11	7,980 00	10,160 00	957,235 11	1 31	962 44
Preston	486,013	158.010 00	1,149,901 74	14.940 00	18,898 00	1,168,799 74	2 36	1,210 69
Pulaski	180,916	113.908 00	898.089 84	22,825 00	29,400 00	927,489 84	4 96	933 87
Putnam	151,016	69.450 00	690.069 40	18,265 00	25.123 00	715.192 40	4 56	718 98
Randolph	2,114,372	27,460 00	1,099.021 49	14.795 00	23,620 00	1,122,641 49	51	1,147 92
Ritchie	597,178	87,044 00	812,440 05	11,525 00	14,465 00	826,905 05	1 36	830 77

Russell	568,966	77,690 00	952,228 98	13,795 00	21,640 00	973,868 78	1 67	979 46
Raleigh	480.507	26 817 00	238,054 32	1,020 00	2,450 00	240,504 32	49	241 68
Scott	1,054,958	117,708 00	717,293 75	14,225 00	16,710 00	734,003 75	68	739 21
Smyth	307,637	184,365 00	1,528,298 49	29,875 00	40,765 00	1,569,063 49	4 96	1,579 73
Tazewell	2,769,974	84.025 00	1,251,153 77	22,465 00	29,145 00	1,280,298 77	45	1,287 05
Tyler	337,947	86,361 00	853 653 26	41,450 00	60,187 00	913,840 26	2 52	931 27
Taylor	148,170	62,625 00	1,068,040 71	34,030 00	46,059 00	1,114,099 71	7 20	1,222 75
Washington	377,452	341,654 00	2,418,856 86	156,100 00	248,035 00	2,666,891 86	6 40	2,720 75
Wayne	183,250	41,325 00	609.082 01	2,385 00	3,555 00	612,637 01	3 32	612 18
Wirt	299,632	39,087 00	500,399 97	7,807 00	11,945 00	512,344 97	1 67	529 19
Wood	348,970	131,550 00	1,441,651 66	190,713 00	290,446 66	1,732,098 32	4 13	1,895 79
Wyoming	164,628	6,770 00	127,397 00			127,397 00	77	127 39
Wythe	699,249	373,861 00	1,984,652 31	120,015 00	170,345 00	2,254,997 31	2 83	2,185 70
Wetzel	214,962	36,556 62	578,372 32	12,175 00	19,965 00	598,337 32	2 69	609 88
	26,644,341	$6,134,129 54	$55,739,994 16	$3,308,734 00	$5.772.934 41	$61,512,928 57	$2 09	$65,324 69

Total amount of property in 1st district,	$77,964,574 52	Average value of land, per acre,	$8 02	Amount that would be payable at present rate of taxation, $91,370 30
Do. 2d do.	77,786,476 99	Do.	7 36	Do. 81,018 43
Do. 3d do.	57,416,246 29	Do.	8 13	Do. 59,346 05
Do. 4th do.	61,512,928 57	Do.	2 09	Do. 65,324 69
	$274,680,226 37			$297,059 47

Total amount of property in 1st district—under assessment of 1838,	$60,704,053 20½	Average per acre, 1st district,	$6 73½
Do. do. 2d district,	69,016,705 97½	Do. 2d do.	6 81½
Do. do. 3d district,	42,992,204 29½	Do. 3d do.	6 44
Do. do. 4th district,	39,217,544 61	Do. 4th do.	1 40
	$211,930,508 08½		

Total amount of property in 1st district—under assessment of 1819,	$71,496,997 00	Average per acre, 1st district,	$8 43
Do. do. 2d district,	78,165,919 00	Do. 2d do.	8 20
Do. do. 3d district,	41.173,512 00	Do. 3d do.	7 33
Do. do. 4th district,	16,057,550 00	Do. 4th do.	92
	$206,893,978 00		

AUDITOR'S OFFICE, Nov. 30th, 1850.

In making up the table I have corrected the additions of the several columns of value and amount found in the assessors' books, but have not attempted to correct the entry of each tract, as it is impossible to tell whether the errors apparent in such entries are in "the number of acres," "the price per acre," "the sum added on account of buildings," or in the extension of the "total value of land and buildings" the books sent to this office being generally copies.

In ascertaining the amount that would be payable by each county, city and town, at the rate of taxation now prescribed by law, I have obtained the tax on lots and buildings in cities and towns from the Commissioners' books of 1850, as that tax is generally laid on the rents, and not on the value. The assessment did not embrace rents, but they are, under the present system, ascertained each year by the Commissioners of the revenue. No amount is here taken of the increase of tax on "lots in cities and towns which are unimproved, or which, though improved, are not occupied by the proprietor nor rented or leased out:" Such lots are taxed as lands, but it was found to be very difficult to separate them, on the Commissioners' books and the books of assessment, from the lots, &c. paying tax on rents. I will, if it is desirable, hereafter ascertain the amount of tax, which will be payable, at the present rate of taxation, under the late assessments, on these lots

Tax on lots in 1850, - - -	$65,295 80
Tax on lands in 1850, - - -	194,725 54
Total in 1850. - - -	$260,021 34

One of the assessors of Lewis county says, in a note to his book, that "some ten or more valuable lots, on a few of which are the most valuable buildings in the town, are not here set down, nor have they been assessed, as they do not appear on the Commissioners' books." He speaks, I suppose, of the town of Weston. I have written to him for an assessment of the omitted property, and will communicate it to the Convention, if it is received.

RO. JOHNSTON,
First Auditor.

STATEMENT

SHOWING THE

AMOUNT PAID OUT OF THE TREASURY

IN EACH YEAR,

FOR

CONVICT SLAVES,

FROM 1800 TO 1850, INCLUSIVE;

DISTINGUISHING BETWEEN THE AMOUNTS PAID

IN

EACH GRAND DIVISION

OF

THE STATE.

STATEMENT

Showing the amount paid out of the Treasury in each year for Convict Slaves, from the year 1800, inclusive, to the 1st day of October, 1850—distinguishing between the amounts paid in each grand division of the State—made in compliance with a resolution of the Convention, passed on the 29th day of October, 1850.

Year.	1st division.	2d division.	3d division.	4th division.	Total.
1800	9285	300			9585
1801	6083 98	566 67			6650 65
1802	8982 63	4936 67			13919 30
1803	3116 65	933 33	333 33	300	4683 31
1804	2151 08	766 67	400	600	3917 75
1805	2000 00	2093 33	650		4743 33
1806	2966 66	633 33	950		4549 99
1807	2099 67	1316 67			3416 34
1808	4462 34	2937 74		350	7750 08
1809	2883 33	766 67	266 67		3916 67
1810	2599 99	800		300	3699 99
1811	5283 33	2400		675	8358 33
1812	2333 33	3200			5533 33
1813	7740 33	1800	600		1140 33
1814	2150	3833 33	850		6833 33
1815	4100	2250	1450		7800
1816	7350	4800	425	700	13275
1817	1730	1500	850	650	4730
1818	6750	4600	1100		12450
1819	5900	6250	3275	550	15975
1820	6110	4600	700	500	11910
1821	4925	3720		675	9320
1822	2500	3500	400	300	6700
1823	5550	2500		60	8110
1824	4080	3125	1150	900	9255
1825	4125	2425		1385	7935
1826	2850	6475		1200	10525
1827	5025	8615		250	13890
1828	3835	4100		400	8335
1829	6205	2725	925	400	10255
1830	6150	2725			8875
1831	15175	3650	400		19225
1832	11700	2820		800	15320
1833	6997	5400	450		12847
1834	6915	4155		1325	12395
1835	4075	1150			5225
1836	5100	5195			10295
1837	8700	8990			17690
1838	3250	5830	1370	600	11050
1839	12200	3350	2350	800	18700
1840	6224 16	6300	1500		14024 16
1841	6921 33	3950	1445		12316 33
1842	3713 33	2580	1234 28	400	7927 61
1843	1703 57	4320			6023 57
1844	1948 88	4770			6718 88
1845	6320	3180 70	450	575	10525 70
1846	2034 58	1095	1350		4479 58
1847	3155	4755		500	8410
1848	6725 47	1680	350	3050	11805 47
1849	4514 51	2080	425		7019 51
1850	4230	2650			6880
	$262926 15	$169095 11	$25649 28	$18245	$475915 54

This table shews the amount paid out of the Treasury for Convict Slaves between the periods mentioned in the caption, exclusive of the cost of the conveyance, &c., of said convicts, and without making any deduction for the amount paid into the Treasury of the proceeds of sales of transported slaves.

Respectfully, &c.

RO: JOHNSTON, First Auditor.

First Auditor's Office, Dec. 8th, 1850.

A STATEMENT

EXHIBITING THE

EXPENDITURES OF THE COMMONWEALTH,

DIVIDED AND ASSIGNED,

AS FAR AS PRACTICABLE,

AMONG THE COUNTIES, CITIES & TOWNS:

SHOWING ALSO,

AS FAR AS CAN BE ASCERTAINED,

THE AMOUNT EXPENDED

FOR

EACH GRAND DIVISION

OF

THE STATE.

A STATEMENT

Exhibiting the Expenditures of the Commonwealth, by warrants from this Office, for the year ending the 30th of September, 1850; divided and assigned, as far as practicable, among the Counties, Cities and Towns for which they were made—shewing also, as well as can be ascertained, the amount expended for each Grand Division of the State—prepared in compliance with a resolution of the Convention, passed October the 17th, 1850.

TRANS-ALLEGHANY DISTRICT.

	Expended for Delegates to General Assembly.	For re-assessment of lands.	For slaves executed and transported.	For guards to jails.	Lunatics' support in jails & conveyance to asylums.	Penitent'y criminal charges; carrying convicts to pen'y.	For commissioners of the revenue.	Crim'l charges—support of persons in jails, &c. &c.	Expenses of representation; comparison of election polls	For transportation of arms.	For pensions.	Contingent expenses of courts; services of attorneys, clerks, &c.	For militia; pay of adjutants, clerks, musicians, &c	From conting't fund; for expenses of quarantine, &c.	General appropriation; over charges in tax &c.	Aggregate for the district.
BARBOUR . . .	with Randolph				$78 66	$	$166 75	$421 66	$23 37			$134 63	$282 25			
BRAXTON . . .	$558					144	179 08	206 83	20 66			194	114			
BOONE	with Logan						153 50	76 72	11 10			220				
BROOKE	592				242 43		163 59	43 20	18 87	21 32		255	65			
CABELL	589 60					195 80	320 10	269 05	24 29			255	107 50			
CARROLL . . .	with Grayson					119 17	179	90 14				302	121			
DODDRIDGE . .	with Tyler &c.				85 90	227 79	164 42	112 81				180	5			
FAYETTE . . .	554 80				190 58		7	69 85				155	134			
FLOYD	524					138 57	313 77	195 33				160	124			
GRAYSON . . .	552					132 40	173 58	294 36				137	44			
GREENBRIER .	512 40				434 72		347 67	181 69	3 77			2194 61	228			
GILES	476				56 25		350 90	136 46				210	171			
GILMER	with Braxton, &c.						146 99	260 66	10 21			157	92			
HANCOCK . . .	with Brooke						134 31		18 59			175	61			
HARRISON . .	538				493 15		243 10	530 29		5 34		192 49	309			
JACKSON . . .	with Mason			402	122 19		163 94	1094 30	5 07			129	112			
KANAWHA . .	526						457 45	332 88				295 25	80			
LEE	602			24	92 57		223 47	327 22	13 29			90	203			
LEWIS	with Braxton, &c.				63 86	355 20	321 86	385 88	20 66			259	275			
LOGAN	533 60					425 20	19 50	362 93	11 78			198 75	103			
MARION . . .	464						124 17	100 33	6 42			198 50	353 75			
MARSHALL . .	580				164 20		169 39	115 86	19 70			155	28			
MASON	592 80				233 32		165	205 16	6 86			130	119			

	Expended for Delegates to General Assembly.	For re-assessment of lands.	For slaves executed and transported.	For guards to jails.	Lunatics' support in jails & conveyance to asylums.	Penitent'y criminal charges; carrying convicts to pen'y.	For commissioners of the revenue.	Crim'l charges—support of persons in jails, &c. &c.	Expenses of representation; comparison of election polls.	For transportation of arms.	For pensions.	Contingent expenses of courts, services of attorneys, clerks, &c	For militia; pay of adjutants, clerks, musicians, &c	From conting't fund; for expenses of quarantine, &c.	General appropriation; over charges in tax &c.	Aggregate for the district.
MERCER . . .	with Giles				279 26		164 42	67 39				216 50	104			
MONONGALIA .	560				231 92	294 91	231 31	249 49				193 50	226			
MONROE . . .	525 20				207 30		102 71	82 21	1 67			174 50	243 25			
MONTGOMERY .	526						138 50	54 06	7 45			232	126			
NICHOLAS . . .	with Fayette				75 04		164 10	21 71	9 49			180	86			
OHIO	582 80				349 68	801 91	339 59	1656 17	10 21			279 14	25			
PRESTON . . .	559 20				397 93		233 37	310 77	6 54	62 95		180	333			
POCAHONTAS .	520						179 17	4 20	13 95			155	43			
PULASKI . . .	with Montg'y, &c.						186 85	11 85	6 40			193	107			
PUTNAM . . .	with Cabell, &c.				361 41		164 35		9 10			245				
RALEIGH . . .	Created from Fayette in 1850								18 60			60				
RANDOLPH . .	512 80				232 08	161 42	163 73	383 26	14 54			265 25	136			
RITCHIE . . .	with Wood, &c						18 13				160	180	172			
RUSSELL . . .	572 80				43 24		225 69	609 01	8 72			175 65	203			
SCOTT	600					249 10	25	407 22	6 79			115	176			
SMYTH	559 20	118 87					223 76	62 99	3 91			180	142 50			
TAYLOR	528						170 30	67 71	24 04			185 62	112			
TAZEWELL . .	562 40						223 69	9 18	10 34			230	80			
TYLER	668				164 63		164	16 55	31 21			180	109 50			
WASHINGTON .	571 20						341 79	281 49	6 62			180	325			
WAYNE	with Cabell, &c.					272 51	164 22	80 16	23 05			145	110			
WETZEL . . .	with Tyler &c.						164 93	15 20				450 50	100			
WIRT	with Wood, &c.				170		163 91	132 85	45 02			185	65			
WOOD	576			6	180 40	571 22	422	1359 24	31 09			217	88			
WYOMING . . .	Created fr. Logan in Jan'y 1850											25				
WYTHE	510 80				153 44		228 90	128 16	6 47			170	100 50			
WHEELING . .	with Ohio													765 52		
	17129 60	118 87		432	4804 36	4089 30	9297 96	11829 48	509 85	89 61	160	11360 89	6344 25	765 52		66931 69

VALLEY DISTRICT.

	Expended for Delegates to General Assembly.	For re-assessment of lands	For slaves executed and transported.	For guards to jails.	Lunatics' support in jails & conveyance to asylums.	Penitent'y crimin'l charges; carrying convicts to pen'y.	For commissioners of the revenue.	Crim'l charges—support of persons in jails, &c. &c.	Expenses of representation; comparison of election polls	For transportation of arms.	For pensions.	Contingent expenses of courts; services of attorneys, clerks, &c.	For militia; pay of adjutants, clerks, musicians &c	From conting't fund; for expenses of quarantine, &c.	General appropriation; over charges in tax &c.	Aggregate for the district.
ALLEGHANY . .	520				266 93		161 73	22 50				276 65	133			
AUGUSTA . . .	970 40				194 39	272 92	368 60	896 61				155	387			
BATH	510	76					143 30	44 75				180	44			
BERKELEY . . .	1017 60				281 76		203 07	144 94	8 76			234	122			
BOTETOURT . .	508				12 02		218 88	40 32	6 65			165	187			
CLARKE . . .	180				126 72		164 31	21 23				120	79			
FREDERICK . .	992				188 49	199 85	287 32	831 04				309	206 50			
HAMPSHIRE . .	964 60				77 28		342 83	281 25				165	241 25			
HARDY . . .	470 80						238 28	94 67				192	176 69			
HIGHLAND . .	with Bath,	&c.			20 52		15	13 95	9 36			195	83 50			
JEFFERSON . .	1011 20				124 64		222 83	150 47	5 10			200	145		7 87	
MORGAN . . .	534 40				33 87		168 80	15 81				188	83			
PAGE	520						168 53	84				182	134			
PENDLETON . .	504				53 77		214 55	34 25	6 60			25	128 75			
ROANOKE . . .	407 60				41		177 10	33 87	8 54			245	85		5	
ROCKBRIDGE . .	967 60				126 12		320 43	318 11	10 66			160	211			
ROCKINGHAM .	932				11 55	65 62	341 18	54 05				215	279			
SHENANDOAH .	954 40		425		17 82		332 25	174 32				220	351	46 16		
WARREN . . .	with Clarke	166 87			38	248 21	30	178 19				170	69			
WINCHESTER .	with Fred'k	126					172 18	119 59								
STAUNTON . .	with Augusta						15	66 80								
	12264 60	368 87	425		1614 88	786 60	4306 17	3537 56	55 67			3596 65	3145 69	46 16	12 87	30160 72

PIEDMONT DISTRICT.

	Expended for Delegates to General Assembly.	For re-assessment of lands.	For slaves executed and transported.	For guards to jails.	Lunatics' support in jails & conveyance to asylums.	Penitent'y criminal charges; carrying convicts to pen'y.	For commissioners of the revenue.	Crim'l charges—support of persons in jails, &c. &c.	Expenses of re-presentation; comparison of election polls.	For transportation of arms.	For pensions.	Contingent expenses of courts, services of attorneys, clerks, &c.	For militia; pay of adjutants, clerks, musicians, &c.	From conting't fund; for expenses of quarantine, &c.	General appropriation; over charges in tax &c.	Aggregate to the district.
ALBEMARLE	944				67 20		653 22	341 75				206	226 50			
AMELIA	458 80				43 20		166 80	5 49				180	128 50			
AMHERST	458 40				294 51		222 42	91 61	7 74			190	64			
APPOMATTOX	468				114 52		164 07	3 50				260	131 50			
BEDFORD	953 60				312 09		481 01	178 16	7 79		60	195 25	201 57			
BRUNSWICK	938 80		1100		5 61		330 38	49 85	9 10			175	166			
BUCKINGHAM	472				79 28		329 33	20 41	5 27			175	139			
CAMPBELL	968				59 93	75 89	342 39	858 28		30		80	296			
CHARLOTTE	480						320 97	28 62	4 87			150	83			
CUMBERLAND	465 60						218 45	22 28				130	28			
CULPEPER	480	129			53 20		226 15	525 61	10 28		90	216	77			
DINWIDDIE	451 20						326 71	49 07	4 23			90	159			
FAUQUIER	1226		350		148 40	71 89	228	288 70	3 34			157	231 25			
FRANKLIN	1000	198 50					322 54	336 87				195 50	236 37			
FLUVANNA	778				45 90		166 03	55 33				158	58			
GREENE	with Orange						164 40	29 82				342	92			
GOOCHLAND	457 20						224 98	77 04	7 37			255	105			
HALIFAX	976 80		650		106 65	64 02	337 89	319 85	8 34			146	327 50			
HENRY	520				72 84	249 54	163 90	1361 91				107 50	135			
LOUDOUN	1509 20				195 10		434 06	313 52				176	276			
LOUISA	461 60				3 84		331 05	94 34				190	171			
LUNENBURG	470						214 08	107 12	4 03			165	75			
MADISON	480				145 83		164 06	9 35				155	132		60	
MECKLENBURG	972 40		1200				298 60	43 68				126	235	34 17		
NELSON	484			12			209 87	266 81				195	124 13			
NOTTOWAY	476						317 35	10 01				185	62			
ORANGE	444						214 04	14 14	5 74	5 79		95	44 75			
PATRICK	542						202 65	490 59				170	440 75			
PITTSYLVANIA	928	238	380		115 55		496 77	453 15				240	529			
PRINCE EDWARD	388			77	49 79		219 90	130 84				180	92			
POWHATAN	895 20				74 81		171 38	71 90				373	58			
RAPPAHANNOCK	490				77		157 41	30 57	3 67			176	126			
LYNCHBURG	with Campbell					52 16	180 56	1023 28			100	130				
	21036 80	5655 50	3680	89	2065 25	513 50	9001 42	7703 45	81 77	35 79	250	5964 25	5250 82	34 17	60	56331 72

TIDE WATER DISTRICT.

	Expended for Delegates to General Assembly.	For re-assessment of lands.	For slaves executed and transported.	For guards to jails.	Lunatics' support in jails & conveyance to asylums.	Penitent'y criminal charges; carrying convicts to pen'y.	For commissioners of the revenue.	Crim'l charges—support of persons in jails, &c. &c.	Expenses of representation; comparison of election polls.	For transportation of arms.	For pensions.	Contingent expenses of courts; services of attorneys, clerks, &c.	For militia; pay of adjutants, clerks, musicians &c	From conti g't fund; for expenses of quarantine, &c.	General appropriation; over charges in tax &c.	Aggregate for the district.
ALEXANDRIA	486				4		220 63	552 86				271	168		122 39	
ACCOMACK	1036 80			64 50	194 51	375 14	325 97	311 10	25 49	51		248	348			
CHARLES CITY	with N	w Kent	650				164 38	76				195	9	9 50		
CAROLINE	463 20				110 42		323 48	176 77				148 50	84			
CHESTERFIELD	445 60			4			324 76	208 46				166	65			
ESSEX	464						300 11	26 61				133	128			
ELIZABETH CITY	472						179 50	29 43	5 26			212				
FAIRFAX	493 60					166 88	222 73	470 40	4 07			319	60		33 29	
GREENSVILLE	466 40						15	3 50				188	73			
GLOUCESTER	470		650				164 18	37 78	3 17			286	125	24 66	15	
HANOVER	448				78 65		332 78	174 81				277 75	117			
HENRICO	440		350		60 80		329 50	2547 13	4 07			617 43	285			
ISLE OF WIGHT	452				28 65		213 65	32 19				177	135			
JAMES CITY	464						164 57	3 50				257	82			
KING GEORGE	473 20				59 70		164 58	49 54				210	86			
KING & QUEEN	456			12			199 06	53 25	3 51			218	96			
KING WILLIAM	448						180 78	64 09	12 41			134	55			
LANCASTER	with Rich	'd 140					164 47	32 28	19 25			170	94			
MATTHEWS	424				34 62		164 30	219 49	4 07			296	104			
MIDDLESEX	with Math	ews.			14 22		160 50	37 09	6 30			145	71			
NANSEMOND	468 80		300				350 42	179 68	3 67			180	141 50	29 30		
NEW KENT	452						166 33	48 80	10 63			163 50	148			
NORFOLK	991 20				44	140 29	630 71	625 51				285	280			
NORTHUMBERL'D	478 80	200					164 69	39 06	13 20			192 25	87			
NORTHAMPTON	847 60	182					164 35	26 69	12 87			187 50	100			
PRINCESS ANNE	479 20						412 76	108 17				163	62			
PRINCE GEORGE	452	214	1130				178 98	156 88	6 07	11 75		152 50	93	7 50		
PRINCE WILLIAM	487 20		450				126 08	174 65	5 34			261	79			
RICHMOND	436 80						149 08	14 92				180	128 50			
STAFFORD	469 20	152					220 73	191 04	11 34			161	90 62			
SOUTHAMPTON	442		700	516	63 72	35 97	329	74 90				120	84			
SPOTTSYLVANIA	464				9 27		330 15	231 72				211	138		1 72	
SURRY	452						298 60	29 42				183	93			
SUSSEX	436 80						215	46 51	5 27			267 50	124			

	Expended for Delegates to General Assembly.	For re-assessment of lands	For slaves executed and transported.	For guards to jails.	Lunatics' support in jails & conveyance to asylums.	Penitent'y criminal charges; carrying convicts to pen'y.	For commissioners of the revenue.	Crim'l charges —support of persons in jails, &c. &c.	Expenses of representation; comparison of election polls.	For transportation of arms.	For pensions.	Contingent expenses of courts, services of attorneys, clerks, &c.	For militia; pay of adjutants, clerks, musicians, &c	From conting't fund; for expenses of quarantine, &c.	General appropriation; over charges in tax &c.	Aggregate for the district.
WARWICK . with	Eliz'h C'y	110					149 77		2 39			143 50				
WESTMORELAND	424					112 09	163 94	271 05		7 01		186	128 19			
YORK . . . . with	James C'y	174					166 46	12 30				183 50	101			
FREDERICKSB'G	with Spott	sylvania					164 26	245 29		6						
NORFOLK CITY	494 40			36	105 58	47 43	192 65	2153 66	5 03			360	222			
PETERSBURG .	448 80				156 02		176 78	1426 79		2		196	186			
RICHMOND CITY	440		1242 85	63	233 98	22 66	317 50	5241 10		47 62		3508 24	142 98	10	8 40	
WILLIAMSB'G with	James C'y	76					179 50	31 68	7 18				10			
	17567 60	1248	5472 85	695 50	1198 14	900 46	9562 67	16436 10	170 59	125 38		11953 17	4623 79	80 96	180 80	70216 01

	Trans-Alleghany District.	Valley District.	Piedmont District.	Tide-Water District.
See Extended.—Aggregate amount for each District of the State, of the sums disbursed under the several heads of the preceding table, and assigned and distributed in said table among the counties and towns of the Commonwealth,	$ 66,931 69	$ 30,160 72	$ 56,331 72	$ 70,216 01
Add the following disbursements, which cannot be assigned to counties or towns, to-wit:				
For pay and mileage of Senators,	3,823 60	3,048	5,238 40	4,098
For salaries, mileage, &c., of Judges of the General Court,	9,817 42	6 823 02	11,558 21	14,632 27
For appropriations from the Treasury to Public Roads,	1,101 50	4,500		
	$ 81,674 21	$ 44,531 74	$ 73,128 33	$ 88,946 28
		81,674 21		73,128 33
		$ 126,205 95		$ 162.074 61

	Western Division. Comprehending Trans-Allegheny and Valley Districts	Eastern Division. Comprehending Tide-Water and Piedmont Districts.
Above expenditures allotted among the districts, combined so as to show the amounts disbursed for the several grand divisions of East and West,	$ 126,205 95	$ 162,074 61
Add—For printing records of Court of Appeals at Lewisburg and Richmond, &c.	2,448 54	4,859 39
For services of Commissioners of public Warehouses in Richmond, Petersburg and Lynchburg,		225 13
" Lunatic Asylums at Williamsburg and Staunton,	47,000 00	43,937 27
	$ 175,654 49	$ 211,096 40
		175,654 49
		$ 386,750 89

Total amount assigned to the grand divisions of East and West (as shown above)	$386,750 89
Add—For disbursements under the following heads, which, being for the entire Commonwealth, cannot be referred to any division or sub-division of State, to wit:	
" Officers of government (part of the payments from this appropriation, salaries &c of judges of General Court, assigned to the four districts)	46,088 85
" Contingent fund, disbursements upon orders of the executive, (partly annexed to counties and towns in the above table)	15,745 59
" General appropriation—for printing and binding law reports, copies of Mayo's Guide to Magistrates, &c. (except sundry payments distributed among the counties in the above table)	26,908 35
" Penitentiary, house expenses and salaries of officers, (expenses $3,084 13—salaries $7,379 50)	10,463 63
" Officers of militia—under this head the only disbursements for the Adjutant General's salary, $99 50—military contingent, for expenses of visitors of Military School at Lexington, firing salutes, &c. &c $1,663 68	1,763 18
" Virginia Military Institute—for annual appropriation and for new barracks	19 210

	Item	Amount
"	Public Guard—for pay, &c.	21,340 18
"	Manufactory of arms—for water rent at the armory, $1,230. Repairs of armory, $274 45. Repairs of arms—pay of artificers at the armory, $4,329,34	5,883 79
"	Deaf and Dumb and Blind—for furniture and on account of appropriation for 1849 and 1850	18,901 29
"	Civil prosecutions—for expenses in civil suits	104 92
"	Furniture and repairs of Governor's house, &c.	1,369 33
"	Warrants on account—refunded to sheriffs and clerks for overpayments into the Treasury, &c.	1,991 67
"	William F. Ritchie—for copies of the New Code	25,801
"	Revision of the laws—to the revisors for superintending publication of the Code	3,000
"	Virginia Volunteers	2,969 84
"	Repairs of the Capitol	647 63
"	Transportation of free negroes to Liberia	605
"	Lands redeemed—refunding erroneous payment into the treasury	75
"	Robert and Anna M. Walsh—refunding part of a sum deposited in the treasury to pay certain taxes	21 08
"	Sinking fund—redemption of an old certificate (of 1782)	7 10
"	State loan—redemption of 5 per cent stock created by act of 1833	239,500
"	Board of public works—for payment of interest on public debt	197,000
"	Washington Monument fund—for purchase of bonds and state stock $995, and for sundry expenses in erection of the monument	29,860 25
"	General Assembly—pay of clerks, public printer, for stationery, &c. &c. (other disbursements divided among counties and districts)	19,609 40
"	Interest on public debt, registered in this office	60,638 63
		$1,136,182 35

RO: JOHNSTON, First Auditor.

Auditor's office, Richmond, Dec 26, 1850.

A STATEMENT

SHEWING THE

AMOUNT OF TAXES

ASSESSED FOR EACH COUNTY, CITY AND TOWN,

AND THE

AMOUNT ON EACH SUBJECT OF TAXATION,

FOR THE YEAR 1850;

ARRANGED INTO THE

FOUR GRAND DIVISIONS OF THE STATE.

TAXATION.

A

A STATEMENT *showing the amount of taxes assessed for each County, City and Town, and the amount of taxes accruing on each subject of taxation, for the year* 1850; *arranged into the four grand divisions of the Commonwealth, prepared, in part compliance, with a resolution adopted by the Convention, on the* 17*th October*, 1850.

No. 1.—Taxes arising on Lots, Lands, Slaves, Horses, Watches Clocks, Carriages, Pianos, Harps, Plate, Interest, Income, Attorneys, Physicians, Dentists, Bridges, Ferries, Free-Negroes, and Collateral Inheritances, and the total amount thereof.	Trans-Alleghany District.
No. 2.—Taxes arising on Lots, Lands, Slaves, Horses, Watches, Clocks, Carriages, Pianos, Harps, Plate, Interest, Income, Attorneys, Physicians, Dentists, Bridges, Ferries, Free-Negroes, and Collateral Inheritances, and the total amount thereof.	Valley District.
No. 3.—Taxes arising on Lots, Lands, Slaves, Horses, Watches, Clocks, Carriages, Pianos, Harps, Plate, Interest, Income, Attorneys, Physicians, Dentists, Bridges, Ferries, Free-Negroes, and Collateral Inheritances, and the total amount thereof.	Piedmont District.
No. 4.—Taxes arising on Lots, Lands, Slaves, Horses, Watches, Clocks, Carriages, Pianos, Harps, Plate, Interest, Income, Attorneys, Physicians, Dentists, Bridges, Ferries, Free-Negroes, and Collateral Inheritances, and the total amount thereof.	Tide-water District.

No. 5.—Taxes on Licenses to Merchants, Pedlars, Studs, Houses of private Entertainment, Ordinaries, Shows, Auctioneers, Brokers, Insurance Offices, Dentists, Venders of patent Medicines, Lottery Offices, Billiard Tables, and Bowling Alleys, and the total amount thereof; on law process, deeds, wills, county seals, fees, of the clerk of the General Court, in the County Courts, Circuit Superior Courts, Hustings Courts, Court of Appeals, and General Court, and the total amount thereof; on notarial seals, and tax on dividends so far as it can be arranged by counties, with the total amount on the foregoing enumerated subjects.	Trans-Alleghany District.
No. 6.—Taxes on Licenses to Merchants, Pedlars, Studs, Houses of private Entertainment, Ordinances, Shows, Auctioneers, Brokers, Insurance Offices, Dentists, Venders of patent Medicines, Lottery Offices, Billiard Tables, and Bowling Alleys, and the total amount thereof; on law process, deeds, wills, county seals, fees of the clerk of the General Court, in the County Courts, Circuit Superior Courts, Hustings Courts, Court of Appeals, and General Court, and the total amount thereof; on notarial seals, and tax on dividends so far as it can be arranged by counties, with the total amount on the foregoing enumerated subjects.	Valley District.
No. 7.—Taxes on Licenses to Merchants, Pedlars, Studs, Houses of private Entertainment, Ordinaries, Shows, Auctioneers, Brokers, Insurance Offices, Dentists, Venders, of patent Medicines, Lottery Offices, Billiard Tables, and Bowling Alleys, and the total amount thereof; on law process, deeds, wills, county seals, fees of the clerk of the General Court, in the County Courts, Circuit Superior Courts, Hustings Courts, Court of Appeals, and General Court, and the total amount thereof; on notarial seals, and tax on dividends so far as it can be arranged by counties, with the total amount on the foregoing enumerated subjects.	Piedmont District.
No. 8.—Taxes on Licenses to Merchants, Pedlars, Studs, Houses of private Entertainment, Ordinaries, Shows, Auctioneers, Brokers, Insurance Offices, Dentists, Venders	Tide-water District.

of patent Medicines, Lottery officers, Billiard Tables, and Bowling Alleys, and the total amount thereof; on law process, deeds, wills, county seals, fees of the clerk of the General Court, in the County Courts, Circuit Superior Courts, Hustings Courts, Court of Appeals, and General Court, and the total amount thereof; on notarial seals, and tax on dividends so far as it can be arranged by counties, with the total amount on the foregoing enumerated subjects.	Tide-water District.

No. 9.—Recapitulation, giving a condensed and comparative view of the foregoing tables, with the addition of such subjects of taxation as could not be brought within a classification by counties, cities and towns.

Notes.—The body of the following tables is made up for each collection district, with the exception of the City of Petersburg, which, being assigned to a different grand division, from the county of Dinwiddie, the sheriff of the county being the collecting officer of both, has been entered separately—at the foot of each grand division, such cities and towns as have a separate commissioner of the revenue, have been added—when the same commissioner of the revenue acts for county and town, the office does not possess the information to give the taxation of the city or town within his limits.

The sums marked thus,* under the head of law process, are supplied from the accounts of the next preceding year, in the absence of those for the one just terminated,—and those marked thus,† under the head of notarial seals, in part, in the same manner—under the head of law process and certain fees of the clerk of the general court, made collectable by clerks, are included, as in some cases, the accounts are so made out that the amount cannot be ascertained, the amount is inconsiderable.

A CORRECTED TABLE,

SHOWING

THE AMOUNT OF TAX

THAT WOULD BE PAYABLE

BY EACH COUNTY, CITY AND TOWN,

UNDER THE RECENT ASSESSMENT OF LANDS,

AT THE

RATE OF TAXATION NOW PRESCRIBED BY LAW

A CORRECTED TABLE,

owing the amount of Tax that would be payable by each county, city and town, under the recent assessment of lands, at the rate of taxation now prescribed by law.

Counties, &c. **First District.**	Amo'nt that would be payable at present rates of taxation.
LEXANDRIA -	4368 41
CCOMACK - -	2800 71
HARLES CITY -	861 57
AROLINE - -	2563 98
HESTERFIELD	3560 24
SSEX - -	1614 30
LIZABETH CITY	797 51
AIRFAX - -	3006 76
REENSVILLE -	563 30
LOUCESTER -	1301 07
ANOVER - -	2332 69
ENRICO - -	4247 39
SLE OF WIGHT -	1256 05
AMES CITY - -	568 55
ING GEORGE -	1086 64
ING AND QUEEN	1337 46
ING WILLIAM -	1366 70
ANCASTER - -	792 11
ATTHEWS - -	634 49
IDDLESEX - -	715 77
ANSEMOND - -	1554 02
ORFOLK CO. -	1738 05
EW KENT - -	708 11
ORTHUMBERL'D	978 53
NORTHAMPTON	1280 55
PRINCESS ANNE	1231 76
PRINCE GEORGE	1484 18
PRINCE WILLIAM	1753 53
RICHMOND - -	811 28
SOUTHAMPTON	1114 21
SPOTTSYLVANIA	1864 39
SURRY - -	726 51
SUSSEX - -	905 97
STAFFORD - -	1340 67
WARWICK - -	309 26
WESTMORELAND	1116 20
YORK - -	666 48
FREDERICKSB'G -	1577 01
NORFOLK - -	8236 60
PETERSBURG -	5816 37
PORTSMOUTH -	2496 51
RICHMOND - -	17716 58
WILLIAMSBURG	330 98
	91533 43

Counties, &c. **Second District.**	Amo'nt that would be payable at present rates of taxation.
APPOMATTOX -	1108 25
ALBEMARLE - -	5648 42
AMELIA - -	1340 55
AMHERST - -	1932 41
BEDFORD - -	3044 74
BRUNSWICK - -	1141 15
BUCKINGHAM -	2151 54
CAMPBELL - -	2633 75
CHARLOTTE - -	2658 83
CULPEPER - -	2573 29
CUMBERLAND -	1556 90
DINWIDDIE - -	1227 51
FLUVANNA - -	1463 06
FAUQUIER - -	6517 15
FRANKLIN -	1823 31
GOOCHLAND - -	2218 76
GREENE - -	723 03
HALIFAX - -	3827 99
HENRY - -	954 09
LOUDOUN - -	9582 30
LOUISA - -	2627 11
LUNENBURG - -	1043 11
MADISON - -	1846 84
MECKLENBURG	2863 04
NELSON - -	2019 69
NOTTOWAY - -	1109 29
ORANGE - -	2093 79
PATRICK - -	741 61
PITTSYLVANIA -	2909 85
POWHATAN - -	1542 92
PRINCE EDWARD	2281 26
RAPPAHANNOCK	2022 65
DANVILLE - -	344 63
LYNCHBURG - -	3421 86
	80994 68

Third District.	
ALLEGHANY - -	635 42
AUGUSTA - -	8349 72
BATH - -	768 02
BERKLEY - -	4639
BOTETOURT - -	2548 52
CLARKE - -	3447 38
FREDERICK - -	3925 57
HARDY - -	2684 82
HAMPSHIRE - -	2992 69
HIGHLAND - -	1274 32
JEFFERSON - -	6626 18
MORGAN - -	719 64
PAGE - -	1721 96
PENDLETON - -	1006 80
ROANOKE - -	1823 85
ROCKINGHAM -	6894 48
ROCKBRIDGE -	3540 13
SHENANDOAH -	3749 64
WARREN - -	1642 83
STAUNTON - -	614 45
WINCHESTER -	1637 39
	61242 81

Counties, &c. **Fourth District.**	Amo'nt that would be payable at present rates of taxation.	Counties, &c. **Fourth District.**	Amo'nt that would be payable at present rates of taxation.
BARBOUR - -	1213 18	MONONGALIA -	2379 07
BOONE - -	228 23	MONTGOMERY -	1464 73
BRAXTON - -	504 80	NICHOLAS - -	799 17
BROOKE - -	1667 78	OHIO - -	6835 22
CABELL - -	1182 29	POCAHONTAS -	962 48
CARROLL - -	471 80	PRESTON - -	1214 06
DODDRIDGE - -	525 84	PULASKI - -	933 97
FAYETTE - -	467 59	PUTNAM - -	719 09
FLOYD - -	659 34	RANDOLPH - -	1148 90
GILES - -	975 70	RITCHIE - -	832 24
GILMER - -	944 59	RUSSELL - -	979 31
GRAYSON - -	581 74	RALEIGH - -	241 62
GREENBRIER -	2867 21	SCOTT - -	739 94
HANCOCK - -	788 79	SMYTHE - -	1579 77
HARRISON - -	2945 72	TAZEWELL - -	1287 65
JACKSON - -	1348 25	TYLER - -	930 46
KANAWHA - -	2951 49	TAYLOR - -	1223 30
LEE - -	1089 13	WASHINGTON -	2719 50
LEWIS - -	1989 59	WAYNE - -	612 55
LOGAN - -	327 68	WIRT - -	529 31
MARION - -	2072 28	WOOD - -	1892 17
MARSHALL - -	2118 57	WYOMING - -	127 39
MASON - -	1853 42	WYTHE - -	2186 28
MONROE - -	2252 88	WETZEL - -	608 34
MERCER - -	422 60		65397 01

Total in 1st District - - - - -	$91,533 43
2d do. - - - - -	80,994 68
3d do. - - - - -	61,242 81
4th do. - - - - -	65,397 01
	$299,167 93

SUPPLEMENTAL ASSESSMENT.

A supplemental assessment of some property, omitted by the assessor of one of the districts in Lewis Co., has been received, and will be found below. An error in the former "statement of the value of lands and lots," &c., "under the re-assessment of 1850", furnished for the Convention on the 28th day of Nov. last, has been corrected. The correction will be found below.

FOURTH DISTRICT.	No. of acres of land:	Sum added to the land on account of buildings:	Total value of land and buildings:	Value of buildings on lots:	Value of lots including buildings:	Aggregate value of land and lots:	Average value of land per acre:	The amount that would be payable at present rates of taxation:
Lewis	1,009,718	162,261 50	1,893,231 42	59,210 00	94,420 00	1,987,651 42	1 87	1984 71
Total in the 4th District	26,644,741	6,134,679 54	55,742,544 16	3,317,474 00	5,785,224 41	61,527,768 57	2 09	65,339 53
THIRD DISTRICT.								
Frederick	270,928	637,408 75	3,916,945 37	48,075 00	65,840 00	3,982,785 37	14 45	3925 57
Aggregate in the 3d District	6,527,368	8,039,750 26	54,960,157 03	2,881,157 00	4,290,589 26	59,250,746 29	8 41	61,180 55

Total amount of property in 1st district,	77,964,574 52	Av. value of land per acre,	$8 02	Amount that would be payable at present rates of taxation,	$91,370 30
2d do.	77,786,476 99		7 36	do.	81,018 43
3d do.	59,250,746 29		8 41	do.	61,180 55
4th do.	61,527,768 57		2 09	do.	65,339 53
	276,529,566 37				298,908 81

RO: JOHNSTON, First Auditor.

Auditor's Office, Richmond, Jan. 3d, 1851.

A STATEMENT

SHEWING THE

AVERAGE VALUE OF LANDS PER ACRE,

FOR THE

YEARS 1800, 1820, 1840 AND 1850,

THE VALUE OF

BUILDINGS ON OTHER THAN TOWN PROPERTY,

ADDED TO THE VALUE OF

LAND FOR THE YEARS 1820, 1840 AND 1850,

IN

ASCERTAINING THE AVERAGE VALUE THEREOF,

AND ALSO THE AVERAGE VALUE OF

BUILDINGS ON TOWN LOTS IN 1820, 1840 AND 1850,

ARRANGED INTO THE FOUR

GRAND DIVISIONS OF THE COMMONWEALTH.

PREPARED IN PART COMPLIANCE WITH A

Resolution adopted by the Convention, on the 17th October, 1850.

AUDITOR'S OFFICE,
Richmond, January 25, 1851.

Sir:—I have the honor of furnishing to you, herewith, for the use of the Convention, "A statement shewing the assessed average value of lands per acre for the years 1800, 1820, 1840 and 1850; the value of buildings, on other than town lots, added to the value of lands in 1820, 1840 and 1850, in ascertaining the average value thereof; and also the value of buildings on town lots in 1820, 1840 and 1850."

I have also enclosed to you, herewith, "A table shewing the aggregate amounts expended by the commonwealth, through this office, in each county, city and town thereof, during the fiscal year ending on the 30th September, 1850."

I am, with great respect, your ob't. servant,

RO: JOHNSTON, First Auditor.

To the Hon: JOHN Y. MASON, Pres't. of the Virginia Convention.

A STATEMENT *shewing the assessed average value of lands per acre, for the years* 1800, 1820, 1840 *and* 1850; *the value of buildings on other than town property, added to the value of land for the years* 1820, 1840 *and* 1850, *in ascertaining the average value thereof, and also the value of buildings on town lots in* 1820, 1840 *and* 1850, *arranged into the four grand divisions of the Commonwealth: prepared, in part compliance with a resolution adopted by the Convention, on the* 17*th Oct*. 1850.

COUNTIES IN THE FIRST DISTRICT.	Assessed average value of land, in 1800.	Assessed average value of land, in 1820.	Value of buildings on land, in 1820.	Value of buildings on town lots, in 1820.	Assessed average value of land, in 1840.	Value of buildings on land, in 1840.	Value of buildings on town lots, in 1840.	Assessed average value of land, in 1850.	Value of buildings on land, in 1850.	Value of buildings on town lots in 1850.
Alexandria,	$	$	$	$	$	$	$	$33 71	$68350	$1228200
Accomack,	1 81	9 55	195608		11 71	249118	21165	11 57	271340	21950
Charles City,	1 50	8 90	142533		7 10	152035		7 75	169688 45	
Caroline,	1 63	8 63	405485	20100	5 98	367734	28050	7 64	431675	27275
Chesterfield,	1 51	10 78	548391	221450	10 35	982510	121700	10 91	1101007 62	147310
Essex,	1 55	8 45	143925	26195	9 08	222938	20925	9 57	246455	29680
Elizabeth City,		10 91	41855	54025	12 31	95850	81060	15 44	121955	116270
Fairfax,	1 59	10 69	415544	26885	6 56	356934 50	20515	11 11	517127 62	36105
Greensville,	1 56	6 13	176472	21070	4 69	204214	11970	2 82	117430 20	22250
Gloucester,	1 51	8 77	254244	1660	8 94	285258		9 50	358781 17	350
Hanover,	1 66	10 75	391728	3720	7 70	434704	520	8 05	432329 88	
Henrico,	1 62	47 63	520020		18 84	741596		25 71	1297621 29	
Isle of Wight,	1 61	6 07	286386		5 51	345474	65220	5 99	382893	69800
James City,	1 57	4 01	64975		4 74	88078	45455	6 20	109690	
King George,	1 59	11 42	147380	5910	8 63	188635		9 61	197120	6525
King and Queen,	1 66	5 42	254708	3660	6 68	286014	1090	7 04	312420	
King William,	1 65	9 50	179450	1000	8 36	213595	500	8 10	157125	
Lancaster,	1 65	6 62	76561		7 45	146990		9 69	164978	
Mathews,	2 20	8 56	86772 46		13 60	170356		11 70	178791	
Middlesex,	1 69	5 42	81579		5 50	87950		8 53	104756 15	4855
Nansemond,	1 50	4 63	176710	71320	5 27	325072	95450	5 12	343627 75	132700
Norfolk County,	1 27				7 49	214400	32200	8 13	418455	21850
New Kent,	1 62	5 76	121905		5 71	176401 83		5 43	185222	
Northumberland,	1 67	7 94	106856		6 32	59925	11850	7 97	192334	15500
Northampton,	1 62	11 49	155723		12 57	202579 25		11 23	218989 98	

COUNTIES IN THE FIRST DISTRICT.	Assessed average value of land in 1800.	Assessed average value of land, in 1820.	Value of buildings on land, in 1820.	Value of buildings on town lots, in 1820.	Assessed average value on land, in 1840.	Value of buildings on land, in 1840.	Value of buildings on town lots, in 1840.	Assessed average value of land, in 1850.	Value of buildings on land, in 1850.	Value of buildings on town lots, in 1850.
Princess Anne,	$1 53	$8 50	$198347	$	$7 13	$275277	$9990	$7 68	$327544	$13110
Prince George,	1 50	6 31	173276	2829	5 57	209732 17	320	7 50	252877 45	310
Prince William,	1 70	9 41	332585	62670	5 31	195815	71615	7 31	164365	67565
Richmond,	1 55	7 45	104270		5 97	148876		6 77	189753 20	
Southampton,	1 67	4 75	396800	19770	4 15	376559 41	13490	2 96	327607	11725
Spottsylvania,	1 68	7 17	366678		5 11	441307 52		7 27	528782 58	
Surry,	1 65	4 81	155192	2825	4 07	162794 21	1575	4 55	192424 31	1075
Sussex,	1 65	5 19	271814		4 08	263905		3 06	243004	
Stafford	1 67	9 01	261372	69950	6 00	211516 32	53731 57	7 10	224239 25	52700
Warwick,	1 67	5 11	29350		6 04	28781		7 20	37840	
Westmoreland,	1 70	6 98	89824	1285	6 37	126049 25	1275	7 71	183426 50	1125
York,	1 67	4 32	33830	8110	5 91	58146 11	11120	8 95	99845 20	15015
Fredericksburg				575080			673360			826780
Norfolk,				2188625			2387365			2811315
Petersburg				1921494			1708378			2449900
Portsmouth,							719000			935450
Richmond,				2639344			4303445			6953133
Williamsburg,				106180			81365			145225
			$7388148 46	$8055157		$9097120 57	$10593699 57		$10921871 60	$16165048

A STATEMENT *shewing the assessed average value of lands per acre, for the years* 1800, 1820, 1840 *and* 1850; *the value of buildings on other than town property, added to the value of land for the years* 1820, 1840 *and* 1850, *in ascertaining the average value thereof, and also the value of buildings on town lots in* 1820, 1840 *and* 1850, *arranged into the four grand divisions of the Commonwealth: prepared in part compliance with a resolution adopted by the Convention, on the* 17*th Oct.* 1850.

COUNTIES IN THE SECOND DISTRICT.	Assessed average value of land in 1800.	Assessed average value of land in 1820.	Value of buildings on land in 1820.	Value of buildings on town lots in 1820.	Assessed average value of land in 1840.	Value of buildings on land in 1840.	Value of buildings on town lots in 1840.	Assessed average value of land in 1850.	Value of buildings on land in 1850.	Value of buildings on town lots in 1850.
Appomattox,	$	$	$	$	$	$	$	$ 5 24	$ 219980	$ 13540
Albemarle,	1 13	10 75	486605	64892	8 93	737971	180110	10 46	838732 34	295850
Amelia,	1 36	7 98	294155	1300	6 92	297650		6 05	248775 50	
Amherst,	1 00	7 11	262230	2900	5 25	231530	11090	6 47	271754 21	10945
Bedford,	98	6 58	263385		4 46	348683 50	48195	6 06	442955	55950
Brunswick,	1 68	5 82	401705	1500	3 21	324563		3 16	322585	20850
Buckingham,	93	8 40	590554	19375	6 39	450762	41825	5 65	331180	42985
Campbell,	98	9 94	356496	504373	6 13	442085	18640	7 85	576047	31950
Charlotte,	1 22	8 33	228125		7 96	356759		8 90	427355	
Culpeper,	1 16	9 62	323294	68146	9 57	153027	62410	10 49	229665	56180
Cumberland,	1 64	9 17	309196	2:220	8 10	314921	22300	8 07	381494	11870
Dinwiddie,	1 57	7 15	531939		3 76	305322		3 80	310451	
Fluvanna,	1 14	8 62	213397	9565	7 48	286452	20420	7 67	285533	23635
Fauquier,	1 19	15 23	729936	84920	11 95	661580	168110	14 70	820168	238475
Franklin,	62	2 49	126359	6450	3 38	204704	12425	4 16	305704 50	14525
Goochland,	1 59	14 38	278780		11 50	236320		12 51	353348 07	
Greene,					5 28	59611	7170	6 65	76720	15800
Halifax,	1 12	7 58	356287	3900	8 10	587130	15000	7 45	659121	13652
Henry,	90	3 25	45360		3 59	52600	11850	4 25	81650	13520
Loudoun,	1 31	23 49	704382	295550	21 71	889806	233316	27 50	1127181	268142
Louisa,	1 20	8 09	369492		6 64	377156 76		8 24	422969 31	
Lunenburg,	1 25	4 82	169031		3 73	178604	5600	3 84	197035	3550
Madison,	1 00	7 60	243700	11550	6 52	187805	32300	7 94	243667	36050
Mecklenburg,	1 20	6 79	383985	10462 80	8 42	512237	115408	6 15	470121	151535
Nelson,		6 65	112000	2450	6 02	252595	31150	6 69	360305	37920

COUNTIES IN THE SECOND DISTRICT.	Assessed average value of land in 1800.	Assessed average value of land in 1820.	Value of buildings on land in 1820.	Value of buildings on town lots in 1820.	Assessed average value of land in 1840.	Value of buildings on land in 1840.	Value of buildings on town lots in 1840.	Assessed average value of land in 1850.	Value of buildings on land in 1850.	Value of buildings on town lots in 1850.
Nottoway,	1 45	8 20	188000		6 09	289956		3 61	296397	
Orange,	1 13	9 46	302198	5962 50	6 10	307687	60800	9 36	339480 20	43800
Patrick,	30	71	47983		59	80611		97	79913	9200
Pittsylvania,	83	5 43	225969	18912	4 62	368972 50	122870	4 62	413318	12825
Powhatan,	1 64	9 98	327657	1562[illegible]	8 15	345522 50	23922	10 12	343595	17115
Prince Edward,	1 24	8 38	245105	16165	8 18	393956	125985	8 41	374937	158447
Rappahannock,					9 81	251654	29175	11 49	276375	47779
Danville,										117500
Lynchburg,							697470			978745
			$9116610	$1165213 30		$10488233 26	$2098841		$12128712 13	$2742335

A STATEMENT *shewing the assessed average value of lands per acre, for the years* 1800, 1820, 1840 *and* 1850; *the value of buildings on other than town property, added to the value of land for the years* 1820, 1840, *and* 1850, *in ascertaining the average value thereof, and also the value of buildings on town lots in* 1820, 1840 *and* 1850, *arranged into the four grand divisions of the Commonwealth; prepared in part compliance with a resolution adopted by the Convention on the* 17*th October*, 1850.

COUNTIES IN THE THIRD DISTRICT.	Assessed average value of land in 1800.	Assessed average value of land in 1820	Value of buildings on land in 1820	Value of buildings on town lots in 1820.	Assessed average value of land in 1840.	Value of buildings on land in 1840.	Value of buildings on town lots in 1840	Assessed average value of land in 1850.	Value of buildings on land in 1850.	Value of buildings on town lots in 1850.
Allegheny,					1 52	78720	31000	1 74	139674	30626
Augusta,	55	10 39	691183	270034	8 70	827210	80315	13 37	1251587 13	97740
Bath,	8	2 04	84382	531 25	2 45	117851 62		1 71	159585 04	
Berkeley,	1 21	11 69	526755	141125	15 66	438110	126590	20 65	511005	225000 00
Botetourt,	39	4 23	320784	89278	3 57	335620	119270	5 17	367266	74073
Clarke,					23 43	308795	24280	29 54	401825	37375
Frederick,	1 24	16 44	853216	386[illegible]75	10 75	533466	46820	7 68	637408 75	48075
Hardy,	46	4 12	78292	16680	2 95	154282	33500	3 78	209287 85	48410
Hampshire,	50	3 74	189267	35935	4 29	258009	57925	4 65	391320	98275
Highland,								5 99	125244	7270
Jefferson,		23 40	339449	166090	33 82	925835	289976	43 98	863780	426245
Morgan,					3 46	117109	27575	4 22	125925 25	56030
Page,					6 69	243029	35750	8 49	284643 66	44720
Pendleton,	20	1 58	68029	11502	1 73	124549 08	15493 25	2 10	129437	18870
Roanoke,					7 29	243780	50350	8 06	319430	59740
Rockingham,	21	9 42	417359	77792 78	9 00	809790 05	110110 50	10 94	977694	179675
Rockbridge,	50	5 40	281298	57429 50	4 40	306424	141733	7 03	472320	238351
Shenandoah	75	8 06	540212	108113 20	8 32	357627 04	117993	10 71	464072 58	144947
Warren,					8 83	161815	28050	12 71	208215	46100
Staunton,							148500			278330
Winchester,							500125			721300
			$4384226	$1360635 73		$6342022 39	$1985355 75		$8039720 26	$2381157

A STATEMENT shewing the assessed average value of lands per acre for the years 1800, 1820, 1840 *and* 1850*; the value of buildings on other than town property, added to the value of land for the years* 1820, 1840 *and* 1850, *in ascertaining the average value thereof, and also the value of buildings on town lots in* 1820, 1840 *and* 1850, *arranged into the four grand divisions of the Commonwealth; prepared in part compliance with a resolution adopted by the Convention on the 17th Oct.* 1850.

COUNTIES IN THE FOURTH DISTRICT.	Assessed average value of land in 1800	Assessed average value of land in 1820.	Value of buildings on land in 1820	Value of buildings on town lots in 1820.	Assessed average value of land in 1840.	Value of buildings on land in 1840	Value of buildings on town lots in 1840	Assessed average value of land in 1850.	Value of buildings on land in 1850.	Value of buildings on town lots in 1850.
Barbour,								4 18	98 20	13415 09
Boone,								70	24010	
Braxton,					33	14532 83	2570	50	23173 67	8375
Brooke,	36	7 67	105613	63117 99	14 68	161347 50	189000	22 66	157825	149425
Cabell,		2 21	20365	5720	3 10	92204	28050	2 52	125948 98	42475
Carroll,								1 19	78016	15690
Doddridge,								1 45	27895	13025
Fayette,					49½	53715		88	59235	
Floyd,					1 59½	53685	6700	2 22	72670	24990
Giles,		48	27908	3727 50	2 49	71015	21635	3 03	94627	33055
Gilmer,								93	36161	13890
Grayson,	14	27	53191	1985	62½	72609	5100	1 21	89320	3725
Greenbrier,	36	1 83	94497	26460	2 95	429019	79135	3 45	448188	111772
Hancock,								14 36	75339	12825
Harrison,	43	1 95	70076	37461 25	2 80	206282	94410	7 28	265021	163195
Jackson,					1 12	17845	5075	1 75	70945	24220
Kanawha,		34	61951	10000	1 33	292075	131475	1 99	452780 66	148150
Lee,	19	18	42010	6520	1 18	90240	11139	2 43	116419	12449
Lewis,		56	22220	831 25	60	79250 84	16487	1 87	161711 50	50470
Logan,					39	29284	3645	33	30990	3380
Marion,								8 37	185391 85	92210
Marshall,					5 51	59980	35740	8 71	143400	72411
Mason,		1 85	29060	6960	3 98	85105	31820	5 46	118881	49250
Monroe,		1 95	79276	13745	4 40	286818 50	30350	5 25	294800	53040
Mercer,					60	6189 75	100	1 06	15655	5780
Monongalia,	21	1 18	190519	44900	4 06	245514 50	80525	7 90	231133 50	124100
Montgomery,	29	2 26	101034	22845	3 17	125183	66845	5 84	196525	76550
Nicholas,					47	29698	4350	59	59673	5740
Ohio,	6	4 11	118569	73700	21 49	158042	16123	20 83	221285	89995
Pocahontas,					1 19	41138	7830	1 31	92517 76	7930
Preston,					1 81	51774	15990	2 36	158010	14940
Pulaski,								4 96	113903	22825
Putnam,								4 56	69450	18265

Randolph		23	12840	9850	31	29265	12280	51	27460	14795
Ritchie								1 36	87044	11525
Russell	5	24	22512	490	49	59870 61	12040	1 67	77690	13795
Raleigh								49	26817	1020
Scott		44	29080	600	56	78032	15630	68	117708	14225
Smyth					4 36	135470	17500	4 96	184365	29875
Tazewell		33	24632	1510	29	37390	12350	45	84025	22465
Tyler		68	20320	2540	1 43	69841	19890	2 52	86361	41450
Taylor								7 20	62625	34030
Washington	33	4 30	251234	78985	4 95	309606	155100	6 40	341654	156100
Wayne								3 32	41325	2385
Wirt								1 67	39087	7807
Wood		4 32	39640	18904	2 53	122795	93465	4 13	131550	190713
Wyoming								77	6770	
Wythe	7	3 94	204658	46215	2 16	329431	81975	2 83	373861	120015
Wetzel								2 60	36556 62	12175
Wheeling							768540			1159835
			$1621205	$481066		$3875247	$2072864		$6134129	$3309732

RECAPITULATION.

	Total value of buildings on land in 1820.	Total value of buildings on town lots in 1820.	Total value of buildings on land in 1840.	Total value of buildings on town lots in 1840.	Total value of buildings on land in 1850.	Total value of buildings on town lots in 1850.
First District, ...	7388148 46	8055157	9097120 57	10593699 57	10921871 60	16165048
Second District, ...	9116610	1165213 30	10488233 26	2098841	12128712 13	2742335
Third District, ...	4384226	1360635 73	6342022 39	1985355 75	8039720 26	2881157
Fourth District, ...	1621205	481066	3875247	2072864	6134129	3309732
	$22510189 46	$11062072 03	$29802623 22	$16750760 32	$37224432 99	$25098272

I have not complied strictly with the resolution of the Convention, in making up this table. Instead of giving the assessed average value of land per acre, and the value of buildings in the several cities, towns, and counties at the periods aforesaid, viz: 1790, 1800, 1810, 1820, 1830, 1840, and 1850, I have given the information mentioned in the caption of this table. There was no valuation of the lands of the Commonwealth made by her, between 1782 and 1819; and none between 1819 and 1839; The taxed value of lands between 1782 and 1820 was not the estimated actual value thereof, but a scaled value (sometimes more and sometimes less than the actual value) fixed by the equalizers of the Land tax, appointed under the act of the General Assembly, passed in October 1782. This taxed value remained the same between 1782 and 1820, and the additions of omitted lands and newly patented lands, it is supposed, did not materially affect the assessed average value per acre, as these additions were put upon the books at a scaled valuation. I have therefore given the average taxed value of land in 1800 and not in 1790 and 1810. I have given the taxed or scaled value not only because I supposed it to be as near the true value in 1790 and 1810 as the assessments of 1782, but because I understand the resolution requires it. If I am correct in supposing that the additions of land made on the Commissioners' books from new patents, &c., do not materially affect the average value per acre, it was unnecessary to look to the Commissioners' books of 1830, and I have not done so. The value of buildings prior to 1820 could not be given because it did not then appear on the Commissioners' books, or on the books of the assessment made in 1782. Respectfully submitted.

RO. JOHNSTON, First Auditor.

Auditor's Office, January 22d, 1851.

A TABLE

SHEWING THE

AGGREGATE EXPENDITURES

BY

COUNTIES.

A TABLE

Shewing the aggregate amounts expended by the Commonwealth through this office, in each county, city and town thereof, during the fiscal year ending 31st Sept. 1850—the details of which are given in a "statement exhibiting the expenditures of the Commonwealth," &c., heretofore furnished to the Convention—prepared in compliance with a Resolution adopted the 20th January, 1851.

TRANS-ALLEGHANY DISTRICT.

BARBOUR	1107 32	MONTGOMERY	1084 01
BRAXTON	1416 57	NICHOLAS	536 34
BOONE	466 32	OHIO	4044 50
BROOKE	1401 46	PRESTON	2083 82
CABELL	1761 34	POCAHONTAS	915 32
CARROLL	811 31	PULASKI	505 10
DODDRIDGE	775 92	PUTNAM	779 86
FAYETTE	1111 23	RALEIGH	78 60
FLOYD	1455 67	RANDOLPH	1874 09
GRAYSON	1333 34	RITCHIE	530 13
GREENBRIER	3602 86	RUSSELL	1838 11
GILES	1400 61	SCOTT	1579 11
GILMER	666 86	SMYTH	1291 28
HANCOCK	388 90	TAYLOR	1087 67
HARRISON	2311 37	TAZEWELL	1115 61
JACKSON	2019 50	TYLER	1333 89
KANAWHA	1691 58	WASHINGTON	1706 10
LEE	1575 55	WAYNE	794 94
LEWIS	1681 55	WETZEL	730 63
LOGAN	1654 76	WIRT	761 78
MARION	1247 17	WOOD	3450 95
MARSHALL	1232 15	WYOMING	25 00
MASON	1452 14	WYTHE	1298 27
MERCER	831 57	WHEELING	765 52
MONONGALIA	1987 13		
MONROE	1336 93		$66931 69

VALLEY DISTRICT.

ALLEGHANY	1380 81	PAGE	1005 37
AUGUSTA	3244 92	PENDLETON	966 92
BATH	998 05	ROANOKE	1003 11
BERKELEY	2012 13	ROCKBRIDGE	2113 92
BOTETOURT	1137 87	ROCKINGHAM	1898 40
CLARKE	991 26	SHENANDOAH	2520 95
FREDERICK	3014 20	WARREN	900 27
HAMPSHIRE	2072 21	WINCHESTER	417 77
HARDY	1172 44	STAUNTON	81 80
HIGHLAND	337 33		
JEFFERSON	1867 11		$30160 72
MORGAN	1023 88		

PIEDMONT DISTRICT.

ALBEMARLE	2438 67	HENRY	2610 69
AMELIA	982 79	LOUDOUN	2903 88
AMHERST	1328 68	LOUISA	1251 83
APPOMATTOX	1141 59	LUNENBURG	1035 23
BEDFORD	2389 47	LYNCHBURG	1486 00
BRUNSWICK	2774 74	MADISON	1146 24
BUCKINGHAM	1220 29	MECKLENBURG	2909 85
CAMPBELL	2710 49	NELSON	1291 81
CHARLOTTE	1067 46	NOTTOWAY	1050 36
CUMBERLAND	864 33	ORANGE	823 46
CULPEPER	1807 24	PATRICK	1845 99
DINWIDDIE	1080 21	PITTSYLVANIA	3380 47
FAUQUIER	2704 58	PRINCE EDWARD	1137 53
FRANKLIN	2289 28	POWHATAN	1644 29
FLUVANNA	1260 76	RAPPAHANNOCK	1060 65
GREENE	628 22		
GOOCHLAND	1126 59		
HALIFAX	2937 05		$56331 72

TIDE-WATER DISTRICT.

ALEXANDRIA	1824 88	NORFOLK	2996 71
ACCOMACK	2980 51	NORTHUMBERL'D	1175 00
CHARLES CITY	1103 88	NORTHAMPTON	1521 01
CAROLINE	1306 37	PRINCESS ANNE	1225 13
CHESTERFIELD	1213 82	PRINCE GEORGE	2402 68
ESSEX	1051 72	PRINCE WILLIAM	1583 27
ELIZABETH CITY	898 19	RICHMOND	909 30
FAIRFAX	1769 97	STAFFORD	1295 93
GREENSVILLE	745 90	SOUTHAMPTON	2365 59
GLOUCESTER	1775 79	SPOTTSYLVANIA	1385 86
HANOVER	1428 99	SURRY	1056 02
HENRICO	4633 93	SUSSEX	1095 08
ISLE OF WIGHT	1038 49	WARWICK	405 66
JAMES CITY	971 07	WESTMORELAND	1292 28
KING GEORGE	1043 02	YORK	637 26
KING & QUEEN	1037 82	FREDERICKSBURG	415 55
KING WILLIAM	894 28	NORFOLK CITY	3616 75
LANCASTER	620 00	PETERSBURG	2592 39
MATTHEWS	1246 48	RICHMOND CITY	11278 33
MIDDLESEX	434 11	WILLIAMSBURG	304 36
NANSEMOND	1653 37		
NEW KENT	989 26		$70216 01

A STATEMENT

SHEWING THE

VALUE OF ALL THE REAL ESTATE

AND

PERSONAL PROPERTY

IN

EACH OF THE COUNTIES, CITIES & TOWNS,

TAXED IN 1849 AND 1850;

AND

EXHIBITING THE VALUE THEREOF

IN

EACH OF THE GRAND DIVISIONS

OF

THE STATE.

AUDITOR'S OFFICE,
RICHMOND, April 15th, 1851.

Sir: I have the honor of furnishing you, herewith, "A Statement shewing the value of all the real estate and personal property in each of the counties, cities and towns of the Commonwealth, taxed in 1849 and 1850; and exhibiting the value thereof in each of the grand divisions of the State—prepared in compliance with a resolution of the Convention adopted on the 21st of October, 1850.

I am, with great respect, your obedient servant,

RO. JOHNSTON, First Auditor.

To the Hon. JOHN Y. MASON, President of the Virginia State Convention.

***A STATEMENT** shewing the value of all the **Real Estate** and **Personal Property** in each of the counties, cities and towns of the Commonwealth, taxed in the years 1849 and 1850, and exhibiting the value thereof in each of the grand divisions of the State; prepared in compliance with a resolution of the Convention, adopted on the 21st October, 1850.*

TIDE WATER DIVISION.	1849.			1850.		
	Real estate taxed.	Personal property taxed.	Aggregate.	Real estate taxed.	Personal property taxed.	Aggregate.
Accomac,	2815680	1126698	3942378	2817010	1241585	4058595
Alexandria,	2156465	743086	2899551	2248753	958517	3207270
Caroline,	2127365	1878588	4005953	2129605	1951350	4080955
Charles City,	824830	606711	1431591	827950	531954	1359904
Chesterfield,	3331758	1799341	5131099	3285008	1836519	5121527
Essex,	1467350	1319808	2787158	1495015	1349429	2844444
Elizabeth City,	606290	380660	936950	624558	392680	1017238
Fairfax,	1980890	662346	2643236	1926183	636112	2562295
Greensville,	880015	688232	1568247	890305	731667	1621972
Gloucester,	1253800	1174056	2427856	1259450	1189604	2449054
Hanover,	2379960	1785572	4165532	2384282	1809414	4193696
Henrico,	3620780	1383876	5004656	3703830	1428816	5132646
Isle of Wight,	1164590	784662	1949252	1155420	907165	2062585
James City,	434910	390383	825293	436750	378099	814849
King George,	1019250	660187	1679437	1082480	717000	1799480
King and Queen,	1353230	1368158	2721388	1360030	1341769	2701799
King William,	1424590	1070116	2494706	1422160	1093225	2515385
Lancaster,	634560	518485	1153045	751220	539977	1291197
Mathews,	722310	548157	1270497	740490	503524	1244014
Middlesex,	546540	453861	1000401	546815	464199	1011014
Nansemond,	1502035	974955	2476990	1503655	1024888	252854[illegible]

TIDE-WATER DIVISION.—Concluded.	1849.			1850.		
	Real estate taxed.	Personal property taxed.	Aggregate.	Real estate taxed.	Personal property taxed.	Aggregate.
New Kent,	750750	611720	1362470	753360	603545	1356905
Norfolk County,	1542140	867984	2410124	1539160	872553	2411713
Northampton,	1369160	896130	2265290	1374360	894674	2269034
Northumberland,	779970	598779	1378749	788070	618624	1406694
Prince George,	1022851	898927	1921778	1027291	965661	1992952
Princess Anne,	1139087	594321	1733408	1126247	571374	1697621
Prince William,	1307585	550592	1858177	1389725	533654	1923379
Richmond,	727550	408915	1136465	735880	419628	1155508
Stafford,	1117472	670617	1788089	1123492	671008	1794500
Southampton,	1567150	1245765	2812915	1598740	1260781	2859521
Spottsylvania,	1707280	1511997	3219277	1734750	1641173	3375923
Surry,	658477	583970	1242447	659957	587876	1247833
Sussex,	1203950	1252306	2456256	1203590	1217907	2421497
Warwick,	261610	184191	445801	272050	186144	458194
Westmoreland,	959155	645840	1604995	963555	646286	1609841
York,	460419	373072	833491	470979	364119	835098
Norfolk City,	4483553	1936301	6419854	4627966	1907681	6535647
Petersburg,	3601309	1498027	5099336	3681192	2789659	6470851
Williamsburg,	166233	204277	370510	169815	193477	363292
Richmond City,	9864515	3727421	13591936	10134590	3810241	13944831
Fredericksburg,	993076	654633	1647709	1035746	705677	1741423
Portsmouth,	1585332	320731	1906063	1654225	325400	1979625
	69515902	40554454	110070356	70655709	42814635	113470344

Piedmont Division	1849. Real estate taxed.	1849. Personal property taxed.	1849. Aggregate.	1850. Real estate taxed.	1850. Personal property taxed.	1850. Aggregate.
Albemarle,	4578740	2896716	7475456	4612679	3018259	7630938
Amelia,	1525950	1210383	2736333	1511310	1290956	2802266
Amherst,	1716255	1058828	2775083	1696385	1048738	2745123
Appomattox,	1058952	796641	1855593	1057337	829524	1886861
Bedford,	2330798	1780272	4111070	2351083	1894176	4245259
Brunswick,	1214570	1666194	2880764	1230500	1703309	2933809
Buckingham,	2638113	1723192	4361305	2641523	1708468	4349991
Campbell,	2262360	1909498	4171858	2313821	1709073	4022894
Charlotte,	2438620	1877987	4316607	2449820	1873322	4323142
Culpeper,	2048576	1320811	3369387	2104206	1334520	3438726
Cumberland,	1544065	1216447	2760512	1546845	1168564	2715409
Dinwiddie,	1246640	1138881	2385521	1251330	1213230	2464560
Fauquier,	5074320	2117290	7191610	5093205	2076458	7169663
Franklin,	1521816	1080121	2601937	1528336	1124597	2652933
Fluvanna,	1526298	921226	2447524	1523638	956078	2479716
Greene,	578970	293440	872410	580100	317196	897296
Goochland,	2123060	1303586	3426646	2128610	1281656	3410266
Halifax,	4376679	3118003	7494682	4400164	3273008	7673172
Henry,	862868	542257	1405125	861808	649630	1511438
Loudoun,	7403681	2070136	9473817	7424348	2084859	9509207
Louisa,	2184050	1914747	4098797	2200990	1967928	4168918
Lunenburg,	1070415	1371425	2441840	1078675	1397633	2476308
Madison,	1557050	889862	2446912	1552010	885647	2437657
Mecklenburg,	2698158	2334619	5032777	2900542	2441132	5341674
Nelson,	1883475	1084169	2967644	1889415	1106297	2995712
Nottoway,	1250810	1161809	2412619	1252020	1214342	2466362
Orange,	1821090	1163860	2984950	1869440	1218246	3087686
Patrick,	545905	465037	1010942	547597	477195	1024792
Pittsylvania,	3276801	2414240	5691041	3268141	2465315	5733456
Prince Edward,	2255806	1450150	3705956	2251680	1445552	3697232
Powhatan,	1397382	973852	2371234	1398362	1007801	2406163
Rappahannock,	1697659	761456	2459115	1718170	790643	2508813
Lynchburg,	1484676	1069056	2553732	1565966	1073436	2639402
	71194608	47096191	118290799	71800056	48046788	119846844

Valley Division.	1849 Real estate taxed.	1849 Personal property taxed.	1849 Aggregate.	1850 Real estate taxed.	1850 Personal property taxed.	1850 Aggregate.
Alleghany,	533964	188273	722237	537034	179793	716827
Augusta,	5385412	1343755	6729167	5419712	1439500	6859212
Town of Staunton,	378710	194421	573131	387689	210480	607169
Bath,	679000	229944	908944	681350	239496	920846
Berkeley,	3362785	647857	4010642	3411184	643059	4054243
Botetourt,	2216187	996501	3212688	2224317	866924	3091241
Clarke,	2781950	752889	3534839	2767090	779170	3546260
Frederick,	3088905	656293	3745198	3105955	655646	3761601
Town of Winchester,	1075275	291894	1367169	1121790	310597	1432387
Hampshire,	2514343	450179	2964522	2523043	476706	2999749
Hardy,	2244175	411765	2655940	2254645	358428	2613073
Highland,	609980	152301	762281	621034	149352	770386
Jefferson,	4927520	1222638	6150158	4964780	1285434	6250214
Morgan,	563107	72337	635444	575171	76316	651487
Page,	1469285	374441	1843726	1478725	401138	1879863
Pendleton,	665277	212750	878027	665217	181873	847090
Roanoke,	1404908	541770	1946678	1414468	580676	1995144
Rockbridge,	2292071	1126615	3418686	2304181	1072934	3377115
Rockingham,	5228091	1102611	6330702	5237167	1147629	6384796
Shenandoah,	2853772	504533	3358305	2877663	514091	3391754
Warren,	1146305	399816	1546121	1155185	401244	1556429
	45421022	11873583	57294605	45727400	11979486	57706886

Trans-Alleghany Division.	1849. Real estate taxed.	1849. Personal property taxed.	1849. Aggregate.	1850. Real estate taxed.	1850. Personal property taxed.	1850. Aggregate.
Barbour,	576785	121171	697956	599195	130086	729281
Braxton,	359599	60695	420294	376348	61390	437738
Boone,	132770	50487	183257	149780	60325	210105
Brooke,	1312780	152723	1465503	1358839	180467	1539306
Cabell,	914306	167842	1082148	876028	153588	1029616
Carroll,	252286	75943	328229	261688	81474	343162
Doddridge,	215010	32312	247322	237610	35365	272975
Fayette,	774280	98671	872951	564160	80236	644396
Floyd,	451650	144482	596132	455410	137178	592588
Grayson.	310030	117721	427751	312390	175275	487665
Greenbrier,	2877294	540287	3417581	2828866	542870	3371736
Giles,	665317	216612	881929	667147	212232	879379
Gilmer,	309545	41119	350664	387635	43460	431095
Hancock,	680150	72583	752733	693652	82858	776510
Harrison,	1695459	286959	1982418	1701844	288717	1990561
Jackson,	776704	87085	863789	721063	80949	802012
Kanawha,	2253596	725883	2979479	2204730	718704	2923434
Lee,	751896	283990	1035886	756676	294153	1050829
Lewis,	952080	166673	1118753	991076	174369	1165445
Logan,	237545	95935	333480	187215	85368	272583
Marion,	984069	169747	1153816	1019009	176256	1195265
Marshall,	1365153	139578	1504731	1367303	143961	1511264
Mason,	1265841	221151	1486992	1275306	224951	1500257
Mercer,	232703	72862	305565	223773	80765	304538
Monongalia,	1455843	241891	1697734	1515958	256944	1772902
Monroe,	1933704	377641	2311345	1932614	387853	2320467
Montgomery,	858641	359145	1217786	861846	354562	1216408
Nicholas,	624680	62856	687536	638380	61958	700338
Ohio,	1546425	122855	1669280	1600290	124456	1724746
Preston,	801152	146847	947999	822650	160184	982834
Pocahontas,	623855	128652	757507	741065	130237	871302
Pulaski,	546140	350607	896747	546520	350333	896853
Putnam,	525479	167685	693164	558982	156005	714987
Raleigh,*				199345	26405	225750

Trans Alleghany Division—Concluded.	1849. Real estate taxed.	1849. Personal property taxed.	1849. Aggregate	1850. Real estate taxed.	1850. Personal property taxed.	1850. Aggregate.
Randolph,	713877	107487	821364	696422	111267	807689
Ritchie,	421445	44273	465718	413270	43390	456660
Russell,	630000	226985	856985	634880	328506	963386
Scott,	531930	531930	1063860	530000	206083	736083
Smyth,	1145800	289588	1435388	1182230	304901	1487131
Taylor,	477697	102896	580593	471567	110965	582532
Tazewell,	863487	302806	1166293	878082	309155	1187237
Tyler,	656108	73365	729473	677578	75650	753228
Washington,	2419195	694944	3114139	2428135	702167	3130302
Wayne,	348153	90961	439114	360895	89615	450510
Wetzel,	383630	48313	431943	425150	49315	474465
Wirt,	314390	45770	360160	316510	46157	362667
Wood,	1474801	195394	1670195	1559996	189671	1749667
Wyoming,*				49140	31333	80473
Wythe,	1557351	564279	2121630	1563741	609727	2173468
Wheeling City,	2695367	98910	2794277	2862014	96831	2958845
Total Trans-Alleghany Division,	43900998	9518591	53419589	44684003	9558667	54242670
Valley Division,	45421022	11873583	57294605	45727400	11979486	57706886
Piedmont Division,	71194608	47096191	118290799	71800056	48046788	119846844
Tide-Water Division,	69515902	40554454	110070356	70655709	42814635	113470344
Grand Total,	230032530	109042819	339075349	232867168	112399576	345266744
Amount of Bank stocks held by individuals, residents of the State,			5424750			5424750
			344500099			350691494
Eastern Division,	140710510	87650645	228361155	142455765	90861423	233317188
Western Division,	89322020	21392174	110714194	90411403	21538153	111949556

* Raleigh created in 1850 out of Fayette.
Wyoming created in 1850 out of Logan.

NOTE.—Instead of giving the value of the property of the commonwealth, on which taxes were paid, in the years 1849 and 1850, I have given the value of property on which taxes were *as sessed*, in those years. It is to be supposed that the delinquencies are tolerably uniform throughout the state. At any rate, the amount of the delinquencies depends more upon the care and diligence of the collectors than upon any other cause. Besides, it is very difficult to arrive at the actual amount of taxes paid in each county, and to reduce the amount of taxable property accordingly. It would not do to deduct the amount of the delinquent land and property lists from the amount of taxes assessed in each county, and reduce the value of the taxable property accordingly; for the amount of the delinquent land list is, as to the greater part thereof, paid into the Treasury, either upon redemptions in this office, or through tax sales of such lands to raise the amount of such delinquencies; and the amount of the delinquent property lists is, in part at least, paid into the Treasury through the Clerks of County Courts, or directly through this office. At any rate, property in existence in the state at the time of the assessment, was in existence when the taxes were collected, and is still in existence, or it has been substituted by other property of equal value.

In making up my estimates of the value of personal property, I have calculated taxed slaves at three hundred dollars each. I am informed that the Legislature, in fixing the rate of tax on slaves, as compared with land and other property, has generally considered them as worth three hundred dollars each. If this average price is considered too high or too low, each Member, desiring to do so, can, from Taxation table A., heretofore furnished to the Convention, and which shews the number of taxed slaves in each county, town, city and grand division of the State in 1850, by putting another value on them, add to or diminish the estimate which I have made for that year.

The number of taxed slaves in 1849 was 905 less than in 1850.

I have reckoned horses, mules, &c. at 40 dollars each; gold watches at 50 dollars each; patent lever and lepine silver watches at 25 dollars each; other watches at 10 dollars each; metallic clocks at 10 dollars each; other clocks at 5 dollars each; stallions and jacks at 200 dollars each; billiard tables at 300 dollars each.

Where the tax imposed by law was upon the business, as taxes on licenses generally were, and not directly upon the capital invested in that business, I have not estimated anything for such capital. Capital invested in trade, which consists of real estate, is taxed as real estate, and so included in my estimate, but not otherwise. I have added nothing, in this table, for the value of stock in joint stock companies, except Banks. The tax on dividends, or the dividends themselves, of such companies, afford no safe rule by which I can judge of the value of such stock. Some of the capital of such companies is invested in real estate, and so taxed and valued. I have added the amount of stock in the Banks of this state, held by citizens of the state, at the foot of this table. I could not distribute it, as it is owned, in counties and divisions, for want of the necessary information. I have put this stock at its par value, because I supposed that as it in part represented real and personal property, taxed and valued as such, elsewhere, the par value, together with the value of the real and personal property, would approximate the true value, or the selling price thereof, in the years 1849 and 1850.

All of which is respectfully submitted.

RO. JOHNSTON, First Auditor.

AUDITOR'S OFFICE, April 15th, 1851.

TABLES

SHEWING THE NUMBER OF

FREE WHITE PERSONS,

OVER THE AGE OF TWENTY YEARS,

IN THE

SEVERAL COUNTIES, CITIES, TOWNS & GRAND DIVISIONS

OF THE

STATE OF VIRGINIA,

WHO CANNOT READ AND WRITE:

THE NUMBER OF

FREE WHITE, FREE COLORED & SLAVE TITHEABLES

IN THE YEARS 1830, 1840 AND 1850;

THE

FREE WHITE, FREE COLORED & SLAVE POPULATION,

DISTINGUISHED,

IN THE SAME YEARS;

AND THE

AMOUNT & PER CENT. OF INCREASE OR DECREASE

OF

EACH CLASS OF POPULATION;

AND THE

AGGREGATE AMOUNT OF TAXES ASSESSED

IN THE YEARS 1840 AND 1850;

Substituting, however, in 1850, the estimated Tax on Lots and Lands in 1851, at the present rate of Taxation, under the late Assessment, for the actual Tax of 1850 under a former Assessment;

TOGETHER WITH THE

AMOUNT & PER CENT. OF INCREASE OR DECREASE

OF

TAXES BETWEEN THE PERIODS AFORESAID.

WILLIAM CULLEY, PRINTER,
146 Main street.

AUDITOR'S OFFICE,
RICHMOND, February 15, 1851.

Sir:—Herewith I have the honor of sending to you, for the use of the State Convention, "A Table shewing the number of free white persons, over the age of twenty years, in the several counties, cities, towns and grand divisions of the State of Virginia, who cannot read and write." Also, "A Table shewing the number of free white, free colored, and slave titheables in the several counties, cities, towns and grand divisions of the State of Virginia, in the years 1830, 1840 and 1850."

I send also, "A Table shewing the free white, free colored, and slave population, distinguished, in each of the counties, cities, towns and grand divisions of the Commonwealth of Virginia, in the years 1830, 1840 and 1850; and the amount and per cent. of increase or decrease in each county, city, town and division aforesaid, of each class of population aforesaid, between the periods aforesaid." Also, "A Table shewing the aggregate amount of taxes assessed in each county, city, town, and grand division, in the State of Virginia, in the years 1840 and 1850; substituting, however, in 1850, the estimated tax on lots and lands in 1851 at the present rate of taxation, under the late assessment, for the actual tax of 1850 under a former assessment; together with the amount and per cent. of increase or decrease of taxes, so ascertained between the periods aforesaid."

I have the honor to be, with great respect, your obedient servant,

RO. JOHNSTON, *First Auditor.*

To the Hon. JOHN Y. MASON, President of the Virginia State Convention.

A TABLE shewing the number of free white persons, over the age of twenty years, in the several counties, cities, towns and grand divisions of the State of Virginia, who cannot read and write, prepared in compliance with a resolution of the State Convention passed on the 2nd day of November, 1850.

TRANS-ALLEGHANY DISTRICT.

BARBOUR,	1305
BRAXTON,	829
BOONE,	553
BROOKE,	162
CABELL,	644
CARROLL,	938
DODDRIDGE,	327
FAYETTE,	364
FLOYD,	1086
GRAYSON,	131
GREENBRIER,	914
GILES,	601
GILMER,	569
HANCOCK,	185
HARRISON,	282
JACKSON,	873
KANAWHA,	1718
LEE,	1822
LEWIS,	1117
LOGAN,	700
MARION,	1203
MARSHALL,	977
MASON,	955
MERCER,	586
MONONGALIA,	1169
MONROE,	910
MONTGOMERY,	456
NICHOLAS,	45
OHIO,	176
PRESTON,	874
POCAHONTAS,	102
PULASKI,	496
PUTNAM,	861
RALEIGH,	108
RANDOLPH,	620
RITCHIE,	845
RUSSELL,	1751
SCOTT,	872
SMYTH,	476
TAYLOR,	107
TAZEWELL,	1517
TYLER,	588
WASHINGTON,	966
WAYNE,	505
WETZEL,	654
WIRT,	74
WOOD,	288
WYOMING,	274
WYTHE,	1705
Total of Trans-Alleghany District,	34280

VALLEY DISTRICT.

ALLEGHANY,	203
AUGUSTA, and town of Staunton,	1025
BATH,	5
BERKELEY,	286
BOTETOURT,	829
CLARKE,	121
FREDERICK, and town of Winchester,	126
HAMPSHIRE,	1229
HARDY,	972
HIGHLAND,	57
JEFFERSON,	436
MORGAN,	434
PAGE,	1004
PENDLETON,	1111
ROANOKE,	300
ROCKBRIDGE,	230
ROCKINGHAM,	2765
SHENANDOAH,	287
WARREN,	435
Total of Valley District,	11855

PIEDMONT DISTRICT.

ALBEMARLE,	759
AMELIA,	147
AMHERST,	238
APPOMATTOX,	321
BEDFORD,	1293
BRUNSWICK,	166
BUCKINGHAM,	485
CAMPBELL,	210
CHARLOTTE,	248
CULPEPER,	345
CUMBERLAND,	81
DINWIDDIE,	563
FAUQUIER,	500
FRANKLIN,	917
FLUVANNA,	384
GREEN,	494
GOOCHLAND,	314
HALIFAX,	548
HENRY,	813
LOUDOUN,	612
LOUISA,	500
LUNENBURG,	157
MADISON,	318
MECKLENBURG,	506
NELSON,	502
NOTTOWAY,	96
ORANGE,	274
PATRICK,	903
PITTSYLVANIA,	1266
PRINCE EDWARD,	105
POWHATAN,	
RAPPAHANNOCK,	426
LYNCHBURG,	152
Total of Piedmont District,	14643

TIDE-WATER DISTRICT.

ALEXANDRIA,	711
ACCOMACK,	1504
CHARLES CITY,	176
CAROLINE,	467
CHESTERFIELD,	1056
ESSEX,	400
ELIZABETH CITY,	203

FAIRFAX,	391
GREENSVILLE,	188
GLOUCESTER,	746
HANOVER,	414
HENRICO,	694
ISLE OF WIGHT,	918
JAMES CITY, and Williamsburg,	45
KING GEORGE,	236
KING WILLIAM,	204
KING & QUEEN,	401
LANCASTER,	156
MATHEWS,	437
MIDDLESEX,	132
NANSEMOND,	1006
NEW KENT,	198
NORFOLK County and P.	618
NORTHUMBERLAND,	416
NORTHAMPTON,	275
PRINCESS ANNE,	960
PRINCE GEORGE,	371
PRINCE WILLIAM,	763
RICHMOND,	569
STAFFORD,	222
SOUTHAMPTON,	1193
SPOTTSYLVANIA,	85
SURRY,	294
SUSSEX,	86
WARWICK,	55
WESTMORELAND,	400
YORK,	109
RICHMOND CITY,	635
NORFOLK CITY,	722
PETERSBURG,	658
FREDERICKSBURG,	32
Total of Tide Water District,	19146
Total of Piedmont District,	14643
Total of Valley District,	11855
Total of Trans-Alleghany District,	34280
Grand Total,	79924

The resolution, under which this Table was prepared, requested me "to report to the Convention the number of free white persons in this Commonwealth, over the age of twenty, who can *neither read nor write*." This I could not do. The schedules of the Assistant Marshals, the only source of information of this kind open to me, shew the number of free white persons, over twenty years of age, in the commonwealth, who cannot read and write. This information I have given above. It will be noticed that the returns from one district in Pittsylvania county, and from the county of Powhatan, are wanting. The schedules of Powhatan contained no information on the subject, and those of one district in Pittsylvania county have not been received at this office.

RO. JOHNSTON, First Auditor.

AUDITOR'S OFFICE, Richmond, February 15th, 1851.

A TABLE shewing the number of Free White, Free Coloured and Slave Titheables, for the years 1830, 1840 *and* 1850, *prepared in compliance with a resolution of the State Convention, adopted on the 17th October*, 1850.

TIDE-WATER DIVISION.	1830.				1840.				1850.			
	Free White.	Free Coloured.	Slave.	Total.	Free White.	Free Coloured.	Slave.	Total.	Free White.	Free Coloured.	Slave.	Total.
Accomac, - -	2043	414	1904	4361	2270	449	2036	4755	2331	513	1824	4668
Alexandria, - -									1361	218	630	2209
Caroline, - -	1582	68	4826	6476	1603	105	4464	6172	1334	112	5051	6497
Charles City, - -	441	155	1531	2127	381	163	1386	1930	438	191	1322	1951
Chesterfield, - -	1658	17		1675	1649	11		1660	1727	80	4552	6359
Elizabeth City, - -	411	25	882	1318	387	19	933	1339	396	23	979	1398
Essex, - -	785	66	2682	3533	678	57	2733	3468	731	81	2836	3648
Fairfax, - -	1254	72	1786	3112	1228	80	1391	2699	1446	75	1381	2902
Gloucester, - -	878	3		881	899	5		904	953	114	2567	3634
Greensville, - -	479	48	2139	2666	499	34	1191	1724	400	33	1812	2245
Hanover, - -	1532	22	4472	6026	1482	74	3732	5288	1490	49	3759	5298
Henrico, - -	1237		1101	2338	1385	180	2955	4520	1827	195	3128	5150
Isle of Wight, - -	1128	233	1969	3330	1210	300	1889	3399	665	282	1741	2688
James City, - -	248	124	865	1237	394	122	858	1374	259	132	884	1275
King George, - -	520	26	1763	2309	512	52	1541	2105	414	52	1574	2040
King William, - -	528			528	299			299	594	50	2601	3245
King & Queen, - -	656	70	3011	3737		95	2419	2514	862	86	2638	3586
Lancaster, - -	451	35	1163	1649	427		1115	1542	448	38	1291	1777
Mathews, - -	883	21	1766	2670	804	20	1417	2241	776	25	1223	2024
Middlesex, - -	409	25	962	1396	381	27	922	1330	469	36	1048	1553
Nansemond, - -	1168	315	2479	3962	1303	398	2356	4057	1153	370	2239	3762
New Kent, - -	644		1603	2247	559	50	1501	2110	581	65	1542	2188
Norfolk County, - -	1729	112	1729	3570	2006	207	2598	4811	1209	282	2106	3597
Northampton, - -	781	210	1806	2797	813	155	2032	3000	739	152	1184	2075
Northumberland, - -	928	98	1609	2635	805	75	1471	2351	800	105	1448	2353
Princess Anne, - -	1218	62	1709	2989	1082	57	1476	2615	1112	53	1387	2552
Prince George, - -	800	109	2172	3081	803	99	2060	2962	696	118	2342	3156
Prince William, - -	1176		1626	2802	1167	117	1252	2536	1176	97	1095	2368
Richmond, - -	638	78	1398	2114	739	103	1296	2138	751	108	1038	1897
Southampton, - -	1605	341	4367	6313	1483	318	3100	4901	1363	315	2716	4394

TIDE-WATER DIVISION CONTINUED.	1830. Free White.	Free Coloured.	Slave.	Total.	1840. Free White.	Free Coloured.	Slave.	Total.	1850. Free White.	Free Coloured.	Slave.	Total.
Spottsylvania, - -	1021	25	3673	4719	1086	51	3106	4243	1088	62	2939	4089
Stafford, - -	934	45	1637	2616	1110	37	1464	2611	672	15	1374	2061
Surry, - -	879		1776	2655	611	172	1430	2213	592	231	1414	2237
Sussex, - -	970	185	3644	4799	839	151	3384	4374	748	171	2978	3897
Warwick, - -	153	4	469	626	137	4	443	584	182	7	498	687
Westmoreland, - -	858	157	1626	2641	779	182	1657	2618	738	204	1640	2582
York, - -	457	148	1176	1781	479	150	1145	1774	417	130	905	1452
Fredericksburg, - -	356	99	597	1052	456	81	637	1174	478	57	557	1092
Norfolk City, - -	1200			1200	1109			1109	2568	94	* 2078	4740
Petersburg, - -	852	195	690	1737	1384	490	891	2765	1415	541	2183	4139
Richmond City, - -	1683	179		1862	2441	277		2718	4159	389	* 5502	10050
Williamsburg, - -	150	21		171	163	18	376	557	155	17	322	494
Total in Tide-Water Division,	37723				37842				41713	5968	82328	130009

PIEDMONT DIVISION.	1830. Free White.	Free Coloured.	Slave.	Total.	1840. Free White.	Free Coloured.	Slave.	Total.	1850. Free White.	Free Coloured.	Slave.	Total.
Albemarle, - -	2423	68	6393	8884	2500	99	6445	9044	2796	128	4986	7910
Amelia, - -	707		3848	4555	724	68	3893	4685	645	49	3287	3981
Amherst, - -	1425		2742	4167	1471	47	2547	4065	1364	49	2482	3895
Appomattox, - -									976	47	2025	3048
Bedford, - -	2860			2860	1232	90	3946	5268	3100	22	4434	7556
Brunswick, - -	1158	105	4305	5568	1749	91	5035	6875	1170	136	3952	5258
Buckingham, - -	1684	62	4734	6480	1863	90	3955	5908	1413	52	3783	5248
Campbell, - -	1830	87	3590	5507	1262		4283	5545	2035	105	3648	5788
Charlotte, - -	1432		4575	6007	1068	45	2425	3538	875	146	3248	4269
Culpeper, - -	3369	38	4478	7885	742	58	3098	3898	643	34	1300	1977
Cumberland, - -	912	51	3300	4263	982	83	3523	4588	711	35	2959	3705
Dinwiddie, - -	1155	94	3423	4672	2055	94	4328	6477	1027	102	3178	4307
Fauquier, - -	2762	76	5041	7879	1051		1833	2884	2499	121	4471	7091
Fluvanna, - -	984		1698	2682	2402	26	2140	4568	1077	51	2186	3314
Franklin, - -	2241	30	2186	4457	840	98	2613	3551	2839	20	2496	5355
Goochland, - -	988			988	563			563	128	123	2804	3055
Green, - -	3126	122	3076	6324	2814	120	6095	9029	650	6	733	1389
Halifax, - -	949		1361	2310	1004		1297	2301	2396	156	6821	9373
Henry, - -	1707			1707	3546	232	2405	6183	1337	37	1486	2860
Loudoun, - -	1582	33	4169	5784	1404	29	3923	5361	3707	286	2589	6582
Louisa, - -	1075	19	3780	4874	1009	29	3669	4707	1520	47	4086	5653
Lunenburg, - -	982			982	937	10	1714	2661	1015	32	3394	4441
Madison, - -	1798	153	5273	7224	1770	248	5421	7439	970	13	1931	2914
Mecklenburg - -	1263		2679	3942	1377		2069	3446	1752	246	5760	7758
Nelson, - -	627	24	3565	4216	570	22	3335	3927	1322	19	2579	3920
Nottoway, - -	1479	27	3044	4550	852	24	2381	3257	576	29	2923	3528
Orange, - -	1233	134	933	2300	1343	90	928	2361	963	20	2670	3653
Patrick, - -	3349		4838	8187	3398	99	5068	8565	1606	31	979	2616
Pittsylvania, - -	660	106	2671	3437	607	91	3581	4279	3596	176	5627	9399
Powhatan, - -	1380	83	4114	5577	1156	101	4114	5371	629	107	2512	3248
Prince Edward, - -					1178	42	1492	2712	1044	142	3604	4790
Rappahannock, - -					704	76	1066	1846	1361	31	1605	2997
Lynchburg, - -	587	56	851	1494					968	78	1221	2267
Total in Piedmont Division,	47727				44173				48710	2676	101759	153145

VALLEY DIVISION,	1830. Free White.	1830. Free Coloured.	1830. Slave.	1830. Total.	1840. Free White.	1840. Free Coloured.	1840. Slave.	1840. Total.	1850. Free White.	1850. Free Coloured.	1850. Slave.	1850. Total.
Alleghany,	536	10	296	842	582	11	284	877	665	11	56	732
Augusta,	3670	47	1805	5522	3518	87	1805	5410	4022	104	2057	6183
Bath,	671	16	509	1196	769	10	485	1264	627	7	391	1025
Berkeley,	1816	36	797	2649	2084	35	840	2959	2036	25	912	2983
Botetourt,	2854	75	1992	4921	2053	88	1383	3524	2267	106	1765	4138
Clarke,						23	1605	1628	835	21	1612	2468
Frederick,	832	92	3548	4472	2492	94	1009	3595	2343	62	853	3258
Hampshire,	2138	21	514	2673	2605	25	645	3275	2827	40	605	3472
Hardy,	1403	55	468	1926	1346	49	473	1868	1765	45	495	2305
Highland,									965	5	188	1158
Jefferson,	2257	91	2213	4561	2298	57	2221	4576	2368	83	2067	4518
Morgan,	583	4	60	647	666	1	50	717	820	2	56	878
Page,					1245	49	407	1701	1569	45	525	2139
Pendleton,	1335	4	252	1581	1534	5	270	1809	1336	7	166	1509
Roanoke,					971	25	731	1727	1267	29	1016	2312
Rockbridge,	2540			2540	2412			2412	2677	80	2084	4841
Rockingham,	3732	113	968	4813	3732	97	900	4729	4221	106	1093	5420
Shenandoah,	3870		1172	5042	2631		583	3214	3123	55	482	3660
Warren,					901	62	605	1568	999	21	703	1723
Staunton,	285	19	258	562	281	12	262	555	447	8	334	789
Winchester,	629	38	244	902		88	281	369	736	117	314	1167
Total in Valley Division,	29151				32120				37915	989	17774	56678

TRANS-ALLEGHANY DIVISION.	1830. Free White.	1830. Free Coloured	1830. Slave.	1830. Total.	1840. Free White.	1840. Free Coloured.	1840. Slave.	1840. Total.	1850. Free White.	1850. Free Coloured.	1850. Slave.	1850. Total.
Barbour,									2045	45	47	2137
Boone,									705		88	793
Braxton,							29	29	978		40	1018
Brooke,	1412	6	91	1509	1778	10	54	1842	1218	8	27	1253
Cabell,	1140	8	241	1389	1619	6	240	1865	1390	4	181	1575
Carroll,									1242	3	68	1313
Doddridge,									617		12	629
Fayette,					899	4	60	963	849	4	90	943
Floyd,					920	2	138	1060	1326	1	175	1502
Giles,	1104	12	259	1375	1022	12	285	1319	1361	7	310	1678
Gilmer,									702		13	715
Grayson,	1524	17	186	1727	1766	16	200	1982	1309	5	242	1556
Greenbrier,	1735	9	489	2233	1899	27	605	2531	2143	64	725	2932
Hancock,									1056	1	2	1059
Harrison,	2591		286	2877	3594		284	3878	2400	6	222	2628
Jackson,					941		35	976	724		21	745
Kanawha,	1736	12	766	2514	2433	25	1277	3735	2417	44	1630	4091
Lee,	1167		247	1414	1549		240	1789	1857	3	349	2209
Lewis,	1131		73	1204	1662		67	1729	2171	4	124	2299
Logan,	719			719	842		64	906	797		46	843
Marion,									2368	3	46	2417
Marshall,					1600	7	31	1638	2127	5	28	2160
Mason,	1233	7	281	1521	1491	17	365	1873	1547	12	261	1820
Mercer,					478	4	60	542	944		88	1032
Monongalia,	2933	19	207	3159	3696	19	141	3956	2732	11	79	2822
Monroe,	1597	14	358	1969	1717	12	473	2202	1873	10	506	2389
Montgomery,	2187	8	893	3088	1274	23	599	1896	1448	7	622	2077
Nicholas,	782	1	61	844	532		32	564	856		34	890
Ohio,	3233		120	3353	2970	50	84	3104	1380		42	1422
Pocahontas,	610	5	114	729	657	6	92	755	829	7	148	984
Preston,	1101		57	1158	1232	2	43	1277	2797	1	45	2843
Pulaski,					693	9	422	1124	821	6	692	1519
Putnam,									1081	2	254	1337
Raleigh,									519	1	12	532
Randolph,	1032	23	123	1178	1217	30	100	1347	1137	8	104	1249
Ritchie,									777		1	778
Russell,	1278		292	1570	1456	2	305	1763	2195	9	410	2614

TRANS-ALLEGHANY DIVISION CONTINUED.	1830.				1840.				1850.			
	Free White.	Free Coloured.	Slave.	Total.	Free White.	Free Coloured.	Slave.	Total.	Free White.	Free Coloured.	Slave.	Total.
Scott,	1161	4	118	1283	1412	5	147	1564	1845	8	190	2043
Smyth,					1164	34	410	1608	1507	35	476	2018
Taylor,									1157	1	83	1341
Tazewell,	1056		307	1363	1215	10	318	1543	1806	11	442	2259
Tyler,	812		44	856	1406		46	1452	1246		19	1265
Washington,	2805	45	1067	3917	2392	31	864	3287	2733	20	1046	3799
Wayne,									1035	2	83	1120
Wetzel,									878	5	2	885
Wood,	1194	9	284	1487	1914	7	264	2185	2129	13	150	2292
Wythe,	2274	7	886	3167	1765	27	758	2550	2108	38	1007	3153
Wyoming,									323		24	347
Wirt,									698		16	714
Wheeling,									2417	28	27	2472
Total in Trans-Alleghany Division,	39547				51205				72620	442	11349	84411
Total Trans-Alleghany,	39547				51205				72620	442	11349	84411
Total Tide-Water,	37723				37842				41713	5968	82328	130009
Total Piedmont,	47727				44173				48710	2676	101759	153145
Total Valley,	29151				32120				37915	989	17774	56678
Grand Total,	154148				165340				200958	10075	213210	424243

This Table is necessarily incomplete: I could not procure the materials therefor. It is complete for the year 1850, except as to the slave titheables of the cities of Richmond and Norfolk. The Commissioners' books of these cities do not give this information, and the city authorities, I was informed, could not furnish it. I have estimated the slave titheables of these two cities.

RO. JOHNSTON, First Auditor.

Auditor's Office, Richmond, February 15th, 1851.

A TABLE shewing the aggregate amount of Taxes assessed in each county, city, town and grand division in the Commonwealth of Virginia, in the years 1840 *and* 1850,*—substituting, however, in* 1850, *the estimated tax on lots and lands in* 1851, *at the present rate of taxation, under the late assessment, for the actual tax of* 1850, *under a former assessment; together with the amounts and per centage of increase or decrease of the taxes, so ascertained between the periods aforesaid;—prepared in part compliance with a resolution of the State Convention, passed on the 25th day of January,* 1851.

TIDE-WATER DISTRICT.	Aggregate amount of taxes payable in 1840.	Aggreg'e am't of taxes that would have b'n payable in 1850 accord'g to the terms of the Resolution.	Amount of increase.	Amount of decrease.	Per centage of increase.	Per centage of decrease.
ALEXANDRIA,*		7539 67	7539 67			
ACCOMACK,	4665 71	6258 01	1592 30		34	
CHARLES CITY,	1521 71	2169 34	647 63		42½	
CAROLINE,	4979 86	6204 85	1224 99		24½	
CHESTERFIELD,	6127 45	7709 68	1582 23		25¾	
ESSEX,	3162 88	4219 07	1056 19		33⅓	
ELIZABETH CITY,	1118 37	1713 28	594 91		53	
FAIRFAX,	2927 31	4841 23	1913 92		65¼	
GREENSVILLE,	2501 21	1949 56		551 65		22
GLOUCESTER,	2881 38	3742 20	860 82		29¾	
HANOVER,	4677 99	5681 10	1003 11		21¼	
HENRICO,	5672 07	8372 43	2700 36		47½	
ISLE OF WIGHT,	2324 83	3202 38	877 55		37¾	
JAMES CITY,	1002 34	1335 92	333 58		33	
KING GEORGE,	1875 39	2583 16	707 77		37½	
KING & QUEEN,	3001 34	3921 32	919 98		30½	
KING WILLIAM,	3030 82	3419 94	389 12		12¾	
LANCASTER,	1346 95	1867 40	520 45		38½	
MATHEWS,	1618 82	1622 75	3 93		¼	
MIDDLESEX,	1256 30	1659 86	403 56		32	
NANSEMOND,	2853 28	3581 75	728 52		25½	

TIDE-WATER DISTRICT.—CONCLUDED.	Aggregate amount of taxes payable in 1840	Aggreg'e am't of taxes that would have been payable in 1850 accord'g to the terms of the Resolution.	Amount of increase.	Amount of decrease.	Per centage of increase.	Per centage of decrease.
NORFOLK County (including Portsmouth,)	5363 44	7697 35	2333 91		43½	
NEW KENT,	1594 29	1928 06	333 77		2¾	
NORTHUMBERL'D,	1630 48	2375 57	745 09		45½	
NORTHAMPTON,	2734 42	3342 72	608 30		22	
PRINCESS ANNE,	2159 08	2485 86	326 78		15	
PRINCE GEORGE,	2426 22	3508 80	1082 58		44½	
PRINCE WILLIAM,	2541 60	3233 51	691 91		27	
RICHMOND	1521 64	1827 05	305 41		20	
SOUTHAMPTON,	3706 52	4993 43	1286 91		24¼	
SPOTTSYLVANIA,	3497 84	4632 22	1134 38		32¼	
SURRY,	1558 24	2156 08	597 84		38¼	
SUSSEX,	3257 53	3224 88		32 65		1
STAFFORD,	2141 94	2725 33	583 39		27	
WARWICK,	505 02	616 52	111 50		22	
WESTMOREL'D,	1977 58	2695 14	717 56		36¼	
YORK,	1060 00	1458 56	398 56		37½	
NORFOLK CITY,	7969 36	13483 26	5513 90		69	
PETERSBURG,	6511 22	11483 41	4972 19		76¼	
WILLIAMSBURG,	632 99	926 39	293 40		46¼	
RICHMOND CITY,	17604 74	28835 50	11230 76		63¾	
FREDERICKSBURG	2667 50	3408 28	740 78		27½	
Total,	$131607 61	$190632 82	$59609 51	$584 30		
Deducted,			584 30			
Nett increase including Alexandria,			59025 21		44¼	
* Alexandria deducted,			7539 67			
Nett increase exclusive of Alexandria,			$51485 54		39	

PIEDMONT DISTRICT.	Aggregate amount of taxes payable in 1840.	Aggreg'e am't of taxes that would have b'n payable in 1850 accord'g to the terms of the Resolution.	Amount of increase.	Amount of decrease.	Per centage of increase.	Per centage of decrease.
APPOMATTOX,*		2722 55	2722 55			
ALBEMARLE,	7839 61	11790 48	3950 87		50¼	
AMELIA,	3573 83	3651 31	77 48		2	
AMHERST,	3189 66	3924 95	735 29		23	
BEDFORD,	4654 41	6600 50	1946 09		41¾	
BRUNSWICK,	3612 10	4091 99	479 89		13¼	
BUCKINGHAM,	6224 74	5266 56		958 18		15 1-4
CAMPBELL, including Lynchburg,	8296 58	12048 86	3752 28		45	
CHARLOTTE,	5323 45	6096 85	773 40		14½	
CULPEPER,	3725 74	5153 74	1428 00		38	
CUMBERLAND,	3340 59	3787 59	447 00		13¼	
DINWIDDIE,	3015 52	3596 03	580 51		19	
FLUVANNA,	2606 43	3238 20	631 77		24	
FAUQUIER,	8406 39	11304 77	2898 38		34¼	
FRANKLIN,	2925 39	4009 62	1084 23		37	
GOOCHLAND,	3746 51	4631 71	885 20		23¼	
GREENE,	959 47	1357 17	397 70		41¼	
HALIFAX,	8234 93	9385 03	1150 10		13¾	
HENRY.	1626 66	2231 99	605 33		37	
LOUDOUN,	10517 80	15001 60	4483 80		42½	
LOUISA,	4401 66	6061 14	1659 48		37½	
LUNENBURG,	2909 72	3539 53	629 81		21½	
MADISON,	2538 14	4394 51	1856 37		73	
MECKLENBURG,	6510 02	7197 98	687 96		10½	
NELSON,	3630 18	4057 23	427 05		11¾	
NOTTOWAY,	2855 37	3236 96	381 59		13¼	
ORANGE.	3302 95	4717 86	1414 91		42¾	
PATRICK,	1098 40	1722 74	624 34		56¾	
PITTSYLVANIA,	6392 75	8197 71	1804 96		28	
POWHATAN,	2987 00	3546 43	559 40		18½	
PRINCE EDWARD,	5420 97	5438 27	17 30		¼	

PIEDMONT DISTRICT.—CONCLUDED.	Aggregate amount of taxes payable in 1840.	Aggreg'e am't of taxes that would have b'n payable in 1850 accord'g to the terms of the Resolution.	Amount of increase.	Amount of decrease.	Per centage of increase.	Per centage of decrease.
RAPPAHANNOCK, - - - -	2728 50	3602 09	873 59		32	
Total,	$136595 47	$175603 95	$39966 66 958 18	958 18		
Total increase,			$39008 48		28 1-2	
APPOMATTOX,* (created since 1840,) - -		2722 55				
BUCKINGHAM, - - - -	6224 74	5266 56				
CAMPBELL, - - - -	8296 58	12048 86				
CHARLOTTE, - - - -	5323 45	6096 85				
PRINCE EDWARD, - - - -	5420 97	5438 27				
Total,	$25265 74	$31573 09	6307 35		28 3-4	

VALLEY DISTRICT.	Aggregate amount of taxes payable in 1840	Aggreg'e am't of taxes that would have b'n payable in 1850 accord'g to the terms of the R solution.	Amount of increase.	Amount of decrease.	Per centage of increase.	Per centage of decrease.
ALLEGHANY,	788 80	1072 93	284 13		36	
AUGUSTA, including Staunton,	8266 47	13805 90	5539 43		67	
BATH,	1419 53	1369 89		49 64		3 1-4
BERKELEY,	4645 58	6712 79	2067 21		44 1-2	
BOTETOURT,	3885 78	4980 01	1094 23		23	
CLARKE,	4354 35	5680 84	1326 49		30 1-4	
FREDERICK,	4369 90	6165 12	1795 22		41	
HARDY,	3105 21	3869 22	764 01		21 1-4	
HAMPSHIRE,	3803 33	5156 51	1353 18		35 1-2	
HIGHLAND,*		1797 34	1797 34			
JEFFERSON,	7460 44	11161 65	3701 21		49 1-2	
MORGAN,	773 78	1123 80	350 02		46 1 2	
PAGE,	1976 97	2814 97	838 00		42 1-4	
PENDLETON,	1550 17	1580 08	29 91		1 3-4	
ROANOKE,	1948 02	3142 88	1194 86		61 1-4	
ROCKINGHAM,	6745 82	10139 48	3393 66		50 1-4	
ROCKBRIDGE,	3912 75	6289 64	2376 89		60 1-2	
SHENANDOAH,	3771 62	5747 74	1976 12		52 1-4	
WARREN,	1810 57	2666 44	855 87		47	
WINCHESTER,	2054 51	3521 61	1467 10		71 1-4	
Total,	$66643 60	$98798 84	$32204 88	49 64		
			49 64			
Total increase,			$32155 24		44 1-4	
BATH,	1419 53	1369 89				
HIGHLAND,* (created since 1840.)		1797 34				
PENDLETON,	1550 17	1580 08				
Total,	$2969 70	$4747 31	$1777 61		59 3-4	

TRANS-ALLEGHANY DISTRICT.	Aggregate amount of taxes payable in 1840.	Aggreg'e am't of taxes that would have b'n payable in 1850 accord'g to the terms of the Resolution.	Amount of increase.	Amount of decrease.	Per centage of increase.	Per centage of decrease.
BARBOUR,*		1905 60	1905 60			
BRAXTON,	429 65	861 18	431 53		100 1-4	
BOONE,*		460 59	460 59			
BROOKE,	2519 28	2431 99		87 29		3 1-4
CABELL,	1793 17	1943 83	150 66		8 1-4	
CARROLL,*		964 80	964 80			
DODDRIDGE,*		762 52	762 52			
FAYETTE,	817 92	839 96	22 04		2 1-2	
FLOYD,	710 10	1099 39	389 29		54 3-4	
GRAYSON,	906 72	1092 62	185 90		20 1-2	
GREENBRIER,	3901 26	4717 98	816 72		20 3-4	
GILES,	1012 80	1669 37	656 57		64 3-4	
GILMER,*		1231 97	1231 97			
HANCOCK,*		1295 14	1295 14			
HARRISON,	3683 67	4209 34	525 67		14 1-4	
JACKSON,	1106 46	1931 23	824 77		70 1-4	
KANAWHA,	4209 68	5413 02	1203 34		28 1 2	
LEE,	1316 95	1872 05	555 10		42	
LEWIS,	1612 24	3019 79	1407 55		87 1 4	
LOGAN,	449 02	606 54	157 52		35	
MARION,*		3048 95	3048 95			
MARSHALL,	1851 26	2978 10	1126 84		60 3 4	
MASON,	2144 74	2656 58	511 84		23 3 4	
MERCER,	397 96	772 19	374 23		94	
MONONGALIA,	3083 71	3802 52	718 81		23 1-4	
MONROE,	2711 41	2564 18	852 77		31 1 4	
MONTGOMERY,	1687 72	2507 70	819 98		48 1-2	
NICHOLAS,	711 44	1053 78	342 34		48	
OHIO, incl'g Wheeling	6888 35	9780 05	2891 70		41 3 4	
PRESTON,	1053 03	2295 27	1242 24		117 3-4	
POCAHONTAS,	874 14	1414 83	540 69		61 3 4	

TRANS-ALLEGHANY DISTRICT.—CONTINUED.	Aggregate amount of taxes payable in 1840.	Aggreg'e am't of taxes that would have b'n payable in 1850 accord'g to the terms of the Resolution.	Amount of increase.	Amount of decrease.	Per centage of increase.	Per centage of decrease.
PULASKI,	992 24	1689 99	697 75		70 1-4	
PUTNAM,*		1268 59	1268 59			
RALEIGH,*		348 60	348 60			
RANDOLPH,	1355 83	1604 41	248 58		18 1-4	
RITCHIE,*		1137 70	1137 70			
RUSSELL,	1217 43	1880 18	662 75		54 1-4	
SCOTT,	1056 28	1439 91	383 63		36 1-4	
SMYTH,	1738 06	2525 82	787 76		45 1-4	
TAYLOR,*		1687 70	1687 70			
TAZEWELL,	1438 60	2216 34	777 74		54	
TYLER,	1362 58	1420 88	58 30		4 1-4	
WASHINGTON,	3819 56	5009 61	1190 05		31	
WAYNE,*		1019 79	1019 79			
WETZEL,*		941 04	941 04			
WIRT,*		921 51	921 51			
WOOD,	2457 17	3563 82	1106 65		45	
WYOMING,*		370 08	370 08			
WYTHE,	2624 15	4208 72	1584 57		60 1-4	
Total,	$63934 58	$105457 75	$41610 46	$87 29		
			87 29			
Total increase,			$41523 17		64 3-4	

* See pp. 38-39.

Counties whose boundaries have been changed, and Counties formed, since 1840.

TRANS-ALLEGHANY DISTRICT.	Aggregate amount of taxes payable in 1840.	Aggreg'e am't of taxes that would have b'n payable in 1850 accord'g to the terms of the Resolution.	Amount of increase.	Per centage of increase.
BARBOUR,*		1905 60		
BOONE,*		460 59		
CABELL,	1793 17	1943 83		
DODDRIDGE,*		762 52		
GILMER,*	—	1231 97		
HARRISON,	3683 67	4209 34		
JACKSON,	1106 46	1931 23		
KANAWHA,	4209 68	5413 02		
LEWIS,	1612 24	3019 79		
LOGAN,	449 02	606 54		
MARION,*		3048 95		
MASON,	2144 74	2656 58		
MONONGALIA,	3083 71	3802 52		
PUTNAM,*		1268 59		
RANDOLPH,	1355 83	1604 41		
RITCHIE,*		1137 70		
TAYLOR,*		1687 70		
TYLER,	1362 58	1420 88		
WAYNE,*		1019 79		
WOOD,	2457 17	3563 82		
WETZEL,*		941 04		
WIRT,*		921 51		
WYOMING,*		370 08		
Total,	$23258 27	$44928 00	$21669 73	93
BROOKE,		2431 99		
HANCOCK,*		1295 14		
Total,	$2519 28	$3727 13	$1207 85	47 3-4

TRANS-ALLEGHANY DISTRICT—CONCLUDED.	Aggregate amount of taxes payable in 1840.	Aggreg'e am't of taxes that would have b'n payable in 1850 accord'g to the terms of the Resolution.	Amount of increase.	Per centage of increase.
FAYETTE, ...	817 92	839 96		
RALEIGH,*		348 60		
Total,	$817 92	$1188 56	379 64	45 1-4
GRAYSON, ...	906 72	1092 62		
CARROLL,*		964 80		
Total,	906 72	$2057 42	$1150 70	126 3-4

* Created since 1840.

RECAPITULATION.

DISTRICTS.	Aggregate amount of taxes payable in 1840.	Aggregate amount of taxes which would have been payable in 1850.	Amount of increase.	Per centage of increase.
TIDE WATER DISTRICT, - - - - - -	$131607 61	$190632 82	$59025 21	44 3-4
PIEDMONT DISTRICT, - - - - - -	136595 47	175603 95	39008 48	28 1 2
VALLEY DISTRICT, - - - - - -	66643 60	98798 84	32155 24	48
TRANS-ALLEGHANY DISTRICT, - - - - -	63934 58	105457 75	41523 17	64 3-4
TIDE WATER & PIEDMONT DISTRICTS, OR EASTERN VIRGINIA, - -	$268203 08	$366236 77	$98033 69	36 1 2
VALLEY & TRANS-ALLEGHANY DISTRICTS, OR WESTERN VIRGINIA, -	130578 18	204256 59	73678 41	56 1-4
COMMONWEALTH, - - - - - -	$398781 26	$570493 36	$171712 10	43

The formation of new Counties in the Trans Alleghany Division, since 1840, has prevented me from making calculations of the per cent. and amount of increase in the Taxes in that region, except as above.

Auditor's Office, Feb. 15, 1851.

RO. JOHNSTON, First Auditor.

A STATEMENT

SHEWING THE

NUMBER OF WHITE MALES & WHITE FEMALES,

OVER TWENTY-ONE YEARS OF AGE,

IN THE

SEVERAL COUNTIES, TOWNS & GRAND DIVISIONS

OF THE

STATE OF VIRGINIA.

AUDITOR'S OFFICE,
Richmond, March 20th, 1851.

Sir—I have the honor of transmitting to you, "A Table shewing the white males and white females over twenty-one years of age, in the several counties, &c., of the commonwealth, in the years 1840 and 1850," prepared in compliance with a resolution of the Convention passed on the 21st day of October, 1850.

I am, with high respect, your obedient servant,

RO. JOHNSTON, First Auditor.

To the Hon. John Y. Mason, President of the Virginia State Convention.

A TABLE shewing the number of White Males and the number of White Females, over the age of 21 years, in each of the counties, cities and towns of the four grand divisions of the commonwealth, for the years 1840 and 1850; prepared in compliance with a resolution of the Convention adopted October 21st, 1850.

Tide Water Division.	1840. Males.	1840. Females.	1840. Aggregate.	1850. Males.	1850. Females.	1850. Aggregate.
Alexandria, - - -				1581	1907	3488
Accomac, - - -	2073	2438	4511	2092	2327	4419
Charles City, - - -	255	389	644	402	386	788
Caroline, - - -	1385	1619	3004	1476	1741	3217
Chesterfield, - - -	1683	1988	3671	1899	2005	3904
Essex, - - -	796	1054	1850	638	753	1391
Elizabeth City, - - -	306	438	744	578	514	1092
Fairfax, - - -	1234	1239	2473	1609	1519	3128
Greensville, - - -	418	468	886	384	417	801
Gloucester, - - -	970	1006	1976	881	920	1801
Hanover, - - -	1309	1617	2926	1377	1609	2986
Henrico, - - -	1403	1446	2849	1969	2058	4027
Isle of Wight, - - -	1064	1202	2266	995	1069	2064
James City and W. - -	414	305	719	391	363	754
King George, - - -	461	531	992	459	513	972
King and Queen, - -	911	1040	1951	768	1001	1769
King William, - - -	670	807	1477	590	657	1247
Lancaster, - - -	400	469	869	391	404	795
Mathews, - - -	840	987	1827	712	856	1568
Middlesex, - - -	406	491	897	380	425	805
Nansemond, - - -	1028	1113	2141	1215	1297	2512
New Kent, - - -	520	587	1107	476	517	993
Norfolk, - - -	1162	1226	2388	1168	1087	2255
Northumberland, - - -	843	905	1748	618	598	1216
Northampton, - - -	765	820	1585	605	658	1263
Princess Anne, - - -	854	874	1728	987	891	1878
Prince George, - - -	630	573	1203	615	640	1255
Prince William, - - -	1019	1135	2154	1048	1181	2229
Richmond, - - -	551	748	1299	660	756	1416
Stafford, - - -	996	1142	2138	1007	1129	2136
Southampton, - - -	1320	1499	2819	1295	1565	2860
Spottsylvania, - - -	979	1107	2086	947	1111	2058
Surry, - - -	601	678	1279	519	551	1070
Sussex, - - -	761	945	1706	623	790	1413
Warwick, - - -	121	132	253	140	123	263
Westmoreland, - - -	751	745	1496	728	792	1520
York, - - -	450	410	860	397	395	792
Fredericksburg, - - -	549	606	1155	576	663	1239
Norfolk City, - - -	1334	1702	3036	2056	2460	4516
Petersburg, - - -	1423	1279	2702	1580	1692	3272
Portsmouth, - - -	878	1012	1890	1892	1396	3288
Richmond City, - - -	2803	2616	5419	4044	3562	7606
Total Tide Water,	37336	41388	78724	42768	45298	88066

Piedmont Division.	1840. Males.	1840. Females.	1840. Aggregate.	1850. Males.	1850. Females.	1850. Aggregate.
Albemarle,	2361	2263	4624	2753	2468	5221
Amelia,	699	760	1459	672	697	1369
Amherst,	1497	1388	2885	1477	1392	2869
Appomattox,				928	973	1901
Bedford,	2430	2293	4723	3300	2848	6148
Brunswick,	1053	1175	2228	945	1052	1997
Buckingham,	1697	1660	3357	1230	1245	2475
Campbell,	1579	1498	3077	1752	1644	3396
Charlotte,	1086	1117	2203	986	1039	2025
Culpeper,	1085	1188	2273	1213	1353	2566
Cumberland,	792	790	1582	689	703	1392
Dinwiddie,	983	1103	2086	1002	1016	2018
Fauquier,	2211	2411	4622	2286	2457	4743
Franklin,	2098	2183	4281	2339	2409	4748
Fluvanna,	956	1010	1966	962	1002	1964
Greene,	545	539	1084	593	611	1204
Goochland,	857	926	1783	877	977	1854
Halifax,	2326	2489	4815	2361	2646	5007
Henry,	869	869	1738	1108	1117	2225
Loudoun,	2975	3206	6181	3456	3610	7066
Louisa,	1383	1513	2896	1534	1559	3093
Lunenburg,	896	1036	1932	936	1056	1992
Madison,	841	833	1674	1002	1105	2107
Mecklenburg,	1835	1732	3567	1626	1718	3344
Nelson,	1380	1320	2700	1513	1496	3009
Nottoway,	527	595	1122	543	515	1058
Orange,	790	846	1636	882	1009	1891
Patrick,	1145	1198	2343	1462	1439	2901
Pittsylvania,	2897	3118	6015	3155	3401	6556
Prince Edward,	1103	1115	2218	944	913	1857
Powhatan,	566	580	1146	587	548	1135
Rappahannock,	1069	1238	2307	1238	1330	2568
Lynchburg	736	670	1406	1204	839	2043
Total,	43267	44662	87929	47555	48187	95742

Valley Division.	1840. Males.	1840. Females.	1840. Aggregate.	1850. Males.	1850. Females.	1850. Aggregate.
Alleghany,	472	441	913	586	572	1158
Augusta, including Staunton,	3398	3145	6543	4495	4188	8683
Bath,	700	677	1377	548	514	1062
Berkeley,	2333	1902	4235	2460	2092	4552
Botetourt,	1737	1827	3564	2536	2275	4811
Clarke,	669	644	1313	866	795	1661
Freder'k, includ'g Winchester,	2454	2426	4880	2885	2958	5843
Hampshire,	2706	2129	4835	3047	2512	5559
Hardy,	1239	1257	2496	1734	1666	3400
Highland,				824	796	1620
Jefferson,	2553	1984	4537	2574	2391	4965
Morgan,	1422	737	2159	777	691	1468
Page,	1063	1040	2103	1324	1335	2659
Pendleton,	1298	1301	2599	1171	1104	2275
Roanoke,	807	805	1612	1220	1170	2390
Rockbridge,	2204	2192	4396	2636	2553	5189
Rockingham,	3134	3082	6216	3643	3820	7463
Shenandoah,	2294	2250	4544	2798	2899	5697
Warren,	886	820	1706	1100	973	2073
Total,	31369	28659	60028	37224	35304	72528

Trans-Alleghany Division.	1840. Males.	1840. Females.	1840. Aggregate.	1850. Males.	1850. Females.	1850. Aggregate.
Barbour,				1652	1598	3250
Braxton,	483	438	921	825	737	1562
Boone,				607	516	1123
Brooke,	1685	1603	3288	1150	922	2072
Cabell,	1465	1336	2801	1207	1137	2344
Carroll,				1063	1114	2177
Doddridge,				526	488	1014
Fayette,	738	622	1360	766	703	1469
Floyd,	753	796	1549	1140	1217	2357
Grayson,	1585	1616	3201	1120	1184	2304
Greenbrier,	1620	1492	3112	1990	1703	3693
Giles,	911	909	1820	1183	1142	2325
Gilmer,				679	606	1285
Hancock,				901	821	1722
Harrison,	3251	3248	6499	2245	2180	4425
Jackson,	902	783	1685	1299	1137	2436
Kanawha,	2278	1782	4060	2584	2092	4676
Lee,	1349	1399	2748	1743	1762	3505
Lewis,	1463	1439	2902	1923	1825	3748
Logan,	752	687	1439	640	597	1237
Marion,				2046	2012	4058
Marshall,	1368	1277	2645	2085	1907	3992
Mason,	1210	1103	2313	1430	1271	2701
Mercer,	366	374	740	772	720	1492
Monongalia,	3408	3254	6662	2373	2504	4877
Monroe,	1502	1494	2996	1899	1900	3799
Montgomery,	1207	1215	2422	1412	1418	2830
Nicholas,	456	446	902	768	680	1448
Ohio,	1229	1068	2297	1100	1338	2438
Preston,	1262	1205	2467	3837	1781	5618
Pochahontas,	541	544	1085	705	693	1398
Pulaski,	586	574	1160	739	710	1449
Putnam,				1004	904	1908
Raleigh,				360	316	676
Randolph,	1105	1078	2183	1022	929	1951
Ritchie,				766	744	1510
Russell,	1301	1304	2605	1902	1812	3714
Scott,	1246	1261	2507	1716	1710	3426
Smyth,	1067	1075	2142	1361	1300	2661
Taylor,				1164	875	2039
Tazewell,	1021	981	2002	1689	1472	3161
Tyler,	1316	1220	2536	1053	970	2023
Washington,	2121	2237	4358	2469	2593	5062
Wayne,				878	732	1610
Wetzel,				821	791	1612
Wirt,				649	580	1229
Wood,	1462	1345	2807	1938	1740	3678
Wyoming,				279	272	551
Wythe,	1484	1520	3004	2008	1971	3979
Wheeling City,	1861	1625	3486	2892	2616	5508
Total,	46354	44350	90704	68380	62742	131122
Valley,	31369	28659	60028	37224	35304	72528
Piedmont,	43267	44662	87929	47555	48187	95742
Tide-Water,	37336	41388	78724	42768	45298	88006
Grand Total,	158326	159059	317385	195927	191531	387458
Total Western Division,	77723	73009	150732	105604	98046	203650
" Eastern "	80603	86050	166653	90323	93485	183748

In ascertaining the white males and females over twenty-one years of age, in the several counties &c. of the commonwealth, in 1840, I have subtracted one-tenth of the males and one-tenth of the females, respectively, between twenty and thirty years of age, from the number of males and females respectively over twenty years of age; the census of 1840 giving, as it does, the white males and white females classed as to age. It has been found necessary to count the white males and the white females respectively over twenty-one years of age, whose names are found on the schedules of the Assistant Marshals in 1850, there being no classification as to age in the returns of that census. I have used a table, prepared under the direction of the Secretary of the Interior at Washington, of the white males over twenty-one years of age in Western Virginia, in making up this table. White males and white females, who are by the census schedules twenty-one years of age, are counted as being over twenty-one years of age. The counties, opposite to the names of which blanks under the head of the year 1840 appear, have been created since that year.

Respectfully submitted.

AUDITOR'S OFFICE, March 20th, 1851. RO JOHNSTON, First Auditor.

REPORT

OF THE

SECOND AUDITOR,

IN RELATION TO THE

VARIOUS INTERNAL IMPROVEMENTS

IN THE

FOUR GRAND DIVISIONS OF THE STATE;

TO THE CONSTRUCTION OF WHICH,

THE STATE HAS CONTRIBUTED BY SUBSCRIPTIONS,

LOANS AND APPROPRIATIONS.

SECOND AUDITOR'S OFFICE,
7th March, 1851.

SIR: I have the honor to transmit herewith sundry statements furnishing the information called for by a resolution of the State Convention adopted on the 17th October last, on the motion of Mr. CARLILE, accompanied by a report explanatory of the same, which you will please lay before that honorable body.

Other statements are being prepared, in compliance with calls of the Convention, which will be transmitted at the earliest practicable moment.

It is a cause of deep regret on my part, that I have been unable to perform this duty sooner; the constant and heavy pressure of the daily current business of the office, added to my personal indisposition since the beginning of January last, having interfered to make it impracticable.

With great respect, I am, sir,
Your obed't serv't,
J. BROWN, Jr. Second Auditor.

To the Hon. J. Y. MASON, Pres't Va. Reform Convention.

SECOND AUDITOR'S OFFICE,
4th March, 1851.

To the Virginia Reform Convention:

In compliance with a resolution of the State Convention, adopted on the 17th October last, a copy of which is hereto annexed, I have now the honor to submit to that honorable body sundry statements, according to the list hereto subjoined, relating to the various internal improvements in the four grand divisions of the Commonwealth, to the construction of which the State has contributed (down to the 30th September, 1850) by subscriptions and loans, and by appropriations on State account.

The *General Statement* affords a compendious view of the results of the information contained in the detailed statements A, B, C, D, E, F, G, and H, and called for by the resolution. As it is impossible, however, to embody distinctly in such a statement all the phases of information which may be derived from it, it may not be amiss that some explanations and additional information should be afforded in this communication.

The aggregate capital of joint stock companies, in which the State is interested, appears by the first column of the general statement to be $33,805,664 56. This sum includes loans made by the State to certain companies, as specified in the detailed statements, to the amount of $2,522,204 69, which, deducted from the above mentioned sum, leaves the true amount of the aggregate joint capital stock at $31,283,459 87.

I deemed it proper to add to the capital authorized, the amount loaned to companies; in order shew the true aggregate (as nearly as possible) embarked in the various joint stock works completed or under construction.

The whole actual appropriations by the State for internal improvements to the 30th September last, is stated in column 2, at $16,241,592 41. Of this amount, $13,013,361 84 has been contributed in subscriptions and loans to joint stock companies, and the remainder, $2,328,230 57, to improvements on State account.

The aggregate expenditures of the State on both accounts, as shown by column 5, amounts to $11,858,772, which, deducted from the sum of $16,241,592 41, (the amount of appropriations as first above stated,) leaves a balance of $4,382,820 41 of State appropriations remaining on the 1st October last, to be thereafter discharged.

In aid of the above expenditure, loans were obtained to the amount of $10,010,208 10, (column 3,) leaving the amount paid out of the general revenue of the State, and out of the fund for internal improvement, at $1,848,563 90, (column 4.)

The aggregate dividends and surplus revenue received from the various joint stock and State improvements, amounted to $1,421,722 15, (column 6.) Included in this amount is the item of $401,450, (statement F, column 14,) for dividends received on 350 shares of the old James River Company stock from October, 1784, to the 1st October, 1850; and another item of $335,-910 84 for the net *surplus revenue* which accrued from the works of the same company from the

1st January, 1820, to 1st June, 1835, whilst under the management of State agents and on State account.

It appeared proper, in stating the dividends received, that those which accrued on 100 shares of the old stock presented by the State to Gen'l. Washington, and by him to the Washington College, in Rockbridge, should be included; they, accordingly, form part of the sum of $401,-450. The *surplus revenue* of the James River Company above mentioned was paid into the treasury, and applied to the payment of the interest on the loans obtained for the prosecution of the James River improvements, under the act of 1820 and subsequent acts.

The additional statements above referred to, contain the details of the aggregates embodied in the general statement. Each of those marked A, B, C and D, presents all that relates to improvements which lie entirely within the limits of one grand division of the State.

Those marked E, F, G and H relate to improvements which lie within the limits of more than one division, and contain in columns 10 and 11, (E and G,) and columns 10, 11 and 12, (F,) the estimated amount of expenditure belonging to each division. These estimated amounts are also embodied in the statements A, B, C and D, thus shewing the approximate aggregate expenditure for each grand division.

Statement I shews the amount originally obtained by loan for the construction of works down to the 30th September last, the aggregate of which was $10,106,909 87. This amount has been reduced by the redemption of certificates of debt issued for the same, amounting to $383,397 33, leaving the existing *debt for internal improvements* on the above day at $9,723,-512 54. Of this amount, $375,912 41 is held by the fund for internal improvement, and $762,-517 33 by the Literary Fund. The remainder, $8,585,082 80, is in the hands of individuals and corporations.

The interest column of this statement shews that there has been paid for interest on the above loans a sum of $5,443,812 19, of which $389,856 99 (general statement, column 7) has been reimbursed by companies to whom loans were made.

The information called for respecting the bonds of improvement companies guarantied by the State is furnished in statement K. A large portion of these bonds was paid to contractors at its par value. At what rates it was disposed of by them, I had no opportunity of ascertaining. For a general statement of the guarantees authorized by law, I beg permission to refer to page 35 of my report to the present General Assembly, respecting the accounts of the fund for internal improvement and of the Commonwealth on the 30th September last.

Respectfully submitted.

J. BROWN, Jr., 2nd Auditor.

(Copy.)

Resolved, That the Second Auditor be requested, as early as practicable, to prepare and lay before this Convention the number and character of the various works of internal improvement authorized to be constructed in the several grand divisions of the State; the amount appropriated and expended, and the amount authorized to be expended for such works, in each of said divisions: also, the times when the sums of money borrowed for the construction of said works are payable, and the rate of interest paid upon such loans: also, the times when the laws authorizing the construction of each of said works were passed, and the several acts increasing the said appropriations were passed; the interest the State has in each of said works, and the dividends received from each of said works: also, the amount guarantied by the State for works of internal improvements; the names of said works; the amount guarantied for each, and the times when the said guarantied bonds are payable, and the amount for which said bonds were sold, and the time when sold; and that he distinguish between the amounts paid for the respective works of internal improvement out of the treasury of the Commonwealth, and those derived from other sources.

Resolution of Mr. Carlile, adopted by the Convention Oct. 17th, 1850.

S. D. WHITTLE, Sec'y.

LIST OF STATEMENTS REFERRED TO.

GENERAL STATEMENT *relating to the Internal Improvements of the State, contained within the four Grand Divisions, the particulars of which are specified in the accompanying Statements, A, B, C, D, E, F, and G, 30th September,* 1850.

Grand Divisions of the State.	Aggregate capital of joint stock companies under original and amendatory acts. including state loans to companies.	Aggregate amount subscribed, loan'd and appropriated by state to each improvement.	Amount expended by State.			Aggregate of dividends or surplus revenue received from improvements from commencem't.	Interest received on loans to companies.
			Paid out of loans obtained by State.	Paid out of revenue of fund for internal improvem't & from pub. tr'y	Aggregate expenditures of state.		
	1	2	3	4	5	6	7
A. 1st Grand Division of the State, from the Seaboard to the head of Tidewater, as per statement A.	1873759 78	793859 78	534614 00	258709 78	793323 78	57000 00	27516 83
B. 2nd Grand Division of the State, from the head of Tidewater to the Blue Ridge Mountains as per statement B.	7417171 00	3386396 80	1931806 01	569617 83	7445585 77	510434 68	30825 41
C. 3d Grand Division of the State from the Blue Ridge Mountains to the Alleghany Mountains, as per statement C.	1699709 60	899994 32	650960 63	97305 04	2115763 85	29138 16	12722 17
D. 4th Grand Division of the State, from the Alleghany Mountains to the Ohio River, as per statement D.	564857 19	813927 85	286373 20	192735 32	1504098 60	3222 56	
Aggregate relating to works which are confined to one Division, except the 5th column, which represents the entire expenditure of the State,	11555497 57	5894178 75	3403753 84	1118367 97	11858772 00	599795 40	71064 41
Add the following amounts, stated under the respective heads relating to improvements which extend over several of the Grand Divisions which are not embodied (except the *total* expenditure in column 5) in statements A, B, C and D, above referred to—viz:							
E. Columns 3, 7, 8 and 9, works extending over 2d and 3d Divisions,	10744040 39	2132561 11	725897 05	117863 11	Expenditures includ'd above	75073 91	

Grand Divisions of the State.	Aggregate capital of joint stock companies under original and amendatory acts, including state loans to companies.	Aggregate amount subscribed, loan'd and appropriated by state to each improvement.	Amount Expended by State.			Aggregate of dividends or surplus revenue received from improvements from commencem't.	Interest received on loans to companies.
			Paid out of loans obtained by state.	Paid out of revenue of fund for internal improvem't & from pub. tr'y.	Aggregate expenditures of State.		
	1	2	3	4	5	6	7
F. Columns 3, 7, 8 and 9, works extending over 2d, 3d and 4th Divisions,	11360126 60	6996490 60	4986300 00	448826 60	Expenditures includ'd above	746852 84	318792 58
G. Columns 3, 7, 8 and 9, works extending over 3d and 4th Divisions,	146000 00	1218361 95	884257 21	163506 22	do		
Totals,	$33805664 56	16241592 41	10010208 10	1848563 90	11858772 00	* 1421722 15	389856 99

RECAPITULATION.

1.	Aggregate capital of joint stock companies under original and amendatory acts, including state loans to companies,		$33805664 56
2.	Aggregate amount subscribed, loaned or appropriated by state to each improvement,		16241592 41
3.	Paid out of loans obtained by state,	$10010208 10	
4.	Paid out of revenue of fund for internal improvement and from treasury,	1848563 90	
5.	Aggregate expenditures of state,		11858772 00
6.	Aggregate of dividends or surplus revenue received from improvements from commencement,		1421722 15
7.	Interest received on loans to companies,		389856 99

* *Note.* The above sum of $1,421,722 15, column 6, represents actual payments into the treasury from dividends, &c. The Board of Public Works are, however, in possession of the bonds of the following companies, bearing 6 per cent. interest, the principal whereof is payable at a stated period, being for dividends declared out of accrued profits of the respective companies, which, when received, will increase the above sum to $1,572,860 15, viz:

Richmond, Fredericksburg and Potomac Railroad Company,	$83,560.
Richmond and Petersburg Railroad Company,	33,408.
Petersburg (and Roanoke) Railroad Company,	15,270.
Louisa Railroad Company,	18,900.
	$151,138.

2nd Auditor's Office, 4th March, 1851. E. E. J. BROWN, Jr., 2d Auditor.

H.

STATEMENT of Expenditures out of the Public Treasury for Internal Improvements, made upon the warrants of the Auditor of Public Accounts, down to Sept. 30, 1850.

FIRST GRAND DIVISION.

Name of Improvement.	Dates of acts making State subscriptions and appropriations.	Amount authorized and appropriated by State.
Road from N. Carolina line thro' certain counties to Manchester	4 Feb. 1811,	208 36
Survey of the Country for Canal from Roanoke River to Dismal Swamp Canal,	14 Feb. 1812, 13 Feb. 1813, 26 Feb. 1816,	764 75
Paid Commissioners of Dismal Swamp Canal Co.	Oct. 1783, 1 Dec. 1787,	136 67
		$1109 78

THIRD GRAND DIVISION.

Name of Improvement.	Dates of acts	Amount
Opening road from Simpson's Creek across North Mountain in Rockbridge Co.	1 Feb. 1808,	1000 00
Opening road from Hot Springs and repairing road to Bratton's run,		812 25
Opening road from Thomas Helms to Wm. Gibson's, in Montgomery,	10 Feb. 1812,	300 00
Opening road from McAvoy's, in Bath, to Gap run,	9 Jan. 1834,	1000 00
Road from Skidmore's to South Fork in Pendleton,	12 Mar. 1849,	1000 00
Road from Harrisonburg to Hardy and Pendleton,	12 Mar. 1849,	1000 00
Moorfield and Alleghany Turnpike Co.	7 Mar. 1849,	4500 00
		$9612 25

FOURTH GRAND DIVISION.

Name of Improvement.	Dates of acts	Amount
This amount certified to have been discounted by the Treasury after the 31st March 1790, expended in opening roads under acts prior to the dates below mentioned,		4602 74
Road from the Eastern to the Western Waters,	17 Oct. 1785,	
Road from the Great Kanawha to Fayette county,	24 Dec. 1788,	5967 34
Road from Elk to the Great Kanawha River,	19 Dec. 1798,	
Carrying into effect last act,	21 June 1798,	
Opening road to Little Kanawha,	Oct. 1786, 23 Dec. 1795, 23 June 1801,	1000 00
Road from Morgantown to Grave Creek,	23 Dec. 1795,	238 56
Road from Morgantown to Fishing Creek,	Oct. 1786,	648 14
Road from Morgantown to Grave Creek,	25 Jan. 1799,	885 00
Road from Russell Court House,	20 Dec. 1791,	100 00
Road from Washington to Cumberland Mountain,	17 Dec. 1792, 18 Dec. 1794,	568 58
Road from Morgantown to Savage River,	23 Dec. 1795, 14 Dec. 1796,	500 00
Road from Lewisburg to Kanawha River,	21 Dec. 1796,	500 00
Road from Copper Creek to Clinch River,	25 June 1799,	300 58
Road from Mocasin Gap to Powell's Valley in Lee County,	14 Jan. 1805,	600 00
State Road through Randolph County,	3 Dec. 1806,	400 00

Name of Improvement.	Dates of acts making state subscriptions and appropriations.	Amount authorized and appropriat'd by State.
Road from Charlestown, in Brooke, to the Virginia and Pennsylvania line,	18 Jan. 1808,	2000
Road from mouth of Blue Stone River to mouth of Lower Loup Creek,	30 Jan. 1811,	1445
Road from Rifle run to Jackson's River, in Randolph County,	13 Feb. 1811,	1301 03
Road from Clarksburg to Point Pleasant,	16 Jan. 1812, 1 Jan. 1813,	1251
Road from Monongalia to the Ohio River,	27 Jan. 1812, 29 Jan. 1813,	1200
Repairing State Road from Monongalia to the Little Kanawha,	27 Jan. 1812,	1000
Paid Commisioners for viewing James River from Lynchburg to Dunlap's Creek,	15 Feb. 1813,	1222
Road from Greenbrier river to near White Oak lick,	24 Dec. 1813,	300
Road from Sistersville to Beverly	23 Jan. 1817,	694
Road from Virginia and Kentucky line to the Richlands,	17 Feb. 1824,	4000
Paid Commissioners opening road from Clarksburg to Point Pleasant,	4 Feb. 1824,	249
Road from Staunton to Little Kanawha,	5 Mar. 1824,	2400
Completing said Road,	19 Mar. 1824,	2038 50
Do do	28 Mar. 1827,	400
Paid Commissioners to lay out road from Green County in Pennsylvania to Middle Creek, Va	8 Mar. 1827,	653
Opening said Road,	20 May 1831,	5000
Completing said Road,	19 Mar. 1834,	1000
Road from Sistersville in Tyler County to Saline in Harrison,	15 Feb. 1826,	1000
Repairing road on the Ohio,	16 Mar. 1832,	9550
Road from the Kentucky line in Cabell to line in Monroe County,	19 Mar. 1832,	5000
Turnpike across Cheat Mountain in Randolph County,	2 Mar. 1835, 5 Mar. 1833,	7724 63
Road from Charleston in Kanawha County to Weston in Lewis County,	19 Jan. 1836,	4178 21
Locating road from Huntersville to Parkersburg,	16 Mar. 1836,	3000
Road from Nicholas Court House to Gauly Bridge,	21 Mar. 1837,	1500
Road from Pound Gap of Cumberland to Fincastle and Cumberland Gap Road,	25 Mar. 1837,	5000
Road from Smyth Court House to Plaster Banks,	30 Mar. 1838,	3000
Road from Blue Ridge at Simmons' Gap,	5 April 1838,	1000
Road from Brandonville to N. Western Turnpike,	7 April 1838,	9999 97
Free Road from Staunton and James River Turnpike to Turnpike across Warm Springs Mountain,	27 Mar. 1838	4833
Road from Pennsylvania line in Monongalia to Beverly and Clarksburg road,	9 April 1838,	9276
Charleston and Western Road,	19 Jan. 1836,	397 50
Beverly and Clarksburg Road,	14 Mar. 1846,	2724
Repairing Cumberland Gap Road,	3 Feb. 1848,	93 45
Appropriation to Kanawha and Logan Road,	2 Mar. 1845,	157 50
Guest Station through Mocasin Gap,	8 April 1839,	6000
Kanawha and Logan Road,	2 Mar. 1846,	21
Fancy Gap Road,	17 Jan. 1848,	12
Huntersville and Parkersburg road,	10 Mar. 1836,	500
Sandy River in Wayne County,	12 Mar. 1849,	3500
Improvement of 12 Pole River,	9 Mar. 1849.	1200
Appropriation to Kanawha and Logan Road,	2 Mar. 1846,	601 50
Eastern section of the Huntersville and Parkersburg Road,	9 Feb. 1840,	500
Bridges on Tygart's Valley,	5 Mar. 1846,	4522 90
Opening road from James River to Kanawha,	1 Feb. 1802 29 Jan. 1803, 27 Jan. 1804 16 Jan. 1805, 20 Jan. 1807, 5 Jan. 1808,	9375 37
Road across the Alleghany Mountain to Pocahontas,	4 Mar. 1834,	1074
		$138205 52

RECAPITULATION.

Amount authorized and appropriated	by State	in	1st	Grand	Division,	.	$1,109 78
do	do	do	do	3d	do	do	.	9,612 25
do	do	do	do	4th	do	do	.	138,205 52
								$148,927 55

The foregoing statement is an extract from a statement furnished by the First Auditor.

4th March, 1851. J. BROWN, Jr., Second Auditor.

L

STATEMENT shewing all the sums of money borrowed by the State for the construction of works of Internal Improvement, when the said sums are payable, and the rate and the amount of interest paid on such loans, down to 30th Sept. 1850.

Name of Corporation or State Improvement.	In what year redeemable.	Sums redeemable in the respective years.	Amounts borrowed on each account.	Interest paid on each account.
Alleghany and Huntersville Road,	1870		5000 00	56 81
Alexandria Canal Company,	1867		272000 00	52313 42
Appomattox Company, (upper,)	1857	7000 00		
	1858	7000 00		
	1859	10000 00		
	1861	12000 00		
	1862	8000 00		
			44000 00	27336 41
Berryville Turnpike Company	1866	3000 00		
	1867	3000 00		
	1868	2000 00		
			8000 00	1513 07
Blue Ridge Rail Road,	1869		32200 00	1038 63
Berryville and Charleston Turnpike Co.	1870		6400 00	172 60
Beverly and Fairmont Turnpike Road,	1868	13450 00		
	1870	10000 00		
	Redeemed	550 00		
			24000 00	2197 89
City Point Rail Road Company,	1857	25500 00		
	1858	34500 00		
	1859	50000 00		
			110000 00	76190 24

NAME OF CORPORATION OR STATE IMPROVEMENT.	In what year redeemable.	Sums redeemable in the respective years.	Amounts borrowed on each account.	Interest paid on each account.
Coal River Navigation Company,	1870		4000 00	113 16
Clarksburg and Buchanan Turnpike Company,	1869	8000 00		
	1850	1000 00	9000 00	302 87
Charleston and Point Pleasant Turnpike Company,	1858	10000 00		
	1859	8000 00		
	1860	4800 00		
	1869	5800 00		
	1870	200 00	28800 00	389 93
Cacapon and North Branch Turnpike Company,	1860	5300 00		
	1861	5700 00		
	Redeemed	1000 00	12000 00	6331 45
Chesapeake and Ohio Canal loan 5 per cent.,	1850	5000 00		
	Redeemed	245000 00	250000 00	210270 34
Dragon Swamp Navigation Company,	1859	1000 00		
	1860	464 00	1464 00	932 04
Dismal Swamp Canal Company	1857		16500 00	12879 61
Goose Creek and Little River Navigation Company,	1870		7000 00	199 97
Giles, Fayette and Kanawha Turnpike Company,	1867	7900 00		
	1819	6700 00		
	1870	6400 00		
	Redeemed	2450 00	23450 00	1949 60
Hardy and Winchester Turnpike Company,	1868	8900 00		
	1869	10900 00	19800 00	1573 82
Howardsville and Rockfish Turnpike Company,	1869		9000 00	490 91
Hampshire and Morgan Turnpike Company,	1870		4600 00	104 38
Harrisville Turnpike Company,	1869		1000 00	40 85

Name of Corporation or State Improvement.	In what year redeemable.	Sums redeemable in the respective years.	Amounts borrowed on each account.	Interest paid on each account.
Holladay's Cove Turnpike Company,	1859	4000 00		
	1860	800 00		
			4800 00	2982 91
Huntersville and Warm Springs Turnpike Company,	1861		300 00	167 87
Ice's Ferry Road,	1860		1358 00	777 63
James River and Kanawha Company,	1857	780000 00		
	1858	1048520 00		
	1859	160780 00		
	Redeemed	1500 00		
			1990800 00	1462426 04
Loan to ditto, (act 25 March, 1842,)	1862		250000 00	75000 00
Do. to do., (act 1 March, 1847,)	1872	242000 00		
	1873	500000 00		
	1874	250000 00		
	1875	244000 00		
			1236000 00	110880 00
James River Company—loans:	1840	90300 00		
5 per ct. $278,000,	1843	199083 33		
5½ per cent. $25,300,	1844	400000 00		
6 per cent.	1845	196400 00		
	1846	200000 00		
	1849	65500 00		
	1851	15000 00		
	1853	4000 00		
	1854	10000 00		
	1860	100000 00		
	Redeemed	44216 67		
			1324500 00	1583315 39
Jordan's Furnace and Rockbridge Turnpike Co.,	1869		3600 00	324 00
Leesburg and Snicker's Gap Turnpike Company,	1867		2000 00	389 59
Lafayette and English's Ferry Turnpike Company,	1861	1900 00		
	1862	650 00		
	Redeemed	1950 00		
			4500 00	2095 98

Name of Corporation or State Improvement.	In what year redeemable.	Sums redeemable in the respective years.	Amounts borrowed on each account.	Interest paid on each account.
	1861		1000 00	558 75
Lewisburg and Blue Sulphur Springs Turnpike Company,	1862	5350 00		
Lynchburg and Buff. Springs Turnpike Company,	1863	3150 00		
	Redeemed	671 00		
			9171 00	3995 28
	1869		3000 00	270 00
Little Stone Gap Road,	1869		9000 00	337 56
Marshall and Ohio Turnpike Company,	1869		15400 00	521 97
Moorfield and North Branch Turnpike Company,	1870		3600 00	72 59
Moorfield aud Alleghany Turnpike Company,	1870		1940 00	17 62
Morgantown and Bridgeport Turnpike Company,	1869		3000 00	270 00
Morgantown and Beverly Road,	1859	5000 00		
Natural Bridge Turnpike Company,	1861	1100 00		
			6100 00	3881 54
	1870		9100 00	173 44
New Market and Sperryville Turnpike Company,	1868		2000 00	203 54
N. Carolina and Wytheville Road,	1851	5000 00		
North Western Road—Loans:	1852	50000 00		
	1854	57250 00		
5 per cent. $152,500,	1855	50000 00		
	1857	65000 00		
	1858	43950 00		
	1859	32584 00		
	1860	17554 73		
	Redeemed	11276 24		
			332614 97	249407 54
	1869	52000 00		
North-Western Turnpike Road—Macadamizing,	1868	8000 00		
	1870	5850 00		
			65850 00	4113 99
	1869		105900 00	2957 24
Orange and Alexandria Railroad Company,	1869	2000 00		
Ohio River and Maryland Road,	1870	6600 00		

Name of Corporation or State Improvement.	In what year redeemable.	Sums redeemable in the respective years.	Amount borrowed on each account.	Interest paid on each account.
Ohio and Maryland Road,	1858	12000 00		
			20600 00	9798 55
Petersburg and Roanoke Rail Road Company—(5,)	1852		80000 00	63484 52
Loan to ditto,	1858		150000 00	107046 41
Portsmouth and Roanoke Railroad Company,	1854	95000 00		
5 per cent. on $190,000, }	1855	95000 00		
6 " " 66,650, }	1857	49000 00		
	1859	16650 00		
	Redeemed	1000 00		
			236650 00	195790 28
Portsmouth and Roanoke Railroad Company—Loan;	1858		150000 00	82200 00
5 per cent. $100,000, 6 per cent. on $50,000,				
Pittsylvania, Franklin and Botetourt Turnpike Co.,	1859	3231 10		
	1860	2500 00		
	1861	3359 00		
	Redeemed	1159 90		
			10250 00	5548 54
Price's Turnpike and Cumberland Gap Road,	1857	10000 00		
	1858	8000 00		
	1859	18400 00		
	1861	23600 00		
	1863	7600 00		
			67600 00	42076 18
Richmond and Petersburg Railroad Company,	1857	112600 00		
	1858	77000 00		
	1859	7350 00		
	Redeemed	3050 00		
			200000 00	150024 30
Richmond and Petersburg Railroad Company—Loans to,	1858	50000 00		
	1860	100000 00		
			150000 00	85213 70
Richmond, Fredericksburg and Potomac Railroad Company,	1855	110000 00		

NAME OF CORPORATION OR STATE IMPROVEMENT.	In what year redeemable.	Sums redeemable in the respective years.	Amounts borrowed on each account.	Interest paid on each account.
5 per cent.	1856	46800 00		
	Redeemed	50000 00		
			206800 00	147183 28
Richmond and Danville Railroad Company,	1868	363878 00		
	1869	20612 00		
			384490 00	20780 97
Rappahannock Company,	1858	12650 00		
	1864	350 00		
	1860	350 00		
			13350 00	9485 11
Rappahannock Company—Loan to,	1873		100000 00	12279 45
Rivanna Navigation Company,	1858	4900 00		
	1863	1400 00		
	Redeemed	700 00		
			7000 00	3378 67
Red and Blue Sulphur Springs Turnpike Company,	1859	3000 00		
	1861	2000 00		
	1865	2350 00		
	Redeemed	106 66		
			7456 66	3740 73
Rocky Mount Turnpike Company,	1869		12000 00	696 41
Rich Patch Turnpike Company,	1870		1100 00	15 91
Richlands and Kentucky Line Road,	1868		10000 00	1456 86
Smith's River Navigation Co.,	1870		2600 00	46 91
Salem and Pepper's Ferry Turnpike Company,	1860	2000 00		
	1861	3400 00		
	Redeemed	600 00		
			6000 00	3343 33
Salem and New Castle Turnpike Company,	1860	2475 00		
	1863	1400 00		
	1864	1400 00		
			5275 00	2235 80

Name of Corporation or State Improvement.	In what year redeemable.	Sums redeemable in the respective years.	Amount borrowed on each account.	Interest paid on each account.
South Western Road—(Eastwardly,)	1869	20000 00		
	1848	63970 00	83970 00	4438 76
Ditto—(Westwardly,)	1868	93662 00		
	1869	60000 00		
	Redeemed	2575 00	156237 00	9445 81
Staunton and Parkersburg Road—Macadamizing,	1869		16510 00	276 28
Staunton and Parkersburg Road—Bridges on,	1868	6750 00		
	1869	3250 00	10000 00	933 45
Staunton and Parkersburg Road, 5 per cent. on $10,000, 6 " " 170,000,	1858	10000 00		
	1859	6400 00		
	1860	8650 00		
	1861	38653 31		
	1862	66244 96		
	1863	11461 00		
	1865	26315 00		
	1866	1435 00		
	Redeemed	10840 73	180000 00	84451 72
Tazewell Court House and Fancy Gap Railroad,	1870		3420 00	60 62
Virginia Central Railroad Company,	1857	42000 00		
	1858	74250 00		
	1859	42675 00		
	1860	6675 00		
	1863	1200 00		
	1867	11800 00		
	1868	129837 00		
	1869	31380 00		
	Redeemed	1600 00	341437 00	146305 56

Name of Corporation or State Improvement.	In what year redeemable.	Sums redeemable in the respective years.	Amounts borrowed on each account.	Interest paid on each account.
Virginia and Tennessee Railroad Company,	1870		66800 00	1549 88
Valley Turnpike Company,	1859	98450 00		
	1860	120588 00		
	1861	10450 00		
	1862	4937 50		
	1863	887 50		
	1864	700 00		
	1867	900 00		
	1869	150 00		
	Redeemed	686 63		
			237749 63	146477 66
Valley Turnpike Company—Loan to,	1861		25000 00	7500 00
Virginia and Maryland Bridge Co.,	1869	8200 00		
	1870	1800 00		
			10000 00	379 20
Winchester and Potomac Railroad Company,	1854	60000 00		
	1855	50000 00		
	1856	10000 00		
			120000 00	97966 01
Winchester and Potomac Railroad Company—Loan to,	1858	149935 00		
5 per cent. on $8,000, } 6 " " 142,000, }	Redeemed	65 00		
			150000 00	93645 15
Weston and Fairmont Turnpike Company,	1869		5000 00	171 67
Weston and Gauley Bridge Turnpike Company,	1870		5000 00	150 00
Wheeling, West Liberty and Bethany Turnpike Company,	1868	12867 61		
	Redeemed	2400 00		
			15267 61	1188 60

Name of Corporation or State Improvement.	In what year redeemable.	Sums redeemable in the respective years.	Amounts borrowed on each account.	Interest paid on each account.
Wellsburg and Bethany Turnpike Co.,	1869		1700 00	69 72
Williamsport Turnpike Company,	1870		1250 00	14 83
Amount issued under the act March 22, 1850,	1875		562649 00	1422 92
			*10106909 87	5443812 19

* *Note.* Of the above amount of		$10,106,909 87
there has been redeemed		383,397 33
leaving		9,723,512 54
Of which there is held by the board of Public Works,	$375,912 41	
by the board of Literary Fund,	762,517 33	
		1,138,429 74
In other hands,		8,585,082 80
		$9,723,512 54

Second Auditor's Office, March 4, 1851.

E. E.

J. BROWN, Jr., 2d Auditor.

K.

STATEMENT concerning Bonds guaranteed by the State for works of Internal Improvement, 1st *October,* 1850.

1. JAMES RIVER AND KANAWHA COMPANY.

Date and chapter of act.	Amount authoris'd to be guaranteed.	Amount guaranteed	When sold.	For how much sold.	When payable.		Amount remaining to be guaranteed.
					Date.	Amount.	
23 March, 1839, ch. 92	1400000 00	1400000 00	1839	12500 00	1 July, 1869	20000 00	
			1840	670500 00	1 July, 1870	929700 00	
			1841	248200 00	1 July, 1873	383600 00	
			1842	56000 00	1 Mar. 1874	66700 00	
			1843	304100 00			
			1844	57700 00			
			1845	46000 00			
			1846	5000 00			
	1400000 00	1400000 00		1400000 00		1400000 00	
9 Mar. 1849, ch. 129	350000 00	114200 00		116639 71	1 June, 1875		235800 00
12 Mar. 1849, ch. 130	150000 00	65900 00		67675 52		180100 00	84100 00
Total,	1900000 00	1580100 00		1584315 23		1580100 00	319900 00

2. CHESAPEAKE AND OHIO CANAL COMPANY.

Date and chapter of act.	Amount authoris'd to be guaranteed.	Amount guaranteed	When sold.	For how much sold.	When payable.		Amount remaining to be guaranteed.
8 Mar. 1847, ch. 107	300000 00	300000 00	Paid to contractors at par value.	300000 00	1882	18000 00	
					1883	131500 00	
					1884	150500 00	
15 Mar. 1849, ch. 128	250000 00	175000 00	Oct. 1849, to Nov. 1850.	164604 28	1 July. 1869	164000 00	25000 00
	500000 00	475000 00		464604 28		464000 00	25000 00

3. VIRGINIA CENTRAL RAIL-ROAD COMPANY.

Date and chapter of act.	Amount authorised to be guaranteed.	Amount guaranteed.	When sold.	For how much sold.	When payable.		Amount remaining to be guaranteed.
					Date.	Amount.	
2 Feb. 1850, ch. 74	100000 00	100000 00	Ap. to Sep. 1850	100730 00	1 April, 1880 1 July, 1880	70000 00 30000 00	
	100000 00	100000 00		100730 00		100000 00	

4. TOWN OF PETERSBURG.

Date and chapter of act.	Amount authorised to be guaranteed.	Amount guaranteed.	When sold.	For how much sold.	Date.	Amount.	Amount remaining to be guaranteed.
26 Jan. 1850, ch. 79	323500 00	323500 00	M'y to Nov. '50	208777 75	1 Aug. 1870 1 Aug. 1875	161750 00 161750 00	
	323500 00	323500 00		208777 75		323500 00	

5. VALLEY TURNPIKE COMPANY.

Date and chapter of act.	Amount authorised to be guaranteed.	Amount guaranteed.	When sold.	For how much sold.	Date.	Amount.	Amount remaining to be guaranteed.
15 Jan. 1845, ch. 86	20874 00	20874 00	Jan. 1845	20874 00	1 July, 1860	20874 00	

Note. The following guarantees have not yet been applied for, viz:

City of Wheeling, under act of 20th March, 1848, ch. 145, . .	$500,000
Alexandria Canal Company, and the Common Council or Corporation of Alexandria, under act of 4th April, 1848, ch. 125, . . .	43,520
Richmond and Danville Rail-Road Co under act of 15th March, 1850, ch. 80,	200,000
James River and Kanawha Company, under act of 15th March, 1850, ch. 68,	360,000
	$1,103,520

2d Auditor's Office, 4th March, 1851. E. E.

J. BROWN, Jr., 2d Auditor.

Errata.—In statement B., "Richmond and Petersburg Rail Road Company," in lieu of "Capital Stock, $585,000," read $535,000. In statement C., "Winchester and Potomac Rail Road Company, in lieu of "Capital stock, $450,000," read $300,000.

J. B. Jr.

A STATEMENT

SHEWING THE

AMOUNT OF APPROPRIATIONS

MADE BY THE LAST

GENERAL ASSEMBLY,

ON

THE PART OF THE STATE,

TO

WORKS OF INTERNAL IMPROVEMENT

IN THE

FOUR GRAND DIVISIONS

OF

THE STATE.

CLERK'S OFFICE,

April 8th, 1851.

Sir—In compliance with the request of the Convention, I have the honor to enclose a statement shewing the amount of appropriations made by the last General Assembly, on the part of the State, to works of Internal Improvement in the four grand divisions of the Commonwealth. As some of the improvements are in parts of several divisions, I have stated them separately.

With great respect, I am yours, &c.

GEORGE W. MUNFORD, C. H. D.

Hon. John Y. Mason, Pres't of the Convention.

STATEMENT shewing the Amount of Appropriations made by the last General Assembly, on the part of the State, to works of Internal Improvement in the four grand divisions of the State.

TIDE-WATER.

Norfolk and Petersburg Railroad—Route to be surveyed at the cost of the State; amount not specified.	
Kempsville Canal Company,	$7,200 00
Lower Appomattox Company—The State's original subscription $20,000; paid up. The stock nominally worth nothing. State's interest in the stock released to the city of Petersburg upon the payment by the city of $588 82, which leaves amount released,	19,411 18
	$26,611 18

PIEDMONT.

Southside Railroad,	$480,000 00
Richmond and Danville, (additional,)	300,000 00
Roanoke Valley Railroad,	150,000 00
Providence Plank road,	4,000 00
James River and Clover Hill Plank road,	18,000 00
Orange and Alexandria Railroad,	60,000 00
Howardsville and Rockfish Turnpike,	6,000 00
Hazle River Turnpike,	9,600 00
Rivanna Navigation Company,	75,675 00
Slate River Company,	21,000 00
Hazle River Navigation Company,	9,600 00
	$1,133,875 00

VALLEY.

Potomac Turnpike,	2,700 00
Berkeley and Hampshire Turnpike,	12,000 00
Morgan and Frederick Turnpike,	9,000 00
North River Turnpike,	4,320 00
Luray and Front Royal Turnpike,	12,000 00
Jefferson and Frederick Turnpike,	6,000 00
Harrisburg and Franklin Turnpike,	12,000 00
Cedar Creek and Opequon Turnpike,	6,000 00
Middlebrook and Brownsburg Turnpike,	9,000 00
Staunton and North River Gap Turnpike,	15,000 00
Fincastle and Covington Turnpike,	7,200 00
Hot Springs and Clifton Forge Turnpike,	3,600 00
Buford's Gap and Buchanan Turnpike,	6,000 00
Union Hall Turnpike,	10,800 00
Millwood and Berryville Turnpike, (see note A.,)	9,000 00
Hardy and Winchester Turnpike,	2,400 00
Front Royal Turnpike,	12,000 00
Sperryville and Rappahannock Turnpike,	18,000 00
Thornton's Gap Turnpike,	6,000 00
New Market and Sperryville Turnpike,	9,000 00
North Frederick Turnpike,	2,400 00
Alleghany and Huntersville Turnpike,	4,500 00
North River Navigation Company,	45,000 00
South Branch Bridge Company,	4,200 00
	$228,120 00

TRANS-ALLEGHANY.

Fayette and Blue Sulphur Springs Turnpike,	$12,000 00
Centreville and Saint Mary Turnpike,	5,040 00
Ritchie and Gilmer Turnpike,	9,000 00
Salem and Harrisville Turnpike,	7,200 00
Simpson's Creek Turnpike,	4,200 00
Holliday's Cove Turnpike,	2,400 00
Leading Creek and Buffalo Creek Turnpike,	6,000 00
Newark Turnpike,	3,600 00
Saint Mary's Turnpike,	6,000 00
Reedy and Harrisville Turnpike,	7,200 00
Mud River and Valley Turnpike,	1,800 00
Sandy River Turnpike,	3,000 00
Jacksonsville and Christiansburg Turnpike,	5,200 00
Martin's Creek Road Company,	2,040 00
Tazewell Courthouse and Saltville Turnpike,	12,000 00
Stone Mountain Free Road,	1,200 00
Kingwood and West Union Turnpike,	6,000 00
Sistersville and Salem Turnpike,	9,000 00
Harrisville Turnpike,	2,100 00
Morgantown and Bridgeport Turnpike,	7,200 00
Clarksburg and Buchanan Turnpike,	3,000 00
Tazewell Courthouse and Fancy Gap Turnpike,	9,000 00
Charlestown and Point Pleasant Turnpike,	2,460 00
Russell and Washington Turnpike,	2,550 00
West Millford and New Salem Turnpike,	3,600 00
Brandonville, Kingwood and Evansville Turnpike,	6,000 00
Logan, Raleigh and Monroe Turnpike, (see note B.,)	18,000 00
Mechanicsburg and Wythe Turnpike,	3,000 00
Road from Wyoming Courthouse to the Bluffs,	3,000 00
Jonesville and Little Stone Gap Turnpike,	3,000 00
Holliday's Cove Turnpike,	15,000 00
Princeton and Red Sulphur Turnpike,	4,200 00
Floyd Courthouse and Hillsville Turnpike,	10,500 00
Walker's Creek and Holston Turnpike,	15,600 00
Black Leek and Plaster Banks Turnpike,	9,600 00
Grave Creek and Pennsylvania Line Turnpike,	4,800 00
Ravenswood and Reedy Turnpike,	3,000 00
Guyandotte Navigation Company,	75,000 00
Survey of Twelve Pole River,	500 00
Morgantown Bridge Company,	6,000 00
Fairmont and Palestine Bridge Company,	12,000 00
Williamsport Turnpike,	3,000 00
Fish Creek Bridge Company,	2,100 00
	$321,090 00

IMPROVEMENTS LYING IN PARTS OF SEVERAL DIVISIONS.

Virginia and Tennessee Railroad, Piedmont, Valley and Trans-Alleghany,	$163,636 00
Virginia Central Railroad—Tide-Water, Piedmont and Valley,	230,000 00
Manassas' Gap Railroad—Piedmond and Valley,	320,000 00
Rockingham Turnpike—Piedmont and Valley, (see note C.,)	60,000 00
Fredericksburg and Valley Plank road—Piedmont and Valley,	30,000 00
Hardy and Randolph Turnpike—Valley and Trans-Alleghany,	18,000 00
Black water Turnpike across the Alleghany,	1,080 00
Blue Ridge Turnpike—Valley and Piedmont,	30,000 00
Danville and Wythesville Turnpike—Piedmont, Valley and Trans-Alleghany,	30,000 00
	$882,716 00

RECAPITULATION.

TIDE-WATER,	$26,611 18
PIEDMONT,	1,133,875 00
VALLEY,	228,120 00
TRANS-ALLEGHANY,	327,090 00
Improvements lying in several divisions,	882,716 00
	$2,598,412 18

E. E.

GEORGE W. MUNFORD, C. H. D.

NOTE A.—*The Millwood and Berryville Turnpike.*—The former act relating to this Company provided that its capital should be $20,000; of which the Board of Public Works were authorized to subscribe for three-fifths. The act of the last session reduces the capital to $15,000, and directs the Board to subscribe for three-fifths of that sum; and gives the Company two additional years to commence its work.

NOTE B.—*Logan, Raleigh and Monroe Turnpike.*—The act incorporating this Company passed March 17, 1849. By it, a subscription of three-fifths was authorized by the Board of Public Works. The act expired on the 17th March, 1851. The act of the last session, passed March 24, 1851, revives the former act, and directs the Board to subscribe for three-fifths of the capital, which is $30,000.

NOTE C.—*Rockingham Turnpike.*—The act of 1850 requires twelve hundred shares of stock to be subscribed by individuals to secure the charter, and authorizes a subscription by the State of $60,000 upon the usual terms. The act of the last Legislature reduces the amount necessary to secure the charter to eight hundred shares, and directs the Board of Public Works to subscribe for $60,000 in like manner. The last act is an amendment of the first.

STATEMENTS FROM THE GOVERNOR,

RELATIVE TO THE

UNFINISHED IMPROVEMENTS,

IN WHICH

THE STATE IS INTERESTED.

EXECUTIVE DEPARTMENT,
May 3d, 1851.

Hon. JOHN Y. MASON, Pres't Va. Reform Convention.

Sir:

In compliance with a resolution of the Convention, I herewith transmit to you the statistical information asked for, so far as it is practicable to furnish it. The delay in making up the tables has been unavoidable. The information heretofore furnished the Convention is full upon such points presented in the resolution as are not answered by these sheets.

I have the honor to be,

With the highest respect,

Your obedient servant,

JOHN B. FLOYD.

A.

STATEMENT relating to unfinished Improvements in which the State is interested, under acts passed previous to the session of the General Assembly 1850–51—*called for by a Resolution of the Virginia Reform Convention of* 13*th March*, 1851. *Sept.* 30*th*, 1850.

LIST OF UNFINISHED IMPROVEMENTS.	In what grand division.	Amount of State appropriation. 1	Length of improvement. 2	Number of miles yet to be constructed. 3	Cost of construction per mile. 4	Probable cost of completion of unfinished works. 5
Allegheny and Huntersville Road,	3d and 4th	5600	14 Miles.	10 Miles.	437 50	4375 00
Blue Ridge Rail Road,	2d and 3d	600000	12	12	50000 00	600000 00
Clarksburg and Philippi Turnpike Company,	fourth	6000	22	7	350 00	2450 00
Floyd Court House and Hillsville Road,	do	9000	29	23¼	418 45	9728 96
Front Royal and Gaines X Roads Turnpike Company,	2d and 3d	9000	17	7	660 00	4620 00
Front Royal Turnpike Company,	third	24000	21	21	2525 00	53025 00
Fairmont and Wheeling Road,	fourth	25800	78½	78½	624 70	51952 00
Giles, Fayette and Kanawha Turnpike Company,	do	30000	12¼	22	600 00	13200 00
Howardsville and Rockfish Turnpike Company,	second	21000	44	19	860 00	16340 00
Huntersville and Huttonsville Road,	fourth	15000	47¾	47¾	471 50	22525 00
Jacksonville and Bent Mountain Turnpike Company,	do	6000	35	30	257 75	7732 50
James River and Kanawha Company, . (Note A.)	1st 2d 3d & 4th	4922204 69	465	293	24704 00	7233222 00
Jordan's Furnace and Rockbridge Turnpike Company,	third	3600	18¾	2¼	240 00	540 00
Kingwood and West Union Turnpike Company,	fourth	6000	38	35	427 00	14945 00
Martinsburg and Potomac Turnpike Company,	third	18000	12½	12½	1900 00	23750 00
Moorfield and North Branch Turnpike Company,	do	33300	75	7	442 00	3094 00
Morgantown and Bridgeport Turnpike Company,	fourth	13200	38	20	348 00	6960 00
New Market and Sperryville Turnpike Company,	2d and 3d	6000	50½	30½	2823 67	86121 93
Orange and Alexandria Rail road Company,	1st and 2d	540000	83⅞	85⅞	20 00 00	1777500 00
Ohio River and Maryland road,	fourth	84534	106	67	700 00	46900 00
Richland and Kentucky Line road,	do	19000	42¾	13	465 00	6045 00

LIST OF UNFINISHED IMPROVEMENTS	In what grand division.	Amount of State appropriation.	Length of improvement.	Number of miles yet to be constructed.	Cost of construction per mile.	Probable cost of completion of unfinished works.
		1	2	3	4	5
Richmond and Danville Rail road Company,	1st and 2d	900000 00	140 Miles.	80 Miles.	18000 00	1440000 00
Russell and Washington Turnpike Company,	fourth	6675 00	21½	1½	714 00	1071 00
Staunton and James River Turnpike Company,	2d and 3d	125000 00	44	40	2500 00	100000 00
Sistersville and Salem Turnpike Company,	fourth	11000 00	38	3	310 40	931 20
Smith's River Navigation Company,	second	7200 00	66	6	150 00	900 00
South Western Turnpike Company, (Note B.)	3d and 4th	548000 00	179	79	2500 00	147500 00
Virginia and Tennessee Rail road Company,	2d 3d and 4th	1636364 00	210	210	17500 00	3675000 00
Virginia Central Rail road Company, (Note C.)	1st 2d and 3d	900000 00	207	100	20000 00	2000000 00
Weston and Gauley Bridge Turnpike Campany,	fourth	27000 00	106	96	422 00	40512 00
Williamsport Turnpike Company,	do	3000 00	15½	6½	298 50	1940 25
			30th	September,	1850.	17397880 84

NOTE.—*Column* 5 represents the *supposed cost* of the distances stated in *column* 3.

NOTE (A) *James River and Kanawha Company.* This estimate is for the distance between the town of Buchanan, in Botetourt, to the Ohio River, *only*, provision having been made to complete the eastern portion of the work to the first mentioned point.

NOTE (B) *South Western Turnpike.* This estimate is for the distance between Wytheville, in Wythe county, and the Tennessee line, after deducting $50,000 advanced on Col. Lewis' contract, which sum will construct the first 20 miles of the road from Wytheville to Marion in Smythe county.

NOTE (C) *Virginia Central R. R. Co.* This estimate is for the distance between Charlottesville and Covington, with the exception of the Tunnel section of 12 miles through the Blue Ridge, now in process of construction by State agents.

B

The following relates to Improvements, respecting the unfinished portions of which, or the probable cost of completing the same, no information can be given. (Under acts passed previous to session of 1850–51.) September 30th, 1850.

LIST OF UNFINISHED IMPROVEMENTS.	In what grand division.	Amount of State appropriation.	Length of improvement.	Number of miles yet to be constructed.
Berryville and Charleston Turnpike Company,	third	21000 00	12½ Miles.	12½ Miles.
Buchanan Turnpike Company,	do	5400 00	16	11
Blue Ridge Turnpike Company,	2d and 3d	80000 00	56	56
Boydton and Petersburg Plank Road,	second	96000 00		
Coal River Navigation Company	fourth	6000 00		
Fancy Gap Road, (North Carolina line to Wytheville,)	do	2000 00	13	9
Fredericksburg and Valley Plank Road,	second	60000 00		
Goose Creek and Little River Navigation Co.,	do	60000 00	12	12
Guyandotte Navigation Company,	fourth	45000 00	98½	98½
Guyandotte and Kanawha Road,	do	5000 00		
Hampshire and Morgan Turnpike Company,	third	14400 00	17¼	17¼
Harrisville Turnpike Company,	fourth	6000 00	23¾	18¼
Hazle River Navigation Company,	second	45000 00		
Junction Valley Turnpike Company,	third	60000 00	48	48
Seed's Manor Turnpike Company,	second	2000 00		
Martinsburg and Winchester Turnpike Company,	third	27000 00	22¼	22¼
Moorfield and Alleghany Turnpike Company,	do	13500 00	26	26
Morgantown Bridge Company.	fourth	10800 00		
New Creek and Hardy Turnpike Company,	third	6000 00		
North Branch Bridge Company,	do	3000 00		
North River Navigation Company,	do	60000 00		
New Manchester Turnpike Company,	fourth	2000 00		

LIST OF UNFINISHED IMPROVEMENTS.	In what grand division.	Amount of State appropriation.	Length of improvement.	Number of miles yet to be constructed.
Pennsylvania, Morgantown and Beverly Road,	fourth	3000 00	56½ Miles.	12 Miles.
Potomac Bridge Company,	second	16000 00		
Patterson's Creek Valley Turnpike Company,	third	8400 00		
Parkersburg and Elizabethtown Turnpike Co.,	fourth	4800 00		
Rich Patch Turnpike Company,	third	7200 00	30	25
Rivanna Navigation Company,	second	75675 00		
Rocky Mount Turnpike Company,	2d and 4th	39000 00	78½	49½
Ravenswood and Reedy Creek Turnpike Company,	fourth	6000 00		
Road from Shannon's to the Bluffs,	do	2000 00		
Road from the Bluffs to the Cumberland Gap Road,	do	2000 00		
Road from Smyth Court House to the Plaster Banks,	do	1500 00		
Raleigh and Grayson Road,	do	26400 00		
Road in Scott County,	do	3600 00		
Rappahannock and Warren Road,	third	1500 00		
Road from South Branch to Brock's Gap,	do	1400 00		
Slate River Navigation Company,	second	496 80		
Sperryville and Rappahannock Company,	do	30000 00		
Shinston Turnpike Company,	fourth	7200 00		
Tazewell Courthouse and Fancy Gap Road,	do	19200 00	82½	82½
Tazewell Court House and Richlands Road,	do	8000 00	23	23
Thornton's Gap Turnpike Company,	second	45000 00		
Wellsburg and Bethany Turnpike Company,	fourth	16200 00	8	2
West Millford and New Salem Turnpike Company,	do	2000 00		
Wilson's Creek and Kanawha Turnpike Company,	do	4000 00		
Winchester and Berry's Ferry Turnpike Company,	third	15000 00		

C.

A list of the Improvements provided for at the late session of the General Assembly has already been laid before the Convention by Col. Munford, Clerk of the House of Delegates. They must necessarily be classed amongst those, respecting which no estimate can be given as to the probable cost of completion.

REPORT

OF THE

SECOND AUDITOR,

IN RELATION TO THE

NUMBER OF POOR CHILDREN SENT TO SCHOOL,

AND THE

NUMBER OF SCHOOLS IN THE STATE;

AND

WHAT PORTION OF THE LITERARY FUND

HAS BEEN

LOANED TO COLLEGES, ACADEMIES, &c.

SECOND AUDITOR'S OFFICE,
14th March, 1851.

Sir—I have the honor to transmit herewith, statements containing the information concerning the number of poor children and primary schools, and concerning loans to colleges, &c., called for by resolutions of the Convention, adopted on the 29th October and 2d November last, so far as the same can be supplied from the records of my office.

Very respectfully, your obed't serv't,

J. BROWN, Jr. Second Auditor.

To the Hon. J. Y. MASON, Pres't Va. Reform Convention.

SECOND AUDITOR'S OFFICE,
13th March, 1851.

To the Virginia Reform Convention:

I have the honor to transmit the accompanying statements, numbered one and two, prepared in compliance with two resolutions of the State Convention of 2nd November and 29th October last, copies of which are hereto annexed.

The first named resolution requires certain information respecting the poor children and schools of the state, based upon the last reports of the school commissioners, those being for the year ending the 30th September, 1849, which are referred to in the report submitted by me to the General Assembly at the commencement of its present session, (Document House of Delegates, No. 4, statements I and K.)

Table number one is an extract from that report. It will be discovered that it does not afford full information on the points desired, owing to the following causes:

First. No reports were received for the year 1849 from the six counties of Alleghany, Alexandria, Bath, Jefferson, Kanawha, and Logan.

Secondly. A portion of the reports of 1849 were made under the primary school system of 1829, which did not require the registration of the children. The number reported in these was consequently merely conjectural, and evidently very wide of the mark, as is proven by the fact that the real number in many of the counties in which the children have since been registered is more than double that previously reported by conjecture.

Thirdly. The reports from nine counties, operating under different free school systems, are not required by law to state, and accordingly do not state, either the number of *poor children* in the county or the number attending school.

On the other hand, it must be observed that, in carrying out the system of education, its benefits are not restricted to the children of those only who would in society, and under the strict meaning of the term, be called indigent or destitute, but are throughout the State extended to children whose parents, however respectable and industrious, can barely procure food, raiment and lodging, and the most common comforts of life, for their families, and who are, therefore, totally unable to contribute any thing towards the education of their children.

Fourthly. Neither under the free school nor the primary school system are any other schools reported, but those with which the school commissioners are respectively connected in their school operations.

Under these circumstances, the table now presented can only be considered as a very imperfect approximation of the real number of indigent children in the State.

It appears from it, that in 126 counties and towns in the year 1849, operating under the primary school system, 31,655 poor children attended school; 41,321 who attended no school, and 3904 schools to which those children were sent. Hence it will be perceived that there must be a very large number of schools not attended by the poor, of the existence of which no accounts have been received.

Appended to the above table is another, showing that the number of children of all classes attending 140 schools in the same year was 8372.

Statement No. 2 furnishes the information called for by the resolution of 2nd November last, in relation to loans made from the Literary Fund to colleges, academies, &c., since the year 1829.

There were only three institutions of this description to which loans have been made, viz: 1st, Emory and Henry College, Washington Co., $18,000; 2nd, the Medical College of Richmond, $25,000; and 3rd, the Medical College in the Valley of Virginia, $5000—in all $48,000.

At the time of the passage of the act of 20th March, 1850, suspending the payment of the interest due on the loan to Emory and Henry College, there was a balance of interest remaining unpaid of $3,780, which, added to the principal, made an amount then due the Literary Fund of $21,780. The said college was permitted to discharge the amount of the above interest, together with the interest hereafter accruing on said loans, by receiving therein sixteen deserving and indigent young men, which number, it is supposed, are now in attendance at said institution. On the 9th March, 1850, the payments of the interest, amounting to $750, on the debt of the Richmond Medical College, was suspended by the act of that date. There was also $150 in arrear on the loan to the Medical College at Winchester, which has not yet been paid.

Respectfully submitted.

J. BROWN, Jr., 2nd Auditor.

(COPY.)

Resolved, That the Second Auditor be requested to furnish the Convention with the number of poor children in this commonwealth sent to school, the number deriving no benefit from the Literary Fund; also, the number of schools in the different counties and cities, basing such report upon the last report of the School Commissioners.

Adopted November 2nd, 1850.

S D. WHITTLE, Sec'y.

(COPY.)

On motion of Mr. LETCHER,

Resolved, That the Second Auditor be requested to lay before this Convention, a statement shewing what portion of the literary fund has been loaned to colleges, academies or other literary or medical institutions, since the year 1829; the names and location of the several institutions to which such loans have been made, and the sum loaned to each; the nature of the securities and their present solvency; the amount of interest paid by each, and when paid, and the amount of interest now due from each; and he will also show on which of said loans the interest has been remitted by the Legislature.

Adopted October 29th, 1850.

S. D. WHITTLE, Sec'y.

No. 1.

STATEMENT of the number of Poor Children sent to School, the number deriving no benefit from the Literary Fund, and the number of Schools in the different counties and towns in the commonwealth of Virginia, as taken from the last reports of the School Commissioners received at the office of the Second Auditor, to 30th September, 1850.

Counties and Towns	Number of poor children sent to school.	Number deriving no benefit from Literary Fund.	Number of schools attended by poor children.	
Albemarle, . . .	698	672	72	
Alleghany, . . .				no report
Alexandria, . . .				no report
Amelia, . . .	61	135	11	
Amherst, . . .	319	469	27	
Accomac, . . .	527	673	37	
Appomattox, . . .	149	111	25	
Augusta, . . .	794	858	103	
Bath, . . .				no repor.
Barbour, . . .	546	3[illegible]8	56	
Braxton, . . .	153	423	26	
Bedford, . . .	681	409	50	
Berkeley, . . .	372	354	42	
Botetourt, . . .	352	68	41	
Brooke, . . .	290	110	52	
Boone, . . .	96	104	9	
Buckingham, . . .	251	301	30	
Brunswick, . . .	204	256	21	
Cabell, . . .	178	212	23	
Campbell, . . .	322	546	43	
Carroll, . . .	227	363	29	
Caroline, . . .	182	313	21	
Clarke, . . .	239	61	17	
Charles City, . . .	64	125	6	
Charlotte, . . .	163	222	20	
Chesterfield, . . .	236	1751	27	
Culpeper, . . .	121	129	19	
Cumberland, . . .	68	150	14	
Dinwiddie, . . .	107	169	19	
Doddridge, . . .	115	85	16	
Essex, . . .	172	147	25	
Elizabeth City, . . .	42	163	5	
Fairfax, . . .	266	257	33	
Fauquier, . . .	236	514	31	
Fayette, . . .	225	456	21	
Franklin, . . .	522	278	50	
Frederick, . . .	444	636	45	
Floyd, . . .	231	219	35	
Fluvanna, . . .	155	230	22	
Grayson, . . .	189	211	23	
Greene, . . .	83	235	13	
Greenbrier, . . .	315	285	59	
Greensville, . . .	80	53	11	
Giles, . . .	233	352	46	
Gilmer, . . .	141	212	18	
Gloucester, . . .	196	273	20	
Goochland, . . .	64	96	18	
Halifax, . . .	358	242	49	
Hampshire, . . .	579	821	60	

Counties and Towns.	Number of poor children sent to school.	Number deriving no benefit from Literary Fund.	No. of schools attended by poor children	
Hanover, .	231	356	30	
Hardy, .	300	734	35	
Harrison, .	482	740	68	
Hancock, .	195	105	24	
Henry, .				Free schools
Henrico, .	187	477	20	
Highland, .	234	172	33	
Isle of Wight, .	218	182	24	
Jackson, .	190	135	54	
James City, .	47	43	10	
Jefferson, .				Free schools
Kanawha, .				Free schools
King and Queen, .	136	414	16	
King George, .	51	99	15	
King William, .	110	136	19	
Lancaster, .	65	55	12	
Lee, .	366	1082	41	
Lewis, .	363	1925	65	
Logan, .				No report
Loudoun, .	563	375	66	
Louisa, .	132	568	24	
Lunenburg, .	127	290	19	
Madison, .	113	37	17	
Mason, .	212	588	36	
Marion, .	646	416	63	
Marshall, .	412	143	45	
Mathews, .	122	128	19	
Mecklenburg, .	199	502	31	
Mercer, .	163	186	33	
Middlesex, .	145	130	11	
Monongalia, .	964	156	74	
Monroe, .	377	523	69	
Montgomery, .	217	183	29	
Morgan, .	226	267	18	
Nansemond, .	108	242	19	
Nelson, .	566	257	48	
New Kent, .	59	144	8	
Nicholas, .	93	207	17	
Northampton, .				Free schools
Norfolk County, .				Free schools
Northumberland, .	130	60	20	
Nottoway, .	57	63	12	
Orange, .	69	231	14	
Ohio, .				Free schools
Patrick, .	462	814	24	
Page, .	203	597	33	
Pendleton, .	283	317	33	
Preston, .	428	910	73	
Prince Edward, .	112	199	21	
Prince George, .	47	83	8	
Prince William, .	544	156	30	
Princess Anne. .				Free schools
Pittsylvania, .	592	1092	53	
Powhatan, .	77	82	15	
Pocahontas, .	111	89	21	
Pulaski, .	145	333	14	
Putnam, .	177	73	20	
Randolph, .	205	405	36	
Rappahannock, .	184	402	19	
Richmond County, .	114	301	9	
Ritchie, .	200	146	20	
Rockbridge, .	390	980	51	
Rockingham, .	747	644	37	
Roanoke, .	167	83	18	
Russell, .	513	137	59	
Stafford, .	159	341	14	
Shenandoah, .	561	239	60	
Smyth, .	339	318	32	
Scott, .	559	693	57	
Southampton, .	237	163	30	

Counties and Towns.	Number of poor children sent to school.	Number deriving no benefit from Literary Fund.	Number of schools attended by poor children.	
Spottsylvania, .	156	74	30	
Surry, . .	77	373	11	
Sussex, .	78	82	16	
Tazewell, .	271	329	33	
Taylor, .	216	132	27	
Tyler, .	180	220	33	
Washington, .				Free schools
Warren, .	180	344	24	
Warwick, .	7	33	3	
Wayne, .	223	960	19	
Wetzel, .	171	79	23	
Westmoreland,	84	116	8	
Wirt, .	103	116	19	
Wythe, .	325	275	49	
Wood, .	350	450	60	
York, .	81	119	11	
Norfolk City, .				Not in report
Petersburg, .	137	138	* 27	
Richmond City, .	538	162	* 45	
Williamsburg, .	11	39	5	
Portsmouth, .				Free schools
Wheeling, .				Free schools
	31655	41321	3904	

* Whole number of schools in those cities.

FREE SCHOOLS.

Counties and Towns.	Number of children of all classes sent to school.	Number not attending school.	Number of schools.	
Henry, .	1391	430	23	
Jefferson, .				No report
Kanawha, .				No report
Northampton, .	495	180	13	
Norfolk County, .	1232		26	
Ohio, .	839		21	
Portsmouth, .	707	984	13	
Princess Anne, .	855		8	
Southampton, .	31		1	
Washington, .	1337		31	
Wheeling, .	1485	867	4	
	8372		140	

Second Auditor's Office, 13th March, 1851. E. E. J. BROWN, Jr., 2d Auditor.

No. 2.

STATEMENT OF LOANS TO COLLEGES,

From the Literary Fund, since 1829, *prepared in accordance with a resolution of the Convention adopted* 2d *November,* 1850, *and of the interest due and paid thereon.*

LOAN TO EMORY AND HENRY COLLEGE, WASHINGTON COUNTY,

of $18,000, under act passed 27th February, 1843.

SEMI-ANNUAL INTEREST.

When due.		When paid.	
1 January, 1844,	540 00	20 January, 1844,	250 00
1 July, 1844,	540 00	14 February, 1844,	290 00
1 January, 1845,	540 00	22 July, 1844,	540 00
1 July, 1845,	540 00	21 February, 1845,	540 00
1 January, 1846,	540 00	28 July, 1845,	500 00
1 July, 1846,	540 00	6 August, 1845,	40 00
1 January, 1847,	540 00	4 February, 1846,	540 00
1 July, 1847,	540 00	7 Dec. 1846,	540 00
1 January, 1848,	540 00		
1 July, 1848,	540 00	Total paid	3240 00
1 January, 1849,	540 00	Balance due discharged by act of	
1 July, 1849,	540 00	Assembly, passed 20 Mar., 1850,	3780 00
1 January, 1850,	540 00		
	7020 00		7020 00

For the security of this loan, a deed of trust on the lands and tenements of said college was duly executed to the President and Directors of the Literary Fund, by the Trustees thereof, on the 24th March, 1843, and recorded in the County Court office of Washington county; together with a bond of Alexander Findlay, and sundry other individuals, in the penalty of $10,000.

The amount of interest which has accrued on said loan to the 1st January, 1850, is $7020, of which sum, $3240 has been paid, as per foregoing statement. By act of 20th March, 1850, the interest unpaid and accruing was remitted, and the individual security released.

The lien upon the lands and tenements of said college was retained.

LOANS TO MEDICAL COLLEGE AT RICHMOND OF $15,000

under act passed 9th Feb., 1844, and $10,000 under act passed 20th Feb., 1845.

SEMI-ANNUAL INTEREST.

When due.		When paid.	
1 January, 1845,	239 18	24 May, 1845,	239 18
1 July, 1845,	450 00	11 August, 1845,	450 00
1 January, 1846,	613 03	13 June, 1846,	613 03
1 July, 1846,	750 00	17 Nov., 1846,	750 00
1 January, 1847,	750 00	5 June, 1847,	750 00
1 July, 1847,	750 00	30 Sept., 1847,	750 00
1 January, 1848,	750 00	27 May, 1848,	550 00

When due.		When paid.	
1 July, 1848,	750 00	30 June, 1848,	200 00
1 January, 1849,	750 00	30 Sept., 1848,	750 00
1 July, 1849,	750 00	2 June, 1849,	400 00
1 January, 1850,	750 00	30 June, 1849,	350 00
		28 Sept., 1849,	750 00
		Total paid,	6552 21
		Balance due discharged by act of the Assemby passed on the 9th March, 1850,	750 00
	7302 21		7302 21

For the security of the loan of $15000, a deed was executed on the 4th July, 1844, to the President and Directors of the Literary Fund, and recorded in the office of the Clerk of the Hustings Court of the city of Richmond, in conformity to law, for the lot of land in the said city whereon the present college now stands. A bond was also received from each of the six Professors of the institution, in the penalty of $5000, for the further security of said debt.

A deed in like manner was executed on the 16th September, 1845, and recorded in the same office, conveying the same property for the security of the loan of $10,000, with six other bonds in the penalty of $3,500 each, executed by the Professors of said college.

The amount of interest which has accrued on said loan to 1st January, 1850, is $7,302 21; of which sum, $6,552 21 has been paid, as per foregoing statement. By act of 9th March, 1850, the interest unpaid and accruing was remitted, but the securities taken for the re-payment of said loans were retained.

The above mentioned personal security consists of the following bonds:

Bond of	Socrates Maupin, dated	31st July, 1844, for	$5,000
Do.	do.	22d Sept. 1845,	3,500
Do.	R. L Bohannon,	31st July, 1844,	5,000
Do.	do.	22d Sept. 1845,	3,500
Do.	L W. Chamberlayne,	31st July, 1844,	5,000
Do.	do.	22d Sept. 1845,	3,500
Do.	Carter P. Johnson,	24th June, 1848,	8,500
Do.	Charles Bell Gibson,	24th June, 1848,	8,500
Do.	Daniel H Tucker,	10th Nov. 1849,	8,500
			$51,000

LOAN TO MEDICAL COLLEGE IN THE VALLEY OF VIRGINIA,

at Winchester, under act passed 11th March, 1847.

SEMI-ANNUAL INTEREST

When due.		When paid.	
1 July, 1848,	274 93	13 November, 1848,	274 93
1 January, 1849,	150 00	30 November, 1849,	300 00
1 July, 1849,	150 00	Total paid,	574 93
1 January, 1850,	150 00	Balance due 1st Jan., 1850,	150 00
	724 93		724 93

For the security of this loan, a deed was executed on the 10th June, 1847, to the President and Directors of the Literary Fund, and recorded in the Hustings Court of Winchester, conveying the land on which the college now stands: also, a joint bond of the five Professors of the institution, in the penalty of $10,000.

The amount of interest which has accrued on said loan to 1st January, 1850, is $724 93; of which sum, $574 93 has been paid as per foregoing statement.

The above mentioned personal security is as follows:

Bond of Hugh H. McGuire,
Daniel Conrad,
John J. H. Straith,
J. Philip Smith,
Wm. A. Bradford, } dated 2d July, 1847, for . . $10,000

RECAPITULATION.

Colleges.	Amount loaned.	Interest to 1st January, 1850.			Remarks.
		Total due.	Total paid.	Bal. unpaid	
Emory and Henry,	18000	7020 00	3240 00	3780 00	Suspended by act Ass'y
Med'l College, Rich'd,	25000	7302 21	6552 21	750 00	do do do
Med'l College, Winch'r,	5000	724 93	574 93	150 00	do do do
	48000	15047 14	10367 14	4680 00	

E. E.

J. BROWN, Jr. 2d Auditor.

Second Auditor's Office, 13th March, 1851.

STATEMENT OF THE SECOND AUDITOR,

SHEWING THE

DEBT, LIABILITIES & RESOURCES

OF THE

STATE OF VIRGINIA,

DOWN TO APRIL 1, 1851.

SECOND AUDITOR'S OFFICE,
15th April, 1851.

Sir:

In compliance in part with a resolution of the Convention of the 18th October last, I have the honor to submit herewith to that honorable body, through you, a statement of the whole debt, liabilities and resources of the State on the 30th September, 1850, in a printed form, marked 1, being the same reported by me to the late Legislature, at the commencement of their session.

I have also prepared an additional statement of the same subjects, brought down to the first day of the present month; in which the "Liabilities" are considered as a debt, and the "Resources" are increased necessarily in a corresponding degree.

A portion of the remaining information called for, by the resolution, has been furnished in different forms to the Convention: the whole will be embodied in a distinct document, and transmitted at an early day.

With great respect, your ob't servant,

J. BROWN, Jr. 2d Auditor

Hon. JOHN Y. MASON, Pres't Va. Reform Convention.

[I.]

DEBT AND RESOURCES OF THE COMMONWEALTH,

September 30, 1850.

[No. 1.]

PUBLIC DEBT OF THE COMMONWEALTH.

(In stating this debt, all that part of it which is held by state authorities and agents for state purposes, as specified in Note (a) below, is considered to be so much redeemed. It is therefore omitted, in order to simplify the statement, by exhibiting only the amount in the hands of individuals and private corporations at this date.)

OUTSTANDING DEBT HELD BY INDIVIDUALS AND PRIVATE CORPORATIONS.

Amount of internal improvement debt, ...	8,585,082 30	
Amount of debt for subscription to banks, . . .	450,107 00	
Outstanding, Notes (b) and (c),		$9.035.189 30

At 6 per cent. per annum,	$7,956,889 30
At 5 " "	1,053,000 00
At 5½ " "	25,300,00

NOTE (*a*)—STATE STOCKS HELD BY STATE AGENTS.

The following stocks held by state corporations are not included in the above statement, viz:

1. By the president and directors of the Literary fund, (increased since 1840,) 9,450	1,105,556 50
2. By the president and directors of the Board of public works, (increased since 1849,) 9,050 . .	375,912 41
Amount held by state agents, . . .	1,481,468 91
Amount outstanding, ...	9,035,189 30
Total apparent debt,	$10,516,658 21

NOTE (*b*)—*The outstanding debt is held as follows, viz:*

In Great Britain, ...	2,369,989 20	
France and Germany, . . .	368,300 00	
Total in Europe,		2,738,289 20
In Virginia, ...	5,651,461 10	
Maryland, ...	392,139 00	
District of Columbia, ...	110,400 00	
Other states, ...	142,900 00	
		6,296,900 10
Total outstanding debt as above,		$9,035,189 30

NOTE (c).—*The periods of redemption of the outstanding debts are as follows, viz:*

Y'rs.	Amounts.		EXPLANATORY NOTES.	
1840	25,300 00	*c*		
1844	300,000 00	*a*		
1845	160,000 00	*c*		
"	100,000 00	*a*		
1846	30,000 00	*c*	The sums marked (*a*) may be redeemed in the respective years designated, but are to be redeemed within a period not exceeding 15 years thereafter. They amount to	623,950 00
1852	50,000 00	*a*		
"	80,000 00	*c*		
1854	20,000 00	*a*		
"	145,000 00	*c*		
1855	50,000 00	*a*		
"	205,000 00	*c*		
1857	25,500 00	*b*		
"	60,000 00	*a*		
"	994,900 00	*c*		
1858	34,500 00	*b*		
"	43,950 00	*a*		
"	1,744,618 59	*c*		
1859	6,400 00	*b*		
"	809,338 10	*c*		
1860	8,650 00	*b*	The sums marked (*b*) are to be redeemed within their respective years . . .	170,143 27
"	317,689 73	*c*		
1861	23,687 31	*b*		
"	87,509 00	*c*		
1863	11,461 00	*b*		
"	14,937 50	*c*		
1862	59,944 96	*b*		
"	245,737 50	*c*		
1864	350 00	*c*		
1865	17,315 00	*c*		
1866	1,435 00	*c*		
1867	277,500 00	*c*	The sums marked (*c*) may be redeemed in the years specified, and afterwards at the pleasure of the General Assembly, . .	8,241,096 03
1868	678,084 61	*c*		
1869	367,072 00	*c*		
1870	140,660 00	*c*		
1872	242,000 00	*c*		
1873	600,000 00	*c*		
1874	250,000 00	*c*		
1875	806,649 00	*c*		
	$9,035,189 30			$9,035,189 30

E. E.

J. BROWN, Jr., 2nd Auditor.

[No. 2.]

LIABILITIES OF THE COMMONWEALTH.

I. *Bonds of corporations guarantied by the Commonwealth:*

Debts of the James River and Kanawha company:			
1. Under act of the 23d March 1839, .	1,400,000 00		
2. Under act of the 9th March 1849, ch. 29, for connecting the basin at Richmond with tidewater through the Richmond dock, ...	350,000 00		
3. Under act of the 12th March 1849, ch. 130, to provide for the Southside and Rivanna connections, . .	150,000 00		
		1,900,000 00	
Debts of the Chesapeake and Ohio canal co:			
4. Under act of the 8th March 1847, for extension of canal . . .	300,000,00		
5. Under act of the 15th March 1849, for repairing canal below dam No 6, .	200,000 00		
		500,000 00	
6. Debt of the Valley turnpike company, under act of 15th January 1845, ...		20,874 00	
7. Debt of the Virginia Central railroad company, under act 2d February 1850, for completing the construction of their road from the Junction to Richmond, . ,		100,000 00	
8. Debt of the town of Petersburg, under act 26th January 1850, for the construction of the Southside railroad, .		323,500 00	
			2,814,374 00

II. *Bonds of corporations to be guarantied by the state:*

1. Debt of the city of Wheeling for subscription to the Baltimore and Ohio railroad company, under act 20th March 1848, ch. 145, ...	500,000 00	
2. Debt of the Alexandria canal company, for construction of wharves, &c. at Alexandria, under act 4th April 1848, ch. 125, ...	43,520 00	
3. Debt of Richmond and Danville railroad company, for the purchase of heavy rails and machinery, under act 15th March 1850, ch. 80, § 57, . . .	200,000 00	
4. Debt of the James river and Kanawha company, under act of 15th March 1850, ch. 68, for extending the company's water line from Buchanan to Covington. .	360,000 00	
		1,103,520 00
		3,947,894 00

III. *Loans which may be called for under existing laws to complete state subscriptions and appropriations for internal improvements, viz:*

1. On account of balances of appropriations, &c. remaining to be paid to complete state subscriptions and appropriations for improvements commenced, (statement B 2,) . . . . , . . .	4,204,768 49	
2. On account of subscriptions which have been made to organized companies, and not yet called for, (Note B 2,)	428,100 00	
	4,632,868 49	
3. On account of subscriptions authorized to companies of whose organization no information has been received, (Statement B 2,)	844,000 00	
		5,476,868 49
		9,424,762 49

E. E.

J. BROWN, Jr. Second Auditor.

[No. 3.]

FUNDS AND RESOURCES OF THE COMMONWEALTH.

30th September, 1850.

(Owing to the character of these funds, their availability or productiveness cannot be classified in a manner perfectly satisfactory; but as every item of which they are composed is particularized in the annexed statements, the means are afforded of modifying the classification here presented to suit the views of those who do not approve of it.)

1. *Productive stocks:*	
Amounts from which interest or dividends have been received during the year, as particularized in statement No. 4, (*a*), . . .	7,060,565 48
2. *Funds unproductive, but more or less available:*	
Amounts secured by mortgages, as per statement No. 4, *b* . . .	152,308 00
3. *Stocks in improvements not completed:*	
These yield no dividends, but a large proportion of them may hereafter become productive or available—they amount as per statement No. 4, *c*	4,801,677 91
4. *Stocks in improvememts completed, but unproductive, and other unproductive funds:*	
About 5-12ths of these may become productive or available—they amount, per statement No. 4, *d*	1,098,280 62
	$13,112,832 01

E. E.

J. BROWN, Jr., Second Auditor.

Note.—The commonwealth has other stocks, investments, &c. specified in the two notes to statement 4, which were not included in the above statement, for reasons specified in said notes. They amount to the sum of $2,382,646 07.

[No. 4.]

PARTICULARS OF THE FUNDS AND RESOURCES OF THE COMMONWEALTH, REFERRED TO IN STATEMENT No. 3.

These funds are held as follows:

By the Commonwealth,		2,677,504 69
Literary Fund,		472,070 00
Board of Public Works,		9,963,257 32
		$13,112,832 01

(*a*) PRODUCTIVE STOCKS AND FUNDS:

Bank of Virginia, 13,766 shares at 70 dols. per share,		963,620 00
Farmers Bank of Virginia, 9626 shares; Bank of the Valley, 4839 shares; Northwestern Bank, 4826 shares; Merchants and Mechanics Bank of Wheeling, 400 shares; Exchange Bank, 8755 shares, (28,446 shares, at $100 each,)		2,844,600 00
Old James River company, 508 shares, at $500 each,		254,000 00
Certificates of debt of the city of Richmond,		8,000 00
Do. Richmond, Fredericksburg and Potomac railroad co.,	82,560 00	
Do. Petersburg railroad co.,	12,000 00	
Do. Louisa railroad co ,	18,900 00	
		113,460 00
Bonds of the James river and Kanawha company, guarantied by the state		4,500 00
Bonds of the Valley Turnpike company, do.		9,500 00
		4,197,680 00

Stocks in railroad companies:

Richmond, Fredericksburg and Potomac railroad company,	275,200 00	
Winchester and Potomac railroad company, subscription $120,000, loan $150,000, available for $83,333 33, at 6 per cent.,	83,333 33	
		358,533 33

Stocks in Turnpike companies:

Ashby's Gap turnpike company, $14,000; Berryville, $6300; Fincastle and Blue Ridge, $2752; Holliday's cove, $4733 33; Little river, $12,550; Lynchburg and Salem, $30,000; Staunton and James river, $20,000; Swift run gap, $4100; White and Salt Sulphur, $4000; Warm springs and Harrisonburg, $12,000; Valley turnpike company, $262,706 13,	359,141 46

Stocks in navigation companies:

Roanoke river, $80,000; Dismal Swamp canal company, $190,000; Upper Appomattox company, $56,500;	326,500 00

Loans:

To James river and Kanawha company, $1,236,000, $250,000, $268,645 33, $57,559 36; Washington college $4000; trustees of the town of Bath, $2500, (secured by mortgages,)	1,818,710 69
Total amount of productive stocks and funds.	$7,060,565 48

(*b*) FUNDS, &c., UNPRODUCTIVE, BUT MORE OR LESS AVAILABLE:

Debt of the Rappahannock company,	100,000 00
Certificates of debt of the Richmond and Petersburg railroad company, for dividends due,	33,408 00
Certificates of debt of the Virginia Central railroad company, for dividends due,	18,900 00
	152,308 00

Brought forward, 152,308 00 7,060,565 48

(*c*) STOCKS IN IMPROVEMENTS NOT COMPLETED:

In the Virginia Central railroad company, $338,301 44; Richmond and Danville railroad company, $512,488; Virginia and Tennessee railroad, $185,000; Orange and Alexandria railroad, $139,552 50; Chesapeake and Ohio canal company, $281,111 11; Coal river navigation company, $4,000; Guyandotte navigation company, $4,500; Goose creek and Little river navigation co., $13,298 86; Smith's river navigation co., $2,557 50; James river and Kanawha company, $3,000,000; Rappahannock company, $45,500; Rivanna navigation company, $35,373 03; Berryville and Charlestown turnpike company, $7,950; Blue Ridge turnpike co., $14,599 74; Buchanan turnpike company, $1,350; Clarksburg and Buckhannon turnpike co., $8,066 22; Clarksburg and Philippi turnpike co., $1,320; Front Royal and Gains' X Roads turnpike co., $2,070; Giles, Fayette and Kanawha turnpike company, $27,491 60; Hardy and Winchester turnpike company, $19 900 50; Howardsville and Rockfish turnpike company, $13,200; Hampshire and Morgan turnpike company, $2,100; Harrisville turnpike company, $3,000; Jacksonville and Bent mountain turnpike company, $472 50; Jordan's furnace and Rockbrige turnpike company, $2,482 50; Junction Valley turnpike company, $4,390 50; Marshall and Ohio turnpike company, $7,822 50; Martinsburg and Potomac turnpike co., $5,025; Martinsburg and Winchester turnpike company, $7,024; Moorfield and North Branch turnpike co., $17,625 50; Moorfield and Alleghany turnpike company, $3,090; Morgantown and Bridgeport turnpike company, $3,600; New Market and Sperryville turnpike co., $29,104 46; Rocky Mount turnpike company, 11,106 dols.; Russell and Washington turnpike company, $3,577 50; Rich Patch turnpike company, $3,834; Weston and Fairmont, $9,000; Weston and Gauley bridge turnpike company, $6,065 33; Wheeling, West Liberty and Bethany turnpike company, $14,541 18; Wellsburg and Bethany turnpike company, $7,144; Williamsport turnpike company, $1,889 32; Cheat river toll-bridge company, $1,153 12, 4,801,677 91

(*d*) STOCKS IN IMPROVEMENTS COMPLETED AND UNPRODUCTIVE:

In the Richmond and Petersburg railroad co., $385,600; Alexandria canal company, $272,000; Lower Appomattox company, $16,000; Dragon swamp navigation company, $1,464; Cacapon and North Branch turnpike company, $12,000; Charleston and Point Pleasant turnpike company, $28,800; Fairfax turnpike company, $5,400; Fallsbridge turnpike company, $32,000; Fauquier and Alexandria turnpike company, $30,000; Huntersville and Warm springs turnpike company, $6,159 24; Jackson's river turnpike company, $8,839 14; Leesburg turnpike company, $41,450; Leesburg and Snicker's gap turnpike company, $16,990 65; Lewisburg and Blue Sulphur springs turnpike company, $4,950; Lexington and Covington, $13,893 58; Lynchburg and Buffaloe Springs turnpike company, $9,171; Middle turnpike company $23,900; Milboro' and Carr's creek turnpike company, $1,978; Pittsylvania and Lynchburg turnpike company, $6,947; Pittsylvania, Franklin and Botetourt turnpike company, $10,250; Red and Blue Sulphur springs turnpike company, $7,456 66; Salem and Pepper's ferry turnpike company, $6000; Salem and Newcastle, $5,275; Shepherdstown and Smithfield turnpike company, $18,575; Snicker's gap turnpike company, $20,000; Smithfield, Charlestown and Harper's ferry turnpike company, $14,000; Tye river and Blue Ridge turnpike company, $2,400; Warm Springs and Harrisonburg turnpike co., $12,000; Wellsburg and Washington turnpike company, $7,071 01; Swift run gap turnpike co., $46,000; Staunton and James river turnpike company, $7,000; Berryville turnpike co., $8,000; Cartersville bridge co., $6,700; Virginia and Maryland bridge company, $10,000. 1,098,280 62

6,052,266 53

$13,112,832 01

NOTES.

1. *The cost of the following stocks in works sold, transferred, abandoned or useless, is omitted in the above statement:*

Monongalia navigation company $8,180, Slate river company $496 80; Augusta springs turnpike company $2,000, Natural bridge turnpike company $6,100; Lafayette and English's ferry turnpike company $4,500, Richmond dock company $62,500; Covington bridge company $5,607 07; Petersburg railroad company $323,500; Portsmouth and Roanoke railroad company $256,650; loan to Portsmouth and Roanoke railroad company $150.000; stock in City Point railroad company $60,000; loan to do. do. $50,000; Winchester and Potomac railroad company $186,666 67, .	1,116,200 54

2. *The following appropriations, &c., for roads constructed on state account, or in conjunction with counties of the state, are also omitted:*

Price's turnpike and Cumberland gap road D.72,769 47; Ohio river and Maryland road D.23,611 08; Morgantown and Beverly road D.1,214 26; Beverly and Fairmont road D.26,745 01; Tazewell courthouse and Fancy gap road D.3,150, Tazewell courthouse and Richlands road D.162 50; Sistersville and Salem road D. 10,512 89; Ice's ferry road D.1.358; Staunton and Parkersburg road D.182,477 51; bridges on do. D.23,778 97; Richlands and Kentucky line road D.9,865 81; Fancy gap road D.1,976 20; Huttonsville and Huntersville road D.750; Floyd courthouse and Hillsville road D.1,410; Alleghany and Huntersville road D.953 18; Little Stone gap road D.3,287 90; Southwestern turnpike road D.425,142 74; Northwestern turnpike road D.327,554 97; Macadamizing Northwestern turnpike road D.62,896 11, Macadamizing Staunton and Parkersburg road D.26,357 52: Blue Ridge railroad D.59,571 41, South Branch and Petersburg road D.900.	1,266,445 53
	$2,382,646 07

E. E.

Second Auditor's Office, 30th September, 1850.

J. BROWN, Jr., Second Auditor.

DEBT AND RESOURCES OF THE COMMONWEALTH,

Down to the 1st *of April,* 1851.

DEBT AND LIABILITIES.

Amount of certificates issued to 1st Oct. 1850, as per doc. House of Delegates, No. 5, page 33,		10,516,658 21	
Ditto from 1st Oct. 1850, to 1st April, 1851,		732,304 00	
(Note *a*.) Total amount certificates of debt,			$11,248,962 21
Amount actual appropriations to be provided for, viz:			
Unpaid 30th Sept. 1850, as per doc. No. 5, page 35,		4,632,868 49	
Subscriptions made since 1st Oct. 1850, down to 1st April, 1851,		217,000 00	
		4,849,868 49	
Deduct amount of subscriptions and appropriations paid between 1st Oct. 1850 and 1st April, 1851,		879,246 31	
Amount of existing obligations to be provided for by loans			3,970 622 18
Total debt per certificates issued and to be issued,			$15,219,584 39

LIABILITIES.

For subscriptions authorized by acts previous to session 1850-51 but not yet applied for or made, being part of $844,000: Doc. No. 5, G. 2, page 30,	647,400		
Subscriptions authorized by acts passed session 1850-51, as per statement thereof, prepared by Geo. W. Munford, Cl'k of the House of Delegates note (*b*)	2,504,001	3,151,401 00	
For bonds guarantied and to be guarantied, as per Doc: No. 5, page 35, above referred to		3,947,894 00	
Contingent liabilities,			7,099,295 00
Aggregate existing debt, obligations and liabilities, including those created by acts of session 1850-51,			$22,318,879 39

RESOURCES.

Productive stocks, from which interest and dividends have been received during the year, ending 30th Sept. 1850, as per statement No. 4, (*a*) Doc. No. 5, page 37,			7,060,565 48
Unproductive,			
Amounts secured by mortgages, statement No. 4. (*c*) Doc. No. 5, page 38,		152,308 00	
Stocks in improvements, not completed, Doc. No. 5 No. 4, (*c*) page 37,	4,801,677 91		
Stocks in improvements completed, but unproductive, No 4 (*d*) Doc. 5, page 38,	1,098,280 62	5,899,958 53	
Unproductive,			6,052,266 53
Add the following as offsets, against the am't of the "*liabilities*" charged in above statement, viz:			
Amount of subscriptions and appropriations at and previous to the session of the Legislature 1850-51, which, when made, will become so much stock held by the state, either productive or unproductive,			3,151,401 00
Amount of bonds of internal improvement companies, guarantied and to be guarantied by the state, and secured on the property of the several companies,			3,947,894 00
Aggregate resources,			$20,212,127 01

(Note a) This amount includes D.1,501,518 91 of certificates of debt, held by the Boards of the Literary Fund and Public Works.

(Note b) This amount is less by D.94,411 18 than the amount reported to the Convention in Col. Munford's statement, being for certain renewals of appropriations, which are included in the preceding items of D.647,400 remaining unsubscribed under acts of sessions preceding the last, and other differences, which cannot be noticed in this statement.

E. E.

SECOND AUDITOR'S Office, 15th April, 1851.

J. BROWN, JR., Second Auditor.

A TABLE *exhibiting the salaries of the Judges of the Court of Appeals and Circuit Courts, together with the mileage paid the said Judges, for attending the regular terms of their several Courts, and to Judges of the Circuit Courts for attending special terms, for the year* 1849; *also, the per diem and mileage for the same period, paid to Judges of the General Court, for attending that Court and the Special Court of Appeals. To which is added a statement of the sum annually paid Attorneys prosecuting for the Commonwealth. Prepared in compliance with resolutions of the Convention, passed on the* 31*st of October*, 1850.

Judges of the Court of Appeals.	Salaries.	Mileage.	Total.
William H. Cabell, *President*,	$2,750 00	$ 88 40	$2,838 40
John J. Allen,	2,500 00	224 00	2,724 00
Francis T. Brooke,	2,500 00	158 80	2,658 80
Briscoe G. Baldwin,	2,500 00	136 80	2,636 80
William Daniel, Jr.,	2,500 00	212 00	2,712 00
	$12,750 00	$820 00	$13,570 00

Districts.	Circuits.	JUDGES OF CIRCUIT COURTS.	SALARIES.	Mileage for Spring Circuit.	Mileage for Fall Circuit.	Mileage for Special Terms.	Mileage and per diem for General Court.	Mileage and per diem for Special Court of Appeals.	Total of Mileage.	Total of Salary, Mileage, &c.	WHERE SPECIAL TERMS OF CIRCUIT COURTS WERE HELD.
			$ cts.	$ cts.	$ cts.	$ cts.	$ cts.	$ cts.	$ cts.	$ cts.	
1	1	Richard H. Barker,	1,500 00	52 00	51 80				103 80	1603 80	
	2	John W. Nash,	1,500 00	79 00	88 88				167 88	1,667 88	
2	3	George P. Scarburg,	1,500 00	66 60	84 00	150 80			301 40	1,801 40	Warwick and Petersburg.
	4	John B. Christian,	1,500 00	50 00	40 00				90 00	1,590 00	
3	5	John T. Lomax,	1,500 00	44 40	45 40		186 00	728 00	173 00	2,503 80	
	6	John Scott, (now dead,)	1,800 00	9 60	46 00		135 60	334 00	145 20	2,325 20	
4	7	John B. Clopton,	1,800 00	29 40	38 40	86 00			153 80	1,953 80	Chesterfield and other Counties.
	21	{ John Robertson, (Chancery,)	2,000 00							2,000 00	
	21	{ John S. Caskie, (Law side,)	2,000 00							2,000 00	
	8	Daniel A. Wilson,	1,500 00	36 40	36 20				72 60	1,572 60	
5	9	William Leigh,	1,500 00	30 80	33 00		152 00	802 00	207 80	2,517 80	
	10	N. N. Taliaferro,	1,500 00	64 50	64 60				129 10	1,629 10	
6	11	Richard H. Field,	1,500 00	62 20	62 20		222 40	731 20	248 00	2,578 00	
	12	Lucas P. Thompson,	2,000 00	48 00	48 00				96 00	2,096 00	
7	13	J. R. Douglass,	1,500 00	52 00	52 00				104 00	1,604 00	
	14	Daniel Smith,	1,500 00	49 80	44 40		204 00	713 60	251 80	2,511 80	
8	15	Benjamin Estill,	1,500 00	59 20	59 20				118 40	1,618 40	

	16	James E. Brown,	1,500 00	62 40	62 40	11 20			136 00	1,636 00	Wytheville and Newbern.
9	17	Edward Johnston,	1,500 00	65 00	65 00				130 00	1,630 00	
	18	George H. Lee,	1,500 00	67 00	128 00				195 00	1,695 00	
10	19	David McComas,	1,500 00	125 80	99 80	28 40			254 00	1,754 00	Jackson County.
	20	Joseph L. Fry,	1,500 00	97 20	97 60				194 80	1,694 80	
	22	The Judge of the 18th circuit has been transferrred to this circuit, established in 1850.	1,500 00							1,500 00	
			$36,600 00	1,151 30	$1,244.88	$276 40	$900 00	$3,308 80	$3,272 58	$43,483 38	

Total—Salaries and Mileage of Judges of Court of Appeals for 1849,	$13,570 00
Total Salaries and paid Judges of the Circuit Courts, General Court, and Special Court of Appeals for the year 1849, (including also the salary of the Judge of the 22d Circuit established In 1850.)	43,483 38
Total annual sum payable from the treasury to the Attorneys prosecuting for the Commonwealth.	14,500 00
	$71,553 38

Auditor's Office, Richmond, Va.,
November 27th, 1850.

It will be observed that there are occasional differences between the mileage of the spring and fall. These may be explained by various reasons; thus in Judge Lee's circuit the spring courts of Putnam and Kanawha were not held, and the spring mileage, is therefore, less than the fall. In Judge McComas's circuit the spring mileage is rather more than the fall, because by a new arrangement of the terms the distance of the circuit has been diminished.

Judge Lee of the 18th circuit, was assigned to the newly created 22d circuit by a resolution of the general assembly, passed in 1850, and Matthew Dunbar is now the Judge of the 18th circuit, having been elected February 27th, 1850, but the name of Judge Lee is continued in the above table for the purpose of shewing the mileage drawn for 1849. Judge John W. Tyler, is also now judge in the place of Judge Scott deceased, and the name of the former judge is retained for the reason above given.

Each circuit court is authorized by law to allow its prosecuting attorney, a sum not exceeding $100 per annum for public services, except that the courts of Norfolk county and city may allow their respective attorneys $150 per annum, and that the attorney for Henrico Court, (which embraces in its jurisdiction Richmond city,) receives a salary of $400 per annum.

There are (including Lynchburg circuit court, the other courts are for counties,) one hundred and thirty-six courts authorized to allow their prosecuting attorneys $100 each, if you add courts for Raleigh and Wyoming counties established in 1850, 138 counties. The pay of these will make annually the sum of - - - $13,800

Attorney for court of Norfolk county, - - -	150
Attorney for court of Norfolk city, - - - -	150
Attorney for court of Henrico, - - - -	400
	14,580

Respectfully submitted,

RO. JOHNSTON,
First Auditor.

ABSTRACT

FROM THE

REPORTS OF THE CLERKS

OF THE COURT OF APPEALS, AND OF THE CIRCUIT SUPERIOR COURTS OF LAW AND CHANCERY,

For the year ending the thirtieth of August, 1837.

COURT OF APPEALS.

JUDGES.	LOCATION OF COURT.	Suits commenced.	Pending.	Decided.	No. of days in session.
Henry St. George Tucker, (*President*)					
Francis T. Brooke	Richmond	63	387	72	134
William H. Cabell	Lewisburg	26	60	31	32
William Brockenbrough					
Richard E. Parker					

CIRCUIT SUPERIOR COURTS OF LAW AND CHANCERY.

Districts.	Circuits.	JUDGES.	COUNTIES.	Suits without discrimination.			Law.			Chancery.			Criminal.			Days in session.			REMARKS.
				Commenced.	Pending.	Decided.	Suits commenced.	Pending.	Decided.	Causes commenced.	Pending.	Decided.	Prosecutions commenced.	Pending.	Decided.	Fall Term.	Spring Term.	Total.	
1st,	1st,	Richard H. Baker,	Southampton,	119	119	85												9	
			Greensville,	65	51	39												5	
			Surry,				51	40	37	11	24	6						5	
			Isle of Wight,	61	18	68												6	
			Nansemond,		28	33	41			2			5	31	6	3	4	7	Note 1.
			Princess Anne,				44	15	57	6	17	14						8	
			Norfolk county,	219	83	159												16	
			Norfolk Borough,				136	99	151	18	57	24	6	16	12	10	12	22	
	2d,	John Y. Mason,	Dinwiddie,	92	56	83							7						Note 2.
			Nottoway,	37	63	29													
			Amelia,				121	58	56	5	21	14				3	3	6	Note 3.
			Brunswick,	144	49	102												9	
			Sussex,				21	18	26	6	20	6						3	
			Prince George,		19	32	36			7			8			2	2	4	
			Petersburg,				150	110	105	24	40	16						34	Note 4.
2d,	3d,	Abel P. Upshur,	Charles City,	31	66	57												10	
			James City and Williamsburg,	82	306	52												9	
			York,	43	52	19												7	
			Warwick,		35	27	29			1								4	
			Elizabeth City,	36	62	45												7	
			Northampton,	16	48	18												4	Note 5.
			Accomack,	52	192	37												5	
	4th,	John B. Christian,	King William,				130	127	138	13	57	5			5			12	Note 6.
			New Kent,	28	31	41												5	

			King and Queen,	78	58	48												7	
			Essex,	93	98	81												9	
			Middlesex,	32	36	28												4	
			Gloucester,	104	121	93										4	6	10	
			Matthews,	55	39	43												7	
3d,	5th,	John T. Lomax,	Lancaster,				39	12	32	1	5	3		7	4	1	2	3	
			Northumberland,	48	35	46												5	
			Richmond county,	124	71	91										2	4	6	
			Westmoreland,				122	51	98	7	29	3				3	4	7	
			King George,	42	47	46							7					5	
			Caroline,				148	34	85	10	56	7				7	4	11	
			Spottsylvania,				81	95	99	11	621	43						42	Note 7.
	6th,	John Scott,	Fauquier,				161	233	165	41	164	20						22	
			Loudoun,				190	87	212	33	96	38						14	Note 8.
			Prince William,	92	149	82										3	3	6	
			Fairfax,				94	106	163	32	86	26				6	5	11	
			Stafford,	32	41	24												4	
4th,	7th,	John B. Clopton,	Chesterfield,	94	150	61							14	17	2			13	
			Powhatan,	103		60		105			34					4	5	9	
			Goochland,	93	72	80												12	
			Hanover,	96	239	44												12	
	21st,	Philip N. Nicholas,	Henrico and City of Richmond,				529	497	321	134	1744	120				64	78	142	
	8th,	William Daniel,	Cumberland,				140	20	110	2	36	5				3	4	7	
			Buckingham,	297	348	216												16	
			Campbell,				160	53	119	16	19	11				4	6	10	Note 9.
			Bedford,				100	153	89	27	155	27				8	6	14	
			Lynchburg,	149		199		119			359					12	14	26	
5th,	9th,	William Leigh,	Halifax,	137	134	105							81	66	11			20	
			Charlotte,	127	50	107												7	Note 10.
			Prince Edward,	106	108	66												7	
			Lunenburg,	55	76	71								26				7	
			Mecklenburg,				239	173	144	21	75	37						15	
	10th,	Fleming Saunders,	Floyd,	32		33		92			26					3	3	6	
			Patrick,	51		14		82			19					judge sick.	3	3	Note 11.
			Henry,	41	89	59							4			4	5	10	Note 12.
			Franklin,	109	112	76									3	5	6	11	
			Pittsylvania,				178	50	85	16	46	25						28	Note 13.

Districts.	Circuits.	JUDGES.	COUNTIES.	*Suits without discrimination.* Commenced.	Pending.	Decided.	*Law.* Suits commenced.	Pending.	Decided.	*Chancery.* Causes commenced.	Pending.	Decided.	*Criminal.* Prosecutions commenced.	Pending.	Decided.	*Days in session.* Fall Term.	Spring Term.	Total.	REMARKS.
6th,	11th,	Richard H. Field,	Fluvanna,	90	97	81										8	7	15	Note 14.
			Louisa,	87	82	51												20	
			Orange,	79	98	90										6	5	11	
			Madison,	7	16	16												5	
			Culpeper,	110	217	178										15	13	28	
			Rappahannock,				16	28	26	10	19	6						8	
	12th,	Lucas P. Thompson,	Amherst,	233	339	145												17	Note 15.
			Rockbridge,				162	169	141	18	71	11		9				13	
			Nelson,				170	187	117	28	65	24				7	7	14	
			Albemarle,	230	357	244												20	
			Augusta,				155	254	85	27	317	43				15	10	25	
7th,	13th,	Isaac R. Douglass,	Jefferson,	541	626	558							7		23			34	Note 16.
			Berkeley,				141	103	100	15	75	18				5	6	11	
			Morgan,	12	20	15												4	
			Hampshire,				70	93	76	27	122	23				7	5	12	
			Frederick,	164	619	112												44	
			Clarke,	63	33	54										3	6	9	
	14th,	Daniel Smith,	Page,	9	14	21												5	Note 17.
			Shenandoah,	26				5	20		30	3		2	1	2	3	5	
			Warren,	55	21	41												5	
			Hardy,	89	151	113										4	2	6	Note 18.
			Pendleton,	11	27	10							16	3	2	3	1	4	Note 19.
			Rockingham,	84	117	64												16	
8th,	15th,	Benjamin Estill,	Lee,	40	19	21												10	Note 20.
			Scott,				37	46	38	7	25	7	5	4	17	3	4	7	
			Russell,	53	146	47							24	12	30	4	6	10	Note 21.
			Tazewell,				40	79	52	5	51	4		6	12			7	

REMARKS OF CLERKS.

FIRST CIRCUIT.

(*Note* 1.)—NANSEMOND.—The clerk has embraced in his report the fall term of 1837. Suits then pending, 7; number then decided, 21; prosecutions commenced, 1; decided, 7; pending, 15; court in session four days.

SECOND CIRCUIT.

(*Note* 2.)—DINWIDDIE.—Among the suits reported there is one appeal and one supersedeas and seven presentments

(*Note* 3.)—AMELIA.—Two of the chancery causes decided were only interlocutory decrees.

(*Note* 4.)—PETERSBURG.—The clerk reports that there are 40 sleeping chancery causes not embraced.

THIRD CIRCUIT.

(*Note* 5.)—NORTHAMPTON.—The suits pending and decided are denominated by the clerk civil and criminal, without giving the number of each.

FOURTH CIRCUIT.

(*Note* 6.)—KING WILLIAM.—Of the law suits decided, 23 are stated to be motions on forthcoming bonds, notices, &c. and judgments on appeals, &c.

FIFTH CIRCUIT.

(*Note* 7.)—SPOTTSYLVANIA.—Of the chancery causes pending, more than 500 were transferred from the late superior court for the Fredericksburg district. Many are sleeping causes, many not ready for action, and others abandoned.

SIXTH CIRCUIT.

(*Note* 8).—LOUDOUN.—Both terms stated by the clerk to have been special sessions.

EIGHTH CIRCUIT.

(*Note* 9.)—CAMPBELL—The clerk states that three causes have been removed to other courts.

			Washington,	103				66	58		44	47	11	5	32			17	
			Smyth,				48	48	57	7	26	6				3	4	7	
	16th,	James E. Brown,	Wythe,	83	216	91										18	14	32	
			Grayson,	92	90	46										3	4	7	Note 22.
			Montgomery,	62	37	100												20	
			Giles,	35	83	53										7	6	13	
			Mercer,	8	13	6											1	1	Note 23.
			Monroe,	79	60	54							25	16	16	5	4	9	
9th,	17th,	John J. Allen,	Botetourt,	205	285	198												28	
			Alleghany,	52	64	42												9	
			Bath,	55	54	60												9	
			Pocahontas,	16	40	10												7	
			Greenbrier,	146	256	159												15	
	18th,	Edwin S. Duncan,	Fayette,	50		45		23			23					4	4	8	
			Nicholas,	11	29	33										3	3	6	
			Randolph	42	73	52										4	6	10	
			Lewis,		77	58	36			14			11			4	5	9	
			Braxton,	93	69	27												3	
			Harrison,	165	244	183												38	Note 24.
10th,	19th,	Lewis Summers,	Wood,	82	119	96							27					20	
			Jackson,				31	33	33	9	19	3				3	3	6	
			Mason,	47	38	24										4	4	8	
			Cabell,	25	9	16							15	40	20			10	
			Logan,	19				7	24		5	8				4	4	8	
			Kanawha,	395	389	308							2	6		16	17	33	
	20th,	Joseph L. Fry,	Preston,	33	29	38												10	
			Monongalia,				21	4	25	9	29	31						16	
			Tyler,	31	48	25												6	
			Brooke,				45	42	39	11	30	12				6	6	12	
			Ohio,	380	346	232												46	
			Marshall,	61	41	28										4	2	6	

E. E.

GEORGE W. MUNFORD, *C. H. D.*

NINTH CIRCUIT.

(*Note* 10.)—Charlotte.—The criminal causes are stated as not embraced in the report.

TENTH CIRCUIT.

(*Note* 11.)—Patrick.—Of the cases pending, 52 are reported on the issue docket, 30 actions of debt on bonds.

(*Note* 12.)—Henry.—The clerk reports, besides the suits commenced and the four pleas of the commonwealth, six original motions, and *ten* days as the total session. The criminal causes are embraced.

(*Note* 13.)—Pittsylvania.—Fifty of the law suits decided were office judgments confirmed.

ELEVENTH CIRCUIT.

(*Note* 14.)—Louisa.—The suits decided are reported to be exclusive of office judgments, of which there were thirty-four confirmed.

TWELFTH CIRCUIT.

(*Note* 15.)—Rockbridge.—Of the law suits pending, two are stated to be writs of supersedeas; of the law suits decided, 29 were motions on forthcoming bonds.

THIRTEENTH CIRCUIT.

(*Note* 16.)—Jefferson.—Of the law suits decided, 155 are stated to be judgments on forthcoming bonds.

(*Note* 17.)—Page.—The criminal cases are stated to be included in the report.

FOURTEENTH CIRCUIT.

(*Note* 18.)—Pendleton.—The suits reported as pending are those pending on the 8th December, 1837, that being the time of the report.

(*Note* 19.)—Rockingham.—The clerk states that the prosecutions are not included.

FIFTEENTH CIRCUIT.

(*Note* 20.)—Scott.—One of the law suits commenced stated to be an appeal.

(*Note* 21.)—Tazewell.—Among the suits and causes commenced, five are stated to be indictments. Among those pending there are nine rules, and six among those decided.

SIXTEENTH CIRCUIT.

(*Note* 22.)—Grayson.—Of the suits commenced, 42 are reported to be criminal cases.

(*Note* 23.)—Mercer.—The court was instituted for the first time at the May term 1837.

EIGHTEENTH CIRCUIT.

(*Note* 24.)—Harrison.—Of the suits commenced, indictments, scire facias, and forthcoming bonds are included.

ABSTRACT

FROM THE

REPORTS OF THE CLERKS

OF THE

COURT OF APPEALS

AND OF THE

CIRCUIT SUPERIOR COURTS OF LAW AND CHANCERY,

FOR THE

YEAR ENDING 30th AUGUST, 1838

ABSTRACT FROM THE REPORTS

OF THE

CLERKS OF THE COURT OF APPEALS,

AND OF THE

CIRCUIT SUPERIOR COURTS OF LAW AND CHANCERY,

For the year ending 30th August, 1838.

COURT OF APPEALS.

JUDGES.	Location of Courts.	Suits commenced.	Pending.	Decided.	No. of days in session.	REMARKS.
Henry St. George Tucker, (*President*,) Francis T. Brooke, - - - William H. Cabell, - - - William Brockenbrough, (dead,) - Richard E. Parker, - - -	Richmond -	76	404	82	132	The court commenced its session at Richmond, on the first of November, 1837, and adjourned on the 3rd day of May, 1838, comprising 138 judicial days, and 22 Sundays, having had within that time two recesses, one of 18 days, and the other of 6 days, and having actually sat 132 judicial days, exclusive of the Sundays comprised within the time of the sessions. Seven of the 82 cases occupied 53 days in the argument.
	Lewisburg, -	40	76	22	*	

* The clerk of the court at Lewisburg, failed to state the number of days the court was in session.

CIRCUIT SUPERIOR COURT OF LAW AND CHANCERY.

Districts.	Circuits.	Judges.	Counties.	Suits at Law.				Causes in Chancery.					Prosecutions.					Terms Days in session			
				No. commenced.	No. pending.	No. decided.	No. removed from other courts.	No. commenced.	No. pending.	No. interlocutory decrees.	No. final decrees.	No. removed from county courts.	No. commenced.	No. pending.	No. decided.	No. nolle prosequis.	Change of venue.	Fall.	Spring.	Total.	
1st,	1st,	Richard H. Baker,	Southampton,	168	108	175	.	8	30	37	9	3	9	10	24	1	.	6	4	10	Note 1.
			Greensville,	76	39	63	.	13	22	8	6	2	11	5	9	5	.	5	4	9	Note 2.
			Surry,	57	25	75	.	5	24	11	3	1	2	5	5	1	.	2	2	4	
			Isle of Wight,	35	39	40	.	4	11	2	1	.	16	18	10	1	.	4	2	6	
			Nansemond,	46	27	43	3	10	13	4	3	.	7	14	8	.	.	5	5	10	Note 3.
			Princess Anne,	76	49	68	.	6	21	3	6	.	5	1	4	1	.	2	3	5	Note 4.
			Norfolk county,	218	78	164	.	12	45	8	9	.	14	22	12	.	.	10	8	18	
			Norfolk borough,	195	98	203	2	19	44	11	16	1	4		13	2	.	9	9	18	
	2nd,	John Y. Mason,	Dinwiddie,	95	75	114	.	8	30	11	13	4	5	6	4	1	.	3	5	8	Note 5.
			Nottoway,	56	44	57	.	5	25	6	5	.	6	12	5	2	.	4	2	6	Note 6.
			Amelia,	101	86	138	.	9	14	5	8	2	1	1	1	.	.	3	2	5	Note 7.
			Brunswick,	118	29	132	.	19	29	11	17	6	5	9	6	2	.	5	7	12	
			Sussex,	36	20	38	.	7	24	12	2	.	1	1	6	.	.	3	2	5	Note 8.
			Prince George,	23	2	21	.	3	5	10	7	.	3	1	12	.	.	2	3	5	
			Petersburg,	239	123	197	2	29	102	31	22	8	6	2	4	2	.	15	20	35	
2d,	3d,	Abel P. Upshur,	Charles City,	40	41	30	11	5	25	8	5	.	.	.	.	.	.	3	3	6	Note 9.
			James City and Williamsburg,	102	137	94	3	15	199	78	27	3	1	2	5	6	.	13	8	21	
			York,	44	40	44	2	2	9	2	2	.	9	14	4	2	.	5	3	8	Note 10.
			Warwick,	26	25	21	1	4	14	8	2	1	1	2	1	.	.	2	2	4	
			Elizabeth City,	36	26	30	.	7	20	8	13	.	8	9	6	.	.	4	4	8	Note 11.
			Northampton,	10	14	16	.	7	23	4	7	.	.	.	1	1	.	2	2	4	Note 12.
			Accomack,	55	57	36	.	15	81	5	5	1	10	34	14	2	.	3	3	6	
	4th,	John B. Christian,	King William,	152	80	153	.	7	43	46	13	2	.	8	1	.	.	6	6	12	
			New Kent,	23	17	26	.	5	10	10	5	.	7	2	4	1	.	2	3	5	
			King and Queen,	97	50	88	.	11	28	6	5	.	2	.	.	2	.	5	3	8	

			Essex,	73	58	69	.	5	33	8	13	-	9	9	6	1	-	7	5	12	Note 13.
			Middlesex,	29	12	20	:	5	20	3	2	-	5	5	-	-	-	2	2	4	
			Gloucester,	94	70	85	1	28	63	12	23	-	2	2	5	-	-	5	6	11	Note 14.
			Mathews,	53	28	45	.	6	23	5	2	-	4	2	5	3	-	4	3	7	
3d,	5th,	John T. Lomax,	Lancaster,	24	23	19	.	1	8	-	1	-	-	6	7	1	-	1	1	2	
			Northumberland,	32	8	43	.	1	14	9	9	:	5	5	3	-	-	3	2	5	Note 15.
			Richmond county,	164	131	198	.	3	25	17	4	-	3	5	3	-	-	3	5	8	Note 16.
			Westmoreland,	11'	92	120	.	6	29	3	8	1	7	6	7	1	-	2	3	5	Note 17.
			King George,	53	34	46	.	1	13	3	4	-	1	6	2	-	-	1	2	3	
			Caroline,	158	77	153	.	22	55	20	17	2	4	13	1	:	-	5	6	11	
			Spottsylvania,	173	67	112	2	18	630	37	26	5	3	8	5	1	-	29	18	47	Note 18.
	6th,	John Scott,	Fauquier,	254	219	219	1	44	172	187	31	1	3	7	22	8	-	11	12	23	Note 19.
			Loudoun,	171	170	156	:	4	111	30	35	1	21	20	10	6	-	6	3	9	
			Prince William,	101	108	115	:	16	78	18	9	2	10	11	1	1	-	5	4	9	
			Fairfax,	92	92	99	:	33	86	53	33	-	2	:	1	4	-	4	4	8	
			Stafford,	76	26	49	.	10	26	16	1	-	6	10	5	-	.	2	4	6	
4th,	7th,	John B. Clopton,	Chesterfield,	97	133	107	.	11	45	12	5	:	8	15	11	5	1	6	9	15	Note 20.
			Powhatan,	121	63	160	2	6	35	20	14	7	-	1	2	-	-	10	4	14	
			Goochland,	190	270	151	.	9	61	9	8	4	2	7	3	3	.	7	5	12	
			Hanover,	109	134	59	.	20	116	26	25	8	9	9	2	-	-	9	5	14	
	21st,	Philip N. Nicholas,	Henrico and City of Richmond,	632	558	583	4	112	1723	159	78	6	22	38	11	2	1	119	82	201	Note 21.
	8th,	William Daniel,	Cumberland,	108	27	9	.	9	59	11	10	7	18	6	4	14	-	7	4	11	Note 22.
			Buckingham,	358	140	361	.	29	80	11	23	4	11	20	5	-	-	6	10	16	
			Campbell,	181	106	173	.	12	42	5	9	2	8	13	5	1	-	7	9	16	Note 23.
			Bedford,	219	167	197	.	36	164	25	21	18	3	5	12	-	-	8	8	16	Note 24.
			Lynchburg,	136	85	135	2	13	350	81	43	1	15	11	4	-	-	16	20	36	
5th,	9th,	William Leigh,	Halifax,	188	137	169	.	26	73	15	10	6	58	61	35	8	-	10	10	20	
			Charlotte,	167	68	190	.	19	35	14	7	7	1	3	8	7	-	4	4	8	Note 25.
			Prince Edward,	169	84	164	2	14	44	20	17	14	4	4	30	7	-	3	5	8	
			Lunenburg,	105	40	81	.	8	30	9	9	-	4	5	14	1	-	3	5	8	Note 26.
			Mecklenburg,	286	121	356	1	21	69	58	27	4	18	18	10	6	-	8	7	15	Note 27.
	10th	Fleming Saunders,	Floyd,	28	75	52	1	4	15	2	3	-	10	38	16	7	-	7	3	10	Note 28.
			Patrick,	91	54	47	.	11	31	3	2	5	13	11	13	4	-	5	6	11	Note 29.
			Henry,	70	64	60	.	12	33	24	11	3	8	10	7		-	5	4	9	Note 30.
			Franklin,	135	96	117	.	13	58	3	4	10	12	13	10	3	-	6	7	13	Note 31.
			Pittsylvania,	226	339	246	.	29	106	5	24	11	30	58	32	4	-	9	17	26	Note 32.
6th,	11th	Richard H. Field,	Fluvanna,	141	147	103	.	21	65	9	13	13	7	9	4	1	-	6	10	16	
			Louisa,	91	57	60	.	23	34	7	4	1	4	1	1	1	-	4	5	9	Note 33.
			Orange,	135	117	121	.	7	38	7	12	1	5	4	7	3	-	7	5	12	

Districts.	Circuits.	Judges.	Counties.	Suits at Law. No. commenced.	Suits at Law. No. pending.	Suits at Law. No. decided.	Suits at Law. No. removed from other courts.	Causes in Chancery. No. commenced.	Causes in Chancery. No. pending.	Causes in Chancery. No. interlocutory decrees.	Causes in Chancery. No. final decrees.	Causes in Chancery. No. removed from county courts.	Prosecutions. No commenced.	Prosecutions. No. pending.	Prosecutions. No. decided.	Prosecutions. No. nolle prosequis.	Prosecutions. Change of venue.	Terms. Days in session. Fall.	Terms. Days in session. Spring.	Terms. Days in session. Total.	
6th	11th		Greene,	1[illegible]	11	-	1	-	-	-	-	-	-	-	-	-	-	-	1	1	
			Madison,	28	22	16	3	3	9	6	2	1	-	-	1	-	-	5	4	9	
			Culpeper,	167	141	153	2	11	83	41	22	11	3	5	6	-	-	17	11	28	
			Rappahannock,	26	42	9	-	7	20	9	6	1	3	8	5	4	-	4	2	6	
	12th	Lucas P. Thompson,	Amherst,	33[illegible]	269	281	1	59	193	22	32	4	5	9	5	-	-	9	9	18	
			Rockbridge,	221	147	225	-	27	85	16	20	1	4	6	7	-	-	6	7	13	Note 34.
			Nelson,	201	138	273	-	38	74	35	27	6	15	18	2	3	–	8	7	15	Note 35.
			Albemarle,	218	266	234	-	27	90	34	48	20	24	22	31	2	-	10	20	30	
			Augusta,	219	231	221	-	21	304	99	34	-	8	16	12	-	-	38	11	49	Note 36.
7th,	13th	Isaac R. Douglass,	Jefferson,	358	261	581	-	51	214	76	27	1	3	9	7	-	-	23	10	33	Note 37.
			Berkeley,	120	58	165	-	27	87	12	15	1	6	10	5	-	-	6	6	12	Note 38.
			Morgan,	19	10	8	-	2	8	4	2	-	16	16	6	-	-	2	2	4	
			Hampshire,	104	114	75	-	[illegible]6	143	65	20	8	3	7	1	2	-	6	7	13	
			Frederick,	80	85	108	1	40	371	57	52	-	4	23	6	-	-	12	8	20	
			Clarke,	71	22	66	-	13	20	6	4	-	7	8	2	-	-	2	3	5	
	14th	Daniel Smith,	Page,	26	17	18	-	6	12	9	4	-	5	8	1	-	-	2	2	4	
			Shenandoah,	67	52	27	-	8	28	13	7	-	3	1	4	-	-	2	3	5	Note 39.
			Warren,	17	5	17	2	11	28	6	2	-	3	4	2	1	-	2	2	4	
			Hardy,	65	36	52	-	11	52	10	1[illegible]	3	1	6	-	-	-	3	3	6	
			Pendleton,	17	12	12	1	5	17	4	2	-	21	1	20	1	-	3	3	6	Note 40.
			Rockingham,	95	64	99	-	9	42	14	13	-	14	13	7	-	-	6	14	20	Note 41.
8th,	15th	Benjamin Estill,	Lee,	51	29	22	-	[illegible]	21	1	1	4	25	12	6	7	-	6	6	12	Note 42.
			Scott,	67	74	39	-	5	26	5	4	-	22	19	6	1	-	6	4	10	Note 43.
			Russell,	75	82	53	-	12	43	10	5	1	15	7	18	-	-	6	5	11	Note 44.
			Tazewell,	52	59	55	-	13	57	52	9	2	24	21	16	18	-	5	4	9	
			Washington,	98	83	102	-	16	40	4	10	5	17	4	7	4	-	16	7	23	Note 45.
			Smyth,	50	34	54	-	19	38	7	5	-	5	9	5	-	-	4	3	7	
	16th,	James E. Brown,	Wythe,	117	46	80	-	17	132	2	20	1	11	8	6	3	-	12	14	26	
			Grayson,	40	30	19	-	6	11	-	3	-	8	23	16	35	-	4	4	8	

			Montgomery,	107	60	65	-	11	18	1	18	-	13	33	18	5	-	7	7	14	
			Giles,	33	41	21	-	2	49	-	1	-	91	42	4	3	-	6	6	12	
			Mercer,	29	15	16	-	7	8	-	-	-	3	6	-	-	-	1	1	2	
			Monroe,	103	26	89	-	10	42	3	3	4	23	14	27	5	-	5	6	11	
9th,	17th	John J. Allen,	Botetourt,	232	160	216	-	32	120	24	30	12	8	29	25	11	-	14	12	26	
			Roanoke,	12	12	-	-	-	-	-	-	-	2	2	-	-	-	1	-	1	
			Alleghany,	62	73	61	-	5	27	2	10	-	9	7	6	3	-	5	6	11	
			Bath,	62	56	52	-	15	46	3	8	1	12	9	4	1	-	5	6	11	
			Pocahontas,	17	18	10	-	9	33	1	4	2	5	7	12	-	-	2	2	4	
			Greenbrier,	170	127	131	-	24	101	24	22	1	77	64	47	11	-	10	9	19	
	18th	Edwin S. Duncan,	Fayette,	62	49	48	1	3	20	6	11	-	5	6	3	1	-	5	5	10	Note 46.
			Nicholas,	41	5	51	-	5	17	-	-	-	-	-	-	-	-	2	2	4	Note 47.
			Randolph,	31	65	27	1	15	23	3	5	-	-	6	4	1	-	4	-	4	Note 48.
			Lewis,	81	122	39	3	13	58	-	14	-	5	11	4	1	-	11	2	13	Note 49.
			Braxton,	93	73	102	1	8	13	-	2	-	7	6	2	-	-	3	3	6	
			Harrison,	152	178	138	3	65	243	26	47	-	6	15	10	1	-	15	15	30	
10th	19th	Lewis Summers,	Wood,	77	85	58	-	12	54	15	14	-	11	13	11	13	-	11	7	18	Note 50.
			Jackson,	72	64	27	4	5	20	-	2	-	11	12	2	-	-	6	4	10	Note 51.
			Mason,	63	57	40	-	1	24	1	1	-	7	6	2	-	-	6	3	9	Note 52.
			Cabell,	18	20	11	2	3	16	8	3	-	33	45	29	3	-	5	9	14	
			Logan,	24	26	14	-	8	9	2	8	-	15	26	14	2	-	4	4	8	Note 53.
			Kanawha,	577	389	523	-	11	74	10	9	1	51	58	4	1	-	15	21	36	Note 54.
	20th	Joseph L. Fry,	Preston,	22	16	26	-	11	7	2	4	-	8	11	13	13	-	5	4	9	Note 55.
			Monongalia,	52	7	32	-	12	26	15	18	1	16	14	11	-	-	9	7	16	Note 56.
			Tyler,	25	29	23	-	7	32	7	10	-	9	7	12	-	-	3	3	6	
			Brooke,	59	65	34	-	6	21	10	16	-	3	4	-	1	-	5	4	9	Note 57.
			Ohio,	470	246	362	4	53	114	11	25	-	31	14	19	3	-	32	45	77	Note 58.
			Marshall,	72	63	47	-	29	38	12	12	1	5	15	6	3	-	6	5	11	
			Total,	13519	10203	12532	71	1613	9094	2086	1514	271	1229	1431	978	288	2	913	719	1632	

E. E.

GEORGE W. MUNFORD, *C. H. D.*

REMARKS OF CLERKS.

FIRST CIRCUIT.

(*Note* 1.)—SOUTHAMPTON —In ascertaining the number of suits at law pending, all cases at rules subject to the action of the court at the succeeding term, are included ; and in the number pending, all cases are embraced in which an order has been made disposing of the case for the term. The same remarks apply to the causes in chancery and to prosecutions.

(*Note* 2.)—GREENSVILLE.—The number of nolle prosequis is included in the number decided. Four causes in chancery have been removed from other circuits to this during the year ending 31st of August, and which are not included in the list of chancery causes.—The number pending is at this date. The number decided includes dismissions at rules.

(*Note* 3.)—NANSEMOND.—New clerk entered on the duties of his office on the 11th of June, 1838. Report made from the docket in the time of his predecessor.

(*Note* 4.)—PRINCESS ANNE.—This report embraces a portion of those suits reported last year. Under the head of suits commenced, scire facias on judgments are embraced, and under the head of those decided, judgments on forthcoming bonds and scire facias are included. Judgments on forthcoming bonds were not embraced in the last report.

SECOND CIRCUIT.

(*Note* 5.)—DINWIDDIE.—Of the 75 suits at law, 42 are issues and writs of enquiry, 30 are office judgments, and 3 at rules ; of the 95 commenced, 4 are appeals and writs of supersedeas ; of the 114 decided, 56 are office judgments ; of the 30 chancery causes, 19 are on the court docket, 6 on the motion docket, 5 at rules. The prosecutions depending and decided are for misdemeanors. Judgments on forthcoming bonds are not embraced in the report.

(*Note* 6.)—NOTTOWAY.—Motions on delivery bonds and by securities against their principals, and contested will cases, not being considered suits, are not embraced.

(*Note* 7.)—AMELIA.—Of the number of suits pending at law, there are 56 on the issue docket, and 30 on the reference docket, up to August rules.

(*Note* 8.)—SUSSEX.—Four causes in chancery have been removed from this court to other courts within the year.

THIRD CIRCUIT.

(*Note* 9.)—CHARLES CITY.—Troublesome business—poor pay, and d—d nonsensical requirement.

(*Note* 10.) YORK.—Twelve judgments on forthcoming bonds rendered.

(*Note* 11.)—ELIZABETH CITY.—One chancery cause was removed from the circuit superior court for the county of James City and city of Williamsburg to this court within the period embraced in this report. Three suits at law were transferred from this court to the circuit court for Nansemond.

(*Note* 12.)—NORTHAMPTON.—Rules against witnesses, &c., motions on forthcoming bonds, &c., contests concerning roads, mills, wills and the like, are not embraced in the report. Decrees which *end* a cause only are considered as final decrees. All others (including decrees final in part only) except decretal orders reinstating a cause, appointing a guardian ad litem, and the like, on an ex parte application, are considered as interlocutory decrees in the meaning of the acts of assembly requiring the report.

FOURTH CIRCUIT.

(*Note* 13.)—Essex.—Judgments on forthcoming bonds not included. The number of such judgments is 28. All other judgments upon notice are embraced. The number of suits pending embrace all at rules and on the court docket on 30th of August, 1838.—Friendly bills and answers in chancery filed in term time, in which no subpœnas are issued, are included. Among the prosecutions, only those are included founded on presentments, indictments, and scire facias on recognizances of witnesses and criminals. Rules taken against witnesses and grand jurors for non-attendance, are not included.

(*Note* 14.)—Gloucester.—Of the number pending, all are embraced which are on the court and rule docket at the time of making out the report, (25th October, 1838.) Among the number decided, dismissions at rules are included. Among the interlocutory decrees are included decrees for accounts, &c. Among prosecutions commenced and decided, grand jury presentments are embraced, and one case of felony. The cases pending are also presentments of the grand jury.

FIFTH CIRCUIT.

(*Note* 15.)—Northumberland.—Judgments on forthcoming bonds included. Abatements and dismissions not embraced.

(*Note* 16.)—Richmond County.—Of the number of suits pending at law, there were 66 instituted anterior to the 30th of August, 1837, but were pending within the year for which this return is made.

(*Note* 17.)—Westmoreland.—Among the suits at law determined and final decrees in chancery, are included several dismissions at rules. Motions and proceedings against witnesses on their recognizances are omitted, it being supposed they were not contemplated by the act of assembly.

(*Note* 18.)—Spottsylvania.—Of the number of chancery causes now pending, more than 550 or 600 were transferred from the late superior court of chancery of Fredericksburg; that many are sleeping causes; many not ready for the action of the court, and others abandoned by the parties.

SIXTH CIRCUIT.

(*Note* 19.)—Fauquier.—Besides the suits there were 64 motions on forthcoming bonds, and 10 against sheriffs, &c. on the law side of the court, and 22 motions on forthcoming bonds on the chancery side, all made and decided within the year. All orders which did not *end* suits and remove them from the docket, are regarded as interlocutory decrees.

SEVENTH CIRCUIT.

(*Note* 20.)—Chesterfield.—Four suits at law were removed from this court to other courts. Of the nine days, three composed the period of an intermediate term held in July 1838.

TWENTY-FIRST CIRCUIT.

(*Note* 21.)—Henrico and City of Richmond.—Some causes are embraced in this list that are not returned to the auditor of public accounts, no tax being assessed thereon.

EIGHTH CIRCUIT.

(*Note* 22.)—Cumberland.—This report does not include office judgments, judgments on delivery bonds, or suits dismissed by consent of parties.

(*Note* 23.)—Campbell.—This report embraces cases depending at rules, as well as those set for hearing.

(*Note* 24.—Bedford.—Of the suits at law pending, 85 were at rules, 82 remained on the docket after the spring term. Of chancery causes, 72 were on the court docket for trial, 92 at rules, 26 judgments at law, and 6 in chancery, on delivery bonds, are not estimate in this report.

NINTH CIRCUIT.

(*Note* 25.)—CHARLOTTE.—A large proportion of the suits at law depending, were brought to the fall term and decided then, leaving only 15 suits on the docket.

(*Note* 26.)—PRINCE EDWARD.—It is respectfully submitted to the legislature when a new duty be imposed under penalty for non-performance, if there should not be allowed some compensation for the services?

(*Note* 27.)—MECKLENBURG.—Award of executions on forfeited forthcoming bonds in either court, is not embraced in this statement. Orders in chancery causes made on motion, are included under "No. interlocutory decrees." The number of prosecutions decided is 10, exclusive of nolle prosequis.

TENTH CIRCUIT.

(*Note* 28.)—FLOYD.—Owing to the alteration of the time of holding the courts at this court-house, from April and September to March and August, this report necessarily embraces three courts, viz: September 1837, March and August 1838.

(*Note* 29.)—PATRICK.—There was no regular term of the court in the fall of 1837, in consequence of the illness of the judge, but a special term was held in November, of five days, and is noted here as a fall term. The criminal prosecutions are included among the other prosecutions for breaches of the peace, misdemeanors, &c. &c.

(*Note* 30.)—HENRY.—No judgment rendered by the court on forthcoming bonds is included in the list of final judgments and decrees.

(*Note* 31.)—FRANKLIN.—There were 9 judgments on delivery bonds at October term 1837, and 5 at May term 1838, which are not included in the number of suits decided. There were 32 office judgments confirmed at October 1837, and 44 at May term 1838, which are included in the number of suits decided at law. The court was engaged three days at October 1837, in trying prisoners charged with felony.

(*Note* 32.)—PITTSYLVANIA.—The number of causes pending is constituted partly of those commenced previous to the beginning of the year, but which still remain at rules, and partly of those which were on the issue docket at the same period, as well as of those commenced within the year. The number of decisions is constituted of 143 office judgments, and 103 cases decided in court. Of the 17 days the court was in session in the spring, 5 were at the special term.

ELEVENTH CIRCUIT.

(*Note* 33.)—LOUISA.—Of the number of suits decided, 40 were office judgments; there were also 11 motions commenced and decided, 10 dismissions of suits in court, and 19 at rules. 10 chancery causes have been dismissed, 3 in court, 7 at rules.

TWELFTH CIRCUIT.

(*Note* 34.)—ROCKBRIDGE.—Many of the chancery causes are pending on interlocutory decrees pronounced previous to the present year.

(*Note* 35.)—NELSON.—The time allowed for the judge to perform his duty in this court, is too limited. The time for commencing the court in Albemarle, should be postponed or extended to the 15th of the months of May and October, instead of the 10th, as at present. The judge is compelled to leave this court to reach his court in Albemarle, leaving a mass of business unfinished. The number of suits decided at law, embraces perhaps 40 judgments on forfeited forthcoming bonds.

(*Note* 36.)—AUGUSTA.—The court had an adjourned term besides the fall term, commencing on the 15th of January, 1838, the fall term being 8 days, the intermediate term 30 days.

THIRTEENTH CIRCUIT.

(*Note* 37.)—JEFFERSON.—The judge was obliged to break up the spring session before going through the docket, in order to attend the general court.

(*Note* 38.)—BERKELEY.—Under the head of interlocutory decrees, only such as settled the principle of a case have been noted.

FOURTEENTH CIRCUIT.

(*Note* 39.)—SHENANDOAH.—Of the prosecutions, 2 were criminal, the other a misdemeanor. Two of those tried commenced before the fall term 1837. Of the suits reported as pending, a large proportion were decided at the fall term 1838, being a few days after the expiration of the year ending 30th August.

(*Note* 40.)—Pendleton.—Sixteen of the prosecutions were by indictment made at May term 1837, but not docketed until October term 1837.

(*Note* 41.)—Rockingham.—The court sat 7 days in August last, holding then an intermediate term, making within the year 20 days—6 in the fall, 7 in the spring, and 7 in the summer.

FIFTEENTH CIRCUIT.

(*Note* 42.)—Lee.—Fifteen of the chancery causes were commenced before the passage of the act of 19th January, 1837, requiring the clerks to make these reports.

(*Note* 43.)—Scott.—The court was in session at the fall term till 12 o'clock on Saturday night, the greater part of the term having been taken up by the trial of an issue out of chancery from the circuit court of Washington county.

(*Note* 44.)—Russell.—On the first day of the terms the court commenced its sessions at 12 o'clock (noon;) on each subsequent day at 9, A. M., and continuing till 6 to 8, P. M., and sometimes till 9.

(*Note* 45.)—Washington.—Of the 102 suits decided, 18 were dismissed by the parties, 1 dismissed for want of security for costs, and 58 office judgments confirmed. Of the causes in chancery, besides those disposed of by final decrees, 5 have been dismissed by the parties, and 4 removed to Wythe county. Of the 17 prosecutions commenced, and 7 decided, 4 were for felony.

EIGHTEENTH CIRCUIT.

(*Note* 46.)—Fayette.—Sunday intervened in each term.

(*Note* 47.)—Nicholas.—This report is not made conformably with the law. It does not shew what proportion of the cases decided were law and what chancery. The remaining requisitions of the law are not complied with.

(*Note* 48.)—Randolph.—Judge Duncan was sick at the spring term, and held no court for this county.

(*Note* 49.)—Lewis.—The judge was sick at spring term 1838, and unable to do business

NINETEENTH CIRCUIT.

(*Note* 50.)—Wood.—A single land cause occupied four days of the September term 1837.

(*Note* 51.)—Jackson.—The judge has always evinced a disposition to dispatch all the causes ready for trial at each term, unless prevented by uncontrollable circumstances.

(*Note* 52.)—Mason.—Under the head "No. decided." are embraced all suits that are finally disposed of, including dismissions. The spring term was a short one. Nearly all of the disputed causes were continued in consequence of the absence of one of the counsel engaged in them.

(*Note* 53.)—Logan.—A special term was held in June, owing to high water.

(*Note* 54.)—Kanawha.—The suits at law decided are exclusive of 109 judgments on forfeited forthcoming bonds. The prosecutions all commenced spring term 1838.

TWENTIETH CIRCUIT.

(*Note* 55.)—Preston.—Judgments on forthcoming bonds not included.

(*Note* 56.)—Monongalia.—The suits now pending are those on the trial docket.

(*Note* 57.)—Brooke.—Interlocutory decrees do not include continuances.

(*Note* 58.)—Ohio.—Of the 45 days, 20 was the term of the intermediate court held i February and March. This court was held as a court of probat to hear the evidence and decide a will cause.

ABSTRACT

FROM THE

REPORTS OF THE CLERKS

OF THE

COURT OF APPEALS

AND OF THE

CIRCUIT SUPERIOR COURTS OF LAW AND CHANCERY

FOR THE

YEAR ENDING 30th AUGUST, 1839.

ABSTRACT FROM THE REPORTS

OF THE

CLERKS OF THE COURT OF APPEALS,

AND OF THE

CIRCUIT SUPERIOR COURTS OF LAW AND CHANCERY,

For the Year ending the 30th August, 1839; *exhibiting the number of Suits, &c.*

COURT OF APPEALS.

JUDGES.	CLERKS.	Location of Court.	Suits commenced.	Pending.	Decided.	No. of days in session.	REMARKS.
Henry St. George Tucker, *President.*	Joseph Allen,	Richmond, -	98	446	53	138	The court commenced its session on the first day of November, 1838, and adjourned the third day of May 1839, comprising 138 judicial days and 22 Sundays, having had within that time two recesses, one of 18 days and the other of 6 days.
Francis T. Brooke, - - -							
Wm. H. Cabell, - - -							
Richard E. Parker, - - -	John A. North,	Lewisburg, -	35	.	28	24	The clerk of the court of Lewisburg omitted to state the number of suits pending.
Robert Stanard, - - -							

CIRCUIT SUPERIOR COURTS OF LAW AND CHANCERY.

Districts.	Circuits.	JUDGES.	CLERKS.	COUNTIES.	Suits at Law. No. commenced.	No. pending.	No. decided.	No. removed from other courts.	Causes in Chancery. No. commenced.	No. pending.	No. interlocutory decrees.	No. final decrees.	No. removed from county courts.	Prosecutions. No. commenced.	No. pending.	No. decided.	Nolle prosequis.	Change of venue.	Terms. Days in session. Fall.	Spring.	Total.	REMARKS.
1st	1st	Rich'd H. Baker,	L. R. Edwards,	Southampton,	127	78	165	.	8	27	23	8	2	9	11	8	.	.	7	6	13	
			Wm. Blow,	Greenesville,	39	28	22	.	3	37	13	3	4	12	10	3	.	.	4	4	8	Note 1.
			W.P.Underwood	Surry,	26	17	34	.	4	24	25	2	1	3	6	3	1	.	3	2	5	Note 2.
			Nath'l Young,	Isle of Wight,	45	26	37	.	5	8	6	4	.	11	12	16	.	.	3	2	5	Note 3.
			Joseph Prentis,	Nansemond,	66	28	55	.	9	16	8	4	.	5	10	12	.	.	5	4	9	
			J. J. Burroughs,	Princess Anne,	34	29	62	.	1	13	1	3	.	1	1	1	.	.	3	2	5	Note 4.
			John Williams,	Norfolk borough,	217	125	197	1	28	60	14	25	.	12	2	10	2	.	8	12	20	
			Wm. H. Wilson,	Norfolk county,	214	65	154	.	12	44	12	11	.	17	21	14	2	.	14	8	22	
	2d	John Y. Mason,	John P. Crump,	Dinwiddie,	42	45	76	.	5	24	9	10	3	2	5	4	1	.	4	3	7	
			F. Fitzgerald,	Nottoway,	52	37	63	.	16	37	19	11	.	1	3	6	4	.	3	3	6	Note 5.
			Egbert G. Leigh,	Amelia,	51	86	69	.	9	30	9	7	.	1	2	.	.	.	2½	2	4½	Note 6.
			R. Turnbull,	Brunswick,	92	50	81	.	5	20	17	22	.	7	8	9	5	1	5	6	11	
			L. Lanier,	Sussex,	38	24	34	.	7	21	12	9	1	.	.	1	.	.	3	2	5	Note 7.
			Robert Gilliam,	Prince George,	48	34	25	3	3	9	4	2	1	14	13	1	1	.	2	2	4	
			Henry B. Gaines,	Petersburg,	156	194	176	1	16	89	29	18	2	14	4	10	.	.	17	17	34	Note 8.
2d	3d	Abel P. Upshur,	R. W. Christian,	Charles City,	39	33	53	.	1	17	7	5	.	.	.	.	.	.	3	4	7	Note 9.
			Thos. O. Cogbill,	James City and Williamsburg,	78	102	83	.	10	197	23	22	.	.	.	1	1	.	8	4	12	
			Samuel Sheild,	York,	40	20	38	.	6	18	.	1	.	3	8	6	1	.	.	5	7	Note 10.
			Wm. Robertson,	Warwick,	20	24	23	.	4	11	8	5	.	.	2	.	.	.	2	3	5	
			W. S. Armistead,	Elizabeth City,	48	16	57	.	6	19	4	6	.	11	7	13	.	.	3	4	7	Note 11.
			N. J. Winder,	Northampton,	27	117	21	.	6	23	5	7	2	7	4	3	.	.	2	5	7	
			Thos. R. Joynes,	Accomack,	151	103	55	.	22	100	28	12	8	9	34	8	1	.	5	4	9	
	4th	Jno B. Christian,	Robert Pollard,	King William,	105	53	30	.	10	39	6	11	2	3	9	1	1	.	6	6	12	Note 12.
			J. D. Christian,	New Kent,	11	13	10	.	6	12	7	3	.	.	1	.	1	.	3	3	6	
			Rob. Pollard, jr.	King and Queen,	87	41	92	.	12	24	2	7	.	4	4	.	.	.	4	4	8	Note 13.
			J. Roy Micou, jr.	Essex,	71	51	70	.	5	39	7	9	5	3	5	8	.	.	5	3	8	Note 14.

3d	5th	John T. Lomax,	Geo. T. R. Healy,	Middlesex,	38	46	25	.	10	29	7	8	1	.	3	7	.	.	2	3	5	
			John R. Cary,	Gloucester,	58	54	81	.	24	59	12	30	.	3	3	2	.	.	6	6	12	Note 15.
			Shep. G. Miller,	Mathews,	36	35	27	.	8	29	2	3	2	5	5	2	.	.	4	3	7	
			Ben. M. Walker,	Lancaster,	26	7	22	3	3	10	1	.	.	.	2	.	4	.	2	1	3	Note 16.
			S. A. M. Leland,	Northumberland	32	8	40	.	1	12	5	1	.	.	3	3	.	.	2	2	4	Note 17.
			Geo. Saunders,	Richmond co'ty,	104	75	118	1	4	22	5	8	4	4	9	1	.	.	4	3	7	
			William Hutt,	Westmoreland,	87	71	108	.	2	25	6	7	1	5	4	7	.	.	3	3	6	Note 18.
			S. J. S. Brown,	King George,	49	37	75	1	1	10	1	2	.	1	2	4	1	.	2	4	6	
	6th	John Scott,	Robert Hudgin,	Caroline,	175	26	203	2	12	61	15	9	2	6	14	2	2	.	5	6	11	Note 19.
			John J. Chew,	Spottsylvania,	191	44	184	1	22	427	35	34	1	8	11	4	.	.	22	26	48	Note 20.
			Wm. F. Phillips,	Fauquier,	226	181	259	3	40	187	139	45	8	7	6	5	3	.	11	11	22	Note 21.
			W. A. Powell,	Loudoun,	178	100	246	6	29	107	34	43	1	4	20	7	4	.	5	6	11	Note 22.
			J. H. Reid,	Prince William,	110	138	112	.	6	76	8	7	.	6	13	4	1	.	2	3	5	
			J. D. Richardson,	Fairfax,	79	77	99	.	26	83	82	17	2	2	.	2	3	.	5	5	10	
			W. H. Conway,	Stafford,	90	31	53	.	5	22	3	6	.	8	.	14	3	.	3	3	6	
4th	7th	John B. Clopton,	P. Poindexter,	Chesterfield,	80	127	96	2	5	50	12	3	.	5	16	4	.	.	9	14	23	Note 23.
			Wm. S. Dance,	Powhatan,	75	72	72	.	8	40	19	7	1	4	3	2	.	.	4	4	8	Note 24.
			W Miller,	Goochland,	106	157	117	1	7	68	5	5	.	5	11	2	.	.	6	5	11	
			Phil. B. Winston,	Hanover,	96	198	73	4	16	110	25	21	.	2	4	7	.	.	14	4	18	Note 25.
	21st	Phil. N. Nicholas,	John Robinson,	Henrico and city of Richmond,	317	502	339	4	113	1718	130	80	3	16	12	40	2	.	138	54	192	Note 26.
	8th	W. Daniel, (dead)	John Daniel,	Cumberland,	91	34	91	.	16	56	11	11	3	5	8	3	4	.	5	4	9	Note 27.
			Rolfe Eldridge,	Buckingham,	263	148	234	.	32	76	9	13	7	15	7	12	3	.	11	9	20	
			J. D. Alexander,	Campbell,	163	99	161	.	35	36	9	5	4	6	11	10	1	.	6	9	15	Note 28.
			Joseph Wilson,	Bedford,	175	134	177	.	24	169	27	40	15	5	6	2	1	.	12	10	22	Note 29.
5th	9th	William Leigh,	David Rodes,	Lynchburg,	66	90	86	2	16	359	62	36	2	10	3	13	4	.	17	24	41	
			William Holt,	Halifax,	138	107	153	.	25	80	15	18	2	46	54	28	23	.	9	10	19	
			Winsl. Robinson,	Charlotte,	118	61	117	.	5	24	11	17	.	3	4	1	1	1	4	6	10	
			B. J. Worsham,	Prince Edward,	87	56	122	1	11	49	21	10	3	1	1	3	.	.	4	2	6	
			Wm. H. Taylor,	Lunenburg,	85	56	53	.	5	22	8	6	3	3	8	3	.	.	3	3	6	
			J. J. Daly,	Mecklenburg,	191	98	214	.	11	65	48	15	2	6	11	12	1	.	7	7	14	
	10th	Flem'g Saunders,	M. Standifur,	Floyd,	23	30	11	.	5	9	.	4	.	6	37	6	6	.	3	3	6	Note 30.
			A. Staples,	Patrick,	53	42	57	.	7	23	4	7	3	13	19	6	1	.	5	6	11	Note 31.
			Ant'y M. Dupuy,	Henry,	32	37	64	.	3	40	20	6	4	8	14	8	1	.	4	3	7	Note 32.
			C. Tate,	Franklin,	101	80	93	.	18	56	6	18	5	37	36	14	7	.	11	4	15	Note 33.
			W. H. Tunstall,	Pittsylvania,	199	357	254	.	19	114	10	17	5	25	56	15	5	.	7	17	24	Note 34.
6th	11th	Rich'd H. Field,	Ab. Shepherd, jr.	Fluvanna,	105	74	87	1	13	22	4	15	2	4	4	.	5	.	6	6	12	
			John Hunter,	Louisa,	67	74	64	.	10	37	8	11	3	3	2	4	1	.	5	4	9	Note 35.
			Rey. Chapman,	Orange,	95	94	118	.	10	42	7	10	4	3	6	1	.	.	4	4	8	
			Philip S. Fry,	Greene,	4	6	7	.	2	2	1	.	.	6	1	5	.	.	1	4	5	

Districts.	Circuits.	JUDGES.	CLERKS.	COUNTIES.	Suits at Law.				Causes in Chancery.					Prosecutions.					Terms. Days in session			REMARKS.
					No. commenced.	No. pending.	No. decided.	No. removed from other courts.	No. commenced.	No. pending.	No. interlocutory decrees.	No. final decrees.	No. removed from county courts.	No. commenced.	No. pending.	No. decided.	No. nolleprosequis	Change of venue.	Fall	Spring.	Total.	
			Belfield Cave,	Madison,	26	40	23	.	9	12	6	5	.	1	1	.	.	.	2	2	4	
				Culpeper,																		
			Wm. J. Menifee,	Rappahannock,	25	28	40	.	8	23	8	6	.	16	11	12	1	.	3	7	10	
	12th	L. P. Thompson,	Robert Tinsley,	Amherst,	216	156	269	6	39	201	85	40	6	5	8	7	.	.	11	9	20	
			Saml. M'D. Reid,	Rockbridge,	152	129	180	1	23	84	14	18	3	10	13	3	.	.	6	8	14	Note 36.
			Rob. C. Cutler,	Nelson,	114	108	206	.	36	83	68	14	3	2	5	14	.	.	7	6	13	Note 37.
			Alex. Garrett,	Albemarle,	112	151	160	.	10	78	18	27	8	26	32	8	1	.	6	8	14	
			N. C. Kinney,	Augusta,	140	182	189	1	50	316	69	33	.	13	22	7	.	.	19	11	30	
7th	13th	I. R. Douglass,	Rob't T. Brown,	Jefferson,	241	271	367	.	28	197	120	46	.	2	6	3	5	.	20	19	39	
			John Strother,	Berkeley,	133	112	79	1	24	90	.	21	1	5	10	5	.	.	6	6	12	Note 38.
			J. Reichard,	Morgan,	22	17	18	.	4	12	6	2	.	5	12	9	.	.	2	2	4	
			John B. White,	Hampshire,	60	87	99	.	16	130	33	28	2	5	9	2	1	.	6	6	12	
			J. Kean,	Frederick,	131	82	119	2	17	349	82	69	.	27	42	15	2	.	7	5	12	
			H'h H. Lee,	Clarke,	95	39	91	1	7	16	4	9	.	3	3	4	2	.	3	3	6	
	14th	Daniel Smith,	W. A. Harris,	Page,	31	23	9	.	3	7	13	7	1	8	7	3	1	.	2	2	4	Note 39.
			P. Williams,	Shenandoah,	55	22	82	1	11	30	8	10	.	1	.	2	.	.	3	3	6	
			Robert Turner,	Warren,	42	10	37	.	7	13	7	21	.	2	3	2	1	.	1	1	2	
			Charles Lobb,	Hardy,	88	98	57	.	27	77	3	5	.	.	4	1	1	.	2	4	6	
			Z. Dyer,	Pendleton,	26	19	5	.	2	16	2	4	.	11	9	7	2	.	3	2	5	
			H. J. Gambill,	Rockingham,	52	117	60	.	12	36	10	14	1	29	13	8	3	.	3	9	12	Note 40.
8th	15th	Benjamin Estill,	W. S. Morison,	Lee,	58	31	56	.	6	23	2	4	.	31	19	12	.	.	4	4	8	
			John S. Martin,	Scott,	47	60	60	1	8	35	11	3	3	8	7	20	1	.	6	6	12	Note 41.
			James P. Carrell,	Russell,	56	54	81	.	7	46	18	7	2	27	28	16	1	.	6	6	12	Note 42.
			G. W. G. Brown,	Tazewell,	52	43	53	.	9	47	42	14	.	42	36	24	.	.	5	4	9	Note 43.
			Con'ly F. Trigg,	Washington,	136	84	146	.	23	54	3	12	6	20	7	11	7	.	13	10	23	Note 44.
			A. B. Moore,	Smyth,	78	63	50	.	16	39	20	15	2	36	18	23	10	.	4	5	9	Note 45.
	16th	James E. Brown	J. R. Miller,	Wythe,	105	82	54	1	23	142	3	7	1	22	17	5	1	.	18	9	27	
			Orv. Anderson,	Grayson,	30	21	36	.	6	17	8	4	.	31	17	19	35	.	4	3	7	

			R. D. Montague,	Montgomery,	93	58	85	-	15	28	8	6	-	6	23	12	1	-	6	7	13	
			Rufus A. French,	Giles,	55	50	15	-	3	50	-	8	-	8	10	55	29	-	7	5	12	Note 46.
			Alex. Mahood,	Mercer,	47	16	42	-	2	6	-	2	-	3	5	1	-	-	2	3	5	
			J. Hutchinson, jr.	Monroe,	86	58	75	6	3	40	3	5	-	12	18	10	2	-	5	5	10	
9th	17th	John J. Allen,	H. W. Bowyer,	Botetourt,	135	115	175	5	21	152	28	34	13	10	14	25	1	18	12	13	25	Note 47.
			F. Johnston,	Roanoke,	64	13	51	-	3	15	3	3	-	7	3	4	1	-	5	3	8	
			Andrew Fudge,	Alleghany,	65	99	87	-	8	41	-	6	-	3	2	5	2	-	4	6	10	
			Ch. L. Francisco,	Bath,	45	21	62	-	6	36	6	9	-	9	3	10	1	-	5	6	11	
			H. M. Moffett,	Pocahontas,	42	24	28	-	9	35	*	5	1	3	3	7	-	-	2	2	4	*Note 48
			John A. North,	Greenbrier,	212	143	199	-	28	120	39	22	2	14	43	22	14	1	12	11	23	Note 49.
			H. M. Dickinson,	Fayette,	88	61	78	2	10	26	5	4	1	9	8	5	2	-	6	5	11	Note 50.
	18th	Edw. S. Duncan,	Rob't Hamilton,	Nicholas,	31	10	18	-	2	23	5	-	-	4	-	2	3	-	2	3	5	Note 51.
			A. Earle,	Randolph,	26	71	50	-	14	37	12	9	-	7	8	3	-	-	6	4	10	
			John Talbott,	Lewis,	110	111	83	-	23	39	5	9	-	9	8	12	3	-	10	8	18	
			W. Newlon,	Braxton,	63	57	67	-	16	22	1	3	-	3	6	-	-	-	4	3	7	
			G. G. Davisson,	Harrison,	172	202	145	-	59	236	21	47	1	8	14	4	3	3	20	19	39	Note 52.
10th	19th	Lewis Summers,	J. H. Neal,	Wood,	116	69	126	1	20	67	3	4	-	4	5	7	4	-	1	6	13	Note 53.
			D. G. Morrill,	Jackson,	84	85	16	-	5	26	1	1	-	13	17	6	-	-	4	4	8	Note 54.
			G. W. Stribling,	Mason,	85	42	74	-	6	28	4	-	-	2	9	2	-	-	7	7	14	Note 55.
			John Samuels,	Cabell,	32	34	15	-	10	15	13	4	-	46	55	26	4	-	5	8	13	
			Edw. Robertson,	Logan,	15	24	16	-	4	10	2	2	-	9	23	6	2	-	-	6	6	Note 56.
			A. W. Quarrier,	Kanawha,	490	427	515	1	17	73	28	8	-	15	55	13	5	-	16	13	29	Note 57.
	20th	Joseph L. Fry,	Charles Byrne,	Preston,	32	20	22	-	15	18	6	6	-	9	14	7	1	-	5	5	10	Note 58.
			Thomas P. Ray,	Monongalia,	95	10	49	-	40	28	23	13	-	9	14	15	2	-	8	6	14	Note 59.
			D. Hickman,	Tyler,	51	70	45	-	12	38	8	6	1	18	20	5	-	-	3	3	6	
			Adam Kuhn,	Brooke,	61	77	69	-	17	27	10	11	-	1	3	2	-	-	4	4	8	Note 60.
			Alex. T. Laidley.	Ohio,	502	312	513	2	59	133	11	36	1	117	20	57	42	-	25	15	48	Note 61.
			James D. Morris.	Marshall,	70	55	8[illegible]	-	18	31	6	16	-	2	6	11	7	-	7	5	12	Note 62.
					11313	9435	1168[illegible]	69	7104	8937	2039	1543	174	1193	1366	970	323	21	862½	766	1638½	

The report of the clerk of Nicholas county has been received and inserted in its proper place since this report was made to the House.

E. E.

GEORGE W. MUNFORD, *C. H. D.*

RECAPITULATION.

CIRCUIT SUPERIOR COURTS OF LAW AND CHANCERY,

Exhibiting the Number of Suits, &c., in each Circuit, August 30th, 1839.

No. of each circuit.	Number of counties in each circuit.	JUDGES.	Suits at Law.				Causes in Chancery.					Prosecutions.					Terms. Days in session.			Miles travelling.			REMARKS.
			No. commenced.	No. pending.	No. decided.	No. removed from other courts.	No. commenced.	No. pending.	No. interlocutory decrees.	No. final decrees.	No. removed from county courts.	No. commenced.	No. pending.	No. decided.	No nolle prosequis	Change of venue.	Fall.	Spring.	Total.	Travelling to general court.	Circuit travelling.	Total once a year.	
1	8	Rich'd H. Baker,	768	396	726	1	70	229	102	60	7	70	73	67	5	.	47	40	87	224	255	479	
2	7	John Y. Mason,	479	470	524	4	61	230	99	79	7	39	35	31	11	1	36½	35	71½	150	380	530	
3	7	Abel P. Upshur,	307	315	330	.	55	385	75	58	10	30	55	31	3	.	23	29	52	348	310	658	
4	7	J. B. Christian,	406	293	435	.	75	231	43	71	10	18	41	30	9	2	30	28	58	120	230	350	
5	7	John T. Lomax,	664	268	750	8	45	567	68	61	8	24	45	21	7	.	40	45	85	140	218	358	
6	5	John Scott,	683	527	769	9	106	475	266	118	11	27	39	32	14	.	26	28	54	220	200	420	
7	4	Jno. B. Clopton,	357	554	358	7	36	268	61	36	1	16	34	15	.	.	33	27	60	12	182	194	
8	5	Wm. Daniel,	758	505	749	2	123	596	118	105	31	41	35	40	13	.	51	56	107	240	180	420	
9	5	Wm. Leigh,	619	578	659	1	57	240	103	66	10	59	78	47	25	1	27	28	55	260	165	425	
10	5	Flem. Saunders,	408	546	479	.	52	242	40	52	17	89	162	49	20	.	30	33	63	380	219	599	
11	7	Rich'd H. Field,	322	286	339	1	52	138	34	47	9	33	25	22	7	.	21	27	48	216	311	527	No return from the county of Culpeper, in consequence of the death of the clerk.—The suits in that court ought to be added to the eleventh circuit.
12	5	L. P. Thompson,	734	726	1004	8	158	762	254	137	20	43	58	32	1	.	49	42	91	242	240	482	
13	6	I. R. Douglass,	682	608	773	5	96	794	245	175	3	47	82	38	10	.	44	41	85	320	200	520	
14	6	Daniel Smith,	294	289	250	1	62	179	45	61	2	51	36	23	80	.	14	21	35	268	257	525	
15	6	Benjamin Estill,	427	335	446	1	69	244	96	55	13	164	115	116	18	.	38	35	73	618	270	888	
16	6	James E. Brown,	416	285	307	7	52	283	22	32	1	82	83	102	6	.	42	32	74	514	309	823	

17	6	John J. Allen,	563	415	602	5	75	399	76	79	16	46	68	73	19	19	40	41	81	330	241	571	The number of interlocutory decrees in the county of Nicholas was so much defaced by the wafer as to be illegible. This number ought to be added to the 17th circuit.
18	6	Edw. S. Duncan,	490	510	441	2	124	383	49	72	2	40	44	26	11	-	48	42	90	590	323	913	
19	6	Lewis Summers,	822	681	762	2	62	219	51	19	-	89	164	60	15	-	33	44	77	694	333	1027	
20	6	Joseph L. Fry,	820	514	780	2	161	275	64	88	2	156	77	95	52	-	52	38	90	714	290	1004	
21	1	Phil. N. Nicholas,	317	502	339	4	113	1718	130	80	3	16	12	40	2	-	138	54	192				
		Total,	11313	9435	11682	69	1704	8937	2039	1543	174	1193	1366	970	323	21	862½	766	1638½				
		Av'rage of the 21 circuits,	539	449	556	3	81	425	97	73	8	57	65	46	16	1	41	36	78				

Judgments at law,	11,682	Number of appeals allowed,	133	being a little over nine-tenths of one per cent. of the total decisions in the circuit courts.
Interlocutory decrees,	2,039	Causes decided,	81	
Final decrees,	1,543			
			54	excess.
Total decisions from which appeals may be had,	15,264	Pending in the court of appeals at Richmond,		446
		At Lewisburg, not stated,		

E. E.

REMARKS OF CLERKS.

FIRST CIRCUIT.

GREENESVILLE.

1. Two appeals at law from county court.

SURRY.

2. Of the 34 suits decided at law, 11 were forthcoming bonds.

ISLE OF WIGHT.

3. There have been 17 judgments on notices not comprised under either of these heads.

PRINCESS ANNE.

4. Under the head of suits at law decided, all motions made by securities for money paid by their principals are included, also all judgments on forthcoming bonds and dismissions at rules.

SECOND CIRCUIT.

NOTTOWAY.

5. Motions on delivery bonds and of securities against their principals not embraced.

AMELIA.

6. Of the suits at law commenced, all those are embraced in which process has been executed But in the number pending, only those in which issue has been made. At the time embraced in this report, there are a number of suits at rules which are not considered as pending until they are matured for the action of the court. They will be embraced in the next annual report.

SUSSEX.

7. Two chancery causes removed to other courts.

PETERSBURG.

8. The only remark I have to make is, that according to what I conceive to be a just and fair interpretation of the middle clause of the 9th article of our bill of rights, it would be cruel and unjust to inflict the fine imposed by the law passed in relation to the duty of making this report, especially as no compensation whatever is thereby allowed; and that the law reminds me of the imposition laid by the Egyptians upon the Israelites of old, who were compelled to make brick and find their own straw.

THIRD CIRCUIT.

CHARLES CITY.

9. Suits and causes at rules not included in those pending.

YORK.

10. No fall term in 1838, but a special term was held on the 23d and 24th of January 1839 by judge Christian. One supersedeas to a judgment of York county court reversed at April term 1839, and seven judgments on forthcoming bonds rendered within the twelve months.

ELIZABETH CITY.

11. The fall term of the court was not held at its regular session in consequence of the indisposition of the judge. A special term thereof was held in January 1839.

FOURTH CIRCUIT.

KING WILLIAM.

12 At the spring term of 1839 the election of members to the Legislature and to Congress commenced on the fourth day of the court and continued until the close of the term, consequently there was but little court business done on those three days.

KING AND QUEEN.

13 One chancery cause removed to Charles City.

ESSEX.

14. The number decided at law embraces all motions on forthcoming bonds, motions for money paid as security and office judgments confirmed. The number of final decrees embraces all dismissions and one judgment on forthcoming bond. Two of the final decrees were final as to part of the subject in controversy and interlocutory as to other matters involved. No orders of revivor, &c. changing the names of parties only have been entered as interlocutory decrees.—Presentments for misdemeanors, *scire facias* on criminal recognizances and on recognizances of witnesses in criminal cases are only noticed. No rules against witnesses in commonwealth's presentments nor against grand jurors are entered, not being deemed within the provisions of the act. One of those entered as being decided was a joint prosecution on a criminal recognizance, judgment being entered against one party and an *alias scire facias* against the other, which is still pending.

GLOUCESTER.

15. The number of suits and causes pending is the number pending at the time of making out the report on the court and rule dockets (October 1839.) The number decided at law and the number of final decrees in chancery includes dismissions at rules. The number of interlocutory decrees includes decrees for accounts. The prosecutions are presentments of the grand jury.

FIFTH CIRCUIT.

LANCASTER.

16. The suits removed from other courts were removed previous to this year, but decided within the period comprehended in this report. The term called spring was a special term held in June.

NORTHUMBERLAND.

17. Motions on forthcoming bonds not being considered original suits (to which it is supposed the acts of the Legislature on this subject have reference) are not included in this list.

WESTMORELAND.

18. Among suits at law determined and final decrees in chancery are included several dismissions at rules. Motions are omitted, it being supposed they are not contemplated by the law; one chancery suit has been removed from the circuit superior court of Spottsylvania, included in the column of suits commenced.

CAROLINE.

19. Of the number of suits commenced at law, fifty-six were forthcoming bonds. Of the fourteen prosecutions pending, seven are proceedings to outlawry.

SPOTTSYLVANIA.

20. The same remark made in my former report in reference to the number of suits pending in chancery applies also to this report. (See journal 1839, document No. 9.)

SIXTH CIRCUIT.

FAUQUIER.

21. Ninety motions on forthcoming bonds and six other motions at law, and eight motions on forthcoming bonds in chancery not included in the foregoing statement. All chancery orders which did not end suits, regarded as interlocutory decrees.

LOUDOUN.

22. In the number of prosecutions decided, the *nolle prosequis* are included.

SEVENTH CIRCUIT.

CHESTERFIELD.

23. Two chancery causes were removed from the circuit superior court of Henrico and city of Richmond, and one chancery cause was removed from this court to the circuit superior court of Petersburg.

POWHATAN.

24. One suit at law has been removed to Chesterfield circuit court, and two suits in chancery have been removed to this court from the circuit court of Henrico and the city of Richmond.

HANOVER.

25. Of the suits at law commenced within the year ending the 30th day of August 1839, and those pending before, sixteen have been dismissed at the rules. Of the chancery causes commenced within the year, two have been dismissed at rules; and of those pending prior to that time, one has been removed to the circuit court of Henrico and city of Richmond.

TWENTY-FIRST CIRCUIT.

HENRICO AND CITY OF RICHMOND.

26. Among the suits at law commenced, 10 writs of *scire facias* reviving judgments are included. Among the causes in chancery commenced, four writs of *scire facias* reviving decrees are included. The number of final decrees includes such suits as were dismissed, agreed in term, or for want of security for costs. The number of prosecutions decided includes two abatements by death.

EIGHTH CIRCUIT.

CUMBERLAND.

27. Injunctions, office judgments and dismissions are included.

CAMPBELL.

28. The number of suits pending embraces only such as are placed upon the court docket and set for hearing, and not the causes pending at rules; and the number decided includes all suits dismissed as well as those in which judgments were rendered.

BEDFORD.

29. Of suits on the law docket pending, 71 were at rules and 63 remaining on the court docket at the spring term 1838. Of chancery causes 104 were at rules - 65 on the court docket for trial. Judgments on delivery bonds are not included in this list: of these there were 48. An intermediate term was held in the fall of 1838.

TENTH CIRCUIT.

FLOYD.

30 Five of the prosecutions depending are against felons who escaped by breaking jail; and the *nolle prosequis* were entered (except two) against persons who had left the state permanently.

PATRICK.

31. In the number of suits decided, those dismissed and also judgments on forfeited forthcoming bonds are included, though there are but few of either.

HENRY.

32. There were also 14 judgments on forfeited forthcoming bonds not included in this report.

FRANKLIN.

33. There were 19 judgments on forthcoming bonds at the fall term of 1838 and 11 at the spring term 1839, which are not included in the number of suits decided at law. There were also 8 chancery causes removed to other courts for trial which are not included in the number of chancery causes decided. There was also one prisoner tried for felony at the spring term.—There was an adjourned court of the fall term held in Feb. 1839, which continued 5 days and is included in the fall term. Sixty of the number of suits at law decided were office judgments, to which there was no defence.

PITTSYLVANIA.

34. The number of suits pending both at law and in chancery embraces all causes whether on the issue or rule docket. The number of decisions includes office judgments as well as motions on delivery bonds and all other causes actually decided by the court. Under prosecutions are included rules against grand jurors, witnesses, &c.

ELEVENTH CIRCUIT.

LOUISA.

35. Of the number of suits decided at law; 44 were office judgments. There were also 10 motions commenced and decided, and 8 dismissions entered in court and 16 at rules. Five chancery causes have been dismissed, two in court and three at rules.

TWELTH CIRCUIT.

ROCKBRIDGE.

36. In addition there were 55 judgments on forthcoming bonds; and many of the chancery causes pending have been substantially decided.

NELSON.

37. The fall term commenced on Saturday the 29th September 1838, and a Sunday intervened in the term. The April term of said court for 1839 commenced on Monday the 29th of the same month, and continued for the week. With all due deference, I would suggest that the law under which I am compelled to make out this report, is unjust, because the Legislature almost yearly adds extra duties to the clerks without adding to their public allowance—which allowance is small at most. If the Legislature are dissatisfied with the clerks of the respective courts, let them make us salaried officers, do away with the tax on law process, receive the amount of the clerks' fees from the sheriff of each county, to be paid in the treasury, appointing some suitable person or persons to examine and certify the list of insolvents, the balance to be paid into the treasury, subject to the sheriff's commission.

THIRTEENTH CIRCUIT.

BERKELEY.

38. This report includes *scire facias*, but not forthcoming bonds.

FOURTEENTH CIRCUIT.

PAGE.

39. This is one of the most troublesome and vexatious duties which the clerks have to perform; and as the objects originally intended by the law have probably been obtained, it is hoped that it may be repealed or that those universal pack-horses, the clerks, may be paid for the labour thus imposed on them.

ROCKINGHAM.

40. At the fall term 1838, the judge was sick.

FIFTEENTH CIRCUIT.

SCOTT.

41. The number of suits commenced at law does not include motions. The number of suits pending at law includes an issue out of chancery and a *scire facias*. The suits decided at law include one *scire facias* and one motion. The causes commenced in chancery include one by supersedeas.

RUSSELL.

42. At the fall term the court adjourned Saturday evening at half past 9 o'clock at night, and at April term about the same time. The judge generally commences business on the first day of each term at twelve or one o'clock; on the other days at 8 or 9 in the morning, and continues each day's session till after night: but even with this attention to business, some of the litigated cases that come up towards the close of the session are continued for want of sufficient time to progress with them. In the enumeration of the causes decided, office judgments, dismissions, and judgments on forthcoming bonds are included.

TAZEWELL.

43. An imposition: more childish than troublesome, more troublesome than useful.

WASHINGTON.

44. Of the 84 suits pending 70 are upon the court docket and 14 at rules. Of the 146 suits decided, 77 were office judgments confirmed, 16 dismissions in the office confirmed; 8 confessions of judgments taken in the office and 4 in court. Of the chancery causes pending, 26 are at rules and 23 upon the court docket, and the final decrees include two causes dismissed agreed. Five of the prosecutions commenced and decided were for felony, and consumed several days at the fall term in the trials.

SMYTH.

45. A number of the suits pending 31st of August were decided at fall term 1839, which commenced 30th Sept. 1839.

SIXTEENTH CIRCUIT.

GILES.

46. Of the 50 suits pending at law, 16 are upon the rule docket. Of the 50 in chancery, 46 stand at rules, and the *nolle prosequis* are upon indictments for gaming. The persons thus released were fined, however, upon other presentments for gaming.

SEVENTEENTH CIRCUIT.

BOTETOURT.

47. Eighteen causes common law and chancery were removed to the county of Roanoke, in pursuance of the law dividing the county of Botetourt. These I have placed under the head of change of venue,

POCHAHONTAS.

48 *The No. of interlocutory decrees so much defaced by the wafer as to be illegible. (C. H. D.)

GREENBRIER.

49. There were 24 judgments on delivery bonds at the fall term, and the same number at the spring term in addition to the number of causes decided.

EIGHTEENTH CIRCUIT.

FAYETTE.

50. Sunday during each term.

NICHOLAS.

51. A number of causes never reached the docket in consequence of compromise by trust deed and otherwise.

HARRISON.

52. In addition there have been 33 motions and award of executions on forthcoming bonds.

NINETEENTH CIRCUIT.

WOOD.

53. The judge was seriously ill and confined to his room during the fall term 1838, except the first day, and one day during the spring term 1839. There was an intermediate term held in August 1839, which lasted six days.

JACKSON.

54 There is not time enough allowed for this court between the sitting of the courts of Wood and Mason counties to transact all the business therein depending.

MASON.

55. A special term was held commencing 21st January 1839, there being no court in the fall of 1838, in consequence of the illness of the judge. The causes pending embrace those on the rule docket as well as those on the court docket. The causes decided include dismissions.

LOGAN.

56 The judge was sick at the fall term and held no court.

KANAWHA.

57. In the No. pending at law, 45 old causes at the rules and office judgments to fall term 1839 are included. The number decided at law includes dismissions and excludes 181 judgments on forthcoming bonds. Of the number of causes in chancery pending, 45 are old cases at the rules.

TWENTIETH CIRCUIT.

PRESTON.

58. Judgments on forthcoming bonds not included.

MONONGALIA.

59. The suits pending are those on the trial docket. The number decided at law includes office judgments, dismissions and causes remanded to rules.

BROOKE.

60. Number of suits at law decided do not include judgments on forthcoming bonds or cases of wills.

OHIO.

61. The causes decided include also forthcoming bonds. There was an intermediate term of eight days duration.

MARSHALL.

62. The number of suits decided does not include judgments on forthcoming bonds.

ABSTRACT

FROM THE

REPORTS OF THE CLERKS

OF THE

COURT OF APPEALS

AND OF THE

CIRCUIT SUPERIOR COURTS OF LAW AND CHANCERY,

FOR THE

YEAR ENDING 30th AUGUST, 1840.

ABSTRACT FROM THE REPORTS

OF THE

CLERKS OF THE COURT OF APPEALS,

AND OF THE

CIRCUIT SUPERIOR COURTS OF LAW AND CHANCERY,

For the Year ending the 30th August, 1840 ; *exhibiting the number of Suits, &c.*

COURT OF APPEALS.

JUDGES.	CLERKS.	Location of Court.	Suits commenced.	Pending.	Decided.	No. of days in session.	REMARKS.
Henry St. George Tucker, *President*, Francis T. Brooke, Wm. H. Cabell,	Joseph Allen,	Richmond,	81	468	57	127	The number of days the court was in session are judicial days, excluding Sundays.
Richard E Parker, (dead,) Robert Stanard,	John A. North,	Lewisburg,	27	90	21	-	The number of days not reported by the clerk at Lewisburg.

CIRCUIT SUPERIOR COURTS OF LAW AND CHANCERY.

Districts.	Circuits.	JUDGES.	CLERKS.	COUNTIES.	Suits at Law.				Causes in Chancery.					Prosecutions.					Terms. Days in session.			REMARKS.
					No. commenced.	No. pending.	No. decided.	No. removed from other courts.	No. commenced.	No. pending.	No. interlocutory decrees.	No. final decrees.	No. removed from county courts.	No. commenced.	No. pending.	No. decided.	Nolle prosequis.	Change of venue.	Fall.	Spring.	Total.	
1st	1st	Rich'd H. Baker,	L. R. Edwards,	Southampton,	178	144	103	-	11	34	10	-	-	1	11	2	-	-	-	6	6	Note 1.
			Wm. Blow,	Greenesville,	46	14	22	-	4	35	9	8	2	7	7	6	1	-	-	4	4	Note 2.
			W. P. Underwood	Surry,	69	30	64	-	4	22	7	12	2	-	2	-	-	4	-	4	4	Note 3.
			Nath'l Young,	Isle of Wight,	47	26	48	-	4	6	1	5	-	6	12	6	1	-	-	3	3	Note 4.
			Joseph Prentis,	Nansemond,	105	119	88	-	5	13	2	8	-	5	9	5	1	-	-	5	5	Note 5.
			J. J. Burroughs,	Princess Anne,	61	25	72	1	3	12	1	2	-	-	-	-	1	-	-	3	3	Note 6.
			John Williams,	Norfolk borough,	299	124	298	1	29	73	15	18	-	8	5	4	-	-	2	27	29	Note 7.
			Arth. Emmerson,	Norfolk county,	292	83	220	1	9	38	7	12	1	4	19	5	2	-	2	9	11	Note 8.
	2d	John Y. Mason,	John P. Crump,	Dinwiddie,	90	49	49	-	8	25	8	5	1	4	2	4		-	5	7	12	
			F. Fitzgerald,	Nottoway,	57	43	89	-	12	41	14	10	-	2	3	1	1	-	2	2	4	Note 9.
			Egbert G. Leigh,	Amelia,	97	87	87	-	8	31	11	6	-	5	7	-	-	-	2	2	4	
			Chas. Turnbull,	Brunswick,	139	75	111	-	8	18	8	13	-	11	8	13	3	-	6	5	11	
			L. Lanier,	Sussex,	44	18	50	-	3	19	8	5	1	3	2	1	-	-	3	2	5	
			Robert Gilliam,	Prince George,	41	7	39	3	2	5	5	4	1	3	5	12	-	-	2	3	5	Note 10.
			Henry B. Gaines,	Petersburg,	265	198	115	1	38	114	47	35	-	15	20	4	1	1	17	14	31	
2d	3d	Abel P. Upshur,	Thos. O. Cogbill,	James City and Williamsburg,	128	102	136	4	14	177	36	37	-	8	8	-	-	-	20	8	28	
			Samuel Sheild,	York,	64	68	37	1	3	21	-	-	-	3	9	4	1	-	3	5	8	Note 11.
			Wm. Robertson,	Warwick,	20	14	27	-	2	12	3	2	-	3	1	4	-	-	4	1	5	Note 12.
			W. S. Armistead,	Elizabeth City,	39	16	41	-	1	19	9	2	-	2	3	-	6	-	3	3	6	
			N. J. Winder,	Northampton,	45	21	43	-	5	19	7	9	-	8	3	5	2	-	3	3	6	
			Thos. R. Joynes,	Accomack,	60	77	75	-	21	120	29	8	8	1	34	-	-	-	6	3	9	
	4th	Jno B. Christian,	Robert Pollard,	King William,	118	112	92	1	4	46	14	9	-	4	4	9	6	-	5	6	11	
			J. D. Christian,	New Kent,	17	15	12	-	4	12	10	3	1	1	2	-	-	-	2	2	4	
			Robert Pollard.	King and Queen,	112	90	109	-	8	30	11	8	1	5	7	2	-	-	3	3	6	
			J. Roy Micou, jr.	Essex,	115	30	115	-	5	38	12	8	-	-	1	4	-	-	4	4	8	Note 13.
			Geo. T. R. Healy,	Middlesex,	64	10	50	-	5	23	6	4	-	7	3	4	-	-	2	2	4	

3d	5th	John T. Lomax,	**John R. Cary,**	Gloucester,	140	105	93	-	21	62	16	21	-	3	1	5	3	-	6	6	12	Note 14.
			Shep. G. Miller,	Mathews,	104	47	51	-	7	29	8	7	-	4	2	2	-	-	3	4	7	
			Ben. M. Walker,	Lancaster,	44	32	39	-	3	8	3	2	-	3	2	3	-	-	1	2	3	
			S. A. M. Leland,	Northumberland	49	4	34	-	2	12	7	3	-	2	3	1	-	-	2	2	4	
			Geo. Saunders,	Richmond co'ty,	130	45	99	-	4	23	13	9	-	-	6	1	3	-	3	4	7	
			William Hutt.	Westmoreland,	77	71	77	-	5	22	5	8	-	6	6	4	-	—	4	2	6	Note 15.
			S. J. S. Brown,	King George,	31	36	31	-	4	11	2	4	-	-	2	-	-	-	3	2	5	
			Robert Hudgin,	Caroline,	269	86	244	1	11	60	37	14	4	4	3	4	2	-	5	3	8	
			John J. Chew,	Spottsylvania,	205	177	169	-	14	389	40	42	-	3	8	5	-	-	23	20	43	Note 16.
	6th	John Scott,	Wm F. Phillips,	Fauquier,	205	206	216	3	49	214	104	31	10	5	7	3	2	-	12	9	21	Note 17.
			W. A. Powell,	Loudoun,	167	75	166	3	25	78	38	41	1	2	3	3	1	-	6	5	11	Note 18.
			P. D Lipscomb,	Prince William,	146	99	153	-	14	76	12	6	-	33	41	4	3	-	4	3	7	
			F. D Richardson,	Fairfax,	123	93	99	-	26	106	65	9	2	3	-	1	-	-	4	3	7	
			J. M. Conway,	Stafford,	18	12	8	-	1	21	5	4	1	5	5	-	-	-	4	1	5	
4th	7th	John B. Clopton,	P. Poindexter,	Chesterfield,	160	191	96	-	13	61	21	2	-	10	13	13	-	-	11	8	20	Note 19.
			Ro. W. Christian,	Charles City,	54	33	92	-	3	19	5	6	-	1	1	-	-	-	6	6	12	Note 20.
			Wm. S. Dance,	Powhatan,	113	96	98	-	12	52	8	5	2	1	2	3	-	-	5	4	9	
			W Miller,	Goochland,	158	151	143	-	15	79	8	7	-	9	13	3	-	-	6	5	11	
			Phil. B. Winston,	Hanover,	79	150	71	-	11	108	25	11	1	-	1	3	-	-	10	11	23	Note 21.
	21st	Phil. N. Nicholas,	John Robinson,	Henrico and city of Richmond,	606	744	377	-	108	1765	107	85	-	17	15	17	1	-	83	80	163	Note 22.
	8th	Dan'l A. Wilson,	John Daniel,	Cumberland,	105	28	104	-	7	66	7	10	-	1	3	3	1	-	3	4	7	Note 23.
			Rolfe Eldridge,	Buckingham,	333	133	313	-	34	123	20	14	6	23	19	20	6	-	10	13	23	
			J. D. Alexander,	Campbell,	180	149	119	-	34	86	11	8	10	6	17	6	3	-	-	7	7	Note 24.
			Joseph Wilson,	Bedford,	145	151	130	-	15	162	26	30	10	9	9	6	2	-	6	9	15	Note 25.
			David Rodes,	Lynchburg,	149	127	112	-	33	347	56	38	2	6	6	4	2	-	2	17	19	Note 26.
5th	9th	William Leigh,	William Holt,	Halifax,	127	54	111	-	17	56	9	24	2	39	24	26	10	-	12	8	20	
			Winsl. Robinson,	Charlotte,	177	81	157	-	12	34	10	2	2	10	11	3	4	-	3	4	7	
			B. J. Worsham,	Prince Edward,	125	66	160	-	21	51	17	16	2	-	-	6	-	-	3	4	7	
			Wm. H. Taylor,	Lunenburg,	90	30	41	-	7	23	7	10	-	11	9	3	-	-	3	3	6	
			J. J. Daly,	Mecklenburg,	208	108	204	-	14	61	27	29	8	18	17	13	4	-	7	5	12	
	10th	Flem'g Saunders,	M. Standifur,	Floyd,	18	37	10	-	3	9	5	5	-	5	16	7	2	-	3	3	6	Note 27.
			A. Staples,	Patrick,	34	38	37	-	9	15	5	7	-	14	21	13	4	-	6	5	11	
			Ant'y M. Dupuy,	Henry,	84	55	61	-	4	37	16	9	2	13	14	8	3	-	5	2	7	Note 28.
			C. Tate,	Franklin,	88	76	79	-	11	71	6	8	1	14	20	26	3	2	9	6	15	Note 29.
			W. H. Tunstall,	Pittsylvania,	276	409	246	2	23	117	20	19	4	29	52	37	5	-	5	10	22	Note 30.
6th	11th	Rich'd H. Field,	John Hunter,	Louisa,	108	112	50	-	7	35	18	18	1	4	3	1	-	-	7	7	16	Note 31.
			Ab. Shepherd, jr	Fluvanna,	106	106	138	1	7	29	2	11	6	3	4	1	3	-	7	4	17	Note 32.
			Rey. Chapman,	Orange,	135	108	104	-	3	34	4	8	1	-	2	1	2	-	6	4	10	
			Philip S. Fry,	Greene,	10	8	10	-	2	3	2	-	1	11	6	5	1	-	2	3	5	Note 33.

Districts.	Circuits.	JUDGES.	CLERKS.	COUNTIES.	SUITS AT LAW.				CAUSES IN CHANCERY.					PROSECUTIONS.					TERMS. Days in session.			REMARKS.
					No. commenced.	No. pending.	No. decided.	No. removed from other courts.	No. commenced.	No. pending.	No. interlocutory decrees.	No. final decrees.	No. removed from county courts.	No. commenced.	No. pending.	No. decided.	No. nolleprosequis	Change of venue.	Fall.	Spring.	Total.	
			Belfield Cave,	Madison,	62	37	40	.	6	11	6	5	.	.	.	1	.	1	.	4	4	
			R. G. Ward,	Culpeper,	229	209	203	.	.	.	.	.	.	.	.	.	.	.	11	11	28	Note 34.
			Wm. J. Menifee,	Rappahannock,	48	36	38	.	7	22	5	6	.	6	13	1	3	.	6	4	10	
	12th	L. P. Thompson,	Robert Tinsley,	Amherst,	227	233	235	5	39	205	80	31	2	6	6	4	5	.	14	8	22	Note 35.
			Saml. M'D. Reid,	Rockbridge,	126	135	155	.	29	88	15	26	1	10	16	9	.	1	8	6	14	Note 36.
			Rob. C. Cutler,	Nelson,	227	227	202	.	47	128	70	19	6	17	19	5	.	.	6	8	14	
			Alex. Garrett,	Albemarle,	132	113	134	2	7	71	22	28	14	84	76	39	30	.	8	7	15	
			N. C. Kinney,	Augusta,	250	245	187	1	42	333	67	25	1	10	16	16	.	.	15	14	29	Note 37.
7th	13th	I. R. Douglass,	Rob't T. Brown,	Jefferson,	391	319	517	.	42	192	63	45	.	4	9	2	.	.	27	15	42	
			John Strother,	Berkeley,	146	100	158	.	38	114	24	14	.	5	5	6	3	.	5	6	11	Note 38.
			J. Reichard,	Morgan,	32	21	21	.	6	15	2	2	.	5	13	7	.	.	2	2	4	
			John B. White,	Hampshire,	158	157	101	.	17	134	29	18	4	6	6	2	8	.	6	5	11	Note 39.
			J. Kean,	Frederick,	142	50	121	.	22	333	37	56	.	24	29	35	.	1	5	4	9	
			H'h H. Lee,	Clarke,	84	40	85	.	9	14	6	5	.	.	3	1	.	.	3	4	7	Note 40.
	14th	Daniel Smith,	W. A. Harris,	Page,	73	9	33	.	2	9	14	2	.	.	3	4	3	.	2	2	4	Note 41.
			P. Williams,	Shenandoah,	66	51	34	2	14	31	6	10	.	3	3	.	.	.	2	3	5	Note 42.
			Robert Turner,	Warren,	35	9	37	.	3	13	5	4	.	5	5	1	2	.	2	2	4	Note 43.
			Charles Lobb,	Hardy,	126	48	78	.	23	88	23	12	1	2	2	1	.	.	3	3	6	
			Z. Dyer,	Pendleton,	16	11	16	.	7	15	2	6	.	15	2	9	2	.	4	1	5	
			H. J. Gambill,	Rockingham,	91	77	70	.	10	41	15	9	.	24	15	20	3	.	7	7	14	Note 44.
8th	15th	Benjamin Estill,	J. W. S Morison,	Lee,	44	70	28	.	3	24	1	1	.	25	15	9	21	.	3	6	9	Note 45.
			John S. Martin,	Scott,	41	57	48	.	11	32	17	10	2	22	16	11	2	.	4	6	10	Note 46.
			James P. Carrell,	Russell,	42	75	61	.	7	36	4	9	.	13	18	24	1	.	6	3	9	Note 47.
			G. W. G. Brown,	Tazewell,	62	94	18	.	9	54	18	2	.	7	41	2	.	.	6	.	6	Note 48.
			Con'ly F. Trigg,	Washington,	199	97	177	.	15	60	5	12	.	27	28	8	1	.	5	6	11	Note 49.
			A. B. Moore,	Smyth,	59	64	52	.	14	44	35	11	.	24	24	18	2	.	4	4	8	
	16th	James E. Brown,	J. R. Miller,	Wythe,	65	141	80	.	14	169	3	12	.	13	17	17	.	.	9	11	20	
			Orv. Anderson,	Grayson,	32	18	31	.	5	20	18	1	1	101	33	30	58	.	6	4	10	
			R. D. Montague,	Montgomery,	92	66	86	.	18	48	6	13	2	23	23	12	5	.	6	6	12	

			Wm. B. Charlton,	Pulaski,	39	18	11	.	.	.	.	.	.	.	.	.	.	.	.	5	5	Note 50.
			Rufus A. French,	Giles,	33	33	31	.	9	53	.	.	.	14	7	11	6	.	4	4	8	
			Alex. Mahood,	Mercer,	30	16	28	1	5	4	.	6	.	6	3	11	.	.	3	2	5	
			J. C. Hutchinson,	Monroe,	114	35	132	.	5	33	2	4	2	9	7	12	4	.	5	5	10	
9th	17th	John J. Allen,	H. W. Bowyer,	Botetourt,	226	89	148	.	24	145	1[illegible]	[illegible]	3	7	8	10	1	.	12	9	21	
			F. Johnston,	Roanoke,	72	20	62	2	31	18	2	6	1	3	3	6	.	.	5	5	10	
			Andrew Fudge,	Alleghany,	48	50	35	.	11	28	4	10	.	6	6	2	.	.	3	4	7	
			Ch. L. Francisco,	Bath,	60	23	58	.	7	38	2	11	.	5	7	6	1	.	4	6	10	
			J. Tallman,	Pocahontas,	45	35	33	.	10	32	1	11	.	1	3	1	.	.	2	1	3	
			John A. North,	Greenbrier,	161	109	186	2	19	114	35	26	.	10	15	18	21	.	9	12	21	Note 51.
	18th	Edw. S. Duncan,	H. M. Dickinson,	Fayette,	106	70	67	.	15	27	7	4	1	1	2	8	1	.	5	4	9	Note 52.
			Rob't Hamilton,	Nicholas,	23	10	25	.	2	17	.	6	.	3	.	1	2	.	2	5	7	
			A. Earle,	Randolph,	14	49	20	.	9	43	17	11	.	8	11	9	.	.	6	4	10	
			John Talbott,	Lewis,	115	108	155	.	24	80	10	7	.	23	11	6	.	.	10	10	20	
			W. Newlon,	Braxton,	46	58	59	.	3	23	.	3	1	6	6	4	2	.	2	3	5	
			G. G. Davisson,	Harrison,	221	229	206	10	57	254	32	36	.	48	43	14	1	2	34	22	56	Note 53.
10th	19th	Lewis Summers,	J. H. Neal,	Wood,	283	140	119	.	38	78	27	9	.	6	7	6	.	.	7	8	19	Note 54.
			D. G. Morrill,	Jackson,	101	76	64	1	18	27	1	5	.	1[illegible]	22	6	.	.	5	5	10	Note 55.
			G. W. Stribling,	Mason,	93	31	87	.	9	31	3	2	.	1[illegible]	16	2	.	.	6	7	13	Note 56.
			John Samuels,	Cabell,	17	23	28	1	16	16	5	7	.	12	39	29	2	.	6	6	12	
			Edw. Robertson,	Logan,	30	26	23	.	4	9	1	8	.	12	20	22	1	.	6	6	12	
			A. W. Quarrier,	Kanawha,	429	282	701	.	12	72	31	10	.	36	45	34	10	.	29	21	50	Note 57.
	20th	Joseph L. Fry,	Charles Byrne,	Preston,	31	25	28	.	17	20	10	6	.	9	11	11	.	.	6	7	13	Note 58.
			Thomas P. Ray,	Monongalia,	79	21	80	2	34	39	26	29	.	13	13	10	2	.	8	8	16	Note 59.
			D. Hickman,	Tyler,	97	66	88	.	14	39	15	14	.	8	11	17	.	.	5	5	10	
			Adam Kuhn,	Brooke,	72	73	76	.	18	35	9	10	.	8	7	3	1	.	7	5	12	
			Alex. T. Laidley,	Ohio,	607	389	678	1	73	147	9	11	.	14	13	16	4	.	22	23	45	Note 60.
			James D. Morris,	Marshall,	72	53	70	.	24	34	8	21	.	5	6	2	3	.	5	7	12	
					14685	10996	13189	53	1832	9417	1970	1545	157	1249	1396	882	313	12	828	813	1652	

The reports of the clerks of Wythe and Nicholas have been received since this report was made, and are inserted in their proper place.

E. E.

GEORGE W. MUNFORD, *C. H. D.*

RECAPITULATION.

CIRCUIT SUPERIOR COURTS OF LAW AND CHANCERY,

Exhibiting the Number of Suits, &c., in each Circuit, August 30th, 1840.

No. of each circuit.	Number of counties in each circuit.	JUDGES.	Suits at Law.				Causes in Chancery.					Prosecutions.					Terms. Days in session			Miles travelling			REMARKS.
			No. commenced.	No. pending.	No. decided.	No. removed from other courts.	No. commenced.	No. pending.	No. interlocutory decrees.	No. final decrees.	No. removed from county courts.	No. commenced.	No. pending.	No. decided.	No nolle prosequis	Changes of venue.	Fall.	Spring.	Total.	Travelling to general court.	Travelling in circuit.	Total once a year.	
1	8	Rich'd H. Baker,	1097	565	915	3	69	233	52	65	5	31	65	28	6	4	4	61	65	224	255	479	
2	7	John Y. Mason,	733	477	540	4	79	253	101	78	3	43	47	75	5	1	37	35	72	150	380	530	
3	6	Abel P. Upshur,	356	298	359	5	46	368	84	50	8	25	58	13	9	-	39	23	62	348	310	658	
4	7	J. B. Christian,	670	409	522	1	74	240	77	60	2	24	20	26	9	-	25	27	52	120	230	350	
5	7	John T. Lomax,	805	451	693	1	43	525	107	82	4	18	30	18	5	-	41	35	75	140	218	358	
6	5	John Scott,	659	485	642	6	115	495	224	91	14	48	56	11	6	-	30	21	51	220	200	420	
7	5	Jno. B. Clopton,	564	621	500	-	54	319	70	31	3	21	30	22	-	-	38	34	75	12	182	194	Intermediate terms of three days.
8	5	Dan'l A. Wilson,	1032	632	889	-	140	840	129	124	30	84	78	65	24	-	33	58	91	240	180	420	
9	5	Wm. Leigh,	727	339	673	-	71	225	70	81	14	78	61	51	15	-	28	24	52	260	165	425	
10	5	Flem. Saunders,	500	615	433	2	50	249	52	48	7	75	123	91	17	2	35	26	61	380	219	199	
11	7	Rich'd H. Field,	698	616	583	1	32	134	37	48	9	24	28	10	8	1	49	37	90	216	311	527	Intermediate terms were held in this circuit. The clerk of the county of Culpeper failed to discriminate between the suits at law, causes in chancery and prosecutions as required by law.
12	5	L. P. Thompson,	962	943	923	8	164	825	254	129	24	127	133	75	35	1	[illegible]1	43	94	242	240	482	
13	6	I. R. Douglass,	953	667	1003	-	134	802	161	140	4	44	65	53	11	[illegible]	48	36	84	320	200	520	
14	6	Daniel Smith,	407	205	268	2	59	197	65	43	1	49	30	35	10	-	20	18	38	268	257	525	

15	6	Benjamin Estill,	443	447	374	·	59	250	80	45	2	118	142	72	27	-	28	25	53	618	270	888	
16	7	James E. Brown,	425	327	399	1	56	327	29	36	5	156	90	93	73	-	33	37	70	514	309	823	
17	6	John J. Allen,	612	326	522	4	102	375	60	102	4	32	42	43	23	-	35	37	72	330	241	571	
18	6	Edw. S. Duncan,	525	524	532	10	110	444	66	67	2	89	73	42	6	2	59	48	107	590	323	913	
19	6	Lewis Summers,	953	578	1022	2	97	237	68	41	·	88	149	99	13	-	59	53	116	694	333	1027	An intermediate term of four days produces the discrepancy in the total of the days on which the court was held.
20	6	Joseph L. Fry,	958	627	1020	3	180	314	77	91	·	57	61	59	10	-	53	55	108	714	290	1004	
21	1	Phil. N. Nicholas,	606	744	377	-	108	1765	107	85	-	17	15	17	1	-	83	80	163				
		Total,	14685	10996	13189	53	1832	9417	1970	1545	157	1249	1396	882	313	12	828	813	1652				
		Av'rage of the 21 circuits,	699	523	628	2	87	448	93	73	7	59	66	42	14	-	39	38	79				

Judgments at law,	13,189
Interlocutory decrees,	1,970
Final decrees,	1,545
Total decisions from which appeals may be had,	16,704

Number of appeals allowed,	108	being a little less than two-thirds of one per cent.
Causes decided in the court of appeals,	78	
	30	excess.

Pending in the court of appeals at Richmond,	468
at Lewisburg,	90

E. E.

GEORGE W. MUNFORD, *C. H. D.*

REMARKS OF CLERKS.

FIRST CIRCUIT.

SOUTHAMTON.

1. Two suits at law which stood referred to arbitration at the last report, and were not then reported, are now embraced in this report. Office judgments in seven cases, and four dismissions at rules, are not included in the cases pending or decided.

GREENESVILLE.

2. No court held in the fall.

SURRY.

3. No fall court in consequence of the indisposition of the Judge, but the docket was disposed of at the spring term. Of the suits decided, one was a motion on a forthcoming bond, and there were motions by securities against their principals.

ISLE OF WIGHT.

4. Of the suits decided at law, five were motions on delivery bonds, and one office judgment.

NANSEMOND.

5. There was no fall court in 1839, owing to the ill health of the judge.

PRINCESS ANNE.

6. Judgments on forthcoming bonds and dismissions at rules included in the number of suits decided.

NORFOLK BOROUGH.

7. The court did not sit at the regular fall term, owing to the sickness of the Judge, but a special term was held on the 20th February 1840, of two days.

NORFOLK COUNTY.

8. In the suits decided, 22 judgments on forthcoming bonds included.

SECOND CIRCUIT.

NOTTOWAY.

9. Motions on delivery bonds and against securities included.

PRINCE GEORGE.

10. There were no motions on delivery bonds this year.

THIRD CIRCUIT.

YORK.

11. Fourteen judgments on forthcoming bonds, one appeal, and one supersedeas still pending.

WARWICK.

12. The number noted under the head of "No. pending," are those suits remaining on the docket undecided on the 31st August 1840.

FOURTH CIRCUIT.

ESSEX.

13. Those decided at law embrace motions on forthcoming bonds, motions for money paid as security office judgments confirmed, and judgments confessed in the office. In two of the suits depending, there were judgments entered against the party on whom process was executed, and continued at rules agains

the other parties for further proceedings. The number of final decrees embraces all dismissals, and two were final as to part of the matter involved, and interlocutory as to other matters. No orders of revivor, changing names of parties, granting leave to file answers and amended bills, have been entered as interlocutory decrees. Only prosecutions for misdemeanours, scire facias in criminal recognizances, and recognizances of witnesses in criminal prosecutions are noticed. Rules against witnesses and grand jurors are not entered. Of the suits depending, all are embraced up to the 1st November 1840, the time of making up the report. The reason so few appear then pending is, that the court completed its session on the 30th October 1840.

GLOUCESTER.

14. Number pending includes those on the court and rule dockets. Number decided includes dismissions at rules and office judgments. Interlocutory decrees includes decrees for accounts. Prosecutions include presentments. A most troublesome duty required by the Legislature, without compensation.

FIFTH CIRCUIT.

WESTMORELAND.

15. One scire facias is included in the number of suits at law commenced.

SPOTTSYLVANIA.

16. The same remarks made in previous reports, in reference to the number of chancery causes pending, apply to this report.

SIXTH CIRCUIT.

FAUQUIER.

17. Seventy motions on forthcoming bonds against sheriffs and others at law, and sixteen like motions in chancery, not included in the statement. For the last 30 years the Legislature, when requiring new duties to be performed by clerks of courts, seems to have forgot to provide for any compensation for the performance. The preparation of these reports consumes no little time, and is exceedingly troublesome and vexatious. The Legislature is respectfully asked to provide for the payment of a LIBERAL fee for it.

LOUDOUN.

18. Exclusive of law causes ended, are sixty-two judgments on forthcoming bonds; scire facias also excluded. Also one chancery decree on forthcoming bond.

SEVENTH CIRCUIT.

CHESTERFIELD.

19. There was an intermediate term of one day. It may not be improper to remark, that since the date of this return, to wit: at October term 1840, 118 common law suits, 6 chancery causes and 5 prosecutions were decided, as will appear by the next annual report; this materially lessens the number of suits pending subsequent to date of this return.

CHARLES CITY.

20. Of the suits at law commenced, one was by scire facias, on which there is no bail. Of the number commenced in chancery, one was by injunction.

HANOVER.

21. Of the suits commenced, six have been dismissed at rules. There was an intermediate term of the court, consisting of two days.

TWENTY-FIRST CIRCUIT.

HENRICO AND CITY OF RICHMOND.

22. In the number of suits at law commenced, 12 writs of scire facias are included (reviving judgments.) In the causes commenced, four are writs of scire facias reviving decrees, and pauper causes. Among the final decrees, causes dismissed in court are embraced.

EIGHTH CIRCUIT.

CUMBERLAND.

23. Injunctions, office judgments and dismissions, are included in this report.

CAMPBELL.

24. There was no fall term, in consequence of the ill health of Judge Daniel, who shortly afterwards died.

BEDFORD.

25. Of the causes pending on the law docket, 75 were at rules, and 76 upon the court docket. Of the chancery causes, 93 were at rules, and 69 on the court docket. Judgments on delivery bonds are not included in this report. These judgments were 33 in number, all at law.

LYNCHBURG.

26. The fall term was commenced by the late Judge Daniel who sat two days, and on the third became too unwell to return to court and sign the orders of the preceding day. The court remained open till the sitting of the general court, when it stood adjourned by law.

TENTH CIRCUIT.

FLOYD.

27. The court sits on the 26th days of March and August, hence the variation in this report from other counties.

HENRY.

28. Four of the prosecutions decided were felonies Thirty five of the causes now depending commenced since the spring term. Judgments and award of executions on forthcoming bonds not reported.

FRANKLIN.

29 There were 28 judgments on forthcoming bonds which are not included in the number of suits decided; 49 of the suits decided were actions of debt, to which there was no defence. There was one prisoner tried for felony at the spring term.

PITTSYLVANIA.

30. Causes pending include those on the rule as well as on the issue and office judgment dockets. Those decided embrace office judgments as well as motions on delivery bonds and other matters. In prosecutions, rules against grand jurors, witnesses, &c., are included. Suits removed includes one appeal from county court. There was an intermediate term of seven days.

ELEVENTH CIRCUIT.

LOUISA.

31 Intermediate term in June of two days Of suits at law decided, 34 were office judgments. There were 17 motions commenced and decided, and 7 dismissions in court, and 5 at rules. Of the chancery causes decided, 2 were dismissed in court, and 3 at rules.

FLUVANNA.

32. There was an intermediate term of the court, commencing 25th day of March and continuing until 31st making six judicial days, not embraced in spring and fall terms.

GREENE.

33. This duty is considered by the clerks a very unnecessary duty.

CULPEPER.

34. There was an intermediate term of six days. In this report, motions on forthcoming bonds are considered as suits commenced and decided, being 11 in number.
The clerk has not separated the suits from the chancery causes or from the prosecutions.

TWELTH CIRCUIT.

AMHERST.

35. This report embraces more than a judicial year, in consequence of changing the court-day from the 1st September to 25th August It includes fall term of 1839, and five days of the fall term of 1840. The court failed to meet at the regular term in the spring, the Judge being engaged in the court of appeals. A special term in lieu thereof, was held on the 30th of March.

ROCKBRIDGE.

36. Suits at law decided include 34 judgments on forthcoming bonds. Causes decided include dismissions and office judgments. The fall term was taken up with the trial of Richard C. Gwatkin for murder, removed from Greenbrier, and he has obtained a new trial.

AUGUSTA.

37. On the chancery side there were 6 motions and judgments in the name of the receiver of the court, for moneys loaned out, not embraced in the return here made.

THIRTEENTH CIRCUIT.

BERKELEY.

38. No notice has been taken in this report of motions on forthcoming bonds.

HAMPSHIRE.

39. In suits at law decided, there are included 13 judgments on forthcoming bonds.

CLARKE.

40. The undersigned respectfully represents to the Legislature, that the object of the law under which this report is made, was to obtain for the Legislature a comparative statement of the labour and duties performed by the several judges of the circuit courts, with a view to the consideration of the subject of increasing the salaries of those functionaries. That subject being not now before the Legislature, as he believes, the reason of the law has ceased, and he humbly conceives the law should cease also. He states further, that the provisions of the act which require these duties to be performed by the clerks of the circuit courts, without annexing any compensation, and impose a penalty for failure in the performance, [although accidental and unintentional,] are unreasonable, unjust, vexatious, and ought to be repealed, which he respectfully prays may be done accordingly. H. H. Lee, C. C.

FOURTEENTH CIRCUIT.

PAGE.

41. A most troublesome and burdensome duty to perform, no pay for doing it, and of no use when it is done. A wise Legislature will repeal the law.

SHENANDOAH.

42 Of the suits pending, some were office judgments confirmed September 1840. Of those decided, some were pending on 31st August 1839.

WARREN.

43. No notice is taken of judgments on forthcoming bonds. As the suits upon which they are taken are reported, the clerk supposes that it is not the intention of the law that they should be again reported as separate causes.

ROCKINGHAM.

44. Suits decided includes judgments on delivery bonds and office judgments. Prosecutions decided includes all kinds.

FIFTEENTH CIRCUIT.

LEE.

45. Fifteen of the chancery causes were upon the docket before the act requiring this report went into operation; since which, five have been decided. At the spring term the court did not adjourn till Saturday night 9 o'clock.

SCOTT.

46. Suits commenced and decided at law do not include motions, but those decided include two writs of scire facias.

RUSSELL.

47. From severe indisposition the Judge only sat 2 days in court at the spring term. Each day's session, except the first, is generally commenced at 9 in the morning, and continued till 8 or 9 in the afternoon.—But even with this severe labour several causes of importance are continued towards the close of the term for want of time. In the suits at law decided, dismissions, office judgments, and judgments on forthcoming bonds, are included; and generally the number of cases decided is no test of the industry of the Judge while holding court, as sometimes a single cause may occupy several days; and at other times many causes are decided in one day.

TAZEWELL.

48. No court was held in the spring, the Judge being prevented by indisposition from attending.

WASHINGTON.

49 Of the suits decided at law, 18 were judgments confessed in the office, eleven dismissed at rules, 2 nonsuits and 106 office judgments confirmed. Of the causes pending in chancery, 35 are on the rule docket.

SIXTEENTH CIRCUIT.

PULASKI.

50. The clerk does not discriminate between the suits at law and causes in chancery and prosecutions.—This is a new county, and the court has been organized since the last abstract.

SEVENTEENTH CIRCUIT.

GREENBRIER.

51. The number of judgments and forthcoming bonds not included.

EIGHTEENTH CIRCUIT.

FAYETTE.

52 Sunday intervened during the court in the fall term. In the spring term detained one day by high water. Sunday intervening during time prescribed by law for holding the court.

HARRISON.

53. Law judgments on forthcoming bonds, 42; decrees in chancery on ditto, 3.

NINETEENTH CIRCUIT.

WOOD.

54. Intermediate term in March of 4 days. Judgments on forthcoming bonds not included, neither as suits commenced or decided.

JACKSON.

55. Business done with satisfactory dispatch. At September term, just closed, the docket has been considerably diminished.

MASON.

56. Causes decided include dismissions, but excludes judgments on forthcoming bonds. Suits pending include suits at rules, and embrace suits brought on 15th October 1840.

KANAWHA.

57. Of the suits pending, those at rules are included. Of those decided, 48 were dismissions, and 186 judgments on forthcoming bonds. Of the causes pending, those at rules are included.

TWENTIETH CIRCUIT.

PRESTON.

59. Office dismissions not included in the number decided.

MONONGALIA.

60. The causes depending are those on the trial docket. Suits decided includes office judgments, dismissions, and suits remanded to rules. Final decrees also include dismissions and causes remanded to rules.

OHIO.

61. Of the number commenced on the law side of the court, nine are writs of scire facias. Of the suits decided at law, 128 were executions on forthcoming bonds. Causes pending include those at rules. Dismissions at rules not embraced in report.

62. Intermediate term of three days.

63. Intermediate terms were held in this circuit. The clerk of the county of Culpeper failed to discriminate between the suits at law, causes in chancery and prosecutions as required by law.

64. An intermediate term of 4 days produces the discrepancy in the total of the days on which the court was held.

ABSTRACT

FROM THE

REPORTS OF THE CLERKS

OF THE

COURT OF APPEALS

AND OF THE

CIRCUIT SUPERIOR COURTS OF LAW AND CHANCERY,

FOR THE

YEAR ENDING 30th AUGUST, 1841

ABSTRACT FROM THE REPORTS

OF THE

CLERKS OF THE COURT OF APPEALS,

AND OF THE

CIRCUIT SUPERIOR COURTS OF LAW AND CHANCERY,

For the year ending 30th August, 1841; exhibiting the number of suits, &c., for each County in the State.

COURT OF APPEALS.

JUDGES.	CLERKS.	Location of Court.	Suits commenced.	Pending.	Decided.	No. of days in session.	REMARKS OF THE CLERKS.
Henry St. George Tucker, *President*, (resigned,)							
Francis T. Brooke, - - - -	Joseph Allen,	Richmond,	76	464	75	160	
Wm. H. Cabell, - - - -							
Robert Stanard, - - - -	John A. North,	Lewisburg,	34	114	13	30	Of the suits commenced 19 are suits at law and 15 causes in chancery. Of the 114 pending, 51 are suits at law and 63 causes in chancery, and of the 13 decided, 7 are of the former and 6 of the latter.
John J. Allen, - - - - -							
			110	578	88	190	

CIRCUIT SUPERIOR COURT OF LAW AND CHANCERY.

Districts.	Circuits.	JUDGES.	CLERKS.	COUNTIES.	Suits at Law. No. commenced.	Suits at Law. No. pending.	Suits at Law. No. decided.	Suits at Law. No. removed from other courts.	Causes in Chancery. No. commenced.	Causes in Chancery. No. pending.	Causes in Chancery. No. interlocutory decrees.	Causes in Chancery. No. final decrees.	Causes in Chancery. No. removed from county courts.	Prosecutions. No. commenced.	Prosecutions. No. pending.	Prosecutions. No. decided.	Prosecutions. No. nolle prosequis	Prosecutions. Change of venue.	Terms. Days in session. Fall.	Terms. Days in session. Spring.	Terms. Days in session. Total.	REMARKS OF THE CLERKS.
1st,	1st,	Rich'd H. Baker,	L. R. Edwards,	Southampton,	313	183	276	4	17	43	40	12	-	9	9	9	3	-	5	8	13	
			Joseph Turner,	Greenesville,	81	51	56	-	6	31	10	11	1	4	7	4	3	-	3	6	9	Note 1.
			W. P. Underwood,	Surry,	37	14	87	-	9	20	16	8	-	3	3	3	-	-	3	3	6	Note 2.
			Nathaniel Young,	Isle of Wight,	156	150	112	1	4	7	2	2	-	5	3	9	-	-	2	2	4	
			Joseph Prentis,	Nansemond,	187	55	185	-	1	6	6	6	-	3	5	4	-	-	4	4	8	
			J. J. Burroughs,	Princess Anne,	62	9	91	1	-	11	2	2	-	3	3	1	-	-	3	4	7	Note 3.
			John Williams,	Norfolk boro',	197	112	220	-	53	65	14	66	-	3	3	6	-	-	13	15	28	
			Ar. Emmerson, jr.	Norfolk county,	243	65	266	3	15	26	9	15	-	6	6	25	-	-	10	5	15	
	2d,	Jas. H. Gholson,	John P. Crump,	Dinwiddie,	90	41	37	-	8	22	13	7	1	3	5	-	-	-	4	3	7	Note 4.
			F. Fitzgerald,	Nottoway,	102	68	78	-	4	45	11	7	1	3	4	2	-	-	2	2	4	Note 5.
			Egbert G. Leigh,	Amelia,	120	37	107	-	1	28	10	2	-	-	5	1	2	-	2	3	5	
			E. R. Turnbull,	Brunswick,	145	94	126	1	13	25	11	11	1	6	7	7	-	-	6	4	10	
			L. Lanier,	Sussex,	89	55	52	-	3	15	10	3	-	1	2	1	-	-	2	2	4	
			Robert Gilliam,	Prince George,	50	8	44	-	4	7	2	2	-	2	2	3	2	-	3	2	5	Note 6.
			Henry B. Gaines,	Petersburg,	215	233	171	4	40	90	42	34	17	26	31	15	3	-	18	20	38	
2d,	3d,	Abel P. Upshur, (resigned,)	Thos. O. Cogbill,	James City and city of Williamsburg,	189	98	198	2	5	151	41	40	-	2	3	3	4	-	12	9	21	
			Samuel Shield,	York,	58	54	62	1	1	16	3	4	1	2	3	4	1	-	2	5	7	Note 7.
			Wm. Robertson,	Warwick,																		
			W. S. Armistead,	Elizabeth City,	19	13	15	-	4	14	7	7	-	-	1	5	-	-	3	3	6	
			N. I. Winder,	Northampton,	37	26	32	-	5	22	2	4	2	3	5	2	-	-	3	4	7	
			Thos. R. Joynes,	Accomack,	197	153	184	-	20	102	32	14	1	-	36	-	-	-	3	6	9	
	4th,	J. B. Christian,	Robt. Pollard,	King William,	202	117	163	-	12	47	13	3	-	-	1	3	-	-	5	6	11	
			J. D. Christian,	New Kent,	27	16	28	-	1	11	3	3	1	5	4	1	2	-	2	3	5	
			Robt. Pollard, jr.	King & Queen,	209	110	157	-	8	36	12	13	1	12	10	11	-	-	4	4	8	Note 8.
			Ja's Roy Micou, jr.	Essex,	90	65	115	1	5	37	13	3	-	9	6	3	-	-	4	3	7	Note 9.
			Geo. T. R. Healy,	Middlesex,	115	33	104	-	8	28	11	6	-	3	8	1	-	-	2	3	5	

			John R. Cary,	Gloucester,	238	99	219	-	21	53	20	17	1	4	3	2	1	-	5	5	10	Note 10.
			Shep'd G. Miller,	Mathews,	166	39	153	-	10	30	9	6	1	1	1	1	-	-	3	3	8	
3d,	5th,	John T. Lomax,	Benj. M. Walker,	Lancaster,	42	38	36	-	3	11	2	4	-	-	-	2	-	-	3	3	6	
			S. A. M. Leland,	Northumb'land,	60	9	58	-	2	10	11	4	-	1	-	-	-	-	2	2	4	Note 11.
			John T.B.Jeffries,	Richmond co'ty	145	31	157	-	9	30	8	-	-	2	6	1	-	-	3	5	8	
			William Hutt,	Westmoreland,	165	116	120	-	10	27	6	5	-	2	6	2	-	-	2	2	4	Note 12.
			S. J. S. Brown,	King George,	35	32	39	-	4	17	4	-	-	2	1	2	1	-	2	2	4	
			Robert Hudgins,	Caroline,	331	162	311	-	21	77	25	9	2	3	4	4	-	-	9	4	13	
			J. J. Chew,	Spottsylvania,	170	111	229	2	19	343	31	46	-	8	11	5	1	-	16	23	39	Note 13.
			Wm. F. Philips,	Fauquier,	404	330	303	1	53	217	113	42	1	4	7	3	1	-	8	10	18	Note 14.
	6th,	John Scott,	Thomas P. Knox,	Loudoun,	204	171	162	-	22	98	50	33	1	1	4	-	-	-	5	3	8	Note 15.
			P. D. Lipscomb,	Prince William,	176	146	129	-	26	116	16	14	1	5	20	24	2	-	3	3	6	
			F. D. Richardson,	Fairfax,																		
			J. M. Conway,	Stafford,	42	31	20	-	3	22	3	1	-	1	4	3	2	-	1	2	3	
4th,	7th,	Jno. B. Clopton,	Parke Poindexter,	Chesterfield,	159	171	188	1	8	58	25	8	-	18	30	10	-	-	7	9	22	Note 16.
			Ro. W. Christian,	Charles City,	58	27	110	-	-	14	5	6	-	-	-	1	-	-	3	3	7	Note 17.
			Wm. S. Dance,	Powhatan,	202	154	140	-	21	59	36	20	1	1	2	1	-	-	3	8	11	Note 18.
			Wm. Miller,	Goochland,	130	141	112	-	8	64	15	12	2	6	13	1	4	-	5	6	13	Note 19.
			Philip B. Winston,	Hanover,	98	167	70	-	16	111	23	12	-	9	11	1	-	-	1	10	15	Note 20.
	21st,	Ph. N. Nicholas,	J. Robinson,	Henrico & City of Richmond,	439	701	556	-	51	-	54	38	-	49	43	15	6	-	90	53	143	Note 21.
	22d,	Jno. Robertson,	Wm. G. Sands,	Henrico & City of Richmond,	-	-	-	-	40	1737	-53	46								24	39	Note 22.
	8th,	Dan. A. Wilson,	John Daniel,	Cumberland,	202	39	194	1	16	68	13	7	4	4	3	2	1	-	5	5	10	Note 23.
			Rolfe Eldridge,	Buckingham,	521	347	328	-	39	88	20	36	4	4	3	12	4	-	12	10	22	
			J. D. Alexander,	Campbell,	128	145	138	2	11	93	7	5	11	27	36	12	-	-	6	10	16	
			Joseph Wilson,	Bedford,	174	166	159	2	28	179	31	30	20	4	7	4	-	-	9	5	14	Note 24.
			David Rodes,	Lynchburg,	142	109	160	5	18	327	76	22	1	19	9	10	2	-	10	17	27	
5th.	9th,	William Leigh,	Wm. Holt,	Halifax,	117	82	128	-	28	54	25	21	5	36	48	17	17	-	10	11	21	Note 25.
			Winsl. Robinson,	Charlotte,	137	92	153	-	12	51	22	10	-	1	5	4	3	-	3	3	6	
			B. J. Worsham,	Prince Edward,	113	65	139	-	22	63	24	29	4	7	6	1	-	-	3	3	6	
			Wm. H. Taylor,	Lunenburg,	120	66	50	-	6	19	9	2	7	12	11	6	1	-	3	3	6	
			J. J. Daly,	Mecklenburg,	239	68	172	-	11	55	11	11	3	26	16	13	4	-	4	6	10	
	10th	Fleming Saunders,	M. Standifur,	Floyd,	18	27	18	-	10	20	7	2	-	10	8	3	-	-	4	3	7	
			A. Staples,	Patrick,	30	47	27	-	6	21	9	8	3	7	13	17	2	-	4	5	9	
			Anth. M. Dupuy,	Henry,	57	32	60	-	3	37	7	5	4	7	14	8	1	-	3	4	7	Note 26.
			C. Tate,	Franklin,	140	100	105	-	12	57	14	17	1	21	17	17	4	1	15	8	23	Note 27.
			W. H. Tunstall,	Pittsylvania,	314	537	354	3	28	126	8	12	1	13	33	13	1	-	10	14	24	Note 28.

Districts.	Circuits.	JUDGES.	CLERKS.	COUNTIES.	Suits at Law.				Causes in Chancery.					Prosecutions.					TERMS. Days in session.			REMARKS OF THE CLERKS.
					No. commenced.	No. pending.	No. decided.	No. removed from other courts.	No. commenced.	No. pending.	No. interlocutory decrees.	No. final decrees.	No. removed from county courts.	No. commenced.	No. pending.	No. decided.	Nolle prosequis.	Change of venue.	Fall.	Spring.	Total.	
6th,	11th	Rich'd H. Field,	John Hunter,	Louisa,	146	145	121	.	8	38	10	16	.	3	5	.	.	.	6	7	13	Note 29.
			Abr. Shepherd, jr.	Fluvanna,	165	144	148	.	14	22	4	11	1	1	.	5	1	.	5	8	13	
			Rey. Chapman,	Orange,	121	162	74	.	8	43	11	4	2	1	3	1	1	.	4	4	10	Note 30.
			Philip S. Fry,	Greene,	11	13	5	.	5	8	1	1	.	18	14	4	.	.	2	3	5	Note 31.
			Belfield Cave,	Madison,	28	73	58	.	4	13	7	2	.	.	1	1	.	.	4	5	9	
			R. G. Ward,	Culpeper,	145	109	234	1	14	93	18	12	1	3	6	1	1	.	9	12	21	Note 32.
			Wm. J. Menifee,	Rappahannock,	56	30	61	.	7	23	20	6	.	6	15	2	1	.	4	7	11	Note 33.
	12th	L.P.Thompson,	Robert Tinsley,	Amherst,	290	237	286	1	20	207	46	19	1	4	7	1	2	.	12	10	22	
			David Hutcheson,	Rockbridge,	203	214	155	1	21	91	36	17	.	6	11	10	.	1	9	8	17	
			Robert C. Cutler,	Nelson,	265	165	262	.	32	121	86	29	7	17	28	6	.	.	6	8	14	Note 34.
			Alex. Garrett,	Albemarle,	186	127	162	2	4	75	14	12	3	31	63	32	5	.	7	9	16	
			Nich. C. Kinney,	Augusta,	371	303	313	.	37	333	76	37	.	3	11	6	2	.	13	20	33	Note 35.
7th,	13th	I. R. Douglass,	Robert T. Brown,	Jefferson,	434	167	525	.	55	207	71	22	1	14	21	3	.	.	13	14	27	Note 36.
			John Strother,	Berkeley,	196	141	160	.	18	105	22	23	.	6	7	6	.	.	5	5	10	Note 37.
			J. Richard,	Morgan,	84	46	30	.	8	24	14	1	.	6	6	12	.	.	2	3	5	
			J. B. White,	Hampshire,	236	310	251	.	38	175	42	20	.	8	15	3	.	.	6	6	12	Note 38.
			J. Kean,	Frederick,																		
			H. H. Lee,	Clarke,	194	42	185	.	10	19	12	2	.	6	5	2	1	.	4	4	8	Note 39.
	14th	Daniel Smith,	W. A. Harris,	Page,	39	17	60	.	5	21	6	3	.	3	8	3	.	.	2	2	4	
			P. Williams,	Shenandoah,	24	16	51	.	14	38	13	6	.	4	5	2	1	.	2	3	5	Note 40.
			Robert Turner,	Warren,	50	12	47	.	8	10	4	11	1	.	2	.	3	.	2	1	3	Note 41.
			Charles Lobb,	Hardy,	157	130	156	.	15	83	32	15	.	2	1	2	.	.	3	3	6	
			Z. Dyer,	Pendleton,	20	21	18	.	7	16	1	5	.	15	1	14	.	.	1	4	5	
			H. J. Gambill,	Rockingham,	175	265	113	12	13	47	16	10	1	11	15	9	1	.	9	10	19	Note 42.
8th,	15th	Benj. Estill,	J. W. S. Morrison,	Lee,	81	29	49	.	3	25	3	2	.	25	12	15	10	.	2	6	8	Note 43.
			John S. Martin,	Scott,	36	48	46	.	9	34	12	5	2	24	25	15	2	.	4	5	9	Note 44.
			James P. Carroll,	Russell,	41	72	69	.	3	39	6	5	.	12	13	12	4	.	6	3	9	Note 45.
			G. W. G. Brown,	Tazewell,	71	75	79	.	7	50	46	12	.	18	44	13	3	.	5	4	9	Note 46.

			Connally F. Trigg,	Washington,	189	97	198	-	29	86	49	18	12	72	71	18	12	-	6	9	15	
			A. B. Moore,	Smyth,	85	58	86	-	12	47	16	6	-	13	14	16	5	-	4	4	8	
	16th	Ja's E. Brown,	James R. Miller,	Wythe,	115	77	123	-	25	87	-	23	1	19	32	19	3	-	10	9	19	
			Orville Anderson,	Grayson,	30	22	18	-	9	28	39	6	3	20	30	51	2	-	4	6	10	
			R. D. Montague,	Montgomery,	145	122	110	-	15	30	16	24	-	8	15	13	3	-	5	8	13	
			Wm. B. Charlton,	Pulaski,	27	24	7	-	4	5	3	1	-	15	6	4	12	-	1	2	3	Note 47.
			Rufus A. French,	Giles,	64	42	88	-	10	51	2	11	1	8	9	10	1	-	5	6	11	Note 48.
			Alex. Mahood,	Mercer,	58	35	43	1	5	6	-	5	-	4	2	5	-	-	2	2	4	
			J. Hutchinson, jr.	Monroe,	166	59	120	-	11	39	3	8	1	8	9	5	-	-	5	5	10	Note 49.
9th,	17th	Edw. Johnston,	H. W. Bowyer,	Botetourt,	186	194	218	-	28	180	12	22	4	1	10	-	1	-	11	8	19	
			F. Johnston,	Roanoke,	76	32	57	5	10	28	-	1	1	6	6	4	-	-	3	3	6	
			Andrew Fudge,	Alleghany,	34	44	47	5	9	31	7	5	-	3	3	7	-	-	4	6	10	
			Chs. L. Francisco,	Bath,	67	19	57	-	9	31	11	9	1	5	2	5	-	-	4	4	8	
			J. Tallman,	Pocahontas,	43	9	50	2	12	21	1	14	-	14	4	12	-	-	2	3	5	
			John A. North,	Greenbrier,	188	137	158	1	11	119	15	14	-	19	19	14	1	-	8	7	15	Note 50.
	18th	E. S. Duncan,	H. M. Dickinson,	Fayette,	81	70	84	-	13	34	6	9	-	9	8	2	-	-	6	6	12	Note 51.
			Robert Hamilton,	Nicholas,	41	49	43	-	1	20	-	8	-	7	4	3	-	-	4	3	7	
			A. Earle,	Randolph,	31	68	30	-	14	47	24	38	-	6	7	6	1	-	4	5	9	Note 52.
			John Talbot,	Lewis,	195	137	151	-	60	71	4	10	-	11	16	11	1	-	13	11	24	Note 53.
			W. Newlon,	Braxton,	57	54	33	-	6	10	1	1	-	4	11	3	1	-	1	3	4	Note 54.
			G. G. Davisson,	Harrison,	248	244	236	-	57	272	42	52	2	28	41	24	4	-	18	7	45	Note 55.
10th	19th	Lew. Summers,	J. H. Neal,	Wood,	174	90	156	-	24	79	33	21	1	37	21	12	1	-	8	7	20	Note 56.
			D. G. Morrill,	Jackson,	66	98	75	-	18	35	1	11	-	9	10	11	-	-	5	5	10	Note 57.
			G. W. Stribbling,	Mason,	105	36	84	-	12	33	2	5	-	10	10	6	-	-	9	5	14	Note 58.
			John Samuels,	Cabell,	24	26	9	1	17	24	21	2	.	12	29	20	2	-	7	6	13	Note 59.
			Edwin Robertson,	Logan,	21	24	25	-	4	8	1	4	-	17	37	3	1	-	-	3	3	Note 60.
			A. W. Quarrier,	Kanawha,	397	266	584	-	11	83	36	23	-	18	28	29	8	-	10	19	29	Note 61.
	20th	Joseph L. Fry,	Charles Byrne,	Preston,	32	25	28	-	13	23	6	4	-	20	25	7	2	-	-	6	6	Note 62.
			Thomas P. Ray,	Monongalia,																		
			D. Hickman,	Tyler,	73	78	107	1	15	44	6	10	-	9	10	10	-	-	3	6	9	
			Adam Kuhn,	Brooke,	73	84	75	1	8	40	18	3	-	2	5	2	2	-	4	7	11	Note 63.
			Alex. T. Laidley,	Ohio,	521	348	512	-	87	132	14	25	-	14	11	9	2	-	19	28	47	Note 64.
			James D. Morris,	Marshall,	48	56	48	-	34	58	2	11	-	10	11	-	5	-	3	6	9	

CIRCUIT SUPERIOR COURTS OF LAW AND CHANCERY.

Exhibiting the Number of Suits, &c. in each Circuit.

Districts.	No. of circuit.	No. of counties in each circuit.	JUDGES.	Suits at Law. No. commenced.	Suits at Law. No. pending.	Suits at Law. No. decided.	Suits at Law. No. removed from other courts.	Causes in Chancery. No. commenced.	Causes in Chancery. No. pending.	Causes in Chancery. No. interlocutory decrees.	Causes in Chancery. No. final decrees.	Causes in Chancery. No. removed from county courts.	Prosecutions. No. commenced.	Prosecutions. No. pending.	Prosecutions. No. decided.	Prosecutions. No. nolle prosequis	Prosecutions. Change of venue.	Terms. Days in session. Fall.	Terms. Days in session. Spring.	Terms. Days in session. Total.	Miles travelling. Travelling to general court.	Miles travelling. Travelling in circuit.	Miles travelling. Total.	REMARKS.
1	1	8	Daniel H. Baker,	1276	639	1293	9	105	209	99	122	1	36	39	61	6	–	43	47	90	224	255	479	
	2	7	James H. Gholson,	811	536	615	5	73	232	99	66	20	41	56	29	7	–	37	36	73	150	380	530	
2	3	6	Abel P. Upshur, (resigned,)	715	577	662	7	75	395	127	103	21	33	79	29	80	–	41	47	88	348	310	658	The county of Warwick is omitted in this abstract, no return having been made by the clerk.
	4	7	John B. Christian,	1137	479	939	1	65	242	81	50	8	34	33	22	3	–	27	27	54	120	230	350	
3	5	7	John T. Lomax,	948	499	932	2	68	515	87	68	2	18	28	26	2	–	37	41	78	140	218	358	
	6	5	John Scott,	426	478	614	1	104	453	182	90	3	11	35	30	5	–	17	18	35	220	200	420	No return from the clerk of the county of Fairfax.
4	7	5	John B. Clopton,	647	660	620	1	53	306	104	58	3	34	56	14	4	–	19	36	68	12	182	194	
	21	2	Philip N. Nicholas,	439	701	556	–	51	–	54	38	–	49	43	15	6	–	90	53	143				
	22	2	John Robertson,	–	–	–	–	40	1737	53	46	–	–	–	–	–	–	–	24	39				
	8	5	Daniel A. Wilson,	1164	806	979	10	112	755	147	100	40	58	58	40	7	–	42	47	89	240	180	420	
5	9	5	Wm. Leigh,	726	373	642	–	79	242	91	73	19	82	86	41	25	–	23	26	49	260	165	425	
	10	5	Fleming Saunders,	559	743	564	3	59	261	45	44	9	58	85	58	8	1	36	34	70	380	219	199	
6	11	7	Richard H. Field,	672	676	701	1	60	240	71	52	4	32	44	14	4	–	34	46	82	216	311	527	
	12	5	L. P. Thompson,	1315	1046	1178	4	114	827	258	114	11	61	120	55	9	1	47	55	102	242	240	482	
7	13	6	Isaac R. Douglass,	1144	706	1151	–	129	530	161	68	1	40	49	21	–	–	26	28	54	320	200	520	No return from the county of Frederick.

	14	6	Daniel Smith,	465	461	441	12	62	215	71	51	2	36	32	30	5	–	19	23	42	268	257	525	
8	15	6	Benjamin Estill,	503	359	527	–	63	281	132	48	14	164	179	87	46	–	27	31	58	618	270	888	
	16	7	James E. Brown,	605	381	509	1	69	246	63	78	6	82	93	107	21	–	32	38	70	514	309	823	
9	17	6	Edward Johnston,	594	435	587	13	79	410	46	65	6	48	44	42	2	–	32	31	63	330	241	571	
	18	6	Edwin S. Duncan,	653	622	577	–	151	454	77	118	2	65	87	49	7	–	46	45	101	590	323	913	
10	19	6	Lewis Summers,	787	531	933	1	86	262	94	66	1	103	135	81	12	–	39	45	89	694	333	1027	
	20	6	Joseph L. Fry,	747	591	770	2	157	297	46	53	–	55	62	28	11	–	29	53	82	714	290	1004	No return from the clerk of Monongalia.
			Total, – –	16333	12309	15790	72	1834	9109	2188	1571	173	1140	1443	879	270	2	743	831	1619				
			Average of circuits, –	777	586	751	3	83	414	99	71	7	54	68	41	13	2	35	37	73				

Judgments at law,	15,790
Interlocutory decrees,	2,188
Final decrees,	1,571
Total decisions from which appeals may be had,	19,549

Number of appeals allowed,	110	being nine sixteenths of one per cent.
Causes decided in court of appeals,	88	
	22	excess.

Pending in the court of appeals at Richmond,	578
at Lewisburg,	90

E. E.

GEORGE W. MUNFORD, *C. H. D.*

REMARKS OF CLERKS.

FIRST CIRCUIT.

GREENESVILLE.

1. One chancery cause and an issue out of chancery in the same cause, have been removed to the circuit superior court of law and chancery for the town of Petersburg.

SURRY.

2. Of the number of suits at law stated to have been decided, 35 were motions on forthcoming bonds and four were dismissions in court. The clerk of this court has heretofore forborne to complain of the duties imposed by the act of Assembly, under which this statement is made, because it was his belief that when the object for which the law was intended, had been attained, it would be repealed; in this expectation, however, he has been disappointed, and he now most respectfully asks that the Legislature will make some provision by which the clerks may be compensated for this most troublesome duty.

PRINCESS ANNE.

3. Judgments on forthcoming bonds and writs of ejectment, and dismissions at rules, are included under the head of suits at law, decided.

SECOND CIRCUIT.

DINWIDDIE.

4. The office judgments and dismissions at rules are not included in this report. It embraces only such cases as were decided in court.

NOTTOWAY.

5. Motions not embraced.

PRINCE GEORGE.

6. It is to be hoped that this is the last list of this kind that will be required, as the object for which this onerous burthen has been imposed upon my brother clerks and myself must by this time have been attained. It is the practice of our Legislature of late to impose on our profession too many duties and two little pay.

THIRD CIRCUIT.

YORK.

7. One judgment of the county court reversed; 17 judgments on forthcoming bonds; 1 chancery suit sent to Gloucester county; 1 do. to James City; 1 civil suit sent from county court; 1 judgment on motion of security against principal; 1 criminal sent to penitentiary.

FOURTH CIRCUIT.

KING AND QUEEN.

8. There were 84 motions on forthcoming bonds and garnishee summons in addition.

ESSEX.

9. The number decided at law embraces motions on forthcoming bonds, for money paid as security, office judgments confirmed, judgments confessed and dismissions at rules. No. orders granting leave to file answers and amend bills, and No. orders of revivor, changing the names of parties, have been entered as interlocutory decrees.

GLOUCESTER.

10. Number pending are those on the court docket. Number decided includes dismissions, &c. Number of prosecutions commenced includes presentments.

FIFTH CIRCUIT.

NORTHUMBERLAND.

11. Judgments on forthcoming bonds included.

WESTMORELAND.

12. One dismission at rules included among the number of final decrees.

SPOTTSYLVANIA.

13. Of the number of chancery causes now pending, fully three-fourths were transferred from the late superior court of chancery for the Fredericksburg district. Many of them are "sleeping causes," many not ready for the action of the court, and others abandoned.

SIXTH CIRCUIT.

FAUQUIER.

14. Sixty-five common law motions and two chancery motions not included in this statement.

LOUDOUN.

15. Fifty-two judgments on forthcoming bonds and one decree in chancery on a forthcoming bond, are not included in this report.

SEVENTH CIRCUIT.

CHESTERFIELD.

16. Two special terms, one in January, of two days, and the other in May, of four days.

CHARLES CITY.

17. Including one day at special term in July.

POWHATAN.

18. Of the 59 chancery causes pending, 1 was removed to this court within the year from the circuit cour of Cumberland, and one from the circuit court of Henrico and Richmond. Of the 8 days' session of the court, 5 were at the regular term in May and 3 at a special term in July.

GOOCHLAND.

19. There was a special term in June of 2 days session.

HANOVER.

20. There was an intermediate term of 4 days. Of the common law suits commenced within the year and pending before, 5 were dismissed at rules, 11 dismissed in court and 3 abated. Of the chancery suits commenced within the year and pending before, one has been dismissed at rules and one removed to the circuit superior court of Henrico and Richmond.

TWENTY-FIRST CIRCUIT.

HENRICO AND CITY OF RICHMOND.

21. Suits at law commenced include 8 writs of scire facias and 1 pauper cause. Suits decided include judgments on forthcoming bonds and by confession in the office. Causes commenced in chancery include 4 writs of scire facias. Final decrees include dismissions in court.

TWENTY-SECOND CIRCUIT.

HENRICO AND CITY OF RICHMOND.

22. The spring term was the first after the organization of the court. The causes commenced embrace those between 1st April, 1841, and 30th August. Final decrees include dismissions in term. There was an intermediate term of 15 days.

EIGHTH CIRCUIT.

CUMBERLAND.

23. Injunctions, office judgments and dismissions are included in this report.

BEDFORD.

24. Of the causes pending on the law docket, 86 were at rules, 74 remaining upon the docket after the April term, 1841. Of chancery causes, 79 were on the docket for trial, 100 at rules. Judgments on delivery bonds are not included in the list. These were 59 in number, 51 at law and 8 in chancery.

NINTH CIRCUIT.

HALIFAX.

25. Of the number of chancery causes pending, includes only those matured for hearing and on the court docket of September term, 1841; the same remark applies to the suits at law.

TENTH CIRCUIT.

HENRY.

26. There were 17 judgments on delivery bonds at the fall term and 14 at the spring term, which are not included in this report.

FRANKLIN.

27. In addition to the number of suits decided at law, there were 24 judgments on forthcoming bonds not here included. In the number decided, 81 were office judgments. At the spring term, a prisoner charged with felony was tried and acquitted.

PITTSYLVANIA.

28. The number of causes pending includes all commenced as well as those remaining on the rule docket, issue docket and office judgment docket. The number decided includes office judgments confirmed at the rising of the court as well as motions on delivery bonds and all other motions.

ELEVENTH CIRCUIT.

LOUISA.

29. Of the number decided at law, 100 were office judgments. There were 28 motions commenced and decided, 9 dismissions entered in court and 10 dismissions and abatements in the office.

ORANGE.

30. There was an intermediate term of 2 days in January.

GREENE.

31. Prosecutions include rules against grand jurors for non-attendance, &c.

CULPEPER.

32. Forty-six were judgments on forthcoming bonds.

RAPPAHANNOCK.

33. Eleven motions on forthcoming bonds are included in this statement, at law, and 1 like motion in chancery. Rules against absent jurors, witnesses, &c. are not included.

TWELTH CIRCUIT.

NELSON.

34. Several of the foregoing judgments and decrees include also judgments on delivery bonds.

AUGUSTA.

35. In the number of suits on the law side, 8 scire facias, 2 writs of supersedeas and 57 motions on forthcoming bonds are included.

THIRTEENTH CIRCUIT.

JEFFERSON.

36. In the number of common law suits decided, are included 215 judgments on forfeited forthcoming bonds.

BERKELEY.

37. Provisions should be made by law for the transmission of these and other reports required of clerks by mail.

HAMPSHIRE.

38. Judgments on forthcoming bonds included in number of cases at law decided.

CLARKE.

39. This does not include judgments upon delivery bonds.

FOURTEENTH CIRCUIT.

SHENANDOAH.

40. Of the number decided at law, 8 were removed to the county of Rockingham. Of the number of final decrees, 1 was removed to the county of Fauquier.

WARREN.

41. In this report, judgments on forthcoming bonds are not noticed.

ROCKINGHAM.

42. There were two intermediate terms ordered within the foregoing year, 1 of which lasted 1 day and the other 2 days, the parties not being ready for the trial of the suit for which the court was ordered.

ABSTRACT

FROM THE

REPORTS OF THE CLERKS

OF THE

COURT OF APPEALS

AND OF THE

CIRCUIT SUPERIOR COURTS OF LAW AND CHANCERY,

FOR THE

YEAR ENDING 30th AUGUST, 1841

ABSTRACT FROM THE REPORTS

OF THE

CLERKS OF THE COURT OF APPEALS,

AND OF THE

CIRCUIT SUPERIOR COURTS OF LAW AND CHANCERY,

For the year ending 30th August, 1842; exhibiting the number of suits, &c., for each County in the State.

COURT OF APPEALS.

JUDGES.	CLERKS.	Location of Court.	Suits commenced.	Pending.	Decided.	No. of days in session.	REMARKS.
Wm. H. Cabell, *President.* Francis T. Brooke, Robert Stanard, John J. Allen, Briscoe G. Baldwin,	Joseph Allen, John A. North,	Richmond, Lewisburg,	77 44	0453 127	73 33	138 41	The term of the court commenced on the 15th day of October, 1841, and ended on the 14th of May, 1842, comprising 160 days, having had within that time two recesses, one of 25 days and the other 26 days, and having actually sat 138 judicial days, exclusive of Sundays.

CIRCUIT SUPERIOR COURTS OF LAW AND CHANCERY.

Districts.	Circuits.	Judges.	Clerks.	Counties.	Suits at Law. No. commenced.	Suits at Law. No. pending.	Suits at Law. No. decided.	Suits at Law. No. removed from other courts.	Causes in Chancery. No. commenced.	Causes in Chancery. No. pending.	Causes in Chancery. No. interlocutory decrees.	Causes in Chancery. No. final decrees.	Causes in Chancery. No. removed from county courts.	Prosecutions. No. commenced.	Prosecutions. No. pending.	Prosecutions. No. decided.	Prosecutions. No. nolle prosequis,	Prosecutions. Change of venue,	Terms. Days in session. Fall.	Terms. Days in session. Spring.	Terms. Days in session. Intermediate.	Terms. Days in session. Total.	
1st	1st	Rich'd H. Baker,	L. R. Edwards,	Southampton,	378	197	365	-	15	36	29	22	-	17	24	7	-	-	6	6	-	12	Note 1.
			Joseph Turner,	Greenesville,	116	61	52	-	9	23	6	9	1	8	11	6	-	-	-	4	-	4	Note 2.
			W. P. Underwood,	Surry,	44	31	31	-	6	18	7	8	-	4	3	3	-	-	2	2	-	4	Note 3.
			Nath'l P. Young,	Isle of Wight,	127	78	101	-	12	14	6	3	-	7	3	6	-	-	3	3	-	6	
			Joseph Prentis,	Nansemond,	167	83	140	-	6	9	4	6	-	12	16	10	-	-	4	4	-	8	
			J. J. Burroughs,	Princess Anne,	87	43	115	-	7	14	2	4	-	2	2	2	-	-	2	2	-	4	Note 4.
			John Williams,	Norfolk borough,	251	139	222	-	28	62	21	23	2	5	3	5	-	-	12	15	8	35	Note 5.
			A. Emmerson, jr.	Norfolk county,	300	67	302	-	18	22	15	15	1	18	17	8	1	-	12	15	-	27	Note 6.
	2d	Jas. H. Gholson,	John P. Crump,	Dinwiddie,	184	125	134	-	7	23	10	13	3	6	7	5	-	-	4	5	-	9	Note 7.
			F. Fitzgerald,	Nottoway,	104	86	105	-	14	37	7	10	-	1	4	-	-	-	2	3	-	5	Note 8.
			Egbert G. Leigh,	Amelia,	277	181	189	-	4	29	10	4	-	3	3	1	2	-	2	3	-	5	Note 9.
			E. R. Turnbull,	Brunswick,	284	121	254	2	23	27	11	16	-	5	8	3	1	-	5	4	-	9	Note 10.
			L. Lanier,	Sussex,	93	22	126	-	5	17	8	7	-	4	3	3	-	-	2	2	-	4	
			Robert Gilliam,	Prince George,	88	15	80	-	3	8	4	2	1	10	8	2	8	-	3	4	-	7	Note 11.
			Henry B. Gaines,	Petersburg,	379	445	311	2	31	118	45	35	2	24	74	33	15	-	22	30	-	52	Note 12.
2d	3d	Thos. H. Bayly,	Thos. O. Cogbill,	James City & city of Williamsburg.	212	106	205	2	10	151	22	11	-	-	3	-	-	-	-	10	-	10	
			Samuel Shield,	York,	50	57	44	-	6	21	1	1	1	-	3	-	1	-	-	5	-	5	Note 13.
			Wm. Robertson,	Warwick,	14	19	13	-	1	8	4	3	-	-	2	2	-	-	-	2	-	2	Note 14.
			W. S Armstead,	Elizabeth City,	22	13	18	-	-	12	5	3	-	2	1	2	1	-	-	4	-	4	Note 15.
			N. I. Winder,	Northampton,	44	23	50	-	4	25	2	3	1	1	3	3	-	-	2	4	-	6	
			Thos. R. Joynes,	Accomack,	139	125	114	-	21	95	25	16	-	3	22	17	1	-	-	6	5	11	Note 16.
	4th	Jno. B. Christian,	Robert Pollard,	King William,	189	231	198	-	13	49	9	12	-	-	1	1	1	-	5	4	-	9	Note 17.
			J. D. Christian.	New Kent,	37	23	37	-	1	10	5	3	-	-	3	1	-	-	4	3	-	7	
			Robert Pollard, jr.	King & Queen,	227	128	198	-	17	38	7	8	3	10	10	7	1	-	7	4	-	11	Note 18.
			Jas. Roy Micou, jr.	Essex,	85	61	118	-	12	39	7	9	2	14	7	9	4	-	3	5	-	8	Note 19.

			John S. Healy,	Middlesex,	140	29	144	1	10	26	11	11	-	3	7	-	-	-	3	3	-	6
			John R. Cary,	Gloucester,	234	138	182	-	19	60	15	12	2	7	6	4	-	-	5	6	-	11 Note 20.
			Shep'd G. Miller,	Matthews,	183	103	136	-	39	59	10	7	1	-	1	-	-	-	4	4	-	8
			Benj. M. Walker,	Lancaster,	41	40	51	-	8	19	6	3	2	1	-	1	-	-	2	3	-	5
3d	5th	John T. Lomax,	S. A. M. Leland,	Northumberland,	52	9	49	-	3	11	4	4	-	3	7	3	-	-	2	2	-	4 Note 21.
			John T. B. Jeffries,	Richmond co'y,	122	46	144	-	9	25	8	7	1	1	6	2	-	-	5	5	-	10
			William Hutt,	Westmoreland,	173	94	195	-	10	29	14	9	1	2	1	6	1	-	3	2	-	5 Note 22.
			S. J. S. Brown,	King George,	66	38	57	-	6	20	6	1	-	7	6	-	-	-	2	2	-	4
			Robert Hudgins,	Caroline,	267	154	241	-	8	60	20	13	-	1	4	4	-	-	4	4	-	8
			J. J. Chew,	Spottsylvania,	114	92	158	-	10	324	33	29	5	8	12	6	3	-	23	15	-	38 Note 23.
	6th	John Scott,	William F. Philips,	Fauquier,	472	406	414	-	90	272	146	45	2	8	6	4	-	-	10	11	-	21 Note 24.
			Thomas P. Knox,	Loudoun,	338	189	313	2	25	106	47	13	1	7	9	2	-	-	6	3	-	9 Note 25.
			P. D. Lipscomb,	Prince William,	138	130	179	-	16	112	18	5	-	-	14	5	1	-	-	5	-	5 Note 26.
			F. D. Richardson,	Fairfax,	173	128	162	-	19	107	48	20	-	10	-	1	-	-	4	4	-	8 Note 27.
			J. M. Conway,	Stafford,	37	9	30	-	2	25	10	1	-	-	3	-	-	-	1	1	-	2
			Parke Poindexter,	Chesterfield,	247	256	169	-	32	91	40	8	1	18	30	11	2	-	8	8	3	19 Note 28.
4th	7th	John B. Clopton,	Ro. W. Christian,	Charles City,	58	52	87	1	2	16	8	2	-	-	-	-	-	-	3	4	1	8 Note 29.
			Wm. S. Dance,	Powhatan,	256	183	206	-	26	79	26	8	1	-	1	1	-	-	6	3	3	12 Note 30.
			William Miller,	Goochland,	169	97	140	-	16	53	7	17	-	4	7	7	2	-	6	8	-	14
			Philip B. Winston,	Hanover,	194	217	133	-	16	112	35	16	-	2	6	4	1	-	7	10	-	17 Note 31.
	21st	Philip N. Nicholas,	John Robinson,	Henrico and city of Richmond.	372	640	462	1	-	-	-	-	-	23	36	24	6	-	52	54	16	122 Note 32.
	22d	John Robertson,	William G. Sands,	Henrico and city of Richmond,	-	-	-	-	149	1650	141	189	4	-	-	-	-	-	38	69	26	133 Note 33.
	8th	Danl. A. Wilson,	John Daniel,	Cumberland,	371	46	147	-	8	57	7	23	2	2	4	1	-	-	5	7	-	12 Note 34.
			Roif Eldridge,	Buckingham,	882	540	663	-	58	100	17	23	7	5	7	5	-	-	10	12	-	22
			Jno. D. Alexander,	Campbell,	308	10[illegible]	192	-	14	62	13	12	-	22	26	7	-	-	8	9	-	17
			Joseph Wilson,	Bedford,	422	300	273	-	31	194	17	19	7	5	5	6	-	-	10	9	-	19 Note 35.
			David Rodes,	Lynchburg,	266	192	197	3	31	345	72	26	2	16	10	11	3	-	12	20	-	32
5th	9th	William Leigh,	William Holt,	Halifax,	315	32	121	-	33	49	16	26	1	95	105	37	11	-	8	9	-	17 Note 36.
			Wins. Robinson,	Charlotte,	270	145	220	-	21	45	20	21	2	10	11	4	-	-	4	5	-	9
			B. J. Worsham,	Prince Edward,	253	181	182	-	27	70	34	18	-	8	9	2	1	-	4	5	-	9
			Wm. H. Taylor,	Lunenburg,	117	53	51	3	17	18	10	5	2	11	10	5	1	-	3	3	-	6
			R. B. Baptist,	Mecklenburg,	469	254	326	-	21	62	36	15	-	16	20	12	5	-	5	7	-	12 Note 37.
	10th	Fleming Saunders,	M. Sandifur,	Floyd,	36	22	42	-	7	21	5	4	-	9	15	5	-	-	4	-	-	4 Note 38.
			A. Staples,	Patrick,	87	83	33	-	6	23	5	5	-	10	15	14	1	-	4	5	-	9
			Ant'y M. Dupuy,	Henry,	163	118	94	-	4	34	13	5	3	12	18	6	-	-	2	3	-	5 Note 39.
			C. Tate,	Franklin,	242	182	161	-	19	72	12	7	3	36	34	13	2	3	6	7	-	13 Note 40.
			Wm. H. Tunstall,	Pittsylvania,	484	720	492	-	38	138	36	26	4	21	41	13	3	-	10	12	11	33 Note 41.
6th	11th	Rich'd H. Field,	John Hunter,	Louisa,	179	161	151		12	39	30	10	-	4	5	4	1	-	6	6	5	17 Note 42.

Districts.	Circuits.	Judges.	Clerks.	Counties.	Suits at Law.				Causes in Chancery.					Prosecutions.					Terms. Days in session.				
					No. commenced.	No. pending.	No. decided.	No. removed from other courts.	No. commenced.	No. pending.	No. interlocutory decrees.	No. final decrees.	No. removed from county courts.	No. commenced.	No. pending.	No. decided.	No. nolle prosequis.	Change of venue.	Fall.	Spring.	Intermediate.	Total.	
			Abr. Shepherd, jr.	Fluvanna,	173	74	188	-	29	30	8	9	-	4	4	-	-	-	5	8	-	13	
			Rey'ds Chapman,	Orange,	142	107	118	-	17	54	5	14	8	8	9	1	1	-	5	6	-	11	
			Philip S. Fry,	Greene,	21	36	5	-	6	10	-	1	-	15	4	14	6	-	3	4	-	7	Note 43.
			Belfield Cave,	Madison,	63	54	37	-	7	20	18	1	-	-	1	-	-	-	9	7	-	16	Note 44.
			R. G. Ward,	Culpeper,	148	130	167	1	33	88	36	18	6	4	5	4	2	-	10	9	2	21	Note 45.
			Wm. J. Menifee,	Rappahannock,	41	37	29	-	18	36	31	5	1	6	9	7	4	-	3	3	-	6	
	12th	L. P. Thompson,	Robert Tinsley,	Amherst,	480	381	336	1	42	219	81	30	-	1	6	2	-	-	10	9	-	19	
			David Hutcheson,	Rockbridge,	337	92	268	-	36	71	35	8	-	5	7	6	-	-	9	8	-	17	
			Robert C. Cutler,	Nelson,	332	393	417	-	38	252	110	45	5	10	27	7	9	-	10	8	-	18	Note 46.
			Alex. Garrett,	Albemarle,	520	341	355	3	12	93	22	18	2	17	22	53	3	-	8	10	-	18	Note 47.
			Nich. C. Kinney,	Augusta,	451	307	367	-	52	331	102	39	1	93	10	4	1	-	23	20	-	43	Note 48.
7th	13th	Isaac R. Douglass,	Robert T. Brown,	Jefferson,	381	233	509	-	83	238	87	51	1	8	11	16	-	-	17	20	-	37	Note 49.
			John Strother,	Berkeley,	171	110	202	4	48	140	24	13	23	9	7	9	-	-	5	6	-	11	Note 50.
			J. Reichard,	Morgan,	110	92	48	4	11	34	9	1	1	4	8	3	-	-	3	-	-	3	Note 51.
			J. B. White,	Hampshire,	241	432	238	-	48	181	43	27	-	11	21	4	-	-	6	8	-	14	Note 52.
			J. Kean,	Frederick,	234	214	240	-	33	323	37	49	-	5	10	4	16	-	5	7	-	12	
			H. H. Lee,	Clarke,	157	51	151	-	17	34	10	8	-	5	7	3	-	-	3	3	-	6	Note 53.
	14th	Daniel Smith,	Wm. C. Lauck,	Page,	24	16	25	-	9	19	9	11	-	3	5	5	1	-	2	4	-	6	
			P. Williams,	Shenandoah,	76	40	55	-	9	43	8	6	-	3	2	5	-	-	3	2	-	5	Note 54.
			Robert Turner,	Warren,	91	16	87	-	12	15	2	7	-	1	2	-	1	-	2	3	-	5	Note 55.
			Charles Lobb,	Hardy,	224	209	166	-	20	80	28	20	-	1	1	-	-	-	4	2	-	6	
			Z. Dyer,	Pendleton,	18	20	17	-	4	16	-	2	-	3	1	2	-	-	2	2	-	4	
			H. J. Gambill,	Rockingham,	218	162	332	-	19	56	16	5	-	16	5	14	3	-	23	7	-	30	Note 56.
8th,	15th	Benjamin Estill,	J. W. S. Morrison,	Lee,	54	88	76	1	5	30	2	3	-	19	24	10	11	-	5	3	-	8	Note 57.
			John S. Martin,	Scott,	66	54	60	-	8	39	25	8	1	10	17	10	8	-	6	4	-	10	Note 58.
			James P. Carroll,	Russell,	64	84	68	-	5	33	5	5	-	11	2	6	7	-	5	5	-	10	Note 59.
			G. W. G. Brown,	Tazewell,	134	117	84	-	17	57	36	9	-	43	36	53	1	-	5	6	-	11	Note 60.
			Connally F. Trigg,	Washington,	155	106	149	1	19	91	60	11	4	13	23	25	36	-	10	11	-	21	
			A. B. Moore,	Smyth,	162	86	124	-	12	47	12	10	-	24	20	17	1	-	6	5	-	11	Note 61.

	16th	James E Brown,	Jas. R. Miller,	Wythe,	75	51	37	-	36	126	8	9	-	45	39	23	6	-	9	10	2	21	
			Orville Anderson,	Grayson,	75	16	74	-	10	21	19	7	1	7	22	12	3	.	4	4	-	8	Note 62.
			Madison D. Carter,	Carroll,	2	22	-	9	-	1	-	-	-	1	1	-	-	-	-	1	-	1	Note 63.
			R. D. Montague,	Montgomery,	202	159	182	-	19	47	21	14	1	4	18	7	1	-	5	5	-	10	
			Wm. B. Charlton,	Pulaski,	45	23	22	-	8	22	-	-	-	-	-	-	-	-	1	3	-	4	Note 64.
			Rufus A. French,	Giles,	93	75	83	-	11	57	14	8	1	5	4	8	-	-	6	4	-	10	Note 65.
			Alex. Mahood,	Mercer,	58	38	50	-	11	13	-	3	–	6	4	7	-	-	3	4	-	7	Note 66.
			J. Hutchison, jr.,	Monroe,	132	109	195	-	9	33	5	13	-	6	6	5	1	-	5	5	.	10	
9th,	17th	Edward Johnson,	H. W. Bowyer,	Botetourt,	242	238	200	-	23	174	16	26	1	39	19	42	28	-	10	12	-	22	
			F. Johnston,	Roanoke,	101	39	62	-	15	19	2	11	-	13	12	3	-	-	6	6	-	12	
			Andrew Fudge,	Alleghany,	78	46	51	-	11	38	6	8	1	2	1	3	1	.	4	4	-	8	
			Chs. L. Francisco,	Bath,	50	23	57	-	17	27	10	4	-	7	6	6	-	-	4	6	-	10	
			H. M. Moffett,	Pocahontas,	64	64	48	-	1	20	1	3	-	3	8	4	-	-	3	3	-	6	
			John A. North,	Greenbrier,	199	153	175	-	30	98	23	21	-	14	18	13	3	-	8	7	-	15	Note 67.
	18th	Edwin S. Duncan,	H. M. Dickinson,	Fayette,	62	65	58	-	5	40	8	5	-	10	17	1	-	-	5	6	-	11	Note 68.
			Jas. M. Stanard,	Nicholas,	24	41	35	-	7	16	1	2	-	10	8	4	3	-	3	3	-	6	
			Edwin D. Wilson,	Randolph,	71	85	19	1	25	52	-	7	-	6	11	1	-	-	6	6	-	12	
			John Talbott,	Lewis,	219	208	270	-	49	175	22	8	2	15	5	21	7	-	11	11	-	22	
			W. Newlon,	Braxton,	87	117	74	-	4	24	1	3	-	5	10	7	-	-	4	5	-	9	
			G. G. Davisson,	Harrison,	396	442	206	-	105	335	29	53	-	27	47	18	2	.	10	18	-	28	Note 69.
10th	19th	Lewis Summers,	J. H. Neal,	Wood,	204	206	115	-	34	99	30	30	1	29	38	24	-	-	9	9	-	18	Note 70.
			D. G. Morrill,	Jackson,	59	108	54	-	15	38	1	16	-	14	14	17	-	-	5	6	-	11	
			G. W. Stribbling,	Mason,	75	58	101	-	6	36	3	6	-	11	18	7	4	-	8	5	-	13	Note 71.
			John Samuels,	Cabell,	15	22	10	-	16	29	13	7	-	13	19	19	2	-	6	8	.	14	
			Edwin Robertson,	Logan,	18	15	29	3	3	9	3	3	-	16	20	18	2	-	4	5	-	9	
			A. W. Quarrier,	Kanawha,	501	347	609	-	18	90	42	26	-	20	26	20	2	-	24	14	-	38	Note 72.
	20th	Joseph L. Fry,	Charles Byrne,	Preston,	60	47	48	-	17	42	17	12	-	9	25	2	10	-	6	8	-	14	Note 73.
			W. T. Willey,	Monongalia,	64	42	67	-	28	47	20	24	-	14	24	8	1	-	13	8	3	24	Note 74.
			James O. Watson,	Marion,	41	41	4	4	6	7	-	-	1	-	-	-	-	-	-	1	-	1	Note 75.
			D. Hickman,	Tyler,	75	78	94	-	22	48	20	38	-	12	6	7	1	-	8	4	-	12	
			Adam Kuhn,	Brooke,	108	70	122	-	35	63	16	12	-	14	13	5	1	-	7	6	-	13	
			Alex T. Laidley,	Ohio,	453	298	527	-	91	161	31	42	-	9	11	8	1	-	21	23	18	62	Note 76.
			James D. Morris,	Marshall,	72	62	63	-	26	65	4	12	-	4	9	3	5	-	6	7	-	13	

CIRCUIT SUPERIOR COURTS OF LAW AND CHANCERY.

Number of Suits, &c. in each Circuit, August 30th, 1842.

Districts.	Circuits.	No. of counties and towns in circuit.	Judges.	Suits at Law.				Causes in Chancery.					Prosecutions,					Terms. Days in session.				Miles Travelling.			Remarks.
				No. commenced.	No. pending.	No. decided.	No. removed from other courts.	No. commenced.	No. pending.	No. interlocutory decrees.	No. final decrees.	No. removed from county courts.	No. commenced.	No. pending.	No. decided.	No. nolle prose-quis.	Change of venue.	Fall.	Spring.	Intermediate.	Total.	To general court.	In circuit.	Total.	
1	1	8	Rich'd H. Baker,	1470	699	1328	-	101	198	90	90	4	73	79	47	1	-	41	51	8	100	224	255	479	
	2	7	Jas. H. Gholson,	1309	995	1199	4	87	322	95	87	6	53	107	47	27	-	40	51	-	91	150	380	530	
2	3	6	Thos. H. Bayly,	481	343	444	2	42	312	59	37	2	6	34	24	3	-	2	31	5	38	348	310	658	
	4	7	John B. Christian,	1095	713	1013	1	111	281	64	62	8	34	35	22	6	-	31	29	-	60	120	230	350	
3	5	7	John T. Lomax,	835	473	895	-	54	488	91	66	9	23	36	22	4	-	41	33	-	74	140	218	358	
	6	5	John Scott.	1158	862	1098	2	152	622	269	84	3	25	32	12	1	-	21	24	-	45	220	200	420	
4	7	5	John B. Clopton,	924	835	735	1	92	351	106	51	2	24	44	23	5	-	30	33	7	70	12	182	194	
	21	2	Philip N. Nicholas,	372	640	462	1	-	-	-	-	-	23	36	24	6	-	52	54	16	122				
	22	2	John Robertson,	-	-	-	-	149	1650	141	189	4	-	-	-	-	-	38	69	26	133				
	8	5	Dan'l A. Wilson,	2249	1179	1472	3	142	758	126	103	18	50	52	39	3	-	45	57	-	102	240	180	420	
5	9	5	William Leigh,	1424	665	900	3	119	244	116	85	5	140	155	60	18	-	24	29	-	53	260	165	425	
	10	5	Fleming Saunders,	1012	1155	822	-	74	288	71	47	10	88	123	51	6	3	26	27	11	64	380	219	199	
6	11	7	Rich'd H. Field,	767	599	695	1	122	277	128	58	15	41	37	30	14	-	41	43	7	91	206	308	514	
	12	5	L. P. Thompson,	2120	1514	1743	4	180	966	350	140	8	126	72	72	13	-	60	55	-	115	242	240	482	
7	13	6	Isaac R. Douglass,	1294	1132	1388	8	240	950	210	149	25	42	64	39	16	-	39	44	-	83	320	200	520	
	14	6	Daniel Smith,	651	471	682	-	73	229	63	51	-	27	16	26	5	-	36	20	-	56	268	257	525	

8	15	6	Benjamin Estill,	635	535	561	2	66	297	140	46	5	120	122	121	64	-	37	34	-	71	618	270	888	
	16	8	James E. Brown,	682	493	643	9	104	320	67	54	3	77	97	62	11	-	33	36	2	71	514	309	823	
9	17	6	Edward Johnston,	894	563	593	-	97	376	58	73	2	78	64	71	32	-	35	38	-	73	330	241	571	
	18	6	Edwin S. Duncan,	859	958	662	1	195	642	61	78	2	73	98	52	12	-	39	49	-	88	590	323	913	
10	19	7	Lewis Summers,	872	756	918	3	92	301	92	88	1	113	135	105	10	-	56	47	-	103	690	333	1023	No return from the county of Wayne.
	20	7	Joseph L. Fry,	873	638	925	4	225	433	108	140	1	62	88	33	19	-	61	57	21	139	714	300	1014	
10	22	128		20976	16218	20178	49	2517	10305	2615	1778	133	1298	1526	973	276	3	828	911	103	1842	6586	5120	11306	
				998	772	960	2	119	490	124	84	6	61	72	46	13	-	39	43	4	87	329	256	565	

Judgments at law,	- -	20,178
Interlocutory decrees,	- -	2,615
Final decrees,	- - -	1,778
Total decisions from which appeals may be had,	- -	24,571

Number of appeals allowed,	- - - -	121 being a fraction less than one half of one per cent.
Causes decided,	- - - - - -	106
Excess,	-	15

Pending in the court of appeals at Richmond,	- -	453
at Lewisburg,	- -	127
Total,	-	580

E. E.

GEORGE W. MUNFORD, *C. H. D.*

REMARKS OF CLERKS.

FIRST CIRCUIT.

(*Note* 1.)—Southampton.—"I refer to my remarks in my last return as explanatory of this."

(*Note* 2.)—Greenesville.—No fall term was held in consequence of the sickness of the judge. This report embraces one delivery bond and suits dismissed at rules.

(*Note* 3.)—Surry.—Of the suits at law decided, six were motions on forthcoming bonds, and one, the motion of a security against his principal.

(*Note* 4.)—Princess Anne.—Judgments on forthcoming bonds and dismissions at rules are included under the head of suits decided and final decrees.

(*Note* 5.)—Norfolk borough.—The intermediate term was held in July 1842, and continued eight judicial days.

(*Note* 6.)—Norfolk county.—The number of suits decided includes judgments on forthcoming bonds.

SECOND CIRCUIT.

(*Note* 7.)—Dinwiddie.—There were 55 motions on delivery bonds and against sheriffs decided during the year, which are not included in the report,

(*Note* 8.)—Nottoway.—Motions not embraced as suits.

(*Note* 9.)—Amelia.—Of the suits at law pending, there are 49 upon the issue docket; 132 at rules. Of those decided at the fall term 70, seven of which were new writs of enquiry and 58 office judgments confirmed. At the spring term 119 decided, 9 of which were new writs of enquiry, and 103 office judgments confirmed, Some of the decisions were old cases of long standing. No notice has been taken of judgments upon motions.

(*Note* 10.)—Brunswick.—Motions not included.

(*Note* 11.)—Prince George.—The lists heretofore returned embraced all motions on delivery bonds, in this list they are not included.

(*Note* 12.)—Petersburg.—"I have consumed a day in making this list, and the law makers in their wisdom and justice, have allowed me nothing for it."

THIRD CIRCUIT.

(*Note* 13.)—York.—1 judgment of security against principal, 1 suit sent to James City superior court, 1 chancery suit sent to ditto. 1 appeal from county court affirmed. 13 judgments on forthcoming bonds.

(*Note* 14.)—Warwick—Two causes were transferred to the circuit superior court of Williamsburg.

(*Note* 15.)—Elizabeth City.—At April term 1842, one appeal was dismissed, and on the last day of the term, 12 writs of habeas corpus were disposed of.

(*Note* 16.)—Accomack.—No court in the fall in consequence of the resignation of Judge Upshur. A special term was held in March by special act of assembly.

FOURTH CIRCUIT.

(*Note* 17.)—KING WILLIAM.—"Considerable trouble without compensation."

(*Note* 18.)—KING AND QUEEN.—58 motions on forthcoming bonds, &c.

Note 19.—ESSEX.—The number decided at law, embraces judgments on forthcoming bonds, all dismissions in court or otherwise, office judgments confirmed and judgments confessed in the clerk's office; the number of chancery causes commenced embraces one from another circuit; no orders of mere revivor, of suggestion of parties' death are embraced in the interlocutory decrees; one of those stated as commenced on the law side, was an application for a divorce, where the applicant filed a statement of charges, and a jury was empannelled to enquire into the truth of the charges, and the verdict ordered to be certified to the legislature.

(*Note* 20.)—GLOUCESTER.—Judgments at law and final decrees in chancery including dismissions. The suits and causes pending are those on the court docket 30th August, 1842.

FIFTH CIRCUIT.

(*Note* 21.)—NORTHUMBERLAND.—Judgments on forthcoming bonds included.

(*Note* 22.)—WESTMORELAND.—Motions not included.

(*Note* 23)—SPOTTSYLVANIA.—Of the chancery causes now pending, more than two-thirds were transferred from the late superior court of chancery for the Fredericksburg district, and are generally abandoned by the parties and their counsel.

SIXTH CIRCUIT.

(*Note* 24.)—FAUQUIER.—154 common law motions and 7 chancery motions not included in this report.

(*Note* 25.)—LOUDON.—89 judgments and one decree on forthcoming bonds are not included in the number of causes decided.

(*Note* 26.)—PRINCE WILLIAM.—There was no fall term held in consequence of the sickness of the clerk.

(*Note* 27.)—FAIRFAX.—In the suits decided, forthcoming bonds are not included.

SEVENTH CIRCUIT.

Note 28.)—CHESTERFIELD.—5 suits, during the year, have been removed to this court from the superior court of chancery for the city of Richmond.

(*Note* 29.)—CHARLES CITY.—Special term in July.

(*Note* 30.)—POWHATAN.—Special term in July. Of the 79 chancery suits now pending, one was removed from the circuit court of Henrico and city of Richmond.

(*Note* 31).—HANOVER.—Of the common law suits commenced and pending, 13 have been dismissed and abated at the rules, and one removed to Henrico. Of the chancery suits commenced and pending, one has been dismissed at rules and one removed to Henrico.

TWENTY-FIRST CIRCUIT.

(*Note* 32.)—HENRICO AND THE CITY OF RICHMOND.—Suits commenced include 12 writs of *scire facias* and three writs of *supersedeas;* those decided include judgments on forthcoming bonds and by confession in the office. 37 days in the fall and 40 in the spring on the civil docket, and 15 in the fall and 14 in the spring on the criminal docket. Intermediate term for criminal causes in July, 1842.

TWENTY-SECOND CIRCUIT.

(*Note* 33.)—HENRICO AND CITY OF RICHMOND.—Of the causes commenced there are 6 appeals from the decisions of the auditor of public accounts. The number of final decrees includes dismissions in court. The four causes removed, were from other superior courts and not from county courts. The terms are October, January and June.

EIGHTH CIRCUIT.

(*Note* 34.)—CUMBERLAND.—Injunctions, office judgments and dismissions are included.

(*Note* 35.)—BEDFORD.—Of the causes pending on the law docket 76 were on the court docket; 224 at rules. Of the chancery causes 93 were upon the court docket and 101 at rules. Judgments upon delivery bonds are not included in the list. These judgments were 58 in number, 52 at law and 6 in chancery.

NINTH CIRCUIT.

(*Note* 36.)—Halifax.—In the number of causes depending, those only are included which have been matured for trial, and on the court docket to September term 1842.

(*Note* 37.)—Mecklenburg.—Award of executions on delivery bonds and other motions not included.

TENTH CIRCUIT.

(*Note* 38.)—Floyd.—There was no court held at March term 1842.

(*Note* 39.)—Henry.—Judgments confessed in the clerk's office and judgments on forthcoming bonds are not included.

(*Note* 40.)—Franklin.—Of the number of suits at law decided 113 were office judgments or plain actions of debt in which there was no defence. In addition to the number decided, there were 52 judgments on forfeited forthcoming bonds, which are not included in the number of suits at law decided.

(*Note* 41.)—Pittsylvania.—Of the number of suits at law decided, 229 are office judgments and 108 are motions on forfeited forthcoming bonds, &c.

ELEVENTH CIRCUIT.

(*Note* 42.)—Louisa.—Of the suits at law decided, 98 were office judgments. There were also 30 motions commenced and decided. 9 dismissions were entered in court and 16 dismissions and abatements were entered at rules.

(*Note* 43.)—Greene.—At the fall term one criminal was indicted, tried and convicted of manslaughter, and at the spring term 2 were indicted, tried and acquitted of murder.

(*Note* 44.)—Madison.—Judgments at law include 11 forthcoming bonds and 23 office judgments.

(*Note* 45.)—Culpeper.—56 are judgments on forthcoming bonds.

TWELFTH CIRCUIT.

(*Note* 46.)—Nelson.—Suits decided and final decrees embrace judgments on forfeited forthcoming bonds. In the suits and causes stated as pending, many are still on the rule docket, which, of course, are not brought to the notice of the court.

(*Note* 47.)—Albemarle.—The judge was confined one day by sickness, at the spring term.

(*Note* 48.)—Augusta.—In the number of suits commenced on the law side are included 1 *scire facias* and 70 motions on delivery bonds. In the number of suits commenced on the chancery side, are included 6 motions on delivery bonds.

THIRTEENTH CIRCUIT.

(*Note* 49.)—Jefferson.—In the number of suits decided, 158 judgments on forfeited forthcoming bonds are included.

(*Note* 50.)—Berkley.—No notice is taken of motions on forthcoming bonds.

(*Note* 51.)—Morgan.—There was no spring term held on account of high waters.

(*Note* 52.)—Hampshire.—Award of executions on forthcoming bonds not included.

(*Note* 53.)—Clarke.—Judgments on delivery bonds are not included, they number 85.

FOURTEENTH CIRCUIT.

(*Note* 54.)—Shenandoah.—Cases decided include judgment in office confirmed; 4 judgments on delivery bonds not included; 2 criminal prosecutions not included. Suits pending include office judgments confirmed.

(*Note* 55.)—Warren.—Judgments and 3 decrees on forthcoming bonds not included.

(*Note* 56.)—Rockingham.—Suits decided include office judgments, motions for fines and judgments on delivery bonds.

FIFTEENTH CIRCUIT.

(*Note* 57.)—Lee.—Judgments on forfeited forthcoming bonds not included. Provision should be made by law for the transmission of these and other reports required of clerks by mail.

(*Note* 58.)—SCOTT.—Motions on forthcoming bonds, rules against jurors and witnesses, and attachments upon orders for witnesses' attendance not included.

(*Note* 59.)—RUSSELL.—In the suits at law decided, dismissions, office judgments and judgments on forthcoming bonds are included.

(*Note* 60.)—TAZEWELL.—The suits at law commenced include a *supersedeas* and prohibition; the suits decided include judgments on forthcoming bonds. The prosecutions include rules against witnesses, jurors, &c.

(*Note* 61.)—SMYTH.—"The enquiry is respectfully suggested, could not the money expended in preparing these reports for the inspection of the legislature, be more advantageously appropriated?"

SIXTEENTH CIRCUIT.

(*Note* 62.)—GRAYSON.—9 common law and 4 chancery suits removed to Carroll county, and 1 common law suit removed to Patrick county.

(*Note* 63.)—CARROLL.—The first circuit superior court of law and chancery held for the county of Carroll, was on the 18th day of August, 1840. I have consequently designated it as the fall term of said court of this report.

(*Note* 64.)—PULASKI.—"Poor pay, Can the acts be furnished? I find it troublesome to comply without.

(*Note* 65.)—GILES.—Of the suits pending, none are on the rule docket, and of causes in chancery 41 are at rules. "The labour required by the clerks in making out a statement under the act, for which this is furnished, is onerous, and for which they should be compensated. The undersigned conceives that but little benefit is likely to result from the act in question, and therefore deems that a repeal of the same would result to the injury of no one."

(*Note* 66.)—MERCER.—This return does not include judgments on forfeited bonds taken for the delivery of property at the day of sale. 41 judgments of this sort were given during the year.

SEVENTEENTH CIRCUIT.

(*Note* 67.)—GREENBRIER.—There were a number of decrees made for the sale of forfeited and delinquent lands which are not embraced.

EIGHTEENTH CIRCUIT.

(*Note* 68.)—FAYETTE.—There were 14 decrees confirming sales of forfeited and delinquent lands.

(*Note* 69.)—HARRISON.—91 judgments at law and 5 in chancery on forthcoming bonds not included.

NINETEENTH CIRCUIT.

(*Note* 70.)—WOOD.—Motions on bonds are not embraced among suits either commenced or decided.

(*Note* 71.)—MASON.—Among causes decided and final decrees, dismissions are included; but judgments on forthcoming bonds and decrees in forfeited land cases, are excluded. The last class of cases is also excluded from interlocutory decrees.

(*Note* 72.)—KANAWHA.—Suits decided include judgments on forthcoming bonds and dismissions.

TWENTIETH CIRCUIT.

(*Note* 73.)——PRESTON.—Judgments on forthcoming bonds not included.

(*Note* 74.)—MONONGALIA.—Causes depending, include those only on the trial docket, Suits decided and final decrees include office judgments, dismissions and cases remanded to rules. The special term commenced on the 29th of August.

(*Note* 75.)—MARION.—The suits stated as decided, were by dismission at rules and confession in the office. The cause removed was not from the county court, but from another county, in pursuance of the act establishing the county of Marion.

(*Note* 76.)—OHIO.—Of the 527 suits decided at law, 59 were forthcoming bonds; dismissions at rules and judgments confessed in the office, are not included. An intermediate term of 18 days was held in February 1842.

ABSTRACT

FROM THE

REPORTS OF THE CLERKS

OF THE

COURT OF APPEALS

AND OF THE

CIRCUIT SUPERIOR COURTS OF LAW AND CHANCERY,

FOR THE

YEAR ENDING 30th AUGUST, 1843.

ABSTRACT FROM THE REPORTS

OF THE

CLERKS OF THE COURT OF APPEALS,

AND OF THE

CIRCUIT SUPERIOR COURTS OF LAW AND CHANCERY,

For the Year ending the 30th August, 1843; *exhibiting the number of Suits, &c.*

COURT OF APPEALS.

JUDGES.	CLERKS.	Location of Court.	Suits commenced.	Pending.	Decided.	No. of days in session.	REMARKS OF CLERKS.
Wm. H. Cabell, *President*, Francis T. Brooke, Robert Stanard.	Joseph Allen,	Richmond,	79	459	61	160	The court sat 160 days, having had within that time two recesses, one of twenty-five, and the other of twenty-six days, and having actually sat 135 days, exclusive of Sundays, comprised within the time of its sessions, and one day in which there were not a sufficient number of judges present to constitute a court.
John J. Allen, Briscoe G. Baldwin.	John A. North,	Lewisburg,*	42	132	36	34	
			121	591	97	194	

*In consequence of the indisposition of judges Cabell and Brooks the session was probably greatly shortened.

CIRCUIT SUPERIOR COURTS OF LAW AND CHANCERY.

Districts.	Circuits.	JUDGES.	CLERKS.	COUNTIES.	Suits at Law. No. commenced.	No. pending.	No. decided.	No removed from other courts.	Causes in Chancery. No. commenced	No. pending.	No. interlocutory decrees.	No final decrees.	No. removed from county courts.	Prosecutions. No. commenced.	No. pending.	No. decided.	No. nolle prosequis.	Change of venue	Terms. Days in Session. Fall.	Spring.	Intermediate.	Total.	Remarks of Clerks.
1st	1st	R. H. Baker.	L. R. Edwards,	Southampton,	474	181	493	1	23	45	33	14	1	16	15	20	-	-	7	6	-	13	
			Joseph Turner,	Greenesville,	183	60	80	-	12	25	14	14	-	5	4	11	1	-	3	7	-	10	Note 1.
			W. P. Underwood,	Surry,	69	31	71	-	7	16	10	8	-	1	2	2	-	-	2	2	-	4	Note 2.
			N. P. Young.	Isle of Wight,	164	70	136	1	12	22	12	4	-	13	9	5	1	-	3	3	-	6	Note 3.
			Joseph Prentis,	Nansemond,	165	40	256	-	10	13	7	5	-	10	14	13	1	-	5	3	-	8	Note 4.
			J. J. Burroughs,	Princess Anne,	125	53	171	1	-	10	4	4	-	1	-	3	-	-	3	4	-	7	Note 5.
			John Williams,	Norfolk Borough	200	106	255	1	15	54	21	24	5	21	11	10	1	-	12	21	10	43	
			A. Emmerson,	Norfolk county,	432	52	439	-	19	21	8	15	-	-	5	13	-	-	11	8	-	19	
	2d	J. H. Gholson,	John P Crump,	Dinwiddie,	26	31	218	-	24	36	10	12	-	6	17	2	-	-	5	6	-	11	
			F. Fitzgerald,	Nottoway,	156	95	141	-	23	50	18	11	1	26	25	1	2	-	3	3	-	6	Note 7.
			E. G. Leigh,	Amelia,	359	177	342	-	17	41	14	5	-	7	9	1	-	-	3	3½	-	6½	
			E. R. Turnbull,	Brunswick,	438	136	424	-	19	38	20	17	3	4	4	10	2	-	4	5	-	9	
			L. Lanier,	Sussex,	92	26	98	-	8	21	11	3	-	3	3	3	-	-	2	2	-	4	
			Robert Gilliam,	Prince George,	107	16	75	-	11	13	8	5	-	8	12	10	4	-	3	4	-	7	Note8.
			H. B. Gaines.	Petersburg,	336	530	430	-	62	133	18	26	-	15	28	21	5	-	21	26	-	47	
2d	3d	T. H. Bayly,	Thos. O. Cogbill,	James City and Williamsburg,	246	83	267	-	30	139	29	42	-	2	2	1	1	-	21	7	-	28	
			Samuel Shield,	York,	127	123	83	-	2	28	2	3	-	1	5	-	-	-	4	5	-	9	
			Wm. Robertson,	Warwick,	56	18	48	-	1	8	-	2	-	1	-	1	-	-	1	1	-	2	
			W. S. Armstead,	Elizabeth City,	61	22	59	-	5	16	1	1	-	-	1	-	-	-	1	2	-	3	
			N J. Winder,	Northampton,	76	52	53	-	9	28	[illegible]	6	-	-	-	3	-	-	2	3	-	5	
			Thos. R. Joynes,	Accomack,	138	10[illegible]	169	2	17	112	30	13	-	7	20	6	-	-	6	9	-	15	
	4th	J. B. Christian,	Robert Pollard,	King William,	199	48	114	-	8	56	17	11	-	-	1	1	-	-	6	6	-	12	
			J. D. Christian,	New Kent,	71	20	83	-	3	11	6	3	1	-	2	-	1	-	3	3	-	6	Note 9.
			Robert Pollard, jr.	King & Queen,	267	95	182	-	8	29	17	7	-	4	3	5	1	-	4	6	-	10	
			Jas. Roy Micou,	Essex,	200	206	165	-	16	51	4	10	-	-	3	4	-	-	3	4	-	7	Note 10.

			John S. Healey,	Middlesex,	187	111	155	-	18	30	15	3	-	-	-	-	-	-	4	3	-	7	
			John R. Cary,	Gloucester,	255	124	283	-	18	62	13	19	1	3	8	-	2	-	6	5	-	11	Note 11
			Shepard G. Miller.	Mathews,	132	76	138	-	21	64	6	9	1	1	1	1	1	-	2	5	-	7	
3d	5th	John T. Lomax,	Ro. T. Dunaway,	Lancaster,	100	19	60	-	8	11	3	3	-	2	-	2	-	-	2	3	-	5	
			S. A. M. Leland,	Northumberland,	67	7	60	-	[illegible]	16	15	2	-	2	5	3	-	-	2	3	-	5	Note 12.
			J. T. B. Jeffries,	Richmond co.	18[illegible]	52	146	-	12	40	12	5	-	2	6	2	-	-	4	4	-	8	
			Wm Hunt,	Westmoreland,	139	79	154	-	8	33	6	4	-	6	3	4	-	-	2	2	-	4	Note 13.
			S. J. S. Brown,	King George,	78	38	61	-	5	23	8	2	-	1		5	-	-	2	3	-	5	Note 14.
			Robert Hudgin,	Caroline,	292	129	304	-	12	62	25	10	2	4	4	6	-	-	4	4	-	8	
			J. J. Chew,	Spotsylvania,	157	88	217	-	14	525	28	20	1	8	12	4	4	-	22	10	-	32	
	6th	John Scott,	Wm. F. Philips,	Fauquier,	416	407	40	7	75	310	207	40	3	1	3	6	-	-	12	11	-	23	Note 15.
			Thomas P. Knox,	Loudoun,	294	211	313	-	42	126	97	13	1	6	10	2	-	-	6	5	-	11	Note 16.
			P. D. Lipscomb,	Prince William,	135	129	135	2	18	131	57	8	1	9	2	3	-	-	4	5	-	9	
			T. D. Richardson,	Fairfax,	188	160	152	-	46	111	45	19	-	4	5	9	-	-	4	5	-	9	Note 17.
			J. M. Conway,	Stafford,	36	17	31	1	1	28	12	1	11	3	4	[illegible]	-	-	2	3	-	5	
4th	7th	J. B. Clopton,	Parke Poindexter,	Chesterfield,	235	246	240	-	24	94	48	15	2	5	24	6	3	3	9	7	3	19	Note 18.
			Ro. W. Christian,	Charles City,	124	46	159	-	-	22	10	1	1	-	-	-	-	-	3	2	1	6	Note 19.
			Wm. S. Dance,	Powhatan,	344	152	406	-	13	86	29	9	-	1	2	-	-	-	8	5	-	13	Note 20.
			Wm. Miller,	Goochland,	169	128	172	-	9	60	9	22	-	3	6	3	-	-	9	12	-	22	
			Phillip B. Winston,	Hanover,	236	200	213	-	28	123	56	16	1	1	5	2	-	-	14	11	-	25	Note 21.
	21st	P. N. Nicholas,	John Robinson,	Henrico and City of Richmond.	263	507	423	-	-	-	-	-	-	48	41	16	5	2	54	53	6	113	Note 22.
	22d	John Robertson,	Wm. G. Sands,	Henrico and City of Richmond,	-	-	-	-	110	1639	212	100	1	-	-	-	-	-	76	26	-	102	Note 23.
	8th	D. A. Wilson,	John Daniel,	Cumberland,	382	108	374	-	20	80	17	15	-	1	6	8	-	-	7	7	-	14	
			Rolfe Eldridge,	Buckingham,	886	68[illegible]	569	-	50	129	25	13	2	6	8	1	-	-	13	-	8	21	Note 24.
			J. D. Alexander,	Campbell,	312	332	205	-	46	134	4	8	5	5	31	7	1	-	7	2	-	9	Note 25.
			Jos. Wilson,	Bedford,	361	451	196	3	34	215	16	11	1	25	31	1	1	-	9	-	-	9	Note 26.
			D. Rodes,	Lynchburg,	160	139	270	4	20	312	79	24	2	3	8	6	1	-	20	11	-	31	
5th	9th	Wm. Leigh,	Wm. Holt,	Halifax,	568	56	542	-	26	47	7	22	4	25	44	56	6	-	11	10	-	21	Note 27.
			W. Robinson,	Charlotte,	342	127	360	-	29	53	20	21	3	8	11	7	-	-	4	5	-	9	
			B. J. Worsham,	Prince Edward,	526	181	617	-	38	87	45	26	2	4	5	3	1	-	5	7	-	12	
			Wm. H. Taylor,	Lunenburg,	278	49	87	-	10	28	15	-	-	9	11	12	1	-	4	4	-	8	Note 28.
			R. B. Baptist,	Mecklenburg,	758	47	597	-	32	31	17	11	-	66	35	33	10	-	7	8	-	15	
	10th	Fleming Saunders,	J. N. Zentmeyer,	Floyd,	23	17	10	1	7	24	9	5	-	13	12	26	2	-	4	4	-	8	Note 29.
			Sam'l G. Staples,	Patrick,	75	89	59	1	4	30	15	10	-	14	16	8	3	1	4	5	-	9	
			A. M. Dupuy,	Henry,	138	57	194	1	10	43	7	8	4	2	7	11	4	-	5	4	-	9	Note 30.
			C. Tate,	Franklin,	238	147	254	-	16	78	28	15	3	15	18	7	14	-	6	8	-	14	Note 31.
			Wm. H. Tunstall,	Pittsylvania,	519	1007	700	-	38	159	21	32	1	34	58	24	5	-	14	12	-	26	Note 32.
			M. D. Carter.	Carroll,	51	45	17	9	14	14	1	-	-	10	9	-	-	1	-	3	-	3	Note 33.

Districts.	Circuits.	JUDGES.	CLERKS.	COUNTIES.	Suits at Law. No. commenced.	No. pending.	No. decided.	No. removed from other courts.	Causes in Chancery. No. commenced.	No. pending.	No. interlocutory decrees.	No. final decrees.	No. removed from county courts.	Prosecutions. No. commenced.	No. pending.	No. decided.	No. nolle prosequis.	Change of venue.	Terms. Days in session. Fall.	Spring.	Intermediate.	Total.	Remarks of Clerks.
6th	11th	R. H. Field,	John Hunter,	Louisa,	239	175	216	-	17	56	25	14	1	1	3	3	-	-	7	6	5	18	Note 34.
			A. Shepherd, jr.	Fluvanna,	253	193	200	-	24	39	8	10	2	10	12	2	1	-	6	7	-	13	
			R. Chapman,	Orange,	130	98	119	-	9	51	14	10	3	5	4	10	-	-	5	5	-	10	
			Philip S. Fry,	Greene,	39	32	32	-	10	18	4	3	-	2	5	2	-	-	3	3	-	6	
			Belfield Cave,	Madison,	93	49	87	-	10	20	9	6	-	2	3	1	-	-	3	8	-	11	Note 35.
			R. G. Ward,	Culpeper,	159	140	206	12	23	91	43	23	1	3	4	2	2	-	11	12	-	23	Note 36.
			Wm. J. Menifee,	Rappahannock,	56	54	36	-	17	38	17	14	-	6	8	5	2	-	6	4	-	10	Note 37.
	12th	L. P. Thompson,	Robert Tinsley,	Amherst,	528	456	453	1	54	260	88	13	-	4	7	2	1	-	9	10	-	19	
			D. Hutcheson,	Rockbridge,	418	136	374	-	40	97	31	14	-	18	19	6	-	-	8	6	-	14	
			Robert C. Cutler,	Nelson,	376	338	483	1	38	270	107	39	2	20	31	11	9	-	9	7	-	16	
			Alex. Garrett,	Albemarle,	4[illegible]5	330	340	-	22	114	14	16	4	34	45	20	6	-	9	10	-	19	Note 38.
			Nich's C. Kinney,	Augusta,	573	490	390	3	77	345	99	44	-	14	113	47	40	-	22	20	-	42	Note 39.
7th	13th	I. R. Douglass,	R. T. Brown,	Jefferson,	441	222	489	-	80	283	88	44	-	81	33	42	24	-	18	24	5	47	Note 40.
			John Strother,	Berkeley,	196	124	182	-	23	133	42	31	-	4	8	3	-	-	8	5	-	13	Note 41.
			J. Reichard,	Morgan,	77	82	140	1	16	34	16	8	1	5	5	6	1	-	3	2	-	5	Note 42.
			John B. White,	Hampshire,	374	549	323	-	34	206	37	32	-	7	22	7	4	-	7	6	-	13	
			J. Kean,	Frederick,	248	110	272	1	29	320	25	39	2	4	15	-	1	-	5	6	-	11	Note 43.
			H. H. Lee,	Clarke,	239	54	228	1	11	34	5	5	-	1	1	5	-	-	3	4	-	7	Note 44.
	14th	Daniel Smith,	Wm. C. Lauck,	Page,	33	21	28	-	1	17	23	4	-	-	-	5	3	-	4	2	-	6	
			P. Williams,	Shenandoah,	115	57	89	-	9	54	23	5	-	5	6	3	-	-	2	2	-	4	Note 45.
			Robert Turner,	Warren,	145	19	142	-	7	13	3	9	1	1	2	1	-	-	3	2	-	5	Note 46.
			C. Lobb,	Hardy,	181	145	231	4	30	108	24	14	1	2	2	1	-	-	3	4	-	7	
			Z. Dyer,	Pendleton,	34	9	20	-	3	13	2	6	-	3	3	4	1	-	2	2	-	4	
			H. J. Gambill,	Rockingham,	380	153	352	-	35	71	28	17	-	7	7	5	-	-	14	10	-	24	Note 47.
8th	15th	Benj. Estill,	J. W. S. Morrison.	Lee,	51	51	79	-	3	34	4	2	-	20	22	16	2	-	6	5	-	11	Note 48.
			John S. Martin,	Scott,	58	42	70	-	8	43	16	5	-	5	11	8	3	-	5	4	-	9	Note 49.
			James P. Carroll,	Russell,	35	57	84	-	11	37	6	5	-	19	15	7	2	-	6	5	-	11	Note 50.
			G. W. G. Browne	Tazewell,	85	118	97	-	38	86	70	6	-	22	44	15	3	-	6	-	6	12	Note 51.
			C. F. Trigg,	Washington,	108	90	120	-	22	107	61	9	1	20	15	16	12	-	18	15	-	33	

			A. B. Moore,	Smyth,	155	81	159	-	14	44	31	17	1	14	10	24	10	-	5	6	-	11	
	16th	Jas. E, Brown,	J. R. Miller,	Wythe,	43	55	11	3	29	180	11	9	1	13	31	19	-	-	8	-	3	11	
			O. Anderson,	Grayson,	29	20	42	-	9	38	12	7	-	15	13	18	-	-	3	-	2	5	Note 52.
			R. D. Montague,	Montgomery,	149	122	203	2	24	92	19	11	2	14	31	7	3	-	8	4	-	12	
			W. B. Charlton,	Pulaski,	34	18	22	-	11	9	2	1	-	-	-	-	-	-	2	2	-	4	Note 53.
			Rufus A. French,	Giles,	69	37	128	-	12	13	7	9	-	26	29	6	-	-	3	6	-	9	Note 54.
			Alex. Mohood,	Mercer,	33	16	49	2	8	17	-	2	-	4	-	3	1	-	3	3	-	6	
			J. Hutchinson,	Monroe,	87	53	120	-	30	66	26	12	-	7	7	11	-	-	5	9	-	14	Note 55.
9th	17th	E. Johnson,	H. W. Bowyer,	Botetourt,	304	214	324	-	45	177	16	26	2	9	11	5	10	-	15	11	-	26	Note 56.
			F. Johnston,	Roanoke,	88	23	65	-	10	6	4	1	-	7	3	5	9	-	6	6	-	12	
			Andrew Fudge,	Alleghany,	78	54	65	-	11	47	8	6	-	3	2	1	-	-	5	3	-	8	
			C. L. Francisco,	Bath,	52	74	58	-	16	42	7	7	-	2	-	7	-	-	5	6	-	11	
			H. M. Moffett,	Pocahontas,	90	15	79	-	5	14	-	4	-	9	5	6	-	-	2	2	-	4	
			John A. North,	Greenbrier,	232	134	245	-	21	99	23	21	-	15	27	6	-	-	7	5	-	12	
	18th	E. S. Duncan,	H. M. Dickinson,	Fayette,	64	95	28	-	11	51	8	6	-	12	22	10	-	-	4	6	-	10	
			Jas. M. Stanard,	Nicholas,	20	38	24	-	6	23	5	3	-	9	9	3	3	-	3	3	-	6	
			B. L. Brown,	Randolph,	77	61	89	5	47	81	17	4	5	18	20	4	5	-	10	4	-	14	Note 57.
			E. D. Wilson,	Barbour,	25	31	18	24	23	19	-	-	16	8	8	-	-	-	2	1	-	3	
			John Talbot,	Lewis,	263	246	225	-	73	196	10	13	-	10	22	4	1	-	11	9	-	20	
			W. Newland,	Braxton,	36	100	44	8	20	51	5	2	-	4	10	2	4	-	-	4	-	4	Note 58.
			G. G. Davisson,	Harrison,	320	278	472	-	122	369	84	90	-	23	46	19	2	-	15	24	-	39	Note 59.
10th	19th	Lewis Summers,	J. H. Neal,	Wood,	108	123	224	-	44	141	64	19	-	23	48	22	2	-	4	6	1	22	
		(dead,)	T. Stinchcomb,	Ritchie,	4	4	-	-	5	6	-	-	1	-	-	-	-	-	1	-	-	1	
			D. G. Morrill,	Jackson,	49	89	67	-	13	47	2	4	-	10	12	3	-	-	-	6	-	6	Note 60.
			G. W. Stribbling,	Mason,	80	74	73	-	3	34	6	5	-	-	12	3	2	-	-	6	-	6	Note 61.
			John Samuels,	Cabell,	13	18	17	-	7	19	15	19	1	6	19	12	-	-	5	9	-	14	
			H. Clarke,	Wayne,	11	10	2	1	7	9	2	-	-	3	-	-	-	-	-	2	-	2	Note 62.
			Edw. Robertson,	Logan,	9	15	8	-	4	10	3	1	-	7	27	11	1	-	-	5	-	5	Note 63.
			A. W. Quarrier,	Kanawha,	370	351	598	-	14	101	28	9	2	33	35	14	8	-	9	31	-	40	Note 64.
	20th	Joseph L. Fry,	John P. Bryne,	Preston,	59	32	52	-	8	19	8	19	-	6	10	14	2	-	6	7	-	13	
			W. T. Willey,	Monongalia,	70	76	56	-	31	80	28	21	-	7	21	7	-	-	1	1	-	2	Note 65.
			James O. Watson.	Marion,	75	49	70	3	43	46	1	10	6	-	-	-	-	-	3	5	-	8	Note 66.
			D. Hickman,	Tyler,	80	62	127	-	2	64	20	19	-	12	9	11	-	-	5	3	-	8	
			Adam Kuhn,	Brooke,	95	55	158	-	50	89	18	25	1	2	5	6	4	-	5	5	.	10	Note 67.
			Alex. T. Laidley,	Ohio,	236	173	448	1	81	146	36	49	-	8	14	9	1	-	16	21	16	53	Note 68.
			James D. Morris.	Marshall,	56	62	64	-	26	77	14	15	1	1	2	4	4	-	8	6	-	14	Note 69.

GEORGE W. MUNFORD, *C. H. D.*

December 15th, 1843.

RECAPITULATION.

CIRCUIT SUPERIOR COURTS OF LAW AND CHANCERY,

Number of Suits, &c., in each Circuit, August 30th, 1843.

Districts.	Circuits.	No. of counties and towns in circuit.	JUDGES.	Suits at Law. No. commenced.	Suits at Law. No. pending.	Suits at Law. No. decided.	Suits at Law. No. removed from other courts.	Causes in Chancery. No. commenced.	Causes in Chancery. No. pending.	Causes in Chancery. No. interlocutory decrees.	Causes in Chancery. No. final decrees.	Causes in Chancery. No. removed from county courts.	Prosecutions. No. commenced.	Prosecutions. No. pending.	Prosecutions. No. decided.	Prosecutions. No. nolle prosequis.	Prosecutions. Change of venue.	Terms. Days in Session. Fall.	Terms. Days in Session. Spring.	Terms. Days in Session. Intermediate.	Terms. Days in Session. Total.	Miles Travelling. To general court.	Miles Travelling. In circuit.	Miles Travelling. Total.	REMARKS.
1	1	8	Richard H. Baker,	1812	593	1901	4	96	206	109	88	6	61	60	77	4	-	46	54	10	110	224	255	479	
	2	7	Jas. H. Gholson,	1749	1111	1728	-	164	332	99	79	4	63	98	48	13	-	41	49½	-	90½	150	380	530	
2	3	6	Thos. H. Bayly,	704	398	679	2	64	331	65	67	-	11	28	11	1	-	35	27	-	62	440	407	847	
	4	7	John B. Christian,	1311	680	1120	-	92	303	78	62	3	8	18	11	5	-	28	32	-	60	120	230	350	
3	5	7	John T. Lomax,	1021	412	1002	-	60	710	97	46	3	25	31	26	4	-	38	29	-	67	140	218	358	
	6	5	John Scott,	1069	924	1032	10	182	706	418	81	16	23	43	22	3	-	28	29	-	57	220	200	420	
4	7	5	John B. Clopton,	1098	766	1190	-	74	385	162	63	4	10	37	11	3	3	43	38	4	85	12	182	194	
	21	2	P. N. Nicholas,	263	507	423	-	-	-	-	-	-	48	41	16	5	2	54	53	6	113				
	22	2	John Robertson,	-	-	-	7	110	1639	212	100	1	-	-	-	-	-	76	26	-	102				
	8	5	Daniel A. Wilson,	2101	713	1614	-	170	876	141	71	10	50	84	23	3	-	56	20	8	84	240	180	420	
5	9	5	William Leigh,	2472	454	2203	12	135	246	104	80	9	112	106	111	18	-	31	34	-	65	260	165	425	
	10	6	Fleming Saunders,	1044	1362	1234	12	89	338	81	7[illegible]	8	88	130	76	28	2	33	36	-	69	390	247	637	
6	11	7	Richard H. Field,	969	741	896	5	110	313	120	80	7	29	39	25	5	-	41	45	5	91	206	308	514	
	12	5	Lucas P. Thompson,	2310	1750	2040	3	231	1086	339	126	6	90	215	86	56	-	57	53	-	110	242	240	482	
7	13	6	J. R. Douglass,	1575	1041	1634	3	193	1009	213	159	3	101	84	63	30	-	44	47	5	96	320	200	520	
	14	6	Daniel Smith,	888	404	1042		85	276	103	55	[illegible]	18	20	19	4	-	28	[illegible]2	-	50	268	257	888	
8	15	6	Benjamin Estill,	492	439	609		96	351	188	44	3	100	117	86	32	-	46	35	6	87	618	270	525	
	16	7	James E. Brown,	444	321	575	7	123	415	77	51	2	79	111	64	4	-	32	24	5	61	514	309	823	

9	17	6	Edward Johnston,	844	514	836	1	108	385	58	65	2	45	48	30	19	-	40	33	-	73	330	241	571
	18	7	Edwin S. Duncan,	805	849	900	37	302	790	129	118	21	84	137	42	15	-	45	51	-	96	590	363	953
10	19	8	L. Summers (dead,)	740	680	989	1	92	361	120	57	3	82	153	65	13	-	18	65	12	95	690	399	1089
	20	7	Joseph L. Fry,	675	513	975	4	265	527	125	149	9	36	61	51	11	-	45	48	16	109	714	300	1014
10	22	130	Total,	24386	15172	24613	109	2843	11579	3038	1721	122	1163	2011	963	276	7	905	850½	77	1832½	6688	5351	12041
			Average of circuits,	1161	722	1172	5	135	551	144	82	5	55	95	45	13	-	41	38	3	83	334	267	602

Judgments at law, - -	24,386
Interlocutory decrees, - -	3,038
Final decrees, - - -	1,721
Total decisions from which appeals may be had, - -	29,145

Number of appeals allowed, - - - - 121 being about three sevenths of one per cent.
Causes decided in the court of appeals, - - 97

24 excess.

Pending in the court of appeals at Richmond, - - 459
at Lewisburg, - - 132

E. E.

GEORGE W. MUNFORD, *C. H. D.*

December 15*th*, 1843.

REMARKS OF CLERKS.

FIRST CIRCUIT.

(*Note* 1.)—GREENESVILLE.—Judgments on forthcoming bonds are included, but those dismissed at rules are not.

(*Note* 2.)—SURRY.—Of the suits at law decided, eight were motions on forthcoming bonds. Of the causes in chancery, four were similar motions.

(*Note* 3.)—ISLE OF WIGHT.—Motions on forthcoming bonds and other motions are not included in this report.

(*Note* 4.)—NANSEMOND.—All judgments on motions, judgments confessed in the office, all dismissions in the court or otherwise, office judgments confirmed, and one appeal from the county court, are embraced in the number of suits decided at law.

(*Note* 5.)—PRINCESS ANNE—Judgments on forthcoming bonds and dismissions at rules are included under the head of suits decided and final decrees.

SECOND CIRCUIT.

(*Note* 6.)—NOTTOWAY.—Judgments on motions not embraced.

(*Note* 7.)—PRINCE GEORGE.—Motions on forthcoming bonds not included.

FOURTH CIRCUIT.

(*Note* 8.)—NEW KENT.—The number of suits at law decided, embraces all judgments on forfeited forthcoming bonds, &c.

(*Note* 9.)—ESSEX.—Among the suits pending, there are 131 garnishee summonses arising out of two cases of insolvency,—52 office judgments and 23 issues. The number decided in civil cases includes judgments on forthcoming bonds and office judgments confirmed in term time. The number of chancery causes decided embraces a few judgments on forthcoming bonds. I have not included among the interlocutory decrees, simple orders making new parties, &c. Two of the number in chancery commenced have been dismissed at rules.

(*Note* 10.)—GLOUCESTER.—Number of suits at law and causes in chancery pending, are those on the court docket. The number decided at law, includes dismissions.

FIFTH CIRCUIT.

(*Note* 11.)—NORTHUMBERLAND.—Judgments on forthcoming bonds not embraced.

(*Note* 12.)—WESTMORELAND.—Motions not included.

(*Note* 13.)—KING GEORGE.—Motions on forthcoming bonds are not included.

SIXTH CIRCUIT.

(*Note* 14.)—FAUQUIER.—137 motions not included in this statement.

(*Note* 15.)—LOUDOUN.—115 judgments on forthcoming bonds not included in this report.

(*Note* 16.)—FAIRFAX.—Forthcoming bonds not included.

SEVENTH CIRCUIT.

(*Note* 17.)—Chesterfield.—Eight chancery causes have been transferred from this court to that of Richmond circuit. The venue, in one criminal prosecution, has been changed from this to the circuit court of Petersburg, and in two others, from the Richmond circuit to this court.

(*Note* 18.)—Charles City.—Same as those of 1837, with this addition, that the further it goes, the worse it is.

(*Note* 19.)—Powhatan.—Of the 86 chancery suits pending on the 30th day of August last, there were removed to this court from the chancery court of Richmond and Henrico, and one from the circuit superior court of law and chancery for Cumberland county.

(*Note* 20.)—Hanover.—Of the suits at law commenced within the year ending 30th August 1843, and those pending before, 28 have been dismissed and abated at rules. Of the chancery causes commenced in the year ending 30th August 1843, three have been dismissed at rules.

TWENTY-FIRST CIRCUIT.

(*Note* 21.)—Henrico and City of Richmond.—Suits commenced include 7 writs of *scire facias* and 6 writs of *supersedeas*. Suits decided include judgments on forthcoming bonds and by confession in the office ; also non-suits and dismissions in court. Prosecutions decided are exclusive of 28 cases discontinned under decisions of the general court.

TWENTY-SECOND CIRCUIT.

(*Note* 22.)—Henrico and City of Richmond.—Number of final decrees include abatements and dismissions in court. The terms of the court commenced in January and June. Judge P. N. Nicholas, the judge of the common law side of the circuit superior court for the county of Henrico and city of Richmond, presided for fifteen days of the 76 the court was in session at the January term, and during that period five of the final and ten of the interlocutory decrees were rendered.

EIGHTH CIRCUIT.

(*Note* 23.)—Buckingham.—The judge by reason of sickness held no court in April, but held a special session in June 1843.

(*Note* 24.)—Campbell.—At the spring term in 1842, in consequence of the ill health of the judge the court sat only two days.

(*Note* 25.)—Bedford.—Of the causes pending on the law docket, 396 were upon the court docket, 115 at rules. Of chancery causes 107 on the court docket, 108 at rules.—Judgments on forthcoming bonds, 53 in number, not included. No court at the spring term in consequence of the sickness of the judge.

NINTH CIRCUIT.

(*Note* 26.)—Halifax.—Suits at law decided, include office judgments and dismissions. Those pending, are suits on the court docket 1st September, 1843, Suits in chancery decided, include dismissions.

(*Note* 27.)—Lunenburg.—Of the suits commenced, a large number went off as office judgments, dismissions, &c.

TENTH CIRCUIT.

(*Note* 28.)—Floyd.—Among the prosecutions decided are three several indictments, each against two persons jointly for unlawful gaming, that were tried and decided jointly and reported only as three causes.

(*Note* 29.)—Henry.—No cases which abated by the sheriff's return, or were dismissed by the parties at the rules, are embraced in the report of cases decided. There were 72 judgments on forfeited forthcoming bonds, which are also excluded from the number of decided cases.

(*Note* 30.)—Franklin.—Of the number of suits decided 198 were office judgments. There were also 85 motions and judgments on forfeited forthcoming bonds, which are not included in the number of suits decided. There were no criminal trials or prosecutions at either term.

(*Note* 31.)—PITTSYLVANIA.—Number commenced includes writs of *scire facias*, writs of error, *supersedeas*, &c. The number decided includes office judgments, abatements, and rules for dismission in the office. Prosecutions include rules *vs.* grand jurors, &c.

(*Note* 32.)—CARROLL.—By act of last session the time of holding the court was changed so that the fall term commenced on the 31st August, 1843, and therefore not included in this report.

ELEVENTH CIRCUIT.

(*Note* 33.)—LOUISA.—Of the suits decided, 148 were office judgments. There were 73 motions commenced and decided; 9 dismissions were entered in court, and 29 dismissions and abatements were entered in the office.

(*Note* 34.)—MADISON.—One indictment and trial for murder at May term 1843.

(*Note* 35.)—CULPEPER.—Forty-nine judgments on forthcoming bonds included in the number of suits decided.

(*Note* 36.)—RAPPAHANNOCK.—Motions on delivery bonds included.

TWELFTH CIRCUIT.

(*Note* 37.)—ALBEMARLE.—The judge was sick one day at the spring term.

(*Note* 38.)—AUGUSTA.—In the number of suits commenced on the law side are included 6 *scire facias*, two appeals from court below to writs of *supersedeas*, one writ of replevin, one writ of prohibition, and one notice on sheriff's bonds. On chancery side of suits commenced are 6 motions on delivery bonds and 3 motions by receiver of the court.

THIRTEENTH CIRCUIT.

(*Note* 39.)—JEFFERSON.—In the number of suits at law decided are included 109 judgments on forfeited forthceming bonds.

(*Note* 40.)—BERKELEY.—This report does not include delivery bonds.

(*Note* 41.—MORGAN.—In this report are included all confessions of judgments in the clerk's office, judgments on forthcoming bonds, dismissions and causes agreed.

(*Note* 42.)—FREDERICK.—There were judgments on 65 forthcoming bonds which are not included in the number decided on the law side. A large number of the 320 suits depending on the 320 suits depending on the chancery side, are suits which were brought in the old district court, and which have remained sleeping ever since from the neglect of parties; this will account for the disproportion between the number pending and the number decided.

(*Note* 43.)—CLARKE.—Fifty-one judgments on delivery bonds not included in the number of causes decided.

FOURTEENTH CIRCUIT.

(*Note* 44.)—SHENANDOAH.—One chancery cause removed to Frederick county. Fifteen judgments on forthcoming bonds. Part of suits depending were judgments at September term, 1843.

(*Note* 45.)—WARREN.—There were within the year seventy judgments on forthcoming bonds which are not included in this report.

(*Note* 46.)—ROCKINGHAM.—Suits at law decided, include office judgments and judgments on forthcoming bonds.

FIFTEENTH CIRCUIT.

(*Note* 47.)—LEE.—Number of suits decided include those dismissed at rules, office judgments and judgments on forthcoming bonds.

(*Note* 48.)—SCOTT.—Judgments on delivery bonds, and rules against jurors, witnesses, &c., not included in this report.

(*Note* 49.)—RUSSELL.—In suits decided at law, dismissions, office judgments, and judgments on forthcoming bonds are included.

(*Note* 50.)—TAZEWELL.—One writ of error among prosecutions pending. No judgments on forthcoming bonds are comprised in this report. A special term was held June 1843, the judge having by reason of sickness failed to hold the regular court. At the fall term 1842, certain issues out of chancery in a case of much importance, and at the spring term 1843, a criminal trial of singular character occupied a large portion of each term, to the exclusion of other business.

SIXTEENTH CIRCUIT.

(*Note* 51.)—GRAYSON.—No spring term, but a special term held in June.

(*Note* 52.)—PULASKI.—"Poor pay."

(*Note* 53.)—GILES.—Of the suits in chancery pending, forty-eight are at rules.

(*Note* 54.)—MONROE.—The spring term having been adjourned from the 10th of May 'til the 25th July, made the term 9 days.

SEVENTEENTH CIRCUIT.

(*Note* 55.)—BOTETOURT.—The column for suits decided at law, and that for final decrees in chancery, embrace all suits finally terminated, whether by judgment, decrees, voluntary dismissions, abatements, confession of judgment or otherwise, both in court and in the clerk's office. There were 21 suits at law and 28 causes in chancery removed to other courts from this court.

EIGHTEENTH CIRCUIT.

(*Note* 56.)—RANDOLPH.—This report includes all causes for the year ending 30th August 1843. A number of causes both at common law and in chancery have been sent to the new county Barbour. Sundays are not included in the number of days given of the session of the court.

(*Note* 57.)—BAXTON.—There was no court at the fall term 1842.

(*Note* 58.)—HARRISON.—Judgments on forthcoming bonds not included. There were 14 such judgments at law and five in chancery.

(*Note* 59.)—JACKSON.—In consequence of sickness, the judge could not hold the fall term.

(*Note* 60.)—MASON.—There was no fall term in 1842, in consequence of the illness of judge Summers. Suits decided include dismissions and exclude judgments on forthcoming bonds. Decrees in forfeited land cases are not included.

(*Note* 61.)—WAYNE.—The court was not organized in the fall of 1842.

(*Note* 62.)—LOGAN.—No court in the fall.

(*Note* 63.)—KANAWHA.—Suits commenced, inclnde old suits at rules; number decided, include dismmissions and judgments on forthcoming bonds. Causes in chancery pending, include old causes at rules.

TWENTIETH CIRCUIT.

(*Note* 64.)—MONONGALIA.—Suits pending, include 9 at rules; causes pending, include 24 at rules. Prosecutions decided, include confessions.

(*Note* 65.)—MARION.—The number of final decrees includes 9 dismissals.

Note 66.—BROOKE.—Suits at law commenced, include writs of *scire facias* against special bail, and to renew judgments out of date. In suits at law decided, are included office judgments and judgments on forthcoming bonds.

(*Note* 67.)—OHIO.—"Business in this court is diminishing—this, together with the hard times, the difficulty of collecting fees, and the bankruptcy of us all, make it important that officers should be paid liberally for what they are bound to do. We implore for compensation for these reports."

(*Note* 68.)—MARSHALL.—"Among the number of suits decided at law, I omitted to include a will case which occupied some time of the fall term of 1842. Judgments on forthcoming bonds are not included."

ABSTRACT

FROM THE

REPORTS OF THE CLERKS

OF THE

COURT OF APPEALS

AND OF THE

CIRCUIT SUPERIOR COURTS OF LAW AND CHANCERY,

FOR THE

YEAR ENDING 30th AUGUST, 1844.

ABSTRACT FROM THE REPORTS

OF THE

CLERKS OF THE COURT OF APPEALS,

AND OF THE

CIRCUIT SUPERIOR COURTS OF LAW AND CHANCERY,

For the Year ending the 30th August, 1844; *exhibiting the number of Suits, &c.*

COURT OF APPEALS.

JUDGES.	CLERKS.	Location of Court.	Suits commenced.	Pending.	Decided.	No. of days in session.	REMARKS OF CLERKS.
Wm. H. Cabell, *President*,	Joseph Allen,	Richmond,	84	471	62	160	The term of the court was 160 days, having had within that time two recesses of twenty-five days each, and having actually sat 138 days exclusive of Sundays.
Francis T. Brooke,							
Robert Stanard.	John A. North,	Lewisburg,	36	138	32	62	
John J. Allen,							
Briscoe G. Baldwin.							
			120	609	94	222	

CIRCUIT SUPERIOR COURTS OF LAW AND CHANCERY.

Districts.	Circuits.	JUDGES.	CLERKS	COUNTIES.	Suits at Law.				Causes in Chancery.					Prosecutions.					Terms. Days in Session.				Remarks of Clerks.
					No. commenced.	No. pending.	No. decided.	No. removed from other courts.	No. commenced.	No. pending.	No. interlocutory decrees.	No. final decrees.	No. removed from county courts.	No. commenced.	No. pending.	No. decided.	No. nolle prosequis.	Change of venue.	Fall.	Spring.	Intermediate.	Total.	
1st	1st	R. H. Baker,	L. R. Edwards,	Southampton,	244	92	343	2	16	37	33	24	-	11	9	17	6	-	6	5	-	11	
			Joseph Turner,	Greenesville,	112	56	77	-	7	19	9	12	2	3	2	4	2	-	3	3	-	6	1
			W. P. Underwood,	Surry,	45	28	61	-	4	14	8	6	-	3	3	2	-	-	2	2	-	4	2
			N. P. Young.	Isle of Wight,	99	35	110	-	11	20	21	5	-	5	6	8	-	-	3	3	-	6	
			Joseph Prentis,	Nansemond,	62	33	114	-	7	12	9	6	-	4	6	11	1	-	3	3	-	6	3
			J. J. Burroughs,	Princess Anne,	79	42	128	-	3	7	4	7	-	1	1	-	-	-	2	2	-	4	
			John Williams,	Norfolk Borough.	179	110	178	1	32	56	19	32	1	9	8	14	-	-	12	18	-	30	4
			A. Emmerson,	Norfolk county,	273	32	311	-	16	30	16	8	1	28	39	6	-	-	10	12	-	22	
	2d	J. H. Gholson,	John P. Crump,	Dinwiddie,	134	52	187	-	25	47	19	22	-	4	14	8	-	-	5	5	-	10	5
			F. Fitzgerald,	Nottoway,	67	39	102	-	8	40	13	14	-	13	22	12	3	-	3	3	-	6	6
			E. G. Leigh,	Amelia,	126	91	234	-	14	37	14	9	-	15	18	2	3	-	4	3	-	7	7
			E. R. Turnbull,	Brunswick,	149	73	186	1	18	32	18	18	2	80	40	40	7	-	5	6	-	11	
			L. Lanier,	Sussex,	57	17	66	-	2	16	6	10	1	1	1	2	1	-	3	2	-	5	
			Robert Gilliam,	Prince George,	76	13	71	-	10	14	5	4	1	5	2	6	2	-	3	3	-	6	
			H. B. Gaines.	Petersburg,	176	279	238	19	44	171	95	62	4	79	96	64	8	-	27	18	-	45	
2d	3d	M. H. Bayly,	Thos. O. Cogbill,	James City and Williamsburg,	170	68	175	-	10	135	35	19	1	2	2	1	1	-	13	11	-	24	
			Samuel Shield,	York,	45	156	95	2	11	24	1	2	-	4	9	3	1	-	4	3	-	7	8
			Wm. Robertson,	Warwick,	35	12	43	-	-	9	-	-	1	-	-	-	-	-	1	1	-	2	
			W. S. Armstead,	Elizabeth City,	25	11	21	-	7	22	2	-	-	1	1	1	-	-	2	2	-	4	
			Louis P. Rogers,	Northampton,	32	27	57	-	10	26	6	10	-	1	-	1	-	-	4	4	-	8	
			Thos. R. Joynes,	Accomack,	66	186	109	7	18	100	23	17	4	6	20	4	2	-	9	6	-	15	
	4th	J. B. Christian,	Robert Pollard,	King William,	84	25	59	1	7	7	-	-	-	2	1	1	-	-	6	3	-	9	9
			J. D. Christian,	New Kent,	34	70	50	-	6	15	9	-	-	2	2	2	-	-	4	2	-	6	
			Robert Pollard, jr.	King & Queen,	92	86	156	-	10	26	16	9	-	6	8	5	-	-	6	4	-	10	10
			Jas. Roy Micou,	Essex,	85	53	271	-	10	50	8	10	-	3	3	3	-	-	4	2	-	6	11

			John S. Healey,	Middlesex,	64	16	104	1	20	43	18	2	1	-	1	1	4	-	3	3	-	6	12
			John R. Cary,	Gloucester,	101	81	145	-	23	76	20	10	-	3	4	3	3	-	6	5	-	11	13
			Shepard G. Miller.	Mathews,	28	41	67	-	17	72	22	11	1	4	3	-	1	-	4	3	-	7	
3d	5th	John T. Lomax,	Ro. T. Dunaway,	Lancaster,	39	105	84	-	7	21	4	7	-	2	2	-	-	-	2	2	-	4	
			S. A. M. Leland,	Northumberland,	37	19	64	-	1	10	11	8	-	3	4	2	1	-	3	4	-	7	14
			J. T. B. Jeffries,	Richmond co.	158	73	138	-	4	37	10	5	-	2	8	3	-	-	3	5	-	8	
			Wm. Hutt,	Westmoreland,	141	79	141	-	10	39	8	4	-	3	5	1	-	-	3	2	-	5	15
			S. J. S. Brown,	King George,	30	25	42	-	4	21	8	1	-	6	6	1	-	-	2	4	-	6	16
			Robert Hudgin,	Caroline,	136	100	150	1	11	60	43	13	2	9	4	9	-	-	4	4	-	8	
			J. J. Chew,	Spotsylvania,	84	58	138	1	12	498	33	27	5	6	11	7	-	-	16	22	-	38	
	6th	John Scott,	Wm. F. Philips,	Fauquier,	279	429	363	-	74	350	193	64	1	12	11	4	3	-	12	11	-	23	17
			Thomas P. Knox,	Loudoun,	225	190	244	-	33	136	85	33	1	2	4	6	2	-	7	7	-	14	18
			P. D. Lipscomb,	Prince William,	84	122	95	-	3	133	38	16	-	9	13	10	2	-	4	5	-	9	
			F. D. Richardson,	Fairfax,	124	147	136	-	37	122	46	18	-	1	-	-	1	-	4	5	-	9	
			J. M. Conway,	Stafford,	22	20	20	1	6	28	6	5	-	9	10	4	1	-	3	4	-	7	
4th	7th	J. B. Clopton,	Parke Poindexter,	Chesterfield,	140	219	176	-	13	92	32	14	-	6	22	4	3	-	9	6	3	18	
			Ro. W. Christian,	Charles City,	57	24	110	1	1	24	15	6	-	1	-	1	-	-	5	3	-	8	19
			Wm. S. Dance,	Powhatan,	144	132	164	1	15	90	23	14	1	2	2	2	-	-	3	7	4	14	
			Wm. Miller,	Goochland,	123	13	193	-	8	65	7	11	1	5	8	3	4	-	8	5	-	13	
			Phillip B. Winston,	Hanover,	132	207	116	-	26	131	38	12	-	2	8	-	-	-	10	6	-	16	
	21st	P. N. Nicholas,	John Robinson,	Henrico and City of Richmond.	108	399	213	1	-	-	-	-	-	26	39	22	7	-	54	52	-	106	20
	22d	John Robertson,	Wm. G. Sands,	Henrico and City of Richmond,	-	-	-	-	78	1623	227	88	-	-	-	-	-	-	78	25	9	112	21
	8th	D. A. Wilson,	John Daniel,	Cumberland,	233	64	237	-	14	95	20	15	2	4	4	4	1	-	5	6	-	11	
			Rolfe Eldridge,	Buckingham,	4[illegible]0	453	838	1	78	162	25	31	2	18	17	9	-	-	25	14	-	39	22
			J. D. Alexander,	Campbell,	225	279	247	-	34	121	10	10	1	10	22	16	8	-	12	10	-	22	23
			Jos. Wilson,	Bedford,	269	263	477	12	33	219	36	33	3	4	10	25	-	-	8	13	6	27	24
			D. Rodes,	Lynchburg,	87	129	132	7	18	327	92	24	-	6	5	5	2	-	10	24	-	34	
5th	9th	Wm. Leigh,	Wm. Holt,	Halifax,	318	62	385	-	44	65	17	17	5	21	52	24	15	-	10	12	-	22	25
			W. Robinson,	Charlotte,	157	97	187	-	19	46	25	26	-	6	9	8	-	-	7	4	-	11	
			B. J. Worsham,	Prince Edward,	183	104	359	3	38	100	56	26	4	3	5	2	-	-	6	5	-	11	
			Wm. H. Taylor,	Lunenburg,	83	38	109	-	17	29	15	-	-	23	19	12	1	-	4	6	-	10	
			R.B. Baptist,	Mecklenburg,	436	53	293	-	34	34	11	22	3	8	28	35	6	-	10	10	-	20	
	10th	N. M. Taliaferro,	J. N. Zentmeyer,	Floyd,	37	20	33	1	5	14	2	8	-	10	10	14	-	2	4	4	-	8	26
			Sam'l G. Staples,	Patrick,	70	79	84	17	17	54	5	7	1	9	14	11	-	-	4	9	-	13	
			A. M. Dupuy,	Henry,	43	49	69	8	5	38	11	10	2	7	9	6	1		3	4	-	7	27
			C. Tate,	Franklin,	179	153	190	2	17	103	17	13	1	17	29	11	1	3	6	8	-	14	28
			Wm. H. Tunstall,	Pittsylvania,	248	629	425	-	43	171	27	19	2	16	45	13	2	-	9	12	-	21	29
			M. D. Carter.	Carroll,	34	53	21	-	10	20	8	4	-	68	57	10	4	-	3	3	-	6	

Districts.	Circuits.	JUDGES.	CLERKS.	COUNTIES.	Suits at Law. No. commenced.	Suits at Law. No. pending.	Suits at Law. No. decided.	Suits at Law. No. removed from other courts.	Causes in Chancery. No. commenced.	Causes in Chancery. No. pending.	Causes in Chancery. No. interlocutory decrees.	Causes in Chancery. No. final decrees.	Causes in Chancery. No. removed from county courts.	Prosecutions. No. commenced.	Prosecutions. No. pending.	Prosecutions. No. decided.	Prosecutions. No. nolle prosequis.	Prosecutions. Change of venue.	Terms. Days in session. Fall.	Terms. Days in session. Spring.	Terms. Days in session. Intermediate.	Terms. Days in session. Total.	Remarks of Clerks.
6th	11th	R. H. Field,	John Hunter,	Louisa,	112	145	138	-	15	63	22	8	-	4	6	1	-	-	6	4	6	16	30
			A. Shepherd, jr.	Fluvanna,	138	118	281	1	12	77	10	12	1	5	8	2	1	-	7	8	-	15	
			Philip S. Fry,	Orange,	113	84	76	4	14	55	14	10	-	4	5	2	-	-	6	7	-	13	31
			Robert Pritchett,	Greene,	29	27	39	5	10	22	12	4	-	2	5	2	-	-	3	3	-	6	
			Belfield Cave,	Madison,	95	31	119	1	11	30	20	6	1	1	5	5	2	-	16	9	-	25	32
			R. G. Ward,	Culpeper,	90	108	202	16	27	95	48	27	4	7	10	2	4	-	19	10	21	50	33
			Wm. J. Menifee,	Rappahannock,	48	49	57	-	3	33	34	8	-	10	8	8	2	-	4	5	-	9	34
	12th	L. P. Thompson,	Robert Tinsley,	Amherst,	300	249	507	2	58	287	148	31	1	7	7	5	2	-	9	13	-	22	35
			D. Hutcheson,	Rockbridge,	210	150	293	10	48	114	65	27	5	8	16	6	1	-	8	12	-	20	
			Robert C. Cutler,	Nelson,	204	360	416	20	61	299	96	37	-	19	27	16	4	-	9	13	-	22	36
			Alex. Garrett,	Albemarle,	268	360	270	-	30	125	17	12	3	60	70	12	3	-	14	11	-	25	
			Nich's C. Kinney,	Augusta,	404	396	500	2	60	460	112	45	-	35	39	20	6	-	17	19	16	52	37
7th	13th	I. R. Douglass,	R. T. Brown,	Jefferson,	223	177	358	6	48	265	91	31	-	5	17	10	5	-	23	21	-	44	38
			John Strother,	Berkeley,	93	108	85	-	17	115	-	24	-	7	3	4	-	-	7	3	-	10	
			J. Reichard,	Morgan,	45	56	83	-	8	36	6	7	-	2	4	3	-	-	2	4	-	6	
			John B. White,	Hampshire,	117	92	216	2	31	151	49	38	-	1	5	7	-	-	7	6	-	13	39
			J. Kean,	Frederick,	86	86	108	-	29	313	29	35	-	13	15	3	3	-	4	6	-	10	40
			H. H. Lee,	Clarke,	113	21	126	2	12	38	15	5	-	4	4	-	1	-	3	4	-	7	41
	14th	Daniel Smith,	Wm. C. Lauck,	Page,	23	18	26	-	4	15	7	7	-	-	-	-	-	-	1	2	-	3	42
			P. Williams,	Shenandoah,	39	12	82	-	2	42	23	7	1	4	4	3	-	-	2	2	-	4	43
			Robert Turner,	Warren,	77	21	75	-	9	12	7	10	1	3	4	-	1	-	3	2	-	5	44
			C. Lobb,	Hardy,	91	71	113	-	12	114	15	9	1	6	3	4	-	-	3	3	-	6	45
			Z. Dyer,	Pendleton,	20	7	11	-	2	13	-	2	1	7	6	7	-	-	3	4	-	7	
			H. J. Gambill,	Rockingham,	202	154	256	-	29	83	32	16	-	10	7	8	-	-	12	23	-	35	46
8th	15th	Benj. Estill,	J. W. S. Morrison,	Lee,	40	56	35	-	4	37	3	1	-	10	24	10	6	-	6	-	-	6	47
			John S. Martin,	Scott,	20	44	26	-	5	43	10	8	1	2	9	1	4	-	4	-	-	4	48
			James P. Carrell,	Russell,	36	43	47	-	2	42	6	5	1	12	15	8	4	-	5	4	-	9	49
			G. W. G. Browne	Tazewell,	46	66	53	-	25	84	20	19	-	17	19	28	10	-	5	4	-	9	50
			A. B. Moore,	Washington,	58	72	99	1	25	110	80	17	-	13	10	11	5	-	17	16	-	33	

			A. B. Moore,	Smyth,	43	58	67	-	9	48	8	9	-	14	19	5	1	-	5	6	-	11	
	16th	Jas. Brown,	J. R. Miller,	Wythe,	40	42	64	-	16	149	7	25	-	21	17	21	3	-	8	10	5	23	
			O. Anderson,	Grayson,	26	20	34	-	5	22	10	4	-	9	3	17	1	-	3	5	-	8	
			R. D. Montague,	Montgomery,	59	64	91	-	14	79	19	11	-	5	12	7	-	-	10	5	-	15	
			W. B. Charlton,	Pulaski,	46	22	34	-	9	17	2	3	2	10	12	3	-	-	3	4	-	7	51
			Rufus A. French,	Giles,	67	41	73	-	12	59	5	8	-	12	35	12	1	-	-	4	-	4	52
			Alex. Mohood,	Mercer,	31	27	33	-	9	30	1	10	-	2	2	1	-	-	3	3	-	6	
			J. Hutchinson,	Monroe,	63	47	103	-	11	75	22	8	-	13	15	4	1	-	5	4	-	9	
9th	17th	E. Johnson,	H. W. Bowyer,	Botetourt,	147	166	195	-	42	201	6	15	2	12	18	6	3	-	11	2	-	13	53
			F. Johnston,	Roanoke,	58	20	69	3	11	20	5	6	4	4	4	2	1	-	5	6	-	11	
			Andrew Fudge,	Alleghany,	38	65	32	-	8	45	4	5	-	-	-	-	-	-	3	-	-	3	54
			C. L. Francisco,	Bath,	74	85	20	1	5	42	5	4	-	5	2	5	-	-	6	-	-	6	
			H. M. Moffett,	Pocahontas,	49	65	47	-	16	29	-	10	-	3	6	3	-	-	2	-	-	2	
			John A. North,	Greenbrier,	149	201	82	-	21	116	18	4	-	11	32	8	-	-	7	-	-	7	
	18th	E. S. Duncan,	H. M. Dickinson,	Fayette,	102	102	89	-	9	42	7	14	1	10	-	12	2	-	7	7	-	14	
			Jas. M. Stanard,	Nicholas,	34	47	28	2	5	31	9	7	-	10	14	8	-	-	3	3	-	6	
			B. L. Brown,	Randolph,	35	59	41	2	17	76	7	20	-	9	13	12	3	-	4	6	-	10	
			E. D. Wilson,	Barbour,	64	53	56	9	45	58	4	2	5	7	10	1	1	-	2	4	-	6	55
			John Talbot,	Lewis,	205	335	199	-	103	227	35	42	2	30	44	8	5	-	12	11	-	23	
			W. Newland,	Braxton,	58	70	83	5	11	67	14	5	-	4	10	2	-	-	3	2	-	5	
			G. G. Davisson,	Harrison,	161	199	251	16	84	339	91	114	1	49	50	36	5	-	27	19	-	46	56
			E. J. Armstrong,	Taylor,	16	17	-	1	6	7	-	-	-	1	1	-	-	-	-	1	-	1	
10th	19th	D. McComas,	J. H. Neal,	Wood,	62	129	32	-	24	136	5	12	-	1	17	6	-	-	-	8	-	8	57
			T. Stinchcomb,	Ritchie,	32	24	8	-	8	5	-	-	-	3	3	-	-	-	-	2	-	2	58
			D. G. Morrill,	Jackson,	43	68	45	1	10	42	2	2	-	5	10	4	-	-	-	6	-	6	59
			G. W. Stribbling,	Mason,	70	49	59	-	14	35	4	15	-	5	8	2	2	-	-	7	-	7	60
			John Samuels,	Cabell,	13	15	18	1	9	13	4	6	1	10	21	10	1	1	-	8	-	8	61
			H. Clarke,	Wayne,	11	7	12	-	12	11	15	7	-	3	4	2	-	-	3	3	-	6	
			Edw. Robertson,	Logan,	22	22	7	-	3	8	2	2	-	20	39	7	-	-	-	4	-	4	62
			A. W. Quarrier,	Kanawha,	293	304	480	-	18	107	24	4	-	29	59	5	6	-	-	18	-	18	63
	20th	Joseph L. Fry,	John P. Bryne,	Preston,	45	75	57	-	37	60	28	10	-	12	16	9	1	-	6	6	3	15	64
			W. T. Willey,	Monongalia,	58	37	81	-	26	57	36	16	-	14	31	5	1	-	7	7	3	17	65
			James O. Watson.	Marion,	59	49	63	4	23	55	4	17	3	17	17	-	-	-	5	4	-	9	66
			D. Hickman,	Tyler,	58	70	73	-	34	68	18	22	-	6	12	7	-	-	5	5	-	10	
			Adam Kuhn,	Brooke,	56	53	83	-	20	86	31	23	1	2	4	2	1	-	6	6	-	12	67
			Alex. T. Laidley,	Ohio,	113	137	190	5	80	191	54	58	4	4	5	4	1	-	21	31	17	59	68
			James D. Morris.	Marshall,	41	37	71	-	19	82	14	18	-	2	2	1	1	-	7	5	-	12	
10	22			Total,	9805	11880	18098	214	2881	12163	3164	1945	104	1339	1735	930	215	6	927	890	93	1910	

RECAPITULATION.

CIRCUIT SUPERIOR COURTS OF LAW AND CHANCERY,

Number of Suits, &c., in each Circuit, August 20th, 1844.

Districts.	Circuits.	No. of counties and towns in circuit.	JUDGES.	Suits at Law.				Causes in Chancery.					Prosecutions.					Terms. Days in Session.				Miles Travelling.			REMARKS.
				No. commenced.	No. pending.	No. decided.	No. removed from other courts.	No. commenced.	No. pending.	No. interlocutory decrees.	No. final decrees.	No. removed from county courts.	No. commenced.	No. pending.	No. decided.	No. nolle prosequis.	Change of venue.	Fall.	Spring.	Intermediate.	Total.	To general court.	In circuit.	Total.	
1	1	8	Richard H. Baker,	1093	428	1322	3	96	195	119	100	4	74	74	62	9	-	41	48	-	89	224	255	479	
	2	7	Jas. H. Gholson,	785	564	1084	20	121	357	170	139	8	197	193	134	24	-	50	40	-	90	150	380	530	
2	3	6	Thos. H. Bayly,	373	460	500	9	56	316	67	48	6	14	32	10	4	-	33	27	-	60	440	407	847	
	4	7	John B. Christian,	478	372	852	2	93	289	93	42	2	20	22	15	8	-	33	22	-	55	120	230	350	
3	5	7	John T. Lomax,	625	459	757	2	49	686	117	65	7	31	40	23	1	-	33	43	-	76	140	218	358	
	6	5	John Scott,	734	908	858	1	181	769	368	136	2	33	38	24	9	-	30	32	-	62	220	200	420	
4	7	5	John B. Clopton,	596	713	759	2	63	402	115	57	2	16	40	10	7	-	35	27	7	69	12	182	194	
	21	2	P. N. Nicholas,	108	399	213	1	-	-	-	-	-	26	39	22	7	-	54	52	-	106				
	22	2	John Robertson,	-	-	-	-	78	1623	227	88	-	-	-	-	-	-	78	25	9	112				
	8	5	Daniel A. Wilson,	1234	1188	1931	20	177	924	183	118	8	42	58	59	11	-	60	67	6	133	240	180	420	
5	9	5	William Leigh,	1177	364	1333	3	152	274	124	85	12	67	113	81	22	-	37	37	-	74	260	165	425	
	10	6	N. M. Taliaferro,	611	983	822	28	117	400	70	61	6	127	164	65	8	5	29	40	-	69	390	265	655	
6	11	7	Richard H. Field,	625	562	912	27	92	375	160	75	6	33	47	22	9	-	61	46	27	134	206	308	514	
	12	5	Lucas P. Thompson,	1386	1515	1986	34	257	1285	438	152	9	129	159	59	16	-	57	68	16	141	242	240	482	
7	13	6	J. R. Douglass,	677	540	976	10	145	918	190	140	-	32	48	27	9	-	46	44	-	90	320	200	520	
	14	6	Daniel Smith,	452	283	563	-	58	279	84	51	4	30	24	22	1	-	24	36	-	60	268	257	525	
8	15	6	Benjamin Estill,	243	339	327	1	70	378	127	59	2	68	96	63	30	-	42	30	-	72	618	270	868	
	16	7	James E. Brown,	332	263	432	-	76	451	66	69	2	72	96	65	6	-	32	35	5	72	514	309	823	

9,	7	6	Edward Johnston,	515	602	445	4	103	453	38	44	6	35	62	24	4	-	34	8	-	42	330	241	571
	18	8	Edwin S. Duncan,	675	862	747	35	280	847	167	204	9	120	142	79	16	-	58	53	-	111	590	363	953
10	19	8	David M'Comas,	546	618	661	2	98	357	56	48	1	76	161	36	9	1	3	56	-	59	640	412	1052
	20	7	Joseph L. Fry,	430	458	618	9	239	599	185	164	8	57	87	28	5	-	57	54	23	134	714	300	1014
10	22	131	Total,	9805	11880	18098	214	2881	12163	3164	1945	104	1339	1735	930	215	6	927	890	93	1910	6638	5382	12020
			Average of circuits,	467	565	861	10	137	579	150	93	5	63	82	44	10	-	42	40	4	87	336	269	601

Judgments at law, - -	18,098
Interlocutory decrees, - -	3,164
Final decrees, - - -	1,945
Total decisions from which appeals may be had, - -	23,207

Number of appeals allowed, - - - - 120 being about eight fifteenths of one per cent. of the total decisions in the circuit courts.

Causes decided inthe court of appeals, - - 94

Excess of new appeals over decisions, - 26

E. E.

GEORGE W. MUNFORD, *C. H. D.*

December 6th, 1844.

REMARKS OF CLERKS.

FIRST CIRCUIT.

(*Note* 1.)—GREENESVILLE.—In this report jndgments on forthcomiug bonds are included; but dismissions at rules are not.

(*Note* 2.)—SURRY.—Of the suits at law decided, 13 were motions on forthcoming bonds, 6 were dismissions in court, and 7 were judgments on motions against garnishees of insolvent debtors.

(*Note* 3.)—NANSEMOND.—All judgments on motions—judgments confessed in the office—all dismissions in court or otherwise, and office judgments confirmed are embracced in suits decided at law.

(*Note* 4.)—NORFOLK BOROUGH.—In the number of suits commenced, are included 13 motions on forthcoming bonds and one writ of *habeas corpus*. In the number decided, 13 judgments on forthcoming bonds, 25 dismissions at rules and one *habeas corpus*. Among chancery causes commenced, one friendly bill is included. Among the final decrees, there are 14 dismissions at rules.

SECOND CIRCUIT.

(*Note* 5.)—DINWIDDIE.—Judgments on motions not embraced.

Note 6.—NOTTOWAY.—Judgments on motions not embraced. Abatements and dismissions included in decisions of law and chancery suits.

(*Note* 7.)—AMELIA.—Of the suits at law decided, 164 were office judgments passed by default. The clerk has not embraced in this report the motions on forfeited forthcoming bonds, as he does not think they can come properly under the head of suits. Of the prosecutions, 14 were misdemeanors and one a criminal offence.

THIRD CIRCUIT.

(*Note* 8.)—YORK.—Thirty-two judgments on forfeited forthcoming bonds and one by security against principal for money paid, &c. rendered.

FOURTH CIRCUIT.

(*Note* 9.)—KING WILLIAM.—The chancery suits were instituted within the rule days intervening between the fall term 1843 and the spring term 1844; consequently, there are no decrees rendered in either of those causes. According to my construction of the act of assembly, it requires that only the causes which are commenced within the year ending on the 30th August preceding the date of the reports, should be embraced in the report.—If this construction be correct, it will be observed that a majority of the chancery causes (the decrees rendered therein) are not reported, because it requires in a great many instances such a length of time to mature such causes for a hearing, as to exclude them altogether—and no decree being rendered, perhaps, at all within twelve months after their institution.

(*Note* 10.)—KING AND QUEEN.—Forty motions.

(*Note* 11.)—Essex.—Among the number of law suits reported as decided, are 117 judgments against garnishees, and 95 office judgments, embracing also judgments on forthcoming bonds. Among the number pending, there are some three or four garnishee cases. I have not noticed orders in chancery merely making new parties, suggesting deaths, &c. as interlocutory decrees. One of the number reported decided was dismissed at rules.

(*Note* 12.)—Middlesex.—The prosecutions herein reported, are presentments of the grand jury.

(*Note* 13.)—Gloucester.—The suits pending are those on the court docket. Suits decided include dismissions; prosecutions commenced include one case of felony, and those decided the same.

FIFTH CIRCUIT.

(*Note* 14.)—Northumberland.—Judgments on forthcoming bonds or motions not embraced, not being considered such suits as were in the contemplation of the legislature.

(*Note* 15.)—Westmoreland.—Motions not included.

(*Note* 16.)—King George.—Motions on forthcoming bonds not included. Quite a considerable falling off in the business of this court since last report.

SIXTH CIRCUIT.

(*Note* 17.)—Fauquier.—One hundred and twenty-eight motions not included in this statement.

(*Note* 18.)—Loudoun.—Ninety judgments on motions not included in this report.

SEVENTH CIRCUIT.

(*Note* 19.)—Charles City.—What a falling off is here, my Lord! Don't you guess it must be the tariff of 1842?

TWENTY-FIRST CIRCUIT.

(*Note* 20.)—Henrico and City of Richmond.—Among the suits commenced, seven writs of *scire facias* are included, two appeals from decisions of the auditor of public accounts, one *caveat* and five writs of *supersedeas*. Among the suits decided, judgments on forthcoming bonds and by confessions in the office are included—also, nonsuits and dismissions and abatements in court, and exclusive of a case removed to another court. Among the *nolle prosequis* there is one case of abatement by death of defendant. Fourteen days of the term were occupied in a case of a contested will.

TWENTY-SECOND CIRCUIT.

(*Note* 22.)—Henrico and City of Richmond.—There were nine causes removed from other circuit superior courts.

EIGHTH CIRCUIT.

(*Note* 23.)—Buckingham.—The regular fall term was in session thirteen days, and adjourned till 23d October following, and was then in session twelve days, making together twenty-five days.

(*Note* 24.)—Campbell.—In addition to the number of suits at law decided, there were seventy judgments on delivery bonds and judgments on the reports of the assessors for assessing damages by occasion of the James river and Kanawha canal passing through the lands of proprietors in two cases. At the fall term the court sat the full time allotted, and being unable to try all causes which were ready for trial, an intermediate term was held on the 11th day of December, 1843, and continued three days—since which time an alteration of the time of holding our court has been made by the legislature, but we are still pressed for the want of time, and are now unable to do the business of the court in the time prescribed by law.

(*Note* 25.)—Bedford.—Of the causes pending on the law docket, 118 were on the court docket, 145 at rules. Of chancery causes, 94 were on the court docket, 125 at rules. Judgments on delivery bonds are not included. These judgments were 176 in number, 173 at law, 3 in chancery.

NINTH CIRCUIT.

(*Note* 26.)—Halifax.—Suits at law decided include office judgments and dismissions. Those pending are suits on the court docket 1st September 1844. Suits in chancery decided include dismissions.

TENTH CIRCUIT.

(*Note* 27.) -Floyd—The two changes of venue removed from Franklin county. One cause at law removed from this to Montgomery county, and one chancery cause removed to Roanoke county.

(*Note* 28.)—Henry.—No causes where there was a confession of judgment in the clerk's office, nor judgments on forfeited forthcoming bonds, are included in the list of causes decided by the court.

(*Note* 29.)—Franklin.—In addition to the number of suits decided, there were 90 motions on forfeited forthcoming bonds and judgments thereon, and 14 other motions and judgments thereon, which are not included in the number decided. There was also a prisoner tried at the spring term for burglary and larceny.

(*Note* 30.)—Pittsylvania.—The number pending includes all causes on the rule, new cause, issue and office judgment docket, as well as motions of all kinds. The number decided includes all office judgments, abatements, dismissions at rules, motions of all kinds, and causes decided on the issue docket.

ELEVENTH CIRCUIT.

(*Note* 31.)—Louisa.- Of the suits at law decided, 91 were office judgments. There were 38 motions commenced and decided. Four dismssions were entered in court and 28 dismissions and abatements were entered in the office.

(*Note* 32.)—Orange.—Judgments on forthcoming bonds and rules for contempt not included.

(*Note* 33.)—Madison.—May term, one conviction for murder. Seven judgments on delivery bonds, in addition to those named as decided.

(*Note* 34.)—Culpeper—Fifty-two judgments on forthcoming bonds included in the number of suits decided.

(*Note* 35.)—Rappahannock.—Forthcoming bonds are included in the suits at law. Rules against witnesses on behalf of the commonwealth and rules against absent grand jurors are included in the prosecutions.

TWELFTH CIRCUIT.

(*Note* 36.)—Amherst.—The chancery suits pending are mostly on the rule docket not ready, or on the sleeping docket having been in the main decided. There are very few remaining on the court docket in which either party was ready.

(*Note* 37.)—Nelson—In the number of suits decided at common law are included many judgments on delivery bonds, and judgments on other motions, on notices, &c.

(*Note* 38.)—Augusta.—In the number of suits commenced on the law side of the court, is included one hundred forthcoming bonds, and six writs of *supersedeas*, leaving 298 suits commenced by writs of *capias ad respondendum*. In the number decided is also included the one hundred forthcoming bonds and six writs of *supersedeas*.

THIRTEENTH CIRCUIT.

Note 39.—Jefferson.—Of the causes decided, 109 are judgments on forfeited forthcoming bonds.

(*Note* 40.)—Hampshire,—Of the common law suits commenced, three are writs of *scire facias*. The causes at law and in chancery pending those remaining on the docket at the end of the spring term undecided. Judgments on forthcoming bonds not included in suits decided, though there were 80 at law and 1 in chancery.

(*Note* 41.)—Frederick.—There are a large number of suits pending from the old chancery district court. They were on the deferred docket when the change in the judicial system was made, and they remain sleeping on that docket. This accounts for the great difference between the number pending and those decided in this report.

(*Note* 42.)—Clarke.—Forty-six motions on delivery bonds not included.

FOURTEENTH CIRCUIT.

(*Note* 43.)—Page.—A decree heretofore rendered by this court was reversed by the court of appeals at Lewisburg, and by said court certified to us, and is reinstated on the docket for further proceedings.

(*Note* 44.)—Shenandoah.—Judgments on forthcoming bonds not included.

(*Note* 45.)—Warren.—There were within the year 31 judgments on forthcoming bonds, which are not included in this report.

(*Note* 46)—Hardy.—Two entire days of the spring term were occupied in a trial for murder and a trial for larceny. Forthcoming bonds are not included in the list of judgments. They were about 50.

(*Note* 47.)—Rockingham.—Suits at law decided include judgments on delivery bonds and office judgments.

FIFTEENTH CIRCUIT.

(*Note* 48.)—Lee.—The number of causes pending includes all commenced as well as those remaining on the rule docket, issue docket and office judgment docket. At the spring term no court was held on account of an epidemic prevailing in town and adjacent thereto.

(*Note* 49.)—Scott.—The spring term was not held. The judge having sprained his ancle, was unable to reach the courthouse for that purpose, although he made an effort to do so. Judgments on delivery bonds and rules against jurors and witnesses are not included in this report.

(*Note* 50.)—Russell.—The greater number of the causes here enumerated are on the rule dockets. There being but few on the court docket, the judge has decided in all the causes that were ready for trial both at law and in equity during each session of the court. Office judgments and judgments on forthcoming bonds are included with the causes decided at law, and dismissions at the rules with those decided at law.

(*Note* 51.)—Tazewell.—I think it time to quit making these reports.

SIXTEENTH CIRCUIT.

(*Note* 52.(—Pulaski.—Poor pay.

(*Note* 53.)—Giles.—Of the causes in chancery 36 are at rules.

SEVENTEENTH CIRCUIT.

(*Note* 54.)—Botetourt.—The judge was taken sick on the second day of April term 1844, and was unable from protracted indisposition to do any more business during that term, having been confined to a sick bed for several weeks. The prosecutions decided include the three *nolle prosequis*.

(*Note* 55.)—Alleghany.—The court did not sit at April term, owing to the indisposition of the judge.

EIGHTEENTH CIRCUIT.

(*Note* 56.)—Barbour.—In the number of suits decided at law, I have included judgments on forthcoming bonds—there were 6. It will be seen by reference to the reports of the clerks of the superior courts west of the mountains, that business is gradually decreasing in this region. It would be no more than justice if the legislature, taking into consideration the present state of things, would increase our fees. We ought to have something for making this report, which, by the by, is a very troublesome job.

(*Note* 57.)—Harrison.—Judgments on forthcoming bonds, and decress in delinquent and forfeited land cases not included.

NINETEENTH CIRCUIT.

(*Note* 58.)—Wood.—No court held at fall term in consequence of the lamented death of judge Summers.

(*Note* 59.)—Ritchie.—Our judge was unable to attend at the regular term, which was the 26th August last, but he holds a special session on the 15th instant.

(*Note* 60.)—JACKSON.—In consequence of the death of Judge Summers, there was no fall term.

(*Note* 61.)—MASON.—No fall term in consequence of the death of Judge Summers.—The column for causes commenced includes *supersedeases*—that for causes decided includes dismissions, but excludes judgments on forthcoming bonds.

(*Note* 62.)—CABELL.—Owing to the death of judge Summers no session was held in the fall of 1813.

(*Note* 63.)—LOGAN.—No fall term.

(*Note* 64.)—No court at fall term 1843. Number of suits pending at law and in chancery includes old suits at rules, The number decided at law includes judgments on forthcoming bonds and dismissions.

TWENTIETH CIRCUIT.

(*Note* 65)—PRESTON.—Judgments on forthcoming bonds not included.

(*Note* 66.)—MONONGALIA.—The number of suits at law decided includes 11 cases dismissed and abated at rules. The number of final decrees in chancery does not include dismissions at the rules. The causes depending are those on the trial docket only.

(*Note* 67.)—MARION.—The cases decided both at law and in chancery include one case each, transferred to the new county of Taylor.

(*Note* 68.)—BROOKE—Suits at law decided include judgments on forthcoming bonds.

(*Note* 69.)—OHIO.—Causes at rules are included in the number pending. Dismissions at rules are not embraced in the number decided. Judgments on forthcoming bonds included in the number disposed of.

ABSTRACT

FROM THE

REPORTS OF THE CLERKS

OF THE

COURT OF APPEALS

AND OF THE

CIRCUIT SUPERIOR COURTS OF LAW AND CHANCERY,

FOR THE

YEAR ENDING 30th AUGUST, 1845.

ABSTRACT FROM THE REPORTS

OF THE

CLERKS OF THE COURT OF APPEALS,

AND OF THE

CIRCUIT SUPERIOR COURTS OF LAW AND CHANCERY,

For the Year ending the 30th August, 1845 ; exhibiting the number of Suits, &c.

COURT OF APPEALS.

JUDGES.	CLERKS.	Location of Court	Suits commenced.	Pending.	Decided.	No. of days in session.	REMARKS OF CLERKS.
Wm. H. Cabell, *President*, Francis T. Brooke, Robert Stanard, John J. Allen, Briscoe G. Baldwin.	Joseph Allen,	Richmond,	100	506	72	137	Nineteen of the one hundred causes commenced, depending upon the same principle, are considered as one case. The term commenced on the 15th day of October, 1844, and ended on the 14th day of May, 1845, making 160 days, the court having had between those periods two sessions of 26 days each, and having actually sat 137 judicial days exclusive of Sundays.
	John A. North,	Lewisburg,	44		51	48	
			144	506	123	165	

CIRCUIT SUPERIOR COURTS OF LAW AND CHANCERY.

Districts.	Circuits.	JUDGES.	CLERKS.	COUNTIES.	Suits at Law. No. commenced.	Suits at Law. No. pending.	Suits at Law. No. decided.	Suits at Law. No removed from other courts.	Causes in Chancery. No. commenced.	Causes in Chancery. No. pending.	Causes in Chancery. No. interlocutory decrees.	Causes in Chancery. No. final decrees.	Causes in Chancery. No. removed from county courts.	Prosecutions. No. commenced.	Prosecutions. No. pending.	Prosecutions. No. decided.	Prosecutions. No. nolle prosequis.	Prosecutions. Change of venue.	Terms. Days in Session. Fall.	Terms. Days in Session. Spring.	Terms. Days in Session. Intermediate.	Terms. Days in Session. Total.	Remarks of Clerks.
1	1	R. H. Baker,	L. R. Edwards,	Southampton,	179	95	175	1	13	36	35	14	-	3	7	7	-	-	3	6	-	9	
			Joseph Turner,	Greenesville,	68	42	57	-	4	17	9	5	-	2	1	3	1	-	2	2	-	4	Note 1.
			W. P. Underwood,	Surry,	21	18	33	-	7	13	9	1	-	1	1	3	-	-	2	2	-	4	Note 2.
			N. P. Young,	Isle of Wight,	37	22	39	-	7	16	11	11	-	3	3	2	4	-	3	3	-	6	Note 3.
			Joseph Prentis,	Nansemond,	29	20	68	1	4	14	5	5	-	-	2	4	-	-	5	4	-	9	Note 4.
			J. J. Burroughs,	Princess Anne,	66	38	99	-	10	12	7	5	-	3	3	1	-	-	4	3	-	7	Note 5.
			John Williams,	Norfolk City.	149	97	172	-	30	64	19	21	2	7	2	13	-	-	12	16	-	28	Note 6.
			A. Emmerson,	Norfolk county,	161	46	207	15	19	22	12	17	-	8	13	19	6	-	12	12	-	24	
	2	J. H. Gholson,	John P Crump,	Dinwiddie,	67	36	89	2	13	46	19	16	1	4	9	11	2	-	5	4	-	9	Note 7.
			C. W. Fitzgerald,	Nottoway,	62	56	50	-	12	38	[illegible]	14	-	1	4	5	14	-	3	2	-	5	Note 8.
			E. G. Leigh,	Amelia,	85	77	111	-	12	47	16	6	-	5	12	9	-	-	3	3	-	6	Note 9.
			E. R. Turnbull,	Brunswick,	95	53	106	1	24	37	15	15	1	5	13	27	22	-	3	5	-	8	
			L. Lanier,	Sussex,	22	20	19	-	3	18	4	2	-	-	-	1	-	-	2	2	-	4	
			Robert Gilliam,	Prince George,	57	2	52	-	3	14	12	5	-	5	3	2	-	-	3	3	-	6	Note 10.
			H. B. Gaines.	Petersburg,	93	180	111	3	45	204	107	62	-	20	44	22	4	-	64	15	-	79	Note 11.
2	3	T. H. Bayly,	Thos. O. Cogbill,	James City and Williamsburg,	77	160	83	11	6	143	22	15	1	8	6	2	2	-	7	11	-	18	
			Samuel Shield,	York,	24	48	47	29	1	20	3	6	-	-	4	-	2	-	4	3	-	7	
			Wm. Robertson,	Warwick,	17	10	17	-	1	10	2	2	1	1	-	1	-	-	1	1	-	2	
			W. S. Armstead,	Elizabeth City,	36	37	31	5	4	24	8	2	1	5	6	-	-	-	4	3	-	7	
			Lewis P. Roger s	Northampton,	14	23	21	1	15	31	20	12	1	-	-	-	-	-	5	4	-	9	
			Thos. R. Joynes,	Accomack,	29	65	62	6	17	[illegible]	29	11	3	4	23	3	-	-	11	12	-	23	
	4	J. B. Christian,	Robert Pollard,	King William,	66	18	86	-	12	44	21	16	1	-	-	1	1	-	5	6	-	11	Note 12.
			J. D. Christian,	New Kent,	18	24	19	1	5	17	5	2	-	-	1	1	-	-	3	4	-	7	
			Robert Pollard, jr.	King & Queen,	70	28	75	8	19	30	18	11	1	4	5	5	1	-	4	4	-	8	Note 13.
			Jas. Roy Micou,	Essex,	60	3	[illegible]	-	10	53	20	8	-	5	4	4	-	-	3	3	-	6	Note 14.

			John S. Healy,	Middlesex,	30	25	55	5	u8	45	24	9	-	1	-	1	-	-	4	2	-	6	Note 15.
				Gloucester,	105	60	123	4	16	69	30	18	-	3	5	2	1	1	5	6	-	11	Note 16.
				Mathews,																			
3	5	John T. Lomax,	Ro T. Dunaway,	Lancaster,	18	26	24	-	5	14	3	5	-	2	3	2	-	-	2	3	-	5	
			J. R. Stith,	Northumberland,	26	20	16	-	2	4	11	5	2	2	4	-	-	-	4	3	-	7	Note 17.
			J. S. Jeffries,	Richmond co.	94	62	107	-	9	34	5	7	-	6	11	3	-	-	3	5	-	8	
			Wm. Hutt,	Wes moreland,	158	104	133	-	10	39	10	10	-	-	1	3	1	-	3	3	-	6	Note 18.
			S. J. S. Brown,	King George,	26	18	27	-	4	22	7	1	-	-	6	2	-	-	2	2	-	4	Note 19.
			Robert Hudgin,	Caroline,	109	90	176	-	25	75	65	11	-	2	3	3	-	1	5	4	-	9	
			John J. Chew,	Spottsylvania,	74	57	102	-	5	485	17	13	3	6	11	6	1	-	7	16	-	23	Note 20.
	6	John Scott,	Wm. F. Phillips,	Fauquier,	217	378	226	-	45	338	189	34	1	-	3	2	6	-	10	12	-	22	Note 21.
			Thos. P. Knox,	Loudoun,	192	200	208	20	32	152	64	19	1	8	5	4	1	-	3	4	7	14	Note 22.
				Prince William,																			
			F. D. Richardson,	Fairfax,	142	154	110	-	35	132	48	24	1	5	-	2	3	-	4	5	-	9	Note 23.
			H. H. Conway,	Stafford,	26	12	30	-	5	16	4	5	-	5	5	11	1	-	4	3	-	7	Note 24.
4	7	Jno. B. Clopton,	P. Poindexter,	Chesterfield,	109	228	124	6	18	89	36	22	2	7	19	5	6	-	9	11	5	25	
			Ro. W. Christian,	Charles City,	17	11	43	-	2	25	9	6	2	1	1	-	-	-	4	4	-	8	Note 25.
			Wm. S. Dance,	Powhatan,	115	123	124	1	11	78	29	23	-	-	1	2	-	-	4	7	4	15	
			Wm. Miller,	Goochland,	100	154	80	-	15	70	27	17	-	-	6	2	-	-	7	5	2	14	
			Phillip B. Winston,	Hanover,	97	155	128	-	21	140	33	6	-	-	6	2	-	1	11	11	-	22	
	21	P. N. Nicholas,	John Robinson,	Henrico and City of Richmond.	153	392	196	-	-	-	-	-	-	10	10	26	13	-	53	54	2	109	Note 26.
	22	John Robertson,	N. P. Howard,	Henrico and City of Richmond,	-	-	-	-	94	1597	196	56	-	-	-	-	-	-	74	25	-	99	
	8	D. A. Wilson,		Cumberland,																			
			Rolfe Eldridge,	Buckingham,	318	240	343	2	53	152	29	32	-	32	20	17	4	-	15	13	-	28	
				Appomattox,																			
			J. D. Alexander,	Campbell,	180	237	168	-	33	146	28	11	-	1	16	1	4	-	7	8	-	15	Note 27.
			Jos. Wilson,	Bedford,	255	293	229	1	42	261	26	12	1	3	8	5	-	-	10	8	-	18	Note 28.
			D. Rodes,	Lynchburg,	89	127	143	11	18	273	91	40	-	8	6	8	-	-	23	30	-	5[illegible]	Note 29.
5	9	William Leigh,	Wm. Holt,	Halifax,	366	57	159	-	40	58	21	35	2	28	58	10	6	-	10	11	-	21	Note 30.
			W. Robinson,	Charlotte,	125	76	146	-	14	44	22	18	2	9	15	2	1	-	5	7	-	12	
			B. J. Worsham,	Prince Edward,	109	88	199	3	26	98	49	29	-	5	7	4	-	-	6	7	-	13	
				Lunenburg,																			
			R. B. Baptist,	Mecklenburg,	189	50	210	-	34	54	29	16	1	25	25	5	6	-	11	8	-	19	Note 31.
	10	N. M. Taliaferro,	J. N. Zentmeyer,	Floyd,	23	19	20	-	12	23	5	4	-	19	20	5	-	-	4	4	-	8	Note 32.
			Sam'l G. Staples,	Patrick,	100	195	73	-	40	75	10	9	2	40	10	28	-	-	9	9	-	18	
			A. M. Dupuy,	Henry,	79	49	72	-	10	46	14	9	1	21	12	14	4	-	7	6	-	13	Note 33.
			M. G. Carper,	Franklin,	221	158	204	-	26	79	52	32	11	69	72	16	8	4	9	8	5	22	Note 34.
			Wm. H. Tunstall,	Pittsylvania,	225	6[illegible]9	28[illegible]	2	48	220	30	51	6	51	134	16	4	-	13	11	-	24	Note 35.

Districts.	Circuits.	JUDGES.	CLERKS.	COUNTIES.	Suits at Law.				Causes in Chancery.					Precutions.					Terms. Days in session.				Remarks of Clerks.
					No. commenced.	No. pending.	No. decided.	No. removed from other courts.	No. commenced.	No. pending.	No. interlocutory decrees.	No. final decrees.	No. removed from county courts.	No. commenced.	No. pending.	No. decided.	No. nolle prosequis.	Change of venue.	Fall.	Spring.	Intermediate.	Total.	
			M. D. Carter,	Carroll,	31	53	42	-	16	20	10	7	1	12	20	26	21	-	4	6	4	14	Note 36.
6	11	R. H. Field,	John Hunter,	Louisa,	8	159	69	-	18	80	26	19	-	12	8	3	4	-	5	7	6	18	Note 37.
			A. Stephen, jr.	Fluvanna,	113	147	216	1	14	50	14	21	3	5	10	1	2	-	5	9	-	14	
			Philip S. Fry,	Orange,	96	121	101	6	21	58	18	17	2	4	4	3	2	-	5	9	-	14	Note 38.
				Greene,																			
			Belfield Cave,	Madison,	36	36	48	6	13	35	13	7	1	-	-	-	-	-	7	6	-	13	
			R. G. Ward,	Culpeper,	73	102	112	2	30	105	44	25	2	12	17	2	2	-	16	12	16	44	Note 39.
			Wm. J. Menifee,	Rappahannock,	21	28	31	1	15	42	19	7	1	2	2	3	-	-	5	7	-	12	
	12	L. P. Thompson,	Robert Tinsley,	Amherst,	168	231	186	4	39	299	118	27	-	11	12	4	2	-	11	9	-	20	
			D. Hutcheson,	Rockbridge,	139	107	117	-	34	127	51	20	2	18	10	13	2	-	10	8	-	18	
			Robert C. Cutler,	Nelson,	181	397	217	-	44	338	105	33	2	6	20	6	7	-	9	11	-	20	Note 40.
			Alex. Garrett,	Albemarle,	214	234	209	-	16	111	19	14	5	25	47	20	15	-	5	12	-	17	Note 41.
			Nich's C. Kinney,	Augusta,	382	419	360	2	54	460	113	33	-	5	22	10	12	-	9	16	-	25	Note 42.
7	13	I. R. Douglass,	R. T. Brown,	Jefferson,	175	122	223	1	47	233	71	45	-	7	19	2	3	1	15	24	-	39	Note 43.
			John Strother,	Berkeley,	130	62	92	-	37	112	-	22	-	1	1	-	-	-	6	6	-	12	
			J. Reichard,	Morgan.	49	40	75	-	9	38	15	9	-	3	7	2	-	1	-	3	-	3	Note 44.
			John B. White,	Hampshire,	125	178	142	2	31	171	42	24	-	11	5	8	2	-	6	8	-	14	Note 45.
			J. Kean,	Frederick,	87	86	87	1	28	322	34	41	-	20	33	4	-	-	4	4	-	8	Note 46.
			H. H. Lee,	Clarke,	38	20	36	-	9	40	20	5	-	7	10	-	-	-	3	3	-	6	Note 47.
	14	Daniel Smith,	Wm. C. Lauck,	Page,	12	13	17	-	4	15	4	4	-	1	1	-	-	-	1	2	-	3	Note 48.
			S. C. Williams,	Shenandoah,	20	15	21	-	5	38	4	11	2	8	8	1	1	-	2	1	-	3	Note 49.
			Robert Turner,	Warren,	38	20	42	3	13	18	7	9	2	2	4	2	-	-	3	3	-	6	Note 50.
			C. Lobb,	Hardy,	63	105	104	1	19	125	16	8	-	4	7	2	1	-	1	4	-	5	
			Z. Dyer,	Pendleton,	27	22	21	-	10	13	2	5	-	7	2	11	1	-	3	2	-	5	
			H. J. Gambill,	Rockingham,	127	108	246	-	24	76	32	21	-	8	9	3	-	-	9	15	-	23	Note 51.
8	15	Benj. Estill,	J. W. S. Morrison.	Lee,	44	69	47	-	10	45	3	5	-	14	13	16	9	-	6	6	-	12	Note 52.
			John S. Martin,	Scott,	37	55	26	-	2	38	19	9	2	22	24	9	-	-	3	3	-	6	Note 53.
			James P. Carroll,	Russell,	26	46	43	-	3	28	5	12	-	37	31	12	2	-	4	4	-	8	Note 54.
			G. W. G. Browne	Tazewell,	58	46	91	-	27	75	19	12	-	22	21	17	12	-	5	4	-	9	Note 55.

			C. F. Trigg,	Washington,	47	63	66	1	28	123	63	13	-	43	35	16	6	-	14	12	-	26	
			A. B. Moore,	Smyth,	49	49	56	-	14	52	40	12	1	16	15	15	4	-	6	4	-	10	
	16	Jas. E, Brown,	J. R. Miller,	Wythe,	32	44	52	-	15	138	14	23	-	13	15	15	3	-	9	3	-	12	
			O. Anderson,	Grayson,	24	21	27	1	8	27	11	7	-	6	6	10	3	-		3	-	6	
			R. D. Montague,	Montgomery,	50	57	60	10	3	59	20	15	-	12	20	7	-	-	3	5	-	11	
				Pulaski,																			
			Rufus A. French,	Giles,	60	43	54	1	8	25	16	6	1	10	13	16	9	-	3	3	-	6	Note 56.
			Allen Mohood,	Mercer,	32	35	36	-	5	21	3	7	-	4	3	1	1	-	2	2	-	4	
			J. Hutchinson,	Monroe,	80	48	71	-	7	70	23	9	-	5	6	16	-	-	5	5	2	12	
9	17	E. Johnson,	H. W. Bowyer,	Botetourt,	95	123	132	-	37	216	21	22	-	7	10	8	-	-	11	11	-	22	
			F. Johnston,	Roanoke,	58	22	29	1	9	27	3	5	2	4	2	2	-	-	6	6	-	12	
			Andrew Fudge,	Alleghany,	28	43	55	-	13	51	14	7	-	1	5	2	-	-	4	3	-	7	
			C. L. Francisco,	Bath,	36	36	95	-	16	70	14	7	-	6	6	-	-	-	5	6	-	11	
				Pocahontas,																			
			John A. North,	Greenbrier,	122	87	251	3	11	88	26	19	-	6	22	16	4	-	7	7	-	14	Note 57.
	18	E. S. Duncan,	H. M. Dickinson,	Fayette,	60	69	94	-	10	41	1	8	2	11	-	9	1	-	7	5	-	12	Note 58.
			Jas. M. Stanard,	Nicholas,	40	27	36	-	7	23	6	1	-	4	7	5	9	-	4	4	-	8	Note 59.
			B. L. Brown,	Randolph,	26	56	40	1	10	67	11	24	-	3	6	7	3	-	4	5	-	9	Note 60.
			E. D. Wilson,	Barbour,	54	70	68	1	17	69	6	20	13	9	12	8	3	-	2	6	-	8	
			John Talbot,	Lewis,	10-	247	205	36	46	239	28	48	1	22	49	22	4	-	8	12	4	24	Note 61.
			W. Newlon,	Braxton,	40	30	42	1	12	36	11	19	-	8	-	-	1	-	3	3	-	6	
			G. G. Davisson,	Harrison,	96	167	156	11	50	206	47	76	-	17	45	18	1	-	22	23	-	45	Note 62.
			E. J. Armstrong,	Taylor,	41	27	33	4	27	33	6	3	-	17	15	3	-	-	2	3	-	5	Note 63.
10	19	D. M'Comas.	J. H. Neal,	Wood,	55	140	49	-	19	135	34	23	-	58	19	44	12	-	5	14	5	24	Note 64.
			T. Stinchcomb,	Ritchie,	30	22	21	-	4	6	-	3	-	12	17	-	-	-	-	2	2	4	Note 65.
			D. G. Morrill,	Jackson,	38	73	46	-	9	36	5	14	-	4	4	5	-	-	5	5	-	10	Note 66.
			G. W. Stribbling,	Mason,	43	37	63	-	2	23	9	13	-	2	2	8	3	-	5	6	-	11	Note 67.
			John Samuels,	Cabell,	10	15	5	3	3	8	5	6	1	28	31	10	2	-	6	8	-	14	
			M. J. Spurlock,	Wayne,	9	5	9	-	8	14	14	6	-	10	14	4	-	-	3	3	-	6	
				Logan,																			
			A. W. Quarrier,	Kanawha,	358	322	559	3	31	131	56	17	-	16	48	26	7	-	18	29	-	47	Note 68.
			Will. Hatcher,	Gilmer,	1	23	5	30	3	12	1	-	-	-	-	-	-	-	-	2	-	2	
	20	Joseph L. Fry,	John P. Bryne,	Preston,	45	50	58	-	21	66	27	8	-	10	10	12	1	-	6	6	-	12	Note 69.
				Monongalia,																			
			James O. Watson,	Marion,	41	50	42	-	21	62	11	13	-	9	21	5	1	-	6	7	-	13	Note 70.
			Jessee Jarvis,	Tyler,																			

Districts.	Circuits.	JUDGES.	CLERKS.	COUNTIES.	SUITS AT LAW.				CAUSES IN CHANCERY.					PROSECUTIONS.					TERMS. Days in Session.				REMARKS OF CLERKS.
					No. commenced.	No. pending.	No. decided.	No removed from other courts.	No. commenced.	No. pending.	No. interlocutory decrees.	No. final decrees.	No. removed from county courts.	No. commenced.	No. pending.	N. decided.	No. nolle prosequis.	Change of venue.	Fall.	Spring.	Intermediate.	Total.	
			James Jarvis,	Doddridge,	7	5	2	-	9	9	2	-	-	-	-	-	-	-	-	1	-	1	Note 71.
			AdamKuhn,	Brooke,	27	39	50	-	15	82	15	19	-	5	8	1	-	-	6	5	-	11	Note 72.
			Alex. T. Laidley,	Ohio,	102	125	84	1	47	201	46	44		7	7	4	-	-	10	17	26	53	Note 73.
			James D. Morris.	Marshall,	26	31	30	-	13	76	11	29	1	3	4	1	-	-	5	7	-	12	Note 74.
				Total,	9994	10971	11888	277	3104	12474	3911	1867	98	1139	1530	861	307	9	890	895	92	1883	

GEORGE W. MUNFORD, *C. H. D.*

December 9th, 1845.

RECAPITULATION.

CIRCUIT SUPERIOR COURTS OF LAW AND CHANCERY,

Exhibiting the Number of Suits, &c., in each Circuit, August 30th, 1845.

Districts.	Circuits.	No. counties, towns and cities in each circuit.	JUDGES.	Suits at Law.				Causes in Chancery.					Prosecutions.					Terms. Days in Session.				Miles Travelling.			REMARKS.
				No. commenced.	No. pending.	No. decided.	No. removed from other courts.	No. commenced.	No. pending.	No. interlocutory decrees.	No. final decrees.	No. removed from county courts.	No. commenced.	No. pending.	No. decided.	No. nolle prosequis.	Change of venue.	Fall.	Spring.	Intermediate.	Total.	To general court.	In circuit.	Total.	
1	1	8	Richard H. Baker,	710	378	850	17	94	94	108	79	2	27	32	52	11	-	43	48	-	91	224	255	479	
	2	7	Jas. H. Gholson,	461	424	538	6	112	398	186	120	2	38	85	77	42	-	83	34	-	117	150	38	530	
2	3	6	Thos. H. Bayly,	197	343	261	52	44	331	84	48	7	18	39	6	4	-	32	34	-	66	440	407	847	
	4	7	John B. Christian,	349	202	435	18	70	258	118	64	2	17	15	14	3	1	24	25	-	49	120	230	350	No return from the cl'k of Mathews co.
3	5	7	John T. Lomax,	505	377	585	-	60	673	118	52	5	18	39	19	2	1	26	36	-	62	140	218	358	
	6	5	John Scott,	577	744	574	20	117	638	305	82	3	18	13	19	11	-	21	24	7	52	220	200	420	No returns from the cl'k of Pr. Wm. co.
4	7	5	John B. Clopton,	441	671	499	7	67	4 2	134	74	4	8	43	11	6	1	35	38	11	84	12	182	194	
	21	2	P. N. Nicholas,	153	392	196	-	-	-	-	-	-	10	10	26	13	-	53	54	2	109				
	22	2	John Robertson,	-	-	-	-	94	1597	196	56	-	-	-	-	-	-	74	25	-	99				
	8	6	Daniel A. Wilson,	482	897	883	14	146	832	1 4	95	1	44	50	31	8	-	55	59	-	114	240	180	420	No returns from the cl'ks of the counties of Cumberland and Appomattox.
5	9	5	William Leigh,	789	371	714	3	114	254	121	98	5	67	105	31	13	-	32	33	-	65	260	165	425	
	10	6	N. M. Taliaferro,	679	1083	692	2	152	463	121	112	21	212	268	105	37	4	46	44	9	99	390	265	655	
6	11	7	Richard H. Field,	422	593	577	16	111	370	134	96	8	35	42	12	10	-	43	50	22	115	206	308	514	No rturn from the clerk of the county of Greene.

Districts.	Circuits.	No. counties, towns and cities in each circuit.	JUDGES.	Suits at Law.				Causes in Chancery.					Prosecutions.					Terms. Days in Session.				Miles Travelling.			REMARKS.
				No. commenced.	No. pending.	No. decided.	No. removed from other courts.	No. commenced.	No. pending.	No. interlocutory decrees.	No. final decrees.	No. removed from county courts.	No. commenced.	No. pending.	No. decided.	No. nolle prosequis.	Change of venue.	Fall.	Spring.	Intermediate.	Total.	To general court.	In circuit.	Total.	
	12	5	Lucas P. Thomson	1084	1285	1090	6	187	1335	1276	127	9	65	111	53	38	-	44	56	-	110	242	240	482	
7	13	6	I. R. Douglass,	604	508	655	4	161	916	182	146	-	49	75	16	5	2	34	48	-	82	320	200	520	
	14	6	Daniel Smith,	287	283	451	4	75	285	65	58	4	39	31	19	3	-	19	27	-	45	268	257	525	
8	15	6	Benjamin Estill,	261	328	329	1	84	361	149	58	3	159	149	85	33	-	38	33	-	71	618	270	888	
	16	7	James E. Brown,	27	248	300	12	46	340	87	67	1	50	63	65	16	-	28	21	2	50	514	309	823	No return from the clerk of the county of Pulaski.
9	17	6	Edward Johnston,	349	311	562	4	86	453	78	60	2	24	45	28	4	-	33	33	2	66	330	241	571	No return from the clerk of the county of Pocahontas.
	18	8	Edwin S. Duncan,	465	693	674	54	179	714	116	190	16	91	134	72	22	-	52	61	4	117	590	363	953	
10	19	9	David M'Comas,	5 44	537	757	36	79	365	120	72	1	130	135	97	24	-	42	69	7	118	640	412	1052	No return from the clerk of the county of Logan.
	20	8	Joseph L. Fry,	248	300	266	1	126	496	112	104	2	34	50	23	2	-	33	43	26	102	714	300	1014	No return from cl'ks of the counties of Monongalia and Tyler.
10	22	134	Total,	9994	10971	11888	277	3104	12474	3911	1867	98	1139	1534	861	307	9	89[illegible]	395	92	1883	6638	5382	1220	
			Average of circuits.	476	522	566	13	143	593	186	89	4	54	73	41	14		40	40	4	85	336	269	601	

Judgments at law, - -	11,888	Number of appeals allowed, - -	144	being nearly five sixths of one per cent. of
Interlocutory decrees, - -	3,911	Causes decided in the court of appeals,	123	[the total decisions in circuit courts.
Final decrees, - - -	1,867			
		Excess of new appeals over decisious,	24	
Total decisions from which appeals may be had,	17,666			

December 9th, 1843.

[*E. E.*]

GEORGE W. MUNFORD, *C. H. D.*

REMARKS OF CLERKS.

FIRST CIRCUIT.

(*Note* 1.)—GREENESVILLE.—Judgments on forthcoming bonds are included, but dismissions at rules are not. One chancery cause has been removed from this court.

(*Note* 2.)—SURRY.—Of the number of suits at law stated to have been decided, two were motions on forthcoming bonds.

(*Note* 3.)—ISLE OF WIGHT.—In this report I have included dismissions at rules, and left out judgments on all motions.

(*Note* 4.)—NANSEMOND.—All judgments on motions, judgments confessed in the office; all dismissions in court or otherwise, and office judgments confirmed, are embraced in the number of suits decided at law.

(*Note* 5.)—PRINCESS ANNE.—Judgments on forthcoming bonds. dismissions at rules, judgments on motions for money paid as security, and one case of divorce, are included under the head of suits decided and final decrees.

(*Note* 6.)—NORFOLK CITY—In the column of suits commenced at law, 11 motions on forthcoming bonds, &c., are included. In the number decided at law, dismissions at rules are included. In the number of final decrees in chancery, dismissions at rules are also included.

SECOND CIRCUIT.

(*Note* 7.)—DINWIDDIE.—Judgments on motions not embraced.

(*Note* 8.)—NOTTOWAY.—Judgments on motions not embraced in this report. Abatements and dismissions at rules and in court included in the number of decisions.

(*Note* 9.)—AMELIA.—Of the number of suits at law, 39 are upon the issue docket, and the remainder at rules.

(*Note* 10.)—PRINCE GEORGE.—In this return, motions on delivery bonds are not included.

(*Note* 11.)—PETERSBURG.—Wise and judicious legislation (in combination with other causes) has demolished litigation throughout the country, and almost produced a state of pauperism among the respectable fraternity of clerks of courts and members of the bar generally.

FOURTH CIRCUIT.

(*Note* 12.)—KING WILLIAM.—Motions on forthcoming bonds are not included in this list; but all dismissions are embraced in suits reported as decided.

(*Note* 13.)—KING & QUEEN.—52 motions on forthcoming bonds.

(*Note* 14.)—ESSEX.—Of the law suits pending, 33 are new suits on the office judgment docket for the present fall term, and 20 are on the issue docket. I did not include in the 43 pending, one rule against a petit juror who failed to attend, and 4 rules against witnesses. The number decided embraces all office judgments confirmed, judgments confessed in the clerk's office, and judgments on forthcoming bonds. In chancery one of those commenced was dismissed at rules. I have included in the interlocutory decrees all orders suggesting deaths, entering revivals appointing guardians *ad litem*, and taking leave to file amended bills. Among the 8 decided, there are some dismissals, two causes were consolidated, and one decree was rendered in them unitedly.

(*Note* 15.)—MIDDLESEX.—Judgments on forthcoming bonds are not included in this report.

(*Note* 16.)—GLOUCESTER.—The suits and causes pending are those on the court docket. Those decided include dismissions. The suits at law removed, are from the county court. The interlocutory decrees include all orders not final.

FIFTH CIRCUIT.

(*Note* 17.)—NORTHUMBERLAND.—*State of Virginia*, *Dr.*
1845...To *J. R. Stith*,
To making out lists of suits from Northumberland superior court clerk's office, $4.

(*Note* 18.)—WESTMORELAND.—Motions not included in this return. Among the final decrees, dismissions at rules are included.

(*Note* 19.)—KING GEORGE. Judgments on forthcoming bonds not included. I have also not included among the interlocutory decrees, simple orders making new parties, &c.

(*Note* 20.)—SPOTTSYLVANIA.—Refer to former reports for remarks in relation to the number of causes pending on the chancery docket.

SIXTH CIRCUIT.

(*Note* 21.)—FAUQUIER.—69 common law and 3 chancery motions not included in this statement.

(*Note* 22.)—LOUDOUN.—An intermediate term of seven days was held in January. 57 judgments on motions not included in this report.

(*Note* 23.)—FAIRFAX.—Judgments on forthcoming bonds and on notices not included.

(*Note* 24.)—STAFFORD.—This list includes one appeal on contested will, three motions on forthcoming bonds, and two criminal prosecutions.

SEVENTH CIRCUIT.

(*Note* 25.)—CHARLES CITY.—The number of days includes an intermediate term 29th May. Nothing to say but what I have before said.

TWENTY-FIRST CIRCUIT.

(*Note* 26.)—HENRICO AND CITY OF RICHMOND.—Of the suits commenced, 5 are writs of *scire facias*. 3 writs of *supersedeas*, 1 *caveat*, and 7 appeals from decisions of the auditor of public accounts. Among the number of suits decided, judgments on forthcoming bonds are included, as well as judgments by confessions in the office, also nonsuits and dismissions in court, and exclusive of judgments entered pursuant to decisions of court of appeals. Number of prosecutions decided include several abatements by death, and a trial of a convict for rebellion and murder in the penitentiary. The special session was held for the trial of said convict for murder in penitentiary.

EIGHTH CIRCUIT.

(*Note* 27.)—CAMPBELL.—In addition to the number of suits decided at law, there were 28 judgments on delivery bonds, and in addition to the number of final decrees in chancery, there was one judgment on a delivery bond. The number of suits commenced includes all *scire facias* and motions, except for judgments on delivery bonds. We are still very much pressed for time, as it is impossible to do the business in the time now prescribed.

(*Note* 28.—BEDFORD.—Of the causes pending on the law docket, 134 were upon the court docket and 159 at rules. Of chancery causes, 112 on the court docket and 149 at rules. Judgments on forthcoming bonds are not included in this list, these judgments are 106 in number. Judgments against garnishees are not inclnded, 35 in number.

(*Note* 29.)—LYNCHBURG.—There was a special session of the court in January, but the number of days are not seperated from the fall term in the report of the clerk.

NINTH CIRCUIT.

(*Note* 30.)—HALIFAX.—Suits at law decided, include office judgments and dismissions. Those pending are such on the court docket 1st September 1845. Suits in chancery decided include dismissions.

(*Note* 31.)—MECKLENBURG.—Motions on forfeited forthcoming bonds are not embraced n this report.

TENTH CIRCUIT.

(*Note* 32)—FLOYD.—Judgments on forfeited forthcoming bonds not included—neithe have I taken into the account several rules made against sheriffs for failing to return process, and against jurors and witnesses for failing to attend when summoned. The number of suits at law embraces three *supersedeases* to judgments of the county court of Floyd.

(*Note* 33.)—HENRY.—Judgments on forfeited forthcoming bonds, suits dismissed at rules, and abatements by the sheriff's returns, are not included in the list of causes determined. Of the commonwealth's cases decided, two were prosecutions for felony.

(*Note* 34.)—FRANKLIN.—In addition to the number of suits decided at law, there were 70 motions and judgments on forthcoming bonds; and 17 other motions and judgments, which are not included in the number of suits at law reported as decided. There was also a prisoner arraigned, tried and convicted of larceny at the fall term of 1844.

(*Note* 35.)—PITTSYLVANIA.—The number of law cases pending is constituted of 225 new causes, 75 on the issue docket, 28 on the rule docket, 149 office judgments, 32 motions on, forfeited forthcoming bonds, and 100 other judgments in cases that were on the issue docket. The number of chancery cases are 46 new causes, 93 on issue docket, 13 on rule docket and 51 final decrees. *Query.*—Is the benefit derived by the people from these reports equal to the amount paid for postage and printing them.

(*Note* 36.)—CARROLL.—The case in the column of cases removed from county courts, was removed from the superior court of Pulaski county.

ELEVENTH CIRCUIT.

(*Note* 37.)—LOUISA.—Of the number decided at law, 35 were office judgments. There were 37 motions commenced and decided, 7 dismissions were entered in court, and 14 dismissions and abatements were entered in the office at rules.

(*Note* 38.)—ORANGE.—Judgments on forthcoming bonds not included.

(*Note* 39.)—CULPEPER.—27 judgments on forthcoming bonds included among suits decided.

TWELFTH CIRCUIT.

(*Note* 40.)—NELSON.—Among the judgments at law, and final decrees in chancery, are embraced a number of judgments on delivery bonds, and on other motions, &c.

(*Note* 41.)—ALBEMARLE.—The judge was sick at the spring term.

(*Note* 42.)—AUGUSTA.—In the number of suits commenced on the law side of the court, is included 94 forthcoming bonds, 2 suits removed, and 1 writ of *supersedeas*, leaving 285 suits commenced by writs of *capias ad respondendum*. In the number decided is included 94 forthcoming bonds.

THIRTEENTH CIRCUIT.

(*Note* 43.)—JEFFERSON.—In the number of common law suits decided, 46 judgments on forfeited forthcoming bonds and 15 suits dismissed at rules are included.

(*Note* 44.—MORGAN.—The courthouse having been destroyed by fire and no place established according to law, the court could not hold its term in October 1844. In this report are comprised all office judgments, not set aside, awards of executions on forthcoming bonds, causes agreed and those dismissed, as well as judgments confessed in the clerk's office.

(*Note* 45.)—HAMPSHIRE—Of the suits commenced, 4 are writs of *scire facias*. No notice of forthcoming bonds. Of the chancery causes depending, 88 are on the trial docket, 65 on the deferred issue docket, and 18 at the rules.

(*Note* 46)—FREDERICK.—Of the chancery causes pending, 203 are found on the deferred docket, of which about 150 are old suits; most, if not all of which descended from the old district chancery court, and have been permitted to sleep by the parties and their counsel until this time. Among the chancery causes decided, the decrees on forthcoming bonds are included. On the law side of this court 26 judgments on forthcoming bonds were rendered.

(*Note* 47.)—CLARKE.—Judgments on forthcoming bonds, 18.

FOURTEENTH CIRCUIT.

(*Note* 48.)—PAGE.—Charles Brown, charged with forgery, was sent on to the circuit superior court by a court of examination, for further trial, but broke jail before an indictment was found against him, and has not been retaken.

(*Note* 49.)—SHENANDOAH.—There were executions awarded on six forthcoming bonds, which are not included in the table.

(*Note* 50.)—WARREN.—There were within the year 17 judgments on forfeited forthcoming bonds, which are not included in this report.

(*Note* 51.)—ROCKINGHAM.—Dismissions, office judgments and judgments on delivery bonds, are included among the number of suits decided.

FIFTEENTH CIRCUIT.

(*Note* 52.—LEE.—The court generally commences at an early hour, and adjourns late in the evening. But business is transacted with industry and despatch. Suits decided and final decrees include dismissions, but exclude judgments on delivery bonds.

(*Note* 53.)—SCOTT.—Suits commenced include one *scire facias*, those pending two issues out of chancery and one *scire facias;* and in those determined, judgments on delivery bonds and rules against witnesses and jurors are not enumerated

(*Note* 54.)—RUSSELL.—The greater number of the causes here enumerated, both at law and in chancery, stand on the rule docket. The judge has decided in all the causes that were ready for trial during each session of the court. Office judgments and judgments on forthcoming bonds are included with the causes decided at law, and dismissions at rules with those decided in chancery.

SIXTEENTH CIRCUIT.

(*Note* 55.)—TAZEWELL.—Judgments on forthcoming bonds and dismissions included.

(*Note* 56.)—GILES.—Judgments on forfeited forthcoming bonds not embraced. But few causes on the chancery docket ready for final decrees. The duty enjoined by the legislature upon the clerks in preparing reports similar to the one now presented. is an onorous one, and especially so when no benefit to the country can possibly accrue therefrom. The object contemplated in the passage of the law was to exhibit the delinquency of the judges, if such delinquency existed on their or the part of any of them. Existing or not, how can the evil be remedied? The law should be repealed, as it is certainly a useless one. If, however, our lawgivers still deem it to be an important enactment, and will retain it upon the statute book, ought not the officer making the report, be paid? or the penalty consequent upon his failure to perform the duty imposed upon him, should not be inflicted.

SEVENTEENTH CIRCUIT.

(*Note* 57.)—GREENBRIER.—In the number of law suits decided, office judgments, dismissions at rules and in court are included. The three suits removed from other courts are appeals from the judgments of the county courts.

EIGHTEENTH CIRCUIT.

(*Note* 58.)—FAYETTE.—Judgments on forfeited forthcoming bonds and notices, also decrees of sales of forfeited lands not included in this report.

(*Note* 59.)—NICHOLAS.—This report embraces all judgments, decrees, suits pending at rules, or on the court docket, with the exception of decrees for the sale of delinquent and forfeited land and dismissions at rules. If such reports be important why not allow the clerks pay for it, as it is troublesome?

(*Note* 60.)—RANDOLPH.—Judgments on forthcoming bonds, confessions in the office and dismissions in court are included amongst the causes decided at law—also one case at law transferred to Barbour county. Amongst the causes decided in chancery 11 were transferred to Barbour county.

(*Note* 61.)—LEWIS—In the number of suits decided at law I have not included judgments on forthcoming bonds, all other motions are included. In the number of final decrees I have not included forthcoming bonds and causes dismissed by the parties. On the 16th September an intermediate term was held by the judge for the trial of chancery causes alone, which continued four days, which are not included in the number of days reported at the fall term

(*Note* 62.)—Harrison.—Motions, rules and decrees against delinquent and forfeited lands not included in this report.

(*Note* 63.)—Taylor.—Suits commenced include 2 writs of supersedeas. Suits decided do not include judgments on forthcoming bonds and by confession in the office.

NINETEENTH CIRCUIT.

(*Note* 64.)—Wood.—Motions on bonds not included either as suits commenced or decided.

(*Note* 65.)—Ritchie.—There was no court at the regular time in the fall of 1844, but we had a special term in November, so that we have had 3 terms since my last report.

(*Note* 66.)—Jackson.—There is not time enough to transact the business of our court between the Wood county and Mason circuit courts.

(*Note* 67.)—Mason.—The column for suits decided and final decrees include dismissions, but exclude judgments on forthcoming bonds. In the column of suits commenced is one writ of supersedeas.

(*Note* 68.)—Kanawha.—The number pending includes old suits at rules. The number decided at law includes judgments on forthcoming bonds and dismissions.

TWENTIETH CIRCUIT.

(*Note* 69.)—Preston.—Law business declining in this county. Fifteen judgments on forthcoming bonds not included in this report.

(*Note* 70.)—Marion—Judgments on forthcoming bonds and other motions not included. Four causes included in the number commenced in chancery were removed from the circuit superior court for Harrison by order of that conrt. Five days of the spring term were taken up in trying three criminals charged with burglary and larceny, and one for murder, two of which were convicted. Cannot the legislature allow the clerks something for making these reports, as it is a very troublesome job, and the present allowances are small?

(*Note* 71.)—Doddridge.—Court organized on the 30th April 1845.

(*Note* 72.)—Brooke.—Of the 50 suits at law decided 9 were judgments on forthcoming bonds.

(*Note* 73.)—Ohio.—Causes at rules are included in those pending.

(*Note* 74.)—Marshall.—Judgments on forthcoming bonds not included. Causes pending embrace those at rules.

ABSTRACT

FROM THE

REPORTS OF THE CLERKS

OF THE

COURT OF APPEALS

AND OF THE

CIRCUIT SUPERIOR COURTS OF LAW AND CHANCERY

FOR THE

YEAR ENDING 30th AUGUST, 1846.

ABSTRACT FROM THE REPORTS

OF THE

CLERKS OF THE COURT OF APPEALS,

AND OF THE

CIRCUIT SUPERIOR COURTS OF LAW AND CHANCERY,

For the Year ending the 30th August, 1846; *exhibiting the number of Suits, &c.*

COURT OF APPEALS.

JUDGES.	CLERKS.	Location of Court.	Suits commenced.	Pending.	Decided.	No. of days in session.	REMARKS.
Wm. H. Cabell, *President*. Francis T. Brooke, - Robert Stanard, (dead,) - John J. Allen, - -	Joseph Allen,	Richmond, -	74	504	84	160	The term of the court commenced on the 15th of October 1845, and ended on the 14th May 1846, comprising 160 days, having had within that time two recesses, one of 25 days and the other of 26 days; and having actually sat 137 days, exclusive of Sundays, comprised withn the time of its sessions, and three days on which there were not a sufficient number of judges present to oonstitute a court.
Briscoe G. Baldwin, -	John A. North,	Lewisburg, -	59	129	68	64	
		Total,	133	633	152	224	

CIRCUIT SUPERIOR COURTS OF LAW AND CHANCERY.

Districts.	Circuits.	JUDGES.	CLERKS.	COUNTIES.	Suits at Law. No. commenced.	Suits at Law. No. pending.	Suits at Law. No. decided.	Suits at Law. No. removed from other courts.	Causes in Chancery. No. commenced.	Causes in Chancery. No. pending.	Causes in Chancery. No. interlocutory decrees.	Causes in Chancery. No. final decrees.	Causes in Chancery. No. removed from county courts.	Prosecutions. No. commenced.	Prosecutions. No. pending.	Prosecutions. No. decided.	Prosecutions. Nolle prosequis.	Prosecutions. Change of venue.	Terms. Days in session. Fall.	Terms. Days in session. Spring.	Terms. Days in session. Intermediate.	Terms. Days in session. Total.	REMARKS.
1st	1st	Rh'd H. Baker,	L. R. Edwards,	Southampton,	129	135	89	-	17	40	24	13	-	5	9	3	-	-	4	2	-	4	
			Joseph Turner,	Greenesville,	39	24	45	-	5	11	6	12	-	2	-	1	1	-	2	2	-	4	Note 1.
			W. P. Underwood	Surry,	14	21	8	-	3	12	6	6	-	1	1	-	-	-	2	-	-	2	Note 2.
			N. P. Young,	Isle of Wight,	55	60	13	-	5	16	11	5	-	4	7	3	-	-	3	-	-	3	Note 3.
			Joseph Prentiss,	Nansemond,	31	23	37	-	11	19	5	3	-	2	3	5	2	-	8	5	-	13	Note 4.
			J. J. Burroughs,	Princess Anne,	40	53	25	-	2	13	3	2	-	-	3	-	-	-	3	-	-	3	Note 5.
			John Williams,	Norfolk City,	171	177	90	-	30	72	10	20	2	4	3	6	-	-	12	5	-	17	Note 6.
			Art. Emmerson,	Norfolk county,	211	37	176	1	26	27	15	14	1	7	9	11	1	-	12	16	-	28	
	2d	J. H. Gholson,	John P. Crump,	Dinwiddie,	56	34	62	1	24	54	25	18	3	9	10	1	3	.	4	4	-	8	Note 7.
			F. Fitzgerald,	Nottoway,	45	32	66	-	8	29	14	8	-	4	6	-	2		2	2	-	4	
			Egbert G. Leigh,	Amelia,	68	59	90	-	5	35	21	18	1	4	8	4	-		3	3	-	6	
			E. R. Turnbull,	Brunswick,	39	30	56	1	9	35	15	15	1	21	22	12	8	•	6	4	-	10	
			J. T. J. Mason,	Sussex,	30	26	28	-	3	10	3	5	-	5	2	3	-	-	2	1	-	3	
			Robert Gilliam,	Prince George,	17	5	24	-	13	14	10	5	1	6	4	3	2	-	3	2	-	5	
			Henry B. Gaines,	Petersburg,	170	243	158	7	44	180	72	53	6	18	31	14	3	-	21	24	-	45	
2d	3d	Th. H. Bayly,	Thos. O. Cogbill,	James City and Williamsburg,	76	75	91	2	20	125	65	40	-	8	4	6	2	-	13	14	-	27	
			Alex'r Garrett,	York,	28	50	15	13	2	20	7	1	-	-	3	-	-	-	5	-	1	6	Note 8.
			Wm. Robertson,	Warwick,	19	19	14	-	4	11	7	2	-	-	-	-	-	-	1	2	-	3	
			W. S. Armistead,	Elizabeth City,	29	11	43	-	1	19	9	6	1	2	2	5	1	-	5	2	-	7	Note 9.
			L. P. Rogers,	Northampton,	31	30	26	1	5	30	12	8	-	3	2	1	-	-	6	4	-	10	
			Thos. R. Joynes,	Accomack,	53	59	55	7	12	95	42	31	3	5	16	5	2	-	17	12	-	29	
	4th	J. B. Christian,	Robert Pollard,	King William,	50	25	41	1	7	50	37	13	1	-	-	-	-	-	5	6	5	16	Note 10.
			J. D. Christian,	New Kent,	6	21	12	2	7	24	14	4	-	3	2	-	1	-	6	3	-	9	
			Rob. Pollard, jr.	King and Queen,	29	25	43	2	10	39	14	11	4	2	3	5	1	-	4	4	-	8	Note 11.
			J. Roy Micou, jr.	Essex,	86	93	72	1	11	42	13	21	-	9	9	4	-	-	4	3	-	7	Note 12.
			John S. Healy,	Middlesex,	34	27	26	3	9	45	31	10	-	-	-	1	-	-	3	2	-	5	Note 13.

			John R. Cary,	Gloucester,	116	77	89	-	19	68	27	17	-	8	3	11	2	-	6	6	-	12	Note 14.
			Shep. G. Miller,	Mathews,	17	26	29	5	9	87	21	6	1	-	-	5	-	-	3	3	-	6	
3d	5th	J. T. Lomax,	R. [illegible] Dunaway,	Lancaster,	22	8	19	-	8	9	2	10	-	-	1	1	-	-	2	2	-	4	Note 15.
			J. L. Stith,	Northumberland	27	8	16	-	2	10	7	3	1	-	2	1	-	-	2	2	-	4	Note 16.
			J. S. Jeffries,	Richmond co'ty,	75	58	82	-	9	40	11	2	3	4	8	6	2	-	4	5	-	9	
			William Hutt.	Westmoreland,	157	111	150	-	25	52	24	12	-	5	1	5	-	-	5	5	-	10	Note 17.
			Wm. S. Brown,	King George,	21	20	20	-	13	29	6	6	-	7	8	4	-	-	3	2	-	5	Note 18.
			Robert Hudgin,	Caroline,	169	104	164	-	12	60	55	14	-	24	8	21	-	-	6	5	-	11	
			John J. Chew,	Spottsylvania,	60	65	70	-	15	473	28	12	-	9	14	8	4	19	17	-	-	36	Note 19.
			Wm. F. Phillips,	Fauquier,	197	373	226	-	76	391	157	39	2	3	5	1	-	-	2	18	-	20	Note 20.
	6th	John Scott,	Thos. P. Knox,	Loudoun,	151	192	163	-	35	150	73	37	1	3	5	3	-	-	5	10	-	15	Note 21.
				Prince William,	-	-	-	-	-	-	-	-	-	-	-	-	-	-	-	-	-	-	Note 22.
			F. D. Richardson,	Fairfax,	100	161	98	2	50	133	73	38	0	6	-	5	1	-	5	5	-	10	Note 23.
			H. H. Conway,	Stafford,	9	10	10	1	15	24	8	8	-	4	5	3	-	-	1	3	-	4	Note 24.
	7th	J. B. Clopton,	P. Poindexter,	Chesterfield,	97	263	80	-	14	102	14	13	3	14	15	6	11	-	12	11	-	23	
4th			E. T. Christian,	Charles City,	9	22	14	2	1	23	-	1	-	3	1	-	2	-	2	2	-	4	
			Wm. S. Dance,	Powhatan,	76	78	121	1	13	79	16	12	2	-	1	1	-	-	10	8	-	18	Note 25.
			Nar. W Miller,	Goochland,	79	98	87	-	10	62	21	18	1	2	1	2	1	-	10	7	-	17	Note 26.
			Phil. B. Winston,	Hanover,	66	169	46	-	28	150	39	20	2	5	6	2	3	-	11	10	-	21	
	21st	P. N. Nicholas,	John Robinson,	Henrico and city of Richmond,	128	364	187	-	-	-	-	-	-	37	5	30	12	-	55	54	1	110	Note 27.
	22d	J. Robertson,	N. P. Howard,	Henrico and City of Richmond,	-	-	-	-	99	1592	211	88	2	-	-	-	-	-	77	26	18	121	Note 28.
	8th	D. A. Wilson,	B. B. Woodson,	Cumberland,	88	49	99	-	6	71	19	26	1	2	18	12	-	-	6	7	-	13	
			Rolfe Eldridge,	Buckingham,	197	285	304	1	46	160	27	43	3	7	15	8	7	-	14	12	-	26	
			H. F. Bocock,	Appomattox,	59	25	31	14	15	13	1	1	-	10	9	-	-	1	3	5	-	8	Note 29.
			J. D. Alexander,	Campbell,	158	210	153	-	27	139	5	15	-	2	11	3	1	-	9	2	5	16	Note 30.
			Joseph Wilson,	Bedford,	188	207	278	4	26	253	39	42	8	39	32	15	-	-	9	10	-	19	Note 31.
			David Rodes,	Lynchburg,	90	125	120	4	15	288	52	22	-	12	16	5	-	-	31	24	-	55	
5th	9th	William Leigh,	William Holt,	Halifax,	209	159	270	-	55	115	34	33	4	18	59	28	8	-	13	13	-	26	
			W. Robinson,	Charlotte,	102	75	103	-	15	45	25	14	-	5	7	13	-	-	5	5	-	10	
			B. J. Worsham,	Prince Edward,	112	76	156	2	25	104	48	25	5	6	8	3	-	-	5	5	-	10	
			Thos. W. Winn,	Lunenburg,	64	50	51	-	6	50	-	25	-	7	8	3	1	-	3	3	-	6	Note 32.
			R. B. Baptist,	Mecklenburg,	142	109	171	-	20	94	41	29	2	18	34	14	17	-	12	11	-	23	Note 33.
	10th	N M Taliaferro	John Zentmeyer,	Floyd,	33	18	36	1	10	28	10	6	-	17	15	18	3	-	4	4	-	8	
			Sam. G. Staples,	Patrick,	76	87	84	-	12	47	25	19	3	23	25	21	-	-	8	7	-	15	
			Ant'y M. Dupuy,	Henry,	110	28	99	-	6	49	16	4	2	4	7	11	-	-	4	6	-	10	Note 34.
			M. G. Carper,	Franklin,	159	169	149	1	23	87	37	21	5	13	24	36	25	-	9	7	-	16	Note 35.
			W. H. Tunstall,	Pittsylvania,	124	353	234	1	34	191	29	53	3	25	42	37	15	-	10	10	-	20	
			M. D. Carter,	Carroll,	51	28	58	-	10	22	20	9	-	23	26	17	1	-	6	6	-	12	

Districts.	Circuits.	JUDGES.	CLERKS.	COUNTIES.	Suits at Law. No. commenced.	Suits at Law. No. pending.	Suits at Law. No. decided.	Suits at Law. No. removed from other courts.	Causes in Chancery. No. commenced.	Causes in Chancery. No. pending.	Causes in Chancery. No. interlocutory decrees.	Causes in Chancery. No. final decrees.	Causes in Chancery. No. removed from county courts.	Prosecutions. No. commenced.	Prosecutions. No. pending.	Prosecutions. No. decided.	Prosecutions. No. nolle prosequis	Prosecutions. Change of venue.	Terms. Days in session. Fall	Terms. Days in session. Spring.	Terms. Days in session. Intermediate.	Terms. Days in session. Total.	REMARKS.
6th	11th	Rd. H. Field,	John Hunter,	Louisa,	86	160	65	1	16	70	23	13	1	4	5	8	3	1	9	6	2	17	Note 36.
			A. Shepherd,	Fluvanna,	105	96	189	.	16	42	18	19	1	5	8	7	1	.	6	6	.	12	
			P. S. Fry,	Orange,	78	141	118	2	13	54	19	19	4	7	9	2	.	.	8	11	.	19	Note 37.
			Rob't Pritchett,	Greene,	37	28	29	2	9	19	12	4	.	2	.	2	.	.	4	3	.	7	
			Belfield Cave,	Madison,	54	46	56	3	10	40	18	7	.	1	2	.	.	.	6	5	.	11	
			R. G. Ward,	Culpeper,	48	83	70	1	18	99	44	20	.	4	14	4	4	.	16	11	6	33	Note 38.
			Wm. J. Menefee,	Rappahannock,	17	24	24	2	5	36	23	11	1	5	3	2	1	.	6	6	20	32	
	12th	L.P Thompson	Robert Tinsley,	Amherst,	156	221	166	2	23	303	82	19	.	3	9	5	1	.	13	12	.	25	
			Saml. M'D. Reid,	Rockbridge,	100	79	127	.	44	149	55	22	2	17	13	14	1	.	9	13	.	22	
			Rob. C. Cutler,	Nelson,	140	312	279	.	32	342	177	32	3	8	22	8	3	.	11	8	.	19	Note 39.
			Alex. Garrett,	Albemarle,	232	378	214	.	24	136	27	26	6	57	55	37	21	.	15	16	.	31	
			N. C. Kinney,	Augusta,	264	375	317	9	47	458	126	49	.	21	35	5	3	.	13	20	.	33	Note 40.
7th	13th	I. R. Douglass,	Rob't T. Brown,	Jefferson,	154	156	206	.	47	282	72	34	.	17	22	16	2	.	23	15	.	38	
			John Strother,	Berkeley,	96	78	117	.	41	116	.	21	.	6	2	.	.	.	6	6	.	12	
			Jacob Reichard,	Morgan,	46	86	79		11	37	16	4	.	4	5	7	.	.	3	3	.	6	
			John B. White,	Hampshire,	127	152	118	.4	37	189	49	24	.	5	12	3	1	.	5	5	.	10	Note 41.
			J. Kean,	Frederick,	81	108	45	.	40	215	48	27	1	4	35	5	2	.	5	5	.	10	Note 42.
			H. H. Lee,	Clarke,	32	46	35	.	8	40	19	10	.	9	7	8	.	.	5	4	.	9	Note 43.
	14th	Daniel Smith,	W. C. Lauck,	Page,	9	10	12	.	3	16	8	3	1	3	2	1	1	.	2	1	.	3	
			S. C. Williams,	Shenandoah,	19	11	20	.	2	35	11	6	1	6	4	9	1	.	2	3	.	5	Note 44.
			Robert Turner,	Warren,	18	12	26	1	10	19	6	10	1	1	2	2	1	.	2	2	.	4	Note 45.
			C. Lobb,	Hardy,	35	48	21	.	14	119	22	13	.	1	7	3	1	.	3	2	.	5	
			Z. Dyer,	Pendleton,	17	19	11	.	5	16	3	2	.	17	1	6	11	.	2	4	.	6	
			H. J. Gambill,	Rockingham,	76	88	99	1	6	57	30	18	1	8	7	4	2	.	8	12	.	20	
8th	15th	Benj. Estill,	J. W. Morrison,	Lee,	30	69	33	.	11	53	8	10	.	17	6	9	3	.	6	6	.	12	Note 46.
			S. H. Morrison,	Scott,	37	65	47	.	6	20	11	7	.	10	21	11	1	.	4	4	.	8	Note 47.
			James P. Carroll,	Russell,	33	50	44	.	7	19	5	6	.	35	37	25	3	.	4	4	.	8	Note 48.
			G. W. G. Browne,	Tazewell,	45	49	76	.	19	73	34	25	.	31	32	19	6	.	4	5	.	9	Note 49.

			Con'ly F. Trigg,	Washington,	31	62	40	1	10	119	48	14	2	36	32	27	9	-	13	17	-	30	
			A. B. Moore,	Smyth,	47	38	62	-	15	59	42	12	-	21	22	10	3	-	6	6	-	12	
	16th	Jas. E. Brown,	J. R. Miller,	Wythe,	34	48	31	1	10	117	20	21	-	32	37	8	4	-	11	11	-	22	
			O. Anderson,	Grayson,	17	18	20	-	6	21	8	10	-	6	4	5	1	-	3	4	-	7	
			R. D. Montague,	Montgomery,	56	58	62	2	19	72	12	19	-	-	14	11	4	-	7	6	-	13	
			W. B. Charlton,	Pulaski,	35	37	18	-	10	24	4	1	-	-	-	-	-	-	5	4	-	9	
			Rufus A. French,	Giles,	68	15	100	-	6	24	26	9	-	11	14	8	2	-	4	3	-	7	
			Alex. Mahood,	Mercer,	29	36	52	-	7	19	3	9	1	4	4	4	-	-	2	3	-	5	
			J. Hutchinson,	Monroe,	49	42	70	1	10	75	14	16	-	8	9	6	-	-	5	5	-	10	
9th	17th	E. Johnston,	H. W. Bowyer,	Botetourt,	71	70	92	-	29	193	20	25	3	12	14	8	-	-	7	8	-	15	Note 50.
			Andrew Fudge,	Alleghany,	32	27	43	-	6	47	14	11	-	-	1	3	1	-	3	3	-	6	
			F. Johnston,	Roanoke,	42	24	42	1	16	31	7	3	-	2	-	2	1	-	6	5	-	11	
			Ch. L. Francisco,	Bath,	69	50	-	-	12	58	3	10	-	11	11	6	-	-	5	6	-	11	
			H. M. Moffett,	Pocahontas,	62	93	60	-	8	20	7	5	-	1	1	-	-	-	2	3	-	5	
			John A. North,	Greenbrier,	199	151	104	-	17	99	48	20	-	10	17	15	-	-	6	8	-	14	Note 51.
	18th	Ed. S. Duncan,	H. M. Dickinson,	Fayette,	57	62	54	-	15	48	4	9	-	10	19	9	-	-	6	5	-	11	Note 52.
				Randolph,	-	-	-	-	-	-	-	-	-	-	-	-	-	-	-	-	-	-	Note 53.
			E. D. Wilson,	Barbour,	51	70	68	-	24	80	10	7	-	14	20	4	-	-	4	6	-	10	
			John Talbot,	Lewis,	87	218	60	15	48	253	18	39	-	15	21	15	17	-	12	11	-	23	Note 54.
			W. Newlon,	Braxton,	23	86	54	4	15	43	10	6	-	21	7	7	1	-	2	4	-	6	
			G. G. Davisson,	Harrison,	104	177	105	12	47	235	54	49	-	40	33	51	4	-	12	22	-	34	Note 55.
			E. J. Armstrong,	Taylor,	22	16	46	-	8	36	24	10	-	3	6	10	2	-	4	3	-	7	Note 56.
				Nicholas,	-	-	-	-	-	-	-	-	-	-	-	-	-	-	-	-	-	-	Note 57
10th	19th	D. M'Comas,	J. H. Neal,	Wood,	66	169	36	-	25	141	16	31	-	28	40	23	2	-	6	12	6	24	Note 58.
			T. Stinchcomb,	Ritchie,	27	36	3	-	9	12	-	-	-	30	40	2	4	-	3	1	-	4	
			D. G. Morrill,	Jackson,	58	86	23	-	19	53	5	15	-	7	7	4	4	-	5	5	-	10	
			G. W. Stribbling,	Mason,	36	31	39	-	8	25	2	6	-	1	1	-	2	-	8	6	-	14	
			John Samuels,	Cabell,	8	11	7	1	3	10	1	2	-	25	26	12	11	-	7	6	-	13	
			Ezekiel Bloss,	Wayne,	7	3	3	-	7	5	5	10	-	21	14	7	-	-	3	4	-	7	
			Evermont Ward,	Logan,	40	18	24	1	7	11	2	4	-	14	27	19	-	1	4	5	-	9	Note 59.
			A. W. Quarrier,	Kanawha,	508	443	538	4	24	130	65	18	1	11	35	20	4	1	48	28	-	76	Note 60.
			Will. Hatcher,	Gilmer,	33	24	22	1	21	32	3	-	-	6	5	1	-	-	2	13	-	5	
	20th	Joseph L. Fry,	Jno. P. Byrne,	Preston,	34	46	46	-	26	80	13	24	-	13	17	10	2	-	6	6	-	12	Note 61.
			W. J. Willey,	Monongalia,	33	40	45	-	27	53	28	22	-	11	30	10	10	-	8	8	-	16	Note 62.
			Jas. O. Watson,	Marion,	39	48	41	-	27	72	19	19	-	11	13	11	3	-	7	7	-	14	Note 63.
			D. Hickman,	Tyler,	35	40	45	-	11	61	23	29	-	6	5	7	-	-	5	4	-	9	
			Friend Cox,	Wetzel,	7	5	2	-	-	-	-	-	-	5	5	-	-	-	-	2	-	2	
			J. Jarvis,	Doddridge,	26	26	10	2	6	13	3	-	1	13	13	-	-	-	2	2	-	4	
			Adam Kuhn,	Brooke,	63	64	39	1	24	85	21	21	-	4	3	4	4	-	6	7	-	13	
			Alex. T. Laidley,	Ohio,	148	136	138	4	68	152	27	54	-	8	1	13	2	-	13	23	21	59	Note 64.

Districts.	Circuits.	JUDGES.	CLERKS.	COUNTIES.	Suits at Law.				Causes in Chancery.					Prosecutions.					Terms. Days in session.				REMARKS.
					No. commenced.	No. pending.	No. decided.	No. removed from other courts.	No. commenced.	No. pending.	No. interlocutory decrees.	No. final decrees.	No. removed from county courts.	No. commenced.	No. pending.	No. decided.	No.nolleprosequis	Change of venue.	Fall.	Spring.	Intermediate.	Total.	
			Jas. D. Morris,	Marshall,	21	33	22	-	23	69	5	26	-	1	2	2	-	-	8	6	-	14	
				Total,	9530	11291	10381	160	2294	12138	3312	2134	109	1291	1561	1030	316	4	1028	948	85	2061	

E. E.

GEORGE W. MUNFORD, *C. H. D.*

December 10th 1846.

RECAPITULATION.

CIRCUIT SUPERIOR COURTS OF LAW AND CHANCERY,

Exhibiting the Number of Suits, &c., in each Circuit, August 30th, 1846.

Districts.	Circuits.	No. of counties, towns & cities in each circuit.	JUDGES.	Suits at Law.				Causes in Chancery.					Prosecutions.					Terms. Days in session.				Miles travelling.			REMARKS.
				No. commenced.	No. pending.	No. decided.	No. removed from other courts.	No. commenced.	No. pending.	No. interlocutory decrees.	No. final decrees.	No. removed from county courts.	No. commenced.	No. pending.	No. decided.	No nolle prosequis	Change of venue.	Fall.	Spring.	Intermediate.	Total.	To general court.	In circuit.	Total.	
1	1	8	Rh'd H. Baker,	[illegible]90	530	483	[illegible]	99	210	80	75	3	25	35	29	4	-	46	28	-	74	224	255	479	
	2	7	[illegible] H. Gholson,	[illegible]25	429	484	[illegible]	106	357	160	122	12	67	83	37	18	-	54	54	-	108	150	380	530	
2	3	6	[illegible]h. H. Bayly,	[illegible]36	244	244	23	44	300	142	88	4	18	27	17	5	-	47	34	1	72	440	407	847	
	4	7	[illegible]. B. Christian,	[illegible]38	294	312	14	72	355	157	82	6	22	17	26	4	-	31	27	5	63	120	230	350	
3	5	7	Jno. T. Lomax,	[illegible]31	374	521	-	84	673	133	59	4	49	42	46	6	-	41	38	-	79	140	218	358	
	6	5	John Scott,	[illegible]57	726	497	3	176	698	311	122	3	16	15	12	1	-	13	36	-	49	220	200	420	No return from the clerk of the county of Prince William.
4	7	5	J. B. Clopton,	327	630	348	3	66	466	90	64	8	24	24	11	17	-	45	38	-	83	12	182	194	
	21	2	P. N. Nicholas,	128	364	187	-	-	-	-	-	-	37	5	30	12	-	55	54	1	110				
	22	2	J. Robertson,	-	-	-	-	99	1592	211	88	2	-	-	-	-	-	77	26	18	121				
	8	6	D. A. Wilson,	770	901	985	23	135	924	143	149	12	72	111	43	8	1	72	60	5	137	240	180	420	
5	9	5	Wm. Leigh,	629	469	751	2	121	408	148	126	11	54	116	61	26	-	38	37	-	75	260	165	425	
	10	6	N. M Taliaferro	553	683	660	3	95	424	137	112	13	105	139	140	44	-	41	40	-	81	390	265	655	
6	11	7	Rh'd H. Field,	425	578	551	11	87	360	157	93	7	28	41	25	9	1	55	48	28	131	206	308	514	
	12	5	L. P. Thompson	892	1365	1103	11	170	1388	467	148	11	106	134	69	29	-	61	69	-	130	242	240	482	
7	13	6	I. R. Douglass,	536	626	600	4	184	879	204	120	1	65	83	39	5	-	47	38	-	85	320	200	520	
	14	6	Daniel Smith,	174	188	189	2	40	262	80	52	4	36	23	27	17	-	19	24	-	43	268	257	525	
8	15	6	Benj. Estill,	223	333	302	1	68	343	148	74	2	150	150	101	25	-	37	42	-	79	618	270	888	
	16	7	Jas. E. Brown,	288	254	353	4	68	352	87	85	1	61	82	42	11	-	37	36	-	73	514	309	823	

9	17	6	Ed. Johnston,	375	415	341	1	88	448	99	74	3	36	44	34	2	.	29	33	.	62	330	241	571	No return from the clerks of the county of Randolph and of the county of Nicholas.
	18	8	E. S. Duncan,	344	629	387	31	157	695	120	120	.	103	106	96	25	.	40	51	.	91	590	363	953	
10	19	9	Dav. M'Comas,	783	821	695	7	123	419	99	86	1	143	195	88	27	2	86	70	6	162	640	412	1052	
	20	9	Joseph L. Fry,	406	438	388	7	212	585	139	195	1	74	89	57	21	.	57	65	21	143	714	300	1014	
10	22	135	Total,	9530	11291	10381	160	2294	12138	3312	2134	109	1291	1561	1030	316	4	1028	948	85	2061	6638	53821	2020	
			Average of circuits,	454	538	494	8	109	578	158	101	5	61	74	49	6	.	46	43	4	94	301	244	546	

Judgments at law,	10,381
Interlocutory decrees,	3,312
Final decrees,	2,134
Total decisions from which appeals may be had,	15.827

Number of appeals allowed,	133—being a little over eleven-thirteenths of one per cent. of the total decisions in the circuit courts.
Causes decided in court of appeals,	152
Excess of decisions over new appeals,	19

E. E.

GEORGE W. MUNFORD, *C. H. D.*

December 10th, 1846.

REMARKS OF CLERKS.

FIRST CIRCUIT.

GREENESVILLE.

Note 1. In this report, judgments on forthcoming bonds are included, but dismissions at rules are not.

SURRY.

2. In consequence of the severe illness of the Judge, there was no court held at the fall term.

ISLE OF WIGHT.

3. The Judge did not hold his court at the spring term in consequence of his illness.

NANSEMOND.

4. All judgments on motions, judgments confessed in the office, all dismissions in court or otherwise, and office judgments confirmed, are embraced in number of suits decided at law.

PRINCESS ANNE.

5. Judgments on forthcoming bonds, dismissions at rules, judgments on motions for money paid a security, are included under the head of suits decided, and final decrees—and writs of scire facias to revive judgments are included under the head of suits commenced. Also under the head of causes pending in Chancery is included one case sent back from the Court of Appeals.

NORFOLK CITY.

6. In the number of suits at law commenced, five motions on forthcoming bonds are included. The spring term of the Court was a special term held in March 1846.

SECOND CIRCUIT.

DINWIDDIE.

7. One suit removed to Circuit Court of Petersburg. Judgments on motions and judgments in the office not included in this report.

THIRD CIRCUIT.

YORK.

8. There was no regular term in the spring. A special term was held on the 26th day of June, on which day the clerk, Samuel Shield, died, in consequence of which the court adjourned till the next term.

ELIZABETH CITY.

9. One Chancery cause transferred to the Circuit Court of James City and Williamsburg, and one removed to this Court from that.

FOURTH CIRCUIT.

KING WILLIAM.

10. Motions on forthcoming bonds not included in this report.

KING AND QUEEN.

11. Forty-five motions.

ESSEX.

12. In the suits at law decided, dismissions in the office and in court are included, also confessions of judgments in both, office judgments called in court and confirmed, and 2 judgments upon notices against an attorney for failing to pay over moneys by him collected. Seven judgments on forthcoming bonds, and 4 rules against witnesses afterwards discharged, are not embraced. On the chancery side, orders suggesting deaths of parties, and orders of revivor, and mere orders of continuance, are not included among interlocutory decrees, but an order on petition reinstating a suit is. Among those reported as decided, are several which were dismissed at Court,

MIDDLESEX.

13. The prosecution mentioned in this report was a presentment of the grand jury. Hard times upon clerks and lawyers in this county. Free trade 'tis said by some good folks is the cause.

GLOUCESTER.

14. The number of suits and causes decided, include dismissions; the interlocutory decrees include all orders not final. This is a most troublesome duty imposed on the clerks without any compensation.

FIFTH CIRCUIT.

LANCASTER.

15. Judgments on forthcoming bonds are not included in this report.

NORTHUMBERLAND.

16. Quere? Has the commonwealth the right to require of officers duties for the performance of which no compensation is allowed? The attention of the Legislature is respectfully called to this.

WESTMORELAND.

17. Motions on forthcoming bonds not included.

KING GEORGE.

18. In the number of suits commenced at law, is included two writs of supersedeas. Causes at rules are embraced in the number pending.

SPOTTSYLVANIA.

19. I have no remarks to submit, farther than that it is extremely irksome and annoying to me to make this report, rendered the more so, as I understand the father of the statute requiring this duty to be performed, entertaining the opinion that the judges were too independent, too far removed from the people, that they should be made more responsible. Assured such to have been his object in procuring the passage of the law. It is to be hoped that the next assembly will repudiate such doctrine by repealing the statute.

SIXTH CIRCUIT.

FAUQUIER.

20. The Judge was sick at the fall term He held a special session of six days in April, and the court sat twelve days at the regular term in May, making in all eighteen days in the spring, 55 law and 3 chancery motions not included in this statement, all of which were decided.

LOUDOUN.

21. Thirty-two judgments and three decrees on motions not included in this report.

PRINCE WILLIAM.

22. No return from this county.

FAIRFAX.

23. Judgments on forthcoming bonds and notices not included.

STAFFORD.

24. Four of these cases were motions on forthcoming bonds, and one a supersedeas.

SEVENTH CIRCUIT.

POWHATAN.

25. Of the ten days stated as the session of the court in the fall of 1845, seven days were at the regular term of the court in November and three at a special term in February. And of the eight days stated as the session of the court in the spring, five were at the regular term in May and three at a special term in June.

GOOCHLAND.

26. There have been eighteen office judgments confirmed within the year, which are not included in the number of suits at law decided. In making out the lists of suits pending at law and in chancery, only such are included as stand on the court docket for trial or decision. All at the rules are consequently excluded.

TWENTY-FIRST CIRCUIT.

HENRICO AND CITY OF RICHMOND.

27. Of the suits at law commenced, one was a writ of scire facias, three were writs of supersedeas, one caveat and one appeal from a decision of the auditor of public accounts, and a case for a divorce. Suits decided, include judgments on forthcoming bonds and on motions in other cases, judgments confessed in the office; also non suits and dismissions in court, and exclusive of judgments in pursuance of decisions of court of appeals. Seventy-seven of the days the court was in session, were for civil business, and the balance for criminal cases. The special term was for the trial of a convict in the penitentiary for rebellion and murder.

TWENTY-SECOND CIRCUIT.

HENRICO AND CITY OF RICHMOND.

28. Besides the number of final decrees, there were seventeen suits dismissed at rules. Three suit have been transferred from this court to other circuit courts, and two have been removed to this court from other Circuit Courts.

EIGHTH CIRCUIT.

APPOMATTOX.

29. In this report, motions on delivery bonds are not included. By law now, our court commences its sessions on the 18th of October and May, and the court of Lynchburg, in the same circuit, on the 23d of those months, giving to our court but five days, (frequently but four,) to get through with its business, a space of time obviously too limited. We trust the Legislature will alter the arrangement so as to give us ten days, if necessary.

CAMPBELL.

30. In addition to the number of suits decided, which includes dismissions and confessions of judgments, there were 48 judgments on delivery bonds on the law side, and two on the chancery side of the court.—In consequence of the sickness of the Judge, the court at its spring term, only sat two days; and a special session was holden in July following, which continued for five days. We have not time enough to do the business of the court, and more time should be given us.

BEDFORD.

31. Of the causes pending on the law docket, 110 are upon the court docket, 97 at rules. Of chancery causes, 118 on the court docket and 135 at rules. Judgments on delivery bonds, 91 in number, are not included in the foregoing list.

NINTH CIRCUIT.

LUNENBURG.

32. In the decisions of chancery causes, I have included judgments on forthcoming bonds, interlocutory as well as final decrees, and dismissions in court and at rules. The motions for judgments on forthcoming bonds are not included in the suits commenced either at law or equity. Judgments on forthcoming bonds, dismissions in court and at rules, are included in the number of causes decided at law.

MECKLENBURG.

33. Of the causes pending at law, 46 only are matured for trial, and of chancery causes 52 are on the court docket.

TENTH CIRCUIT.

HENRY.

34. Neither judgments on forthcoming bonds nor causes dismissed at rules, are embraced in this report

FRANKLIN.

35. Motions on forfeited forthcoming bonds and other motions on which judgments are rendered, are not included among the suits and causes decided There were two prisoners tried at the spring term, one for malicious stabbing and the other for horsestealing. The first was acquitted, and the latter convicted and sentenced to five years imprisonment in the penitentiary.

ELEVENTH CIRCUIT.

LOUISA.

36 Of the suits at law decided, 53 were office judgments. There were five awards of executions on forfeited delivery bonds There were 22 dismissions in court, and 24 dismissions and abatements were entered at rules. The change of venue case was the case of William Norment, sent here from Hanover county, to be tried for a rape. It took six days to try him.

ORANGE.

37. An intermediate term was held in the month of March.

CULPEPER.

38. Eleven judgments on forthcoming bonds included in number of suits decided,

TWELFTH CIRCUIT.

NELSON.

39. In the number of suits decided at common law, embraced in this report, judgments on delivery bonds and judgments on other motions, notices, &c. are included.

AUGUSTA.

40 In the number of suits commenced on the law side of the court, is included 79 forthcoming bonds, and one scire facias, leaving 184 suits commenced by writs of capias ad respondendum. In the number decided, is included the 79 forthcoming bonds. On the chancery side, in the number commenced and decided, is included three forthcoming bonds and one motion.

THIRTEENTH CIRCUIT.

HAMPSHIRE.

41. The suits depending are those remaining on the docket on the 31st of August 1846; of the suits commenced, two are writs of scire facias. No notice is taken of forthcoming bonds. Of the chancery suits depending, 25 are at rules, 72 on the deferred issue docket, and 82 on the trial docket.

FREDERICK.

42 The large difference between the number of chancery causes pending and the number commenced, and the number of interlocutory and final decrees, is accounted for by the fact that at least two-thirds of those pending are old suits, brought in the old superior court of chancery, and left sleeping on the deferred docket by the parties concerned. There were also 35 judgments on forthcoming bonds this year.

CLARKE.

43. Judgments on delivery bonds not included.

FOURTEENTH CIRCUIT.

SHENANDOAH.

44. Of the suits at law, the number decided includes office judgments, but not judgments on forthcoming bonds. Causes in chancery: interlocutory decrees include all orders—final decrees—mere dismissions. Prosecutions include those for larceny, &c.

WARREN.

45. There were seven judgments on forfeited forthcoming bonds, and one motion on a notice to recover money paid as security, which are not enumerated in this report. The last term commenced on the 31st August, and closed on 1st Sept. 1846. I have thought it proper to notice it here.

LEE.

46. No notice has been taken in this report of motions on forthcoming bonds.

FIFTEENTH CIRCUIT.

SCOTT.

47. The suits pending include one issue out of chancery, one scire facias; and in those determined are included 22 in which judgments entered at rules were made final, but judgments on delivery bonds and rules against witnesses are not included

RUSSELL.

48 Office judgments entered as of the last day of term, dismissions in the office, and motions on forthcoming bonds, are included with causes decided at law. The Judge passed through the docket at each term, deciding all the causes ready for trial.

TAZEWELL.

49. Judgments at law on forthcoming bonds and dismissions at rules, both at law and chancery, are included in this report. I do not perceive the justice of imposing new duties yearly on clerks, and at the same time forgetting to allow them compensation. It may be that the air of the capitol is favorable to such developments of statesmanship.

SEVENTEENTH CIRCUIT.

BOTETOURT.

50. There were also 35 judgments upon forfeited forthcoming bonds which are not embraced in the num. of suits decided. Of the 3 causes removed, only one was from the county court, and the other two from other courts.

GREENBRIER.

51. No judgments on forfeited forthcoming bonds, or notices against securities, included in the number of judgments reported. Of the 99 causes depending, a number are causes that were commenced in the late superior court of chancery. No steps have been taken in them for several years.

EIGHTEENTH CIRCUIT.

FAYETTE.

52. No judgments on forthcoming bonds or notices included in this report.

RANDOLPH.

53. No return from this county.

LEWIS.

54. In the number of suits here reported. I have excluded motions on forthcoming bonds. All other motions included. It will be seen by reference to the reports of the different clerks, that litigation in this region is rapidly decreasing. hostilities to a considerable extent have abated, a unanimity of feeling is now beginning to prevail among the people here which hitherto has never existed. The flag of civil war has been prostrated, and the standard of union and concurrence has been reared in its stead.

HARRISON.

55. Motions, rules and decrees against delinquent and forfeited lands, not included in this report.

TAYLOR.

56. Of the number of suits at law, nine are judgments on forthcoming bonds.

NICHOLAS.

57. No return from this county.

NINETEENTH CIRCUIT.

WOOD.

58. Motions on bonds not included either as suits commenced or decided.

LOGAN.

59. Notices are included with civil suits, but not on forthcoming bonds. Suits decided are not confined to those commenced during the fiscal year, nor is the number pending.

KANAWHA.

60. The number of suits and causes pending, include all the suits at rules, many of them very old. The number decided at law include judgments on forthcoming bonds and dismissions. The number of days at the fall term includes an adjourned term held in January and February 1846.

TWENTIETH CIRCUIT.

PRESTON.

61. Motions and judgments on forthcoming bonds not included.

MONONGALIA.

62. The number of causes reported as pending, does not include such as were at the rules, only such as were on the docket for trial. Your report to the Legislature last winter represents me as delinquent. It may be proper, therefore, to state here that more business was done in our courts that year than in many years past, his honor Judge Fry having held an intermedite term of ten days duration.

MARION.

63. In the number of causes commenced in chancery, I have included one cause removed from the circuit court of Monongalia by order of that court; and the number of prosecutions decided includes two judgments of outlawry.

OHIO.

64. Causes at rules are included in those pending, and dismissions and judgments confessed in office in those decided. Years ending August 30th: 1837, 46 days; 1838, 77 days; 1839 48 days; 1840, 45 days; 1841, 47 days; 1842, 62 days; 1843, 53 days; 1844, 59 days; 1845, 53 days; 1846, 59 days. Grand total in 10 years, 549 days.

ABSTRACT

FROM THE

REPORTS OF THE CLERKS

OF THE

COURT OF APPEALS

AND OF THE

CIRCUIT SUPERIOR COURTS OF LAW AND CHANCERY,

FOR THE

YEAR ENDING 30th AUGUST, 1847.

ABSTRACT FROM THE REPORTS

OF THE

CLERKS OF THE COURT OF APPEALS,

AND OF THE

CIRCUIT SUPERIOR COURTS OF LAW AND CHANCERY,

For the Year ending the 30th August, 1847 ; exhibiting the number of Suits, &c.

COURT OF APPEALS.

JUDGES.	CLERKS.	Location of Court.	Suits commenced.	Pending.	Decided.	No. of days in session.	REMARKS OF CLERKS.
Wm. H. Cabell, *President*, Francis T. Brooke, John J. Allen, Briscoe G. Baldwin. William Daniel,	Joseph Allen,	Richmond,	117	564	56	130	Of the causes depending there are 23 depending upon the same questions. The term of the court commenced on the 15th October 1346, and ended on the 13th May 1847, comprising 159 days. there being within that time two recesses, one of 25 days and the other of 26 days, the court having actually sat 130 days, exclusive of Sundays, and five days in which there was not a sufficient number of judges present to constitute a court.
	John A. North,	Lewisburg,	62	115	69	60	
		Total,	179	679	125	190	

CIRCUIT SUPERIOR COURTS OF LAW AND CHANCERY.

Districts.	Circuits.	JUDGES.	CLERKS.	COUNTIES.	Suits at Law. No. commenced.	Suits at Law. No. pending.	Suits at Law. No. decided.	Suits at Law. No. removed from other courts.	Causes in Chancery. No. commenced.	Causes in Chancery. No. pending.	Causes in Chancery. No. interlocutory decrees.	Causes in Chancery. No. final decrees.	Causes in Chancery. No. removed from county courts.	Prosecutions. No. commenced.	Prosecutions. No. pending.	Prosecutions. No. decided.	Prosecutions. No. nolle prose-quis.	Prosecutions. Change of venue.	Terms. Days in Session. Fall.	Terms. Days in Session. Spring.	Terms. Days in Session. Intermediate or sp eial.	Terms. Days in Session. Total.	Remarks of Clerks.
1	1	R. H. Baker,	L. R. Edwards,	Southampton,	60	40	155	-	15	33	20	22	-	5	5	2	7	-	5	3	-	8	Note 1.
			Joseph Turner,	Greenesville,	38	20	40	-	6	15	5	3	-	3	1	1	1	-	2	4	-	6	Note 2.
			W. P. Underwood,	Surry,	14	12	24	-	6	13	10	8	-	2	1	2	-	-	2	2	-	4	Note 3.
			N. P. Young.	Isle of Wight,	55	22	72	-	12	25	11	3	-	5	4	7	-	-	5	3	-	8	
			Joseph Prentis,	Nansemond,	35	18	47	-	13	22	8	9	-	3	3	2	1	1	6	4	-	10	Note 4.
			J. J. Burroughs,	Princess Anne,	53	37	77	1	6	9	2	10	-	-	-	3	-	-	2	5	-	7	Note 5.
			John Williams,	Norfolk City,	189	82	250	-	16	54	23	34	-	-	1	2	-	-	4	21	50	75	Note 6.
			A. Emmerson,	Norfolk county,	114	24	191	6	15	27	30	17	-	37	38	8	1	-	12	24	-	36	Note 7.
	2	J. H. Gholson,	John P. Crump,	Dinwiddie,	66	51	52	5	16	49	23	20	-	2	3	8	1	-	4	3	-	7	Note 8.
			F. Fitzgerald,	Nottoway,	88	40	64	-	14	31	11	13	-	9	6	3	8	-	2	3	-	5	Note 9.
			E. G. Leigh,	Amelia,	106	70	99	1	11	25	12	13	1	6	10	-	4	-	3	3	-	6	Note 10.
			E. R. Turnbull,	Brunswick,	37	21	38	-	8	24	8	15	-	4	18	8	4	-	3	4	-	7	
			J. T. J. Mason,	Sussex,	36	26	36	-	10	17	8	5	-	-	2	-	-	-	2	1	-	3	Note 11.
			Robert Gilliam,	Prince George,	38	2	36	-	3	11	17	9	-	17	16	1	-	-	3	2	-	5	Note 12.
			H. B. Gaines.	Petersburg,	158	262	125	1	31	164	81	42	2	22	32	20	8	-	15	16	-	31	
2	3	G. P. Scarburg,	Thos. C. Cogbill,	James City and Williamsburg,	84	64	103	16	9	123	40	20	-	3	3	4	-	-	10	10	-	20	
			Alex'r. Garrett,	York,	16	40	32	10	3	18	12	-	-	12	15	-	-	-	4	2	-	6	
			Wm. Robertson,	Warwick,	15	12	14	2	3	10	5	1	-	3	1	2	-	-	2	2	-	4	
			W. C. Armstead,	Elizabeth City,	37	15	33	2	8	25	16	2	1	1	2	-	-	-	3	3	-	6	
			Louis P. Rogers	Northampton,	22	23	33	2	4	27	13	11	6	-	-	1	-	-	5	4	-	9	
			Thos. R. Joynes,	Accomack,	50	70	59	7	12	97	30	10	-	12	18	11	1	-	9	9	-	18	
	4	J. B. Christian,	Robert Pollard,	King William,	6[illegible]	16	69	-	5	46	18	11	-	-	-	-	-	-	5	4	-	9	Note 13.
			Robert Pollard, jr.	King & Queen,	51	39	40	-	10	31	12	12	-	2	2	3	1	-	3	3	-	6	
			Jas. Roy Micou,	Essex,	54	91	60	5	9	38	15	12	-	1	1	2	1	-	3	3	-	6	Note 14
			Robert N. Trice,	Middlesex,	20	36	30	1	6	49	14	5	1	1	1	-	-	-	3	4	-	7	Note 15.

			John R. Cary,	Gloucester,	112	102	98	4	22	65	27	19	-	2	4	1	-	-	5	12	-	17	Note 16.
			Shep'd G. Miller,	Mathews,	43	30	14	-	25	88	15	6	-	-	-	-	-	-	5	5	-	10	
3	5	John T. Lomax,	Ro. T. Dunaway,	Lancaster,	18	22	21	-	5	9	3	10	-	1	2	2	-	-	2	2	-	4	
			J. R. Stith,	Northumberland,	51	65	25	2	2	10	5	3	1	1	-	4	-	-	2	4	-	6	Note 17.
			J. S. Jeffries,	Richmond co.	102	64	96	1	10	36	21	9	-	-	4	5	1	-	6	4	-	10	
			Wm. Hutt,	Westmoreland,	165	150	131	5	13	50	16	15	-	1	2	-	-	-	4	2	-	6	Note 18.
			Wm. S. Brown,	King George,	27	16	31	1	-	17	12	9	-	1	4	1	4	-	5	2	-	5	Note 19.
			Robert Hudgin,	Caroline,	76	59	108	2	11	54	51	4	4	6	3	4	-	-	5	5	-	10	
			John J. Chew,	Spottsylvania,	54	51	63	-	8	461	44	12	-	7	11	6	1	-	19	8	-	27	
	6	John Scott,	Wm. F. Phillips,	Fauquier,	167	382	265	-	69	395	230	63	1	9	8	4	3	-	12	11	-	23	Note 20.
			Thos. P. Knox,	Loudoun,	158	181	170	1	46	174	98	2	-	1	1	3	2	-	7	11	-	18	Note 21.
			P. D. Lipscomb,	Prince William,	83	110	125	2	23	135	30	17	-	7	10	10	3	-	4	5	-	9	
			F. D. Richardson,	Fairfax,	97	144	93	-	48	152	71	33	2	2	-	2	4	-	8	4	-	12	Note 22.
			Cassius F. Lee,	Alexandria,	58	189	68	-	25	130	12	9	-	-	12	-	-	-	-	7	-	7	Note 23.
			H. H. Conway,	Stafford,	19	6	23	-	14	29	7	9	-	1	2	4	1	-	2	3	-	5	Note 24.
4	7	Jno. B. Clopton,	W. W. T Cogbill,	Chesterfield,	92	223	149	9	18	111	46	14	1	6	12	6	3	-	9	9	7	25	Note 25.
			Ed. T. Christian,	Charles City,	11	14	11	2	2	23	2	1	-	-	1	-	1	-	2	2	2	6	
			John D. Christian,	New Kent,	22	19	17	-	3	18	21	6	-	2	2	-	1	-	4	5	-	9	
			Wm. S. Dance,	Powhatan,	113	100	91	6	11	76	35	15	1	1	2	-	-	-	4	7	2	13	Note 26.
			N. W. Miller,	Goochland,	69	129	98	7	9	62	14	15	1	2	3	1	-	-	5	12	-	17	No e 27.
			Phillip B. Winston,	Hanover,	48	140	7[illegible]	2	32	139	64	36	2	5	8	-	2	-	10	11	3	24	Note 28.
	21	P. N. Nicholas,	John Robinson,	Henrico and City of Richmond.	169	345	199	9	-	-	-	-	-	18	6	17	1	-	49	53	-	102	Note 29.
	22	John Robertson,	Pow. Roberts,	Henrico and City of Richmond,	-	-	-	-	91	1598	276	87	3	-	-	-	-	-	77	26	21	124	Note 30.
	8	D. A. Wilson,	B. B. Woodson,	Cumberland,	125	78	99	1	18	88	7	5	-	3	16	4	-	-	10	8	-	18	
			Rolfe Eldridge,	Buckingham,	155	269	183	3	58	212	26	42	3	8	10	10	3	-	12	14	-	26	
			H. F. Bocock,	Appomattox,	58	50	33	-	11	21	5	3	3	6	10	3	2	-	4	5	-	9	Note 31.
			J. D. Alexander,	Campbell,	123	228	83	-	16	142	3	12	-	2	5	6	1	-	8	4	-	12	Note 32.
			Jos. Wilson,	Bedford,	226	204	237	7	22	252	35	34	11	23	36	19	-	-	11	11	-	22	Note 33.
				Lynchburg,																			Note 34.
5	9	William Leigh,	Wm. Holt,	Halifax,	187	168	197	-	8	94	38	52	2	46	-	28	[illegible]	-	10	13	-	23	Note 35.
			W. Robinson,	Charlotte,	79	59	95	-	20	50	11	15	-	4	4	2	1	-	7	4	-	11	
			B. J. Worsham,	Prince Edward,	95	86	116	4	33	111	65	14	3	4	7	3	4	-	6	8	-	14	
			T. W. Winn,	Lunenburg,	79	51	92	-	14	42	9	9	-	15	17	4	1	-	3	4	-	7	Note 36.
			R. B. Baptist,	Mecklenburg,	132	118	110	-	27	122	21	18	-	14	22	5	9	-	4	9	-	13	Note 37.
	10	N. M. Taliaferro,	J. N. Zentmeyer,	Floyd,	33	19	29	-	18	37	11	7	-	14	14	11	3	-	4	4	-	8	Note 38.
				Patrick,																			Note 39.
			A. M. Dupuy,	Henry,	92	77	106	3	6	38	14	21	1	13	12	7	3	-	3	5	-	8	Note 40.
			M. G. Carper,	Franklin,	187	168	209	-	30	101	58	52	16	19	25	8	7	-	9	9	-	23	Note 41.

Districts.	Circuits.	JUDGES.	CLERKS.	COUNTIES.	Suits at Law.				Causes in Chancery.					Prosecutions.					Terms. Days in session				Remarks of Clerks.
					No. commenced.	No. pending.	No. decided.	No. removed from other courts.	No. commenced.	No. pending.	No. interlocutory decrees.	No. final decrees.	No. removed from county courts.	No. commenced.	No. pending.	No. decided.	No. nolle prosequis.	Changes of venue.	Fall.	Spring.	Intermediate or special.	Total.	
			Wm. H. Tunstall,	Pittsylvania,	184	312	180	-	52	144	37	50	2	10	51	18	13	-	11	17	-	28	Note 42.
			M. D. Carter,	Carroll,	55	32	52	-	12	21	17	10	1	31	37	15	5	-	6	5	-	11	Note 43.
6	11	R. H. Field,	John Hunter,	Louisa,	59	102	126	-	8	67	50	16	3	1	2	3	1	-	7	7	6	20	Note 44.
			A. Shepherd, Jr.,	Fluvanna,	99	84	142	1	16	49	26	23	1	6	12	6	3	-	6	5	-	11	
			Philip S. Fry,	Orange,	86	80	115	1	6	43	16	14	2	1	5	3	4	-	8	5	-	13	
			Robert Pritchett,	Greene,	66	40	27	1	5	20	2	7	-	-	2	-	2	-	4	4	-	8	Note 45.
			Belfield Cave,	Madison,	39	45	45	-	5	35	20	5	1	-	3	1	1	-	5	3	-	8	
			R. G. Ward,	Culpeper,	80	53	100	7	19	96	46	23	1	10	22	2	3	-	15	9	9	33	Note 46.
			Wm. J. Menifee,	Rappahannock,	14	17	18	-	9	35	8	10	-	7	9	-	1	-	4	3	-	7	
	12	L. P. Thompson,	Robert Tinsley,	Amherst,	185	228	178	2	27	300	130	31	2	4	10	-	3	-	11	11	-	22	
			Sam'l M'D. Reid,	Rockbridge,	89	54	121	-	34	136	43	16	-	9	8	10	-	-	10	10	-	20	
			How. L. Brown,	Nelson,	135	300	261	4	43	336	74	35	2	7	16	9	7	-	11	13	-	24	Note 47.
			Alex. Garrett,	Albemarle,	225	155	238	-	39	121	32	23	2	16	44	60	12	-	15	11	13	39	
			Nich's C. Kinney,	Augusta,	270	351	294	1	62	455	119	68	-	5	7	20	13	-	35	23	-	58	Note 48.
7	13	I. R. Douglass,	R. T. Brown,	Jefferson,	153	145	2.8	-	44	302	95	37	-	9	12	7	8	-	18	19	-	37	Note 49.
			John Strother,	Berkeley,	136	77	112	-	38	131	-	24	-	3	6	-	-	-	6	7	-	13	
			Isaiah Buck,	Morgan.	44	66	47	-	10	43	7	2	-	3	7	3	-	-	4	2	-	6	
			John B. White,	Hampshire,	142	111	19	1	42	182	48	43	-	6	13	2	2	-	5	5	-	10	Note 50.
			J. Kean,	Frederick,	145	86	149	1	39	329	44	40	-	4	23	4	5	-	5	4	-	9	Note 51.
			H. H. Lee,	Clarke,	57	28	48	-	8	30	8	5	-	1	11	1	-	-	3	2	-	5	Note 52.
	14	Daniel Smith,	Wm. C. Lauck,	Page,	13	9	16	2	3	11	5	7	-	4	4	2	-	-	2	2	-	4	
			S. C. Williams,	Shenandoah,	29	15	29	-	7	38	22	8	3	1	1	3	1	-	2	2	-	4	Note 53.
			Robert Turner,	Warren,	20	13	25	-	7	20	10	6	-	1	2	1	-	-	2	3	-	5	Note 54.
			C. Lobb,	Hardy,	42	86	36	2	19	128	22	15	-	1	11	4	-	-	3	3	-	6	
			Z. Dyer,	Pendleton,	6	13	11	-	4	15	1	3	-	5	2	12	-	-	3	2	-	5	
			L. W. Gambill,	Rockingham,	109	152	139	-	19	62	5	9	-	5	4	5	-	-	8	7	-	15	
8	15	Benj. Estill,	J. W. S. Morrison,	Lee,	21	70	43	-	7	53	10	6	-	23	27	14	3	-	12	4	6	22	Note 55.
			S. J. Morison,	Scott,	25	60	23	2	7	33	5	11	-	15	26	5	1	-	5	6	-	11	Note 56.
			James P. Carroll,	Russell,	37	53	47	1	3	19	3	5	-	23	31	27	5	-	6	6	-	12	Note 57.

			G. W. G. Browne,	Tazewell,	58	48	70	-	27	63	14	40	-	30	35	14	-	-	3	5	-	8	Note 58.
			C. F. Trigg,	Washington,	29	50	44	-	15	111	38	23	-	7	10	29	7	-	16	16	-	32	
			A. B. Moore,	Smyth,	72	49	67	-	12	51	31	18	-	14	14	17	5	-	6	6	-	12	
	16	Jas. E. Brown,	W. Allen Stuart,	Wythe,	36	36	39	-	10	106	17	16	1	31	22	31	7	-	12	10	6	28	
			O. Anderson,	Grayson,	42	23	24	-	8	26	1	4	-	9	10	2	1	-	4	3	-	7	
			R. D. Montague,	Montgomery,	41	42	50	-	7	70	5	17	-	3	12	4	-	-	6	6	-	12	
			Wm. B. Charlton,	Pulaski,	25	24	9	-	5	24	15	14	-	19	20	3	4	-	4	5	-	9	
			Rufus A. French,	Giles,	84	62	96	-	7	17	11	7	-	11	17	8	-	-	3	3	-	6	Note 59.
			Alex. Mohood,	Mercer,	32	23	37	-	3	19	3	11	1	9	8	5	-	-	2	4	-	6	Note 60.
			J. Hutchinson,	Monroe,	37	44	62	-	12	63	26	11	-	3	6	8	-	-	5	5	-	10	
9	17	E. Johnson,	H. W. Bowyer,	Botetourt,	96	100	106	3	32	192	25	44	1	3	14	4	-	-	9	8	-	17	Note 61.
			Andrew Fudge,	Alleghany,	32	34	21	3	5	37	4	11	-	5	5	1	-	-	3	3	-	6	
			F. Johnston,	Roanoke,	40	19	47	-	12	24	5	12	-	8	4	4	-	-	6	5	-	11	
			C. L. Francisco,	Bath,	68	62	57	-	10	60	28	14	-	5	5	9	1	-	6	6	-	12	
				Highland,																			Note 62.
			H. M. Moffett,	Pocahontas,	32	23	39	2	14	22	2	4	-	5	6	-	-	-	2	2	-	4	
			John A. North,	Greenbrier,	98	102	76	3	16	99	25	16	-	12	18	10	1	-	6	4	-	10	Note 63.
	18	E. S. Duncan,	H. M. Dickinson,	Fayette,	47	80	31	-	16	51	8	7	-	28	34	6	8	-	5	-	-	5	Note 64.
			B. L. Brown,	Randolph,	35	47	30	-	13	55	13	22	-	8	9	8	-	-	5	4	-	9	
			E. D. Wilson,	Barbour,	49	64	68	-	22	70	11	12	-	12	16	13	2	-	7	6	-	13	
			John Talbot,	Lewis,	93	213	148	9	23	246	17	35	-	50	47	14	1	-	12	16	-	28	Note 65.
			W Newlon,	Braxton,	51	46	30	4	21	50	10	20	-	6	19	10	-	-	2	5	-	7	Note 66.
			G. G. Davisson,	Harrison,	94	198	102	1	40	298	37	34	-	11	28	10	3	-	17	14	-	31	
			E. J. Armstrong,	Taylor,	11	11	23	-	19	31	12	22	-	6	7	6	1	2	3	4	-	7	
			Robert Hamilton,	Nicholas,	10	10	24	-	4	20	5	5	-	6	7	3	-	-	2	4	-	6	Note 67.
10	19	D. M'Comas.	J. H. Neal,	Wood,	69	167	70	-	19	144	32	14	-	15	43	30	5	-	7	15	9	31	
			S. Stinchcomb,	Ritchie,	17	27	14	-	11	16	3	1	-	6	31	8	12	-	2	3	-	5	
			D. G. Morrill,	Jackson,	84	108	59	-	25	55	10	18	-	30	29	7	1	-	5	5	13	23	Note 68.
			G. W. Stribbling,	Mason,	48	44	38	-	9	26	3	3	-	9	56	1	1	-	8	8	-	16	Note 69.
			John Samuels,	Cabell,	10	7	8	-	4	6	9	3	-	8	16	9	2	-	7	7	-	14	
			E. Bloss.	Wayne,	13	8	7	-	5	19	3	10	-	13	19	30	-	-	4	4	-	8	
				Logan,	13	10	19	-	4	3	7	6	-	15	21	12	-	-	4	3	-	7	Note 70.
			B. E. Barrett,	Boone,	7	7	-	-	4	4	-	-	-	1	1	-	-	-	-	2	-	2	Note 71.
			A. W. Quarrier,	Kanawha,	551	458	742	-	40	157	61	16	-	27	36	28	3	-	40	37	-	77	Note 72.
				Gilmer,																			Note 73.
	20	Joseph L. Fry,	John P. Bryne,	Preston,	46	30	45	-	10	59	16	9	-	7	5	9	1	-	5	5	-	10	Note 74.
			W. T. Willey,	Monongalia,	71	51	56	-	30	45	29	33	-	7	14	16	7	-	8	8	-	16	Note 75.
			James O. Watson,	Marion,	53	41	61	1	25	64	28	32	-	16	16	11	2	-	9	7	-	16	Note 76.
				Tyler,																			Note 77.

Districts.	Circuits.	JUDGES.	CLERKS.	COUNTIES.	SUITS AT LAW.				CAUSES IN CHANCERY.					PROSECUTIONS.					TERMS. Days in Session.				REMARKS OF CLERKS.
					No. commenced.	No. pending.	No. decided.	No removed from other courts.	No. commenced.	No. pending.	No. interlocutory decrees.	No. final decrees.	No removed from county courts.	No. commenced.	No. pending.	N. decided.	No. nolle prosequis.	Change of venue.	Fall.	Spring.	Intermediate or special.	Total.	
			Friend Cox,	Wetzell,	17	14	7	4	2	2	.	.	-	7	6	4	1	-	2	2	-	4	Note 78.
			F. D. Hickman,	Doddridge,	10	24	16	-	8	20	4	3	-	4	15	2	2	-	2½	1½	-	4	
			AdamKuhn,	Brooke,	60	65	60	1	16	72	18	29	-	8	10	1	-	-	6	7	-	13	
			Alex. T. Laidley,	Ohio,	160	155	153	1	43	131	24	70	-	94	35	34	20	-	13	18	11	42	Note 79.
			James D. Morris.	Marshall,	34	37	36	-	20	59	8	33	-	-	-	1	1	-	5	4	-	9	Note 80.
				Total,	9864	10702	11888	180	2251	11646	3370	2256	89	1105	1592	929	293	3	957½	930½	163	2051	

E. E.

GEORGE W. MUNFORD, *C. H. D.*

RECAPITULATION.

CIRCUIT SUPERIOR COURTS OF LAW AND CHANCERY,

Exhibiting the Number of Suits, &c., in each Circuit, August 30th, 1847.

Districts.	Circuits.	No. counties, towns and cities in each circuit.	JUDGES.	Suits at Law.				Causes in Chancery.					Prosecutions.					Terms. Days in Session.				Miles Travelling.			REMARKS.
				No. commenced.	No. pending.	No. decided.	No. removed from other courts.	No. commenced.	No. pending.	No. interlocutory decrees.	No. final decrees.	No. removed from county courts.	No. commenced.	No. pending.	No. decided.	No. nolle prosequis.	Change of venue.	Fall.	Spring.	Intermediate.	Total.	To general court.	In circuit.	Total.	
1	1	8	Richard H. Baker,	558	255	856	7	89	198	109	106	-	55	53	27	10	1	38	66	50	154	224	255	479	
	2	7	Jas. H. Gholson,	5 9	472	450	7	93	321	160	117	3	60	87	40	25	-	32	32	-	64	150	380	530	
2	3	6	Geo. P. Scarburg,	224	224	274	39	39	300	116	44	7	31	39	18	1	-	33	30	-	63	440	407	847	
	4	6	John B. Christian,	343	314	311	10	77	317	101	65	1	6	8	6	2	-	24	31	-	55	120	230	350	
3	5	7	John T. Lomax,	493	427	475	11	49	217	152	62	5	17	26	22	6	-	41	27	-	68	140	218	358	
	6	6	John Scott,	582	1012	744	3	225	1015	448	153	3	20	33	23	13	-	36	41	-	74	220	292	512	
4	7	6	John B. Clopton,	355	625	444	26	75	429	182	87	5	16	28	7	7	-	34	46	14	94	12	211	223	
	21	2	P. N. Nicholas,	169	345	199	9	-	-	-	-	-	18	6	17	1	-	49	53	-	102				
	22	2	John Robertson,	-	-	-	-	91	1598	276	87	3	-	-	-	-	-	77	26	21	124				
	8	6	Daniel A. Wilson,	687	779	635	11	125	715	76	96	17	42	77	42	6	-	45	42	-	87	240	180	420	No return has been received from the clerk of the circuit court of Lynchburg.
5	9	5	William Leigh,	572	482	610	4	102	419	144	108	5	83	50	42	17	-	30	38	-	68	260	165	425	
	10	6	N. M. Taliaferro,	5[illegible]1	608	576	3	118	341	137	140	20	87	139	59	31	-	33	40	5	78	390	265	655	No return from the clerk of the circuit court of Patrick county.
6	11	7	Richard H. Field,	443	421	573	10	68	345	168	98	8	25	55	15	15	-	49	36	15	100	206	308	514	
	12	5	Lucas P. Thompson,	904	1088	1092	7	205	1348	398	173	6	41	85	99	35	-	82	68	13	163	242	240	482	

Districts.	Circuits	No. counties, towns and cities in each circuit.	JUDGES.	Suits at Law. No. commenced.	No. pending.	No. decided.	No. removed from other courts.	Causes in Chancery. No. commenced.	No. pending.	No. interlocutory decrees.	No. final decrees.	No. removed from county courts.	Prosecutions. No. commenced.	No. pending.	No. decided.	No. nolle prosequis.	Change of venue.	Terms. Days in Session. Fall.	Spring.	Intermediate.	Total.	Miles Travelling. To general court	In circuit.	Total.	REMARKS.
7	13	6	I. R. Douglass,	677	513	764	2	181	1017	202	151	-	28	72	17	15	-	41	39	-	80	310	200	520	
	14	6	Daniel Smith,	219	290	256	4	59	274	65	48	3	17	24	27	1	-	20	19	-	39	268	257	525	
8	15	6	Benj. Estill,	242	330	294	3	71	330	101	103	-	42	143	106	21	-	48	43	6	97	618	270	888	
	16	7	J. E. Brown,	297	254	317	-	52	325	78	80	2	85	95	61	12	-	36	36	6	78	514	309	823	
9	17	7	E. Johnston,	366	340	348	3	89	434	89	101	1	38	52	28	2	-	32	28	-	60	330	240	570	
	18	8	E. S. Duncan,	390	669	456	14	168	821	113	157	-	127	167	70	15	2	53	53	-	106	590	363	953	
10	19	10	D. M'Comas,	812	836	957	-	121	430	128	71	-	124	252	125	24	-	77	84	22	183	640	425	1065	No return has been received from the clerk of the circuit court of Gilmer county, but he has notified the auditor that he has transmitted one by mail.
	20	9	Joseph L. Fry,	451	418	434	7	154	452	127	209	-	143	101	78	34	-	50½	52½	11	114	714	364	1078	No return has been received from the clerk of the circuit court of Tyler county.
			Total,	9864	10702	11065	180	2251	11646	3370	2256	89	1105	1592	929	293	3	957½	930½	163	2051	6638	5579	12217	
			Average of circuits,	479	509	526	8	107	554	160	107	4	52	75	44	13	-	43	42	7	93	331	278	610	

Judgments at law, - - - - - - 11,065
Interlocutory decrees, - - - - - 3,370
Final decrees, - - - - - - 2,250

Total decisions from which appeals may be had, 16,691

Number of appeals allowed, - 179—being something more than one per cent. of the total decisions in the circuit courts.

Causes decided in court of appeals, 125

Excess of new appeals over decisions, 54

GEORGE W. MUNFORD, *C. H. D.*

[*E. E.*]

REMARKS OF CLERKS.

SOUTHAMTON.

Note 1. In this return the judgments on forthcoming bonds are omitted.

GREENESVILLE.

2. In this report dismissions at rules and judgments on forthcoming bonds are embraced.

SURRY.

3. Of the suits at law decided, eight were dismissions in court; of those in chancery decided two were dismissions in court. The prosecutions commenced were criminal, one of which is now pending.

NANSEMOND.

4. Judgments on motions, judgments confessed in the office, dismissions in court or otherwise, and office judgments confirmed, are embraced in the number of suits decided at law.

PRINCESS ANNE.

5. Judgments in court and dismissions at rules are included under the head of suits decided, and writs of scire facias to revise judgments are included under the head of suits commenced. There is also one chancery cause sent back from court of appeals with instructions, &c.

NORFOLK CITY.

6 In the number of suits commenced, there are included 10 motions on forthcoming bonds, 1 other motion and 12 writs of habeas corpus; in the number decided, there are included 10 judgments on forthcoming bonds, one on another motion, 12 judgments or decisions on writs of habeas corpus and the dismissions of causes. In the number of final decrees, dismissions of causes are included. The intermediate term commenced 4th January 1847, and concluded 23d February.

NORFOLK COUNTY.

7. There was an intermediate term held in July 1847.

DINWIDDIE.

8. Judgments on motions and dismissions at rules are not included. Three chancery suits removed to other courts. Office judgments are embraced.

NOTTOWAY.

9. Motions on delivery bonds and by securities against their principals and co-securities not embraced in this report.

AMELIA.

10. Of the prosecutions, two in which *nolle prosequis* were entered were for felony, the parties having absented themselves--two others, breach of the peace, by fighting.

SUSSEX.

11. One chancery cause transferred from the circuit superior court of Dinwiddie county to this court.

PRINCE GEORGE.

12. Motions on delivery bonds are not included in the foregoing list. Among the suits in chancery decided, is embraced changes of venue. I sincerely hope that this is the last of these odious and perfectly useless lists which will be required of other clerks of this commonwealth and myself.

KING WILLIAM.

13. Motions on forfeited forthcoming bonds not included in this report.

ESSEX.

14. Suits at law commenced embrace one issue out of chancery. Those pending include 12 rules, one against a sheriff for failing to return a subpœna for a witness, and eleven rules against witnesses for failing to attend court. One motion against a sheriff for failing to pay over fees collected by him; and a motion to recover money paid as security. The number decided at law includes dismissions in the clerk's office and in court, judgments on forthcoming bonds, office judgments called in court and confirmed, and rules discharged. In chancery the interlocutory decrees embrace orders of revivor allowing parties to file answers and amended bills. Final decrees include dismissions in court.

MIDDLESEX.

15. This report includes causes from 31st August 1846, to 31st August 1847. Motions on forfeited forthcoming bonds and motions for judgments against securities where the original judgment had been discharged by any one of the original obligors, and motions by securities against the principal obligors in a contract, they having first discharged the execution or judgment, are not included; because the institution of and decision having been heretofore reported, if again reported it would seem that a number exceeding what was really in existence would be received.

GLOUCESTER.

16. The number of suits at law and in chancery pending, embrace those on the court docket on the 30th August; those decided include dismissions.

NORTHUMBERLAND.

17. In my younger days I was a lawyer, and while at the bar I contracted the habit of never making remarks unless I received a fee therefor. I hope therefore the clerk of the House of Delegates will excuse me for not making any remarks in this place.

WESTMORELAND.

18. Notices on forthcoming bonds not included in this return.

KING GEORGE.

19. Causes at rules included in number pending, and those pending are suits remaining undecided on the 30th August 1847.

FAUQUIER.

20. Eighty-one common law motions and 9 chancery motions not included in this statement.

LOUDOUN.

21. Thirty-four judgments on forthcoming bonds, and 2 decrees on motion not included in this report.

FAIRFAX.

22. Judgments on forthcoming bonds and notices not included.

ALEXANDRIA

23. The prosecutions consist of those cases pending in the late criminal court of the United States at the time of the retrocession of Alexandria county to Virginia. There are no others.

STAFFORD.

24. One notice, 1 ditto on forthcoming bond, and 1 scire facias reviving an old judgment embraced in suits at law commenced.

CHESTERFIELD.

25. Among the suits at law decided, are included office judgments confirmed, dismissions and abatements, but not judgments on forthcoming bonds, or motions of any kind. Among decrees in chancery, 4 have been set down as both interlocutory and final, being final in some respects and interlocutory in others Among prosecutions commenced, one case of felony is included, and among those decided, a capital felony, for which the party was convicted and executed. Among suits at law commenced are included writs of scire facias to revive judgments, but not those to revive pending actions. The suits removed from other courts were all from the county court of this county.

POWHATAN.

26. Of the 9 days stated as the session of the court in the spring of 1847, seven days were at the regular term of the court in May, and two days at a special term in August 1847.

GOOCHLAND.

27. In making out the lists of suits pending at law and in chancery, only such are included as stand on the court docket for trial or decision. All at the rules are consequently excluded. Forty-seven office judgments have been confirmed within the year, which are not included in the number of suits at law decided.

HANOVER.

28. Three days at a special term in January 1847.

HENRICO AND CITY OF RICHMOND.

29. The suits commenced include 4 writs of scire facias, 7 writs of supersedeas, 2 appeals from decisions of the auditor of public accounts, and a case for a divorce. Of the suits decided, judgments on forthcoming bonds, and on motions in other cases are included. Also judgments confessed in the office, nonsuits and dismissions in court, and excluding decisions on 2 writs of habeas corpus ad subjiciendum awarded in term; two causes removed to another court, and judgments entered in pursuance of decisions of the court of appeals.

HENRICO AND CITY OF RICHMOND.

30. Of the whole number of days the court was in session, Judge P. N. Nicholas sat 34 days for the trial of such causes as Judge Robertson could not properly decide. Of the whole number of interlocutory decrees, 26 were rendered by Judge Nicholas, and of the final decrees 6 were rendered by him. Six suits have been transferred to this court from circuit superior courts, and are embraced in this report. The number of final decrees is the number of suits actually disposed of by the court, and does not include dismissions at rules in the clerk's office.

APPOMATTOX.

31. Judgments on delivery bonds are not included in this report.

CAMPBELL.

32. The number of suits commenced embraces only original suits, and writs of scire facias are not included, and in the number decided, judgments on delivery bonds are not included. In consequence of the ill health of the judge he was unable to hold his spring term longer than four days, and consequently unable to call through the docket.

BEDFORD.

33. Of the causes depending on the common law docket, 90 are at rules, and 114 upon the court docket. In chancery, 131 at rules, and 121 on the court docket. Judgments on delivery bonds not included. These judgments are 62 in number—59 at law, and 3 in chancery.

LINCHBURG.

34. No report has been received from the clerk of Lynchburg.

HALIFAX.

35. Suits at law decided include office judgments and dismissions; those pending are suits on the court docket at the September term 1847. In causes in chancery, final decrees include dismissions.

LUNENBURG.

36. In the number of suits pending at law is included an appeal from a judgment of the county court, and in the chancery causes pending, a cause from Brunswick circuit court removed here by consent.

MECKLENBURG.

37. The sickness of the judge at the fall term prevented his trying all of the causes.

FLOYD.

38. Among the prosecutions were 4 cases of felony and 3 convictions. Motions for award of executions on forthcoming bonds are not included in this report.

PATRICK.

39. No report has been received from the clerk of Patrick.

HENRY.

40. Of the causes decided on the law side of the court, 21 were on forthcoming bonds

FRANKLIN.

41. Judgments on delivery bonds and other motions, and judgments, (of which there were many,) are not included in the number of suits commenced and decided. A prisoner charged with felony was indicted, tried and convicted at the fall term, and a new trial granted him by the general court. He was again tried and convicted at the spring term, and sent to the penitentiary. Another prisoner charged with horse stealing was also indicted, tried and convicted at the spring term, and a new trial granted him by this court.

PITTSYLVANIA.

42. No. pending includes all motions as well as cases remaining at rules, and cases decided No. decided includes as well other suits as all office judgments, motions on forfeited forthcoming bonds and other motions.

CARROLL.

43. There are 14 motions on delivery bonds, notices &c., not included in suits commenced, and five felonies not included under the head of prosecutions, and not heretofore reported.

LOUISA.

44. of the suits at law decided, 40 were office judgments, and 18 were motions. There were also 8 dismissions in chancery in court; 5 dismissions of cases at law in court, and 20 abatements and dismissions at rules.

GREENE.

45. Three judgments on forthcoming bonds included in number of suits decided.

CULPEPER.

46. Thirteen judgments on forthcoming bonds included in number of suits decided.

NELSON.

47. For this as well as in previous years, in the number of suits decided at common law, are included many judgments on delivery bonds and on other motions, notices, &c.

AUGUSTA.

48. In the number of suits commenced on the law side of the court is included 71 forthcoming bonds, leaving 199 suits commenced by writs of capias ad respondendum. In the number decided is also included the 71 forthcoming bonds.

JEFFERSON

49. In the number of common law suits decided are included 37 judgments on forthcoming bonds.

HAMPSHIRE.

50. Of the chancery causes 78 are on the trial docket, 76 on the deferred issue docket and 28 at rules.

FREDERICK.

51. There were judgments on 21 forthcoming bonds which are not included in the number decided on the law side. A large number of the suits depending on the chancery side are suits which were brought in the old district court, and which have remained sleeping ever since from the neglect of parties.

CLARKE.

52. Thirteen judgments on forthcoming bonds are not included. There was one suit at law removed to another court.

SHENANDOAH.

53. Suits decided at common law do not include judgments on forthcoming bonds; causes in chancery, interlocutory decres include all orders except mere continuances; final decrees include all dismissions.

WARREN.

54 There were within the year seven judgments on forfeited forthcoming bonds, and 1 motion on a notice to recover money paid as security which are not counted.

LEE.

55. There was an intermediate term in November of six days. The number of causes pending includes all commenced as well as those remaining on the rule docket, issue and office judgment docket. The court generally commences at an early hour and adjourns late in the evening

SCOTT.

56. The suits pending include one scire facias and 4 rules; and in those determined are included one in which the venue was changed to the county of Russell and 9 in which the judgments entered at rules were made final; but judgments on delivery bonds and rules against witnesses are not included.

RUSSELL.

57. Office judgments entered as of the last day of the term, dismissions in the office and motions on forthcoming bonds are included with suits at law decided. The judge passed through the docket, deciding all causes ready at the fall term; but at the spring term there was not time to try all the causes standing for trial.

TAZEWELL.

58 Dismissions at law and chancery both at rules and in court included in this report. Judgments on forthcoming bonds not embraced herein.

GILES.

59. The causes reported in chancery do not embrace the suits at rules, none of which were in a condition for trial or decision.

MERCER.

60. This return does not embrace judgments on forthcomngbonds.

BOTETOURT.

61. Of the sutis at law decided, 18 were judgments upon forfeited forthcoming bonds. Of the final decrees in chancery, 5 were also judgments on delivery bonds. Of the causes pending in chancery 84 were at rules.

HIGHLAND.

62. New county formed at the last session of the Legislature.

GREENBRIER.

63. Judgments on forthcoming bonds not included.

FAYETTE.

64. Judgments on notices and forthcoming bonds are not included in this report. There was no court held at the spring term 1847, on account of the small pox prevailing at Fayette court-house at this time.

LEWIS.

65. In the number of suits at law decided and final decrees in chancery, I have included judgments on forthcoming bonds, notices, &c., and in the number of prosecutions commenced and decided are included rules against witnesses, &c. I have nothing unusual to report, except that litigation is becoming rather dull; cannot the wit and wisdom of the Virginia legislature devise some means by which it may be restored to life, and thereby save from inevitable ruin an oppressed and grateful people.

BRAXTON.

66. There are 17 judgments on forthcoming bonds not included in this list.

NICHOLAS.

67. Motions on forthcoming bonds not included in this report.

JACKSON.

68. There is not sufficient time allowed us for the transaction of the business of the court.

MASON.

69. The column of suits commenced includes writs of supersedeas. The column of suits dceided includes dismissions, but excludes judgments on forthcoming bonds.

LOGAN.

70. Like the poor boy at the frolic.

BOONE.

71. There was no fall term prior to 31st August 1847. This county having been created last winter.

KANAWHA.

72. Number of suits at law and in chancery pending include those at rules. The number decided at law include judgments on forthcoming bonds and dismissions. There were special terms in January and August.

GILMER.

73 No return has been received from the clerk of this court, though a letter has been received by the first auditor, stating that one has been sent by mail.

PRESTON.

74. Judgments on forthcoming bonds not included.

MONONGALIA.

75. The number of suits commenced at law includes 14 motions on forthcoming bonds, and 5 other notices. The number decided at law includes the same number of motions and notices. The number commenced in chancery includes 3 motions on forthcoming bonds. The number of final decrees includes 6 dismissions at rules.

MARION.

76. Judgments on forthcoming bonds not ncluded.

TYLER.

77. No return has been received from the clerk of this court.

WETZEL.

78. The column of the number decided includes dismissions.

OHIO.

79. Causes at rules are included in those pending, and in those decided are embraced dismissions at rules.

MARSHALL.

80. The final decrees include dismissions. Many orders made in preparing causes for submission are not embraced in the number of interlocutory decrees, such as revivals, appointing guardians *ad litem*.

ABSTRACT FROM THE REPORTS

OF THE

CLERKS OF THE COURT OF APPEALS,

AND OF THE

CIRCUIT SUPERIOR COURTS OF LAW AND CHANCERY,

For the Year ending the 30th August, 1848; *exhibiting the number of Suits, &c.*

COURT OF APPEALS.

JUDGES.	CLERKS.	Location of Court.	Suits commenced.	Pending.	Decided.	No. of days in session.	REMARKS.
Wm. H. Cabell, *President*,	Joseph Allen,	Richmond, -	71	550	72	138	The term of the court commenced on the 15th day of October 1847, and ended on the 14th day of May 1848, comprising 162 days, having had within that time two recesses, one of 25 days and the other of 27 days, and having actually sat 138 days, exclusive of Sundays.
Francis T. Brooke, -							
John J. Allen, - -							
Briscoe G. Baldwin, -							
William Daniel, -	John A. North,	Lewisburg, -	45	139	20	30	
		Total,	116	689	92	168	

CIRCUIT SUPERIOR COURTS OF LAW AND CHANCERY.

Districts.	Circuits.	JUDGES.	CLERKS.	COUNTIES.	Suits at Law.				Causes in Chancery.					Prosecutions.					Terms. Days in session.				REMARKS.
					No. commenced.	No. pending.	No. decided.	No. removed from other courts.	No. commenced.	No. pending.	No. interlocutory decrees.	No. final decrees.	No. removed from county courts.	No. commenced.	No. pending.	No. decided.	Nolle prosequis.	Change of venue.	Fall.	Spring.	Intermediate or special.	Total.	
1st	1st	Rh'd H. Baker,	G. R. Edwards,	Southampton,	63	45	58	1	10	31	27	12	-	10	10	5	-	-	3	3	-	6	
			Joseph Turner,	Greenesville,	32	18	36	-	1	11	6	7	2	1	-	2	1	-	3	3	-	6	
			W. P. Underwood	Surry,	15	10	11	-	2	7	11	6	1	3	3	1	-	-	4	2	-	6	Note 1.
			N. P. Young,	Isle of Wight,	26	14	18	-	8	15	9	14	-	5	5	3	1	-	3	3	-	6	
			Joseph Prentiss,	Nansemond,	24	6	37	-	6	13	12	12	-	8	11	1	-	-	4	3	-	7	Note 2.
			J. J. Burroughs,	Princess Anne,	48	33	66	-	8	13	2	4	-	-	-	-	-	-	2	2	-	4	Note 3.
			John Williams,	Norfolk City,	181	130	163	2	17	50	25	26	4	7	2	5	2	-	18	17	-	35	Note 4.
			Art. Emmerson,	Norfolk county,	135	31	80	2	11	24	13	16	-	18	14	11	6	-	13	11	-	24	
				Total in circuit,	524	287	469	4	63	164	105	97	7	52	45	28	10	-	50	44	-	94	
	2d	J. H. Gholson, (dead,)	John P. Crump,	Dinwiddie,	47	49	14	1	9	43	9	10	-	3	4	1	-	-	4	-	-	4	Note 5.
			F. Fitzgerald,	Nottoway,	92	107	34	1	15	50	10	2	2	4	10	3	2	-	3	-	-	3	
		J. W. Nash,	Egbert G. Leigh,	Amelia,	84	145	32	1	12	32	6	5	1	6	14	2	-	-	3	-	-	3	Note 6.
			E. R. Turnbull,	Brunswick,	44	47	10	1	9	29	6	6	1	12	23	2	5	-	3	-	-	3	Note 7.
			J. T. J Mason,	Sussex,	27	31	22	-	12	24	6	4	-	3	4	1	-	-	2	-	-	2	Note 8.
			Robert Gilliam,	Prince George,	9	3	19	1	5	11	3	12	-	4	22	11	1	-	4	-	-	4	Note 9.
			Henry B. Gaines,	Petersburg,	181	163	106	1	23	133	41	12	1	19	23	4	-	-	15	-	-	15	
				Total in circuit,	484	545	237	6	85	322	81	51	5	51	100	24	8	-	34	-	-	34	
2d	3d	G. P. Scarburg	Thos. O. Cogbill,	James City and Williamsburg,	73	49	88	2	16	121	52	15	-	38	34	7	-	-	7	9	-	16	
			Bolivar Sheild,	York,	32	24	8	-	6	16	-	5	-	9	17	6	-	-	5	5	-	10	
			Wm. B. Jones,	Warwick,	10	17	4	-	2	10	6	-	-	5	6	-	2	-	3	2	-	5	

			S. S. Howard,	Elizabeth City,	56	28	45	1	7	26	17	5	.	5	1	1	4	.	4	3	.	7	
			L. P. Rogers,	Northampton,	48	25	46	.	1	19	12	10	.	.	.	.	.	.	5	4	.	9	
			J. J. Ailworth,	Accomack,	70	73	67	1	24	50	46	11	.	19	19	4	4	.	10	14	.	24	
				Total in circuit,	289	216	258	4	56	242	133	46	.	76	79	18	10	.	3	734	.	71	
	4th	J.B. Christian,	Robert Pollard,	King William,	59	20	57	1	6	32	23	12	.	1	.	1	1	.	6	4	.	10	Note 10.
			Rob. Pollard, jr.	King and Queen,	47	32	38	.	18	36	16	19	.	12	5	7	2	.	6	6	.	12	Note 11.
			J. Roy Micou, jr.	Essex,	49	60	67	1	10	30	25	9	1	5	1	5	.	.	4	4	.	8	Note 12.
			Ro. N. Trice.	Middlesex,	16	20	31	.	5	40	10	15	.	1	1	1	.	.	5	3	.	8	Note 13.
			John R. Cary,	Gloucester,	67	76	100	3	21	72	24	16	.	6	7	3	.	.	6	5	.	11	Note 14.
			Shep. G. Miller,	Mathews,	15	37	19	1	8	92	13	.	1	1	.	1	.	.	2	4	.	6	
				Total in circuit,	253	245	312	6	68	302	111	71	2	26	14	18	3	.	29	26	.	55	
3d	5th	J. T. Lomax,	R. T. Dunaway,	Lancaster,	15	19	21	.	2	6	1	3	.	.	1	2	.	.	2	2	.	4	
			J. R. Stith,	Northumberland	31	5	51	2	2	6	9	4	2	2	.	2	1	.	5	2	.	7	
			J. S. Jeffries,	Richmond co'ty,	60	63	72	5	17	36	23	14	.	1	5	.	.	.	5	4	.	9	
			William Hutt,	Westmoreland,	79	121	108	2	14	54	15	10	.	2	1	3	.	.	4	3	.	7	Note 15.
			Wm. S. Brown,	King George,	35	17	22	.	5	15	8	7	.	4	4	2	2	.	3	2	.	5	
			Robert Hudgin,	Caroline,	84	66	110	.	1	50	43	5	.	3	5	2	.	.	4	3	.	7	
			John J. Chew,	Spottsylvania,	80	49	84	2	7	443	41	18	.	6	8	6	2	.	18	17	.	35	
				Total in circuit,	374	340	468	11	48	610	140	61	2	18	24	17	5	.	41	33	.	74	
	6th	John Scott,	Wm. F. Phillips,	Fauquier,	151	268	173	.	50	406	239	45	1	2	3	7	3	.	11	10	.	21	Note 16.
			Thos. P. Knox,	Loudoun,	159	189	155	4	33	167	98	41	1	1	1	1	.	.	6	7	6	19	Note 17.
				Prince William,																			
			F. D. Richardson,	Fairfax,	145	125	137	1	44	151	70	26	1	2	.	3	1	.	5	4	.	9	Note 18.
			Cassius F. Lee,	Alexandria,	95	125	92	.	28	95	13	35	2	2	.	2	.	.	6	5	.	11	Note 19.
			H. H. Conway,	Stafford,	22	12	14	.	12	33	7	8	.	3	1	3	1	.	2	4	.	6	Note 20.
				Total in circuit,	572	719	571	5	167	852	427	155	5	10	5	16	5	.	30	30	6	66	
4th	7th	J. B. Clopton,	R. W. Flournoy,	Chesterfield,	77	126	140	5	24	113	38	26	2	43	45	6	2	.	8	7	3	18	Note 21.
			E. T. Christian,	Charles City,	11	17	15	3	4	20	4	2	.	2	2	.	.	.	3	3	4	10	
			J. D. Christian,	New Kent,	18	22	22	1	2	23	26	7	.	2	1	2	1	.	5	8	.	13	
			Wm. S. Dance,	Powhatan,	74	64	110	2	11	71	19	16	2	1	1	2	.	.	9	6	6	21	Note 22.
			Nar. W. Miller,	Goochland,	78	167	79	.	3	72	20	19	1	5	5	3	.	.	8	9	.	17	Note 23.

Districts.	Circuits.	JUDGES.	CLERKS.	COUNTIES.	SUITS AT LAW.				CAUSES IN CHANCERY.					PROSECUTIONS.					TERMS. *Days in session.*				REMARKS.
					No. commenced.	No. pending.	No. decided.	No. removed from other courts.	No. commenced.	No. pending.	No. interlocutory decrees.	No. final decrees.	No. removed from county courts.	No. commenced.	No. pending.	No. decided.	No. nolle prosequis	Change of venue.	Fall.	Spring.	Intermediate or special.	Total.	
			Ph. B. Winston,	Hanover,	52	156	40	2	17	147	43	15	1	2	4	3	3	-	12	11	-	23	
				Total in circuit,	310	552	416	13	61	466	150	85	6	55	58	16	6	-	45	44	13	102	
	21st	P. N. Nicholas,	John Robinson,	Henrico and city of Richmond,	230	433	143	7	-	-	-	-	-	26	16	13	2	-	52	55	-	107	Note 24.
	22d	J. Robertson,	P. Roberts,	Henrico and City of Richmond,	-	-	-	-	106	1604	184	94	4	-	-	-	-	-	75	25	14	114	Note 25.
	8th	D. A. Wilson,	B. B. Woodson,	Cumberland,	98	73	125	-	9	56	22	28	1	-	13	-	5	-	8	9	-	17	
			Rolfe Eldridge,	Buckingham,	96	180	143	-	30	130	17	23	2	2	1	-	9	-	-	12	-	12	Note 26.
			H. F. Bocock,	Appomattox,	37	63	24	1	12	32	8	3	-	1	6	3	-	-	-	6	-	6	Note 27.
			J. D. Alexander,	Campbell,	110	194	145	-	20	168	4	5	-	1	8	1	-	-	-	13	-	13	Note 28.
			David Rodes,	Lynchburg,	83	197	43	1	17	293	47	17	-	19	7	4	12	-	6	31	-	37	
				Total in circuit,	424	707	480	2	88	679	98	76	-	23	35	8	26	-	14	71	-	85	
5th	9th	William Leigh,	William Holt,	Halifax,	101	57	167	-	36	92	43	34	2	10	6	6	7	-	13	13	-	26	
			W. Robinson,	Charlotte,	76	57	78	-	16	46	14	20	-	7	4	5	2	-	5	5	-	10	
			B. J. Worsham,	Prince Edward,	73	83	97	1	15	105	67	30	-	10	9	5	-	-	6	8	-	16	
			Thos. W. Winn,	Lunenburg,	61	49	80	3	10	35	9	29	3	3	12	6	3	-	6	4	-	10	Note 29.
			R. B. Baptist,	Mecklenburg,	85	96	125	-	16	101	22	19	-	11	22	16	8	-	10	8	-	18	
				Total in circuit,	396	342	547	4	93	379	156	132	5	41	47	38	20	-	42	38	-	80	
	10th	N M Taliaferro	J. N. Zentmeyer,	Floyd,	22	19	22	3	8	35	28	10	-	51	39	23	1	-	6	4	-	10	
			Sam. G. Staples,	Patrick,	89	76	85	-	24	42	49	20	3	16	17	8	2	-	9	9	-	18	
			Ant'y M. Dupuy,	Henry,	86	84	97	1	10	42	28	37	-	22	21	16	5	-	5	6	-	11	Note 30.

			M. G. Carper,	Franklin,	244	148	237	-	31	94	77	35	4	15	22	17	6	-	9	11	-	20	Note 31.
			W. H. Tunstall,	Pittsylvania,	162	324	173	-	41	195	98	49	3	20	44	25	2	-	9	13	-	22	Note 32.
			Joseph Wilson,	Bedford,	182	201	191	8	24	233	34	44	1	8	23	21	-	-	11	11	-	22	Note 33.
			M. D. Carter,	Carroll,	72	44	77	3	15	34	36	6	2	29	30	24	8	-	6	5	-	11	Note 34.
				Total in circuit,	657	696	682	15	153	675	350	201	13	161	196	134	24	-	55	59	-	114	
6th	11th	Rd. H. Field,	John Hunter,	Louisa,	43	94	51	-	7	65	26	11	-	6	5	2	-	-	6	6	-	12	Note 35.
6th	11th		A. Shepherd, jr.	Fluvanna,	96	82	95	1	25	38	18	33	1	4	8	3	-	-	7	7	-	14	Note 36.
6th	11th		P. S. Fry,	Orange,	50	66	55	4	9	51	14	2	3	7	11	1	-	-	5	5	-	10	
6th	11th		Rob't Pritchett,	Greene,	56	38	18	-	7	23	7	3	-	8	4	4	-	-	4	4	-	8	
6th	11th		Belfield Cave,	Madison,	65	45	51	-	8	43	12	8	-	2	3	-	1	-	5	6	-	11	
6th	11th		R. G. Ward,	Culpeper,	67	83	87	-	24	119	28	11	1	1	15	5	4	-	17	11	25	53	Note 37.
6th	11th		Wm. J. Menefee,	Rappahannock,	17	15	17	3	8	43	35	5	3	10	13	6	1	-	5	6	-	11	Note 38.
				Total in circuit,	394	423	374	8	88	382	140	73	8	38	59	21	6	-	49	45	25	119	
6th	12th	L. P Thompson	Robert Tinsley,	Amherst,	114	216	126	2	22	307	71	15	1	3	9	4	-	-	6	9	-	15	
6th	12th		D. Hutchison,	Rockbridge,	78	56	65	-	35	156	77	16	1	47	42	17	2	-	9	11	-	20	
6th	12th		H. L. Brown,	Nelson,	124	220	223	-	47	335	99	43	-	4	11	7	2	-	13	13	-	26	Note 40.
6th	12th		Alex. Garrett,	Albemarle,	246	402	191	1	27	138	21	12	3	35	64	28	4	-	14	15	-	29	
6th	12th		N. C. Kinney,	Augusta,	108	307	152	3	42	428	105	69	-	3	3	5	-	-	16	30	3	49	Note 41.
				Total in circuit,	670	1201	757	6	173	1364	373	155	5	92	129	61	8	-	58	78	3	139	
7th	13th	J. R. Douglass,	Rob't T. Brown,	Jefferson,	150	154	192	1	35	255	67	62	1	1	3	18	-	-	17	16	-	33	Note 42.
7th	13th		John Strother,	Berkeley,	101	130	120	-	24	175	-	27	1	2	6	2	-	-	6	5	-	11	Note 43.
7th	13th		Isaiah Buck,	Morgan,	33	52	48	-	7	32	6	11	-	9	10	5	-	-	3	5	-	8	Note 44.
7th	13th		John B. White,	Hampshire,	126	151	176	2	31	197	52	32	-	7	15	7	2	-	5	5	-	10	Note 45.
7th	13th		J. Kean,	Frederick,	62	99	58	-	21	329	53	32	-	8	14	16	4	-	5	4	-	9	Note 46.
7th	13th		H. H. Lee,	Clarke,	70	94	25	-	12	53	5	-	-	2	9	-	-	-	2	2	-	4	Note 47.
				Total in circuit,	542	680	619	3	131	1021	193	164	2	29	57	48	6	-	38	37	-	75	
7th	14th	Daniel Smith,	W. C. Lauck,	Page,	10	12	10	3	1	11	4	2	1	2	5	1	-	-	2	2	-	4	
7th	14th		S. C. Williams,	Shenandoah,	19	16	17	-	6	39	15	3	-	-	1	-	-	-	-	1	2	3	
7th	14th		Robert Turner,	Warren,	23	12	25	-	9	21	10	8	-	3	3	2	-	-	-	3	4	7	Note 48.
7th	14th		C. Lobb,	Hardy,	55	57	44	2	23	134	44	18	1	1	3	1	-	-	3	3	-	6	
7th	14th		Z. Dyer,	Pendleton,	7	5	9	-	1	12	1	-	-	11	10	1	4	-	3	3	-	6	

Districts.	Circuits.	JUDGES.	CLERKS.	COUNTIES.	Suits at Law.				Causes in Chancery.					Prosecutions.					Terms. Days in session				REMARKS.
					No. commenced.	No. pending.	No. decided.	No. removed from other courts.	No. commenced.	No. pending.	No. interlocutory decrees.	No. final decrees.	No. removed from county courts.	No. commenced.	No. pending.	No. decided.	No.nolleprosequis	Change of venue.	Fall.	Spring.	Intermediate or special.	Total.	
			L. W. Gambill,	Rockingham,	125	157	91	2	25	62	16	8	-	6	9	3	2	-	8	9	.	17	
				Total in circuit,	239	259	196	7	65	279	90	39	2	23	31	8	6	.	16	21	6	43	
8th	15th	Benj. Estill,	J. W. S. Morrison	Lee,	28	51	47	3	4	44	14	13	.	10	25	7	-	1	5	7	1	13	Note 49.
			S. H. Morrison,	Scott,	39	49	55	1	4	34	6	3	2	17	25	16	1	.	6	5	.	11	Note 50.
			James P. Carroll,	Russell,	24	50	42	.	6	22	4	3	.	26	34	21	4	.	6	4	.	10	Note 51.
			W. Y. Brown,	Tazewell,	57	67	58	.	14	55	46	24	.	21	26	29	5	.	5	3	.	8	Note 52.
			Con'ly F. Trigg,	Washington,	26	41	35	.	8	104	27	15	.	27	28	9	4	.	12	9	.	21	Note 53.
				Smyth,																			
				Total in circuit,	174	258	237	4	36	259	97	58	2	101	138	72	14	1	34	28	1	63	
	16th	Jas. E. Brown,	W. A. Stuart,	Wythe,	55	40	40	.	11	115	8	13	1	37	36	26	4	.	10	8	.	18	Note 54.
			O. Anderson,	Grayson,	26	24	32	3	2	22	13	8	.	6	14	8	.	.	4	5	.	9	Note 55.
			R. D. Montague,	Montgomery,	63	52	58	.	12	57	4	24	1	35	16	14	2	.	6	5	.	11	
			J. B. Baskerville,	Pulaski,	30	47	34	.	6	22	8	13	.	7	.	.	3	.	.	.	.	8	
			Rufus A. French,	Giles,	69	57	67	.	12	19	10	3	.	8	13	5	1	.	3	3	.	6	Note 56.
			Alex. Mahood,	Mercer,	27	20	25	23	3	16	5	3	.	2	2	6	1	.	5	5	.	10	Note 57
			J. Hutchinson,	Monroe,	41	39	43	.	13	67	23	9	.	19	16	8	1	.	5	5	.	10	
				Total in circuit,	311	279	299	26	59	318	61	73	2	114	97	67	12	.	33	31	.	64	
9th	17th	E. Johnston,	H. W. Bowyer,	Botetourt,	71	108	110	8	39	220	13	27	2	58	66	5	.	.	10	11	.	21	Note 58.
			Andrew Fudge,	Alleghany,	16	28	25	.	6	40	6	8	.	.	.	5	.	.	3	3	.	6	
			F. Johnston,	Roanoke,	17	9	14	.	12	18	2	6	.	.	3	1	.	.	6	5	.	11	
			Ch. L. Francisco,	Bath,	30	34	46	.	14	56	19	5	.	.	3	4	1	.	5	5	.	10	
			A. Stephenson jr	Highland,	25	22	7	4	2	1	.	1	.	.	.	.	.	.	.	1	.	1	
			Wm. S. Keen,	Pocahontas,	39	35	29	.	14	23	5	11	.	4	5	2	.	.	4	4	.	8	

			John A. North,	Greenbrier,	53	74	93	-	10	95	9	13	-	22	24	7	-	-	4	5	-	9 Note 59.
				Total in circuit,	251	310	324	12	97	453	54	71	2	84	101	24	1	-	32	34	-	66
	18th	Ed. S. Duncan, (resigned.) George H. Lee	H. M. Dickinson,	Fayette,	36	53	65	3	14	55	6	15	-	6	20	16	3	-	6	5	-	11 Note 60.
			A. W. Quarrier,	Kanawha,	278	379	523	-	19	136	72	18	-	69	75	15	15	-	22	33	-	55 Note 61.
			H. H. Forbs,	Putnam,	11	22	1	11	2	4	-	-	3	-	-	-	-	-	-	2	-	2 Note 62.
			B. S. Brown,	Randolph,	19	64	12	1	5	54	-	6	-	-	8	4	-	-	5	-	-	5 Note 63.
			John Talbot,	Lewis,	90	222	86	3	38	250	12	19	1	13	45	11	2	-	17	-	-	17
			W. Newlon,	Braxton,	47	81	69	1	21	54	14	12	-	15	18	7	5	-	6	4	-	10 Note 64.
			G. G. Davisson,	Harrison,	87	162	95	2	39	310	28	31	-	15	25	16	1	-	15	11	-	26
			A. Armstrong,	Taylor,	17	19	12	-	2	24	10	10	-	4	6	4	-	1	4	4	-	8 Note 65.
			Robt. Hamilton,	Nicholas,	17	6	27	-	6	24	3	6	-	6	9	1	-	-	2	5	-	7 Note 66.
				Total in circuit,	602	1008	900	21	146	911	145	117	4	128	206	74	26	1	77	64	-	141
10th	19th	D. M'Comas,	J. H. Neal,	Wood,	82	185	54	-	28	147	25	16	-	47	72	14	3	-	9	8	-	17
			A. G. Stringer,	Wirt,	15	14	3	2	5	5	-	-	-	9	9	-	-	-	1	1	-	2
			T. Stinchcomb,	Ritchie,	17	22	-	-	12	28	11	4	-	33	32	8	7	-	3	3	-	6
			D. G. Morrill,	Jackson,	58	121	45	1	15	54	4	16	-	40	59	10	-	-	5	9	-	14
			G. W. Stribbling,	Mason,	37	41	46	-	8	23	8	9	-	59	40	9	4	-	7	6	-	13 Note 67.
			John Samuels,	Cabell,	16	18	11	1	6	7	5	6	-	34	46	10	-	-	6	5	-	11
			Ezekiel Bloss,	Wayne,	11	8	8	-	12	3	3	1	-	17	22	22	-	-	4	3	-	7
			No signature to this report.	Logan,	7	19	19	-	3	4	2	3	-	19	39	5	10	-	5	3	-	8
			B. E. Barrett,	Boone,	8	4	4	-	3	7	-	-	2	12	13	-	-	-	2	2	-	4
			Will. Hatcher,	Gilmer,	50	33	76	7	18	29	5	2	-	4	11	6	-	-	7	4	-	11 Note 68.
				Total in circuit,	301	465	256	11	110	307	63	57	2	274	343	84	24	-	49	44	-	93
	20th	Joseph L. Fry,	Jno. P. Byrne,	Preston,	59	39	44	1	12	55	18	10	-	10	12	6	2	-	6	6	-	12 Note 69.
			W. T. Willey,	Monongalia,	44	35	74	-	31	66	33	30	-	12	12	11	1	-	8	8	-	16 Note 70.
			Jas. O. Watson,	Marion,	38	34	45	-	12	54	24	22	-	17	14	15	2	-	8	8	-	16 Note 71.
			D. Hickman,	Tyler,	29	48	28	-	4	51	13	12	-	1	4	1	9	-	4	4	-	8
			Friend Cox,	Wetzel,	9	6	3	-	6	5	-	1	-	22	19	3	-	-	2	2	-	4 Note 72.
			F. D. Hickman,	Doddridge,	8	17	12	-	4	16	2	5	3	-	5	10	2	-	5	2	-	7
			Adam Kuhn,	Brooke,	26	48	39	-	8	68	22	18	-	2	6	5	1	-	7	7	-	14
			Alex. T. Laidley,	Hancock. Ohio,	154	130	142	1	61	168	36	39	-	20	41	17	1	-	11	14	11	36 Note 73.

Districts.	Circuits.	JUDGES.	CLERKS.	COUNTIES.	Suits at Law.				Causes in Chancery.					Prosecutions.					Terms. Days in Session.				Remarks of Clerks.
					No. commenced.	No. pending.	No. decided.	No. removed from other courts.	No. commenced.	No. pending.	No. interlocutory decrees.	No. final decrees.	No. removed from county courts.	No. commenced.	No. pending.	No. decided.	No. nolleprosequis.	Change of venue.	Fall.	Spring.	Intermediate or special.	Total.	
			Jas. D. Morris,	Marshall,	32	43	34	-	9	52	5	13	-	16	13	1	2	-	6	5	-	11	
			E. D. Wilson,	Barbour,	36	58	43	1	23	95	5	12	1	19	20	10	1	-	6	6	-	12	
				Total in circuit.	435	458	464	3	170	630	158	162	4	119	146	79	21	-	63	62	11	136	

E. E.

GEORGE W. MUNFORD, *C. H. D.*

RECAPITULATION.

CIRCUIT SUPERIOR COURTS OF LAW AND CHANCERY,

Exhibiting the Number of Suits, &c., in each Circuit, August 30th, 1848..

Districts.	Circuits.	No. of counties, towns & cities in each circuit.	JUDGES.	Suits at Law.				Causes in Chancery.					Prosecutions.					Terms. Days in session.				Miles travelling.			REMARKS.
				No. commenced.	No. pending.	No. decided.	No. removed from other courts.	No. commenced.	No. pending.	No. interlocutory decrees.	No. final decrees.	No. removed from county courts.	No. commenced.	No. pending.	No. decided.	No nolle prosequis	Change of venue.	Fall.	Spring.	Intermediate.	Total.	To general court.	In circuit.	Total.	
1	1	8	Rh'd H. Baker,	524	287	469	4	63	164	105	97	7	52	45	28	10	-	50	44	-	94	-	255	255	
	2	7	J. H. Gholson, (dead,) and John W. Nash,	484	545	237	6	85	322	81	51	5	51	100	24	8	-	34	-	-	34	-	380	380	
2	3	6	G. P. Scarburg	289	216	258	4	56	242	133	46	-	76	79	18	10	-	34	37	-	71	-	407	407	
	4	7	J. B. Christian,	253	245	312	6	68	302	111	71	2	26	14	18	3	-	29	26	-	55	-	230	230	
3	5	7	Jno. T. Lomax,	374	340	468	11	48	610	140	61	2	18	24	17	5	-	41	33	-	74	140	218	358	
	6	5	John Scott,	572	719	571	5	167	852	427	155	5	10	5	16	5	-	30	30	6	66	220	292	512	No report has been received from the county of Prince William.
4	7	5	J. B. Clopton,	310	552	416	13	61	466	150	85	6	55	58	16	6	-	45	44	13	102	-	211	211	
	21	2	P. N. Nicholas,	230	433	143	7	-	-	-	-	-	-	26	16	13	2	52	55	-	107				
	22	2	J. Robertson,	-	-	-	-	106	1604	184	94	4	-	-	-	-	-	75	25	14	114				
	8	6	D. A. Wilson,	424	707	480	2	88	679	98	76	-	23	35	8	26	-	14	71	-	85	-	180	180	
5	9	5	Wm. Leigh,	396	342	547	4	93	379	156	132	5	41	47	38	20	-	42	38	-	80	260	165	425	
	10	6	N. M Taliaferro	657	696	682	15	153	675	350	201	13	161	196	134	24	-	55	59	-	114	-	265	265	
6	11	7	Rh'd H. Field,	394	423	374	8	88	382	140	73	8	38	59	21	6	-	49	45	25	119	206	308	514	
	12	5	L. P. Thompson	670	1201	757	6	173	1364	373	155	5	92	120	61	8	-	53	78	3	139	-	240	240	
7	13	6	I. R. Douglass,	542	680	619	3	131	1021	193	164	2	29	57	48	6	-	38	37	-	75	-	200	200	
	14	6	Daniel Smith,	239	259	196	7	65	279	90	39	2	23	31	8	6	-	16	21	6	43	268	257	525	

Districts.	Circuits.	No. of counties, towns & cities in each circuit.	JUDGES.	Suits at Law.				Causes in Chancery.					Prosecutions.					Terms. Days in Session.				Miles Travelling.			REMARKS.
				No. commenced.	No. pending.	No. decided.	No. removed from other courts.	No. commenced.	No. pending.	No. interlocutory decrees.	No. final decrees.	No. removed from county courts.	No. commenced.	No. pending.	No. decided.	No. nolle prosequis	Change of venue.	Fall.	Spring.	Intermediate.	Total.	To general court.	In circuit.	Total.	
8	15	6	Benj. Estill,	174	258	237	4	36	259	97	58	2	101	138	72	14	1	34	28	1	63	-	270	270	No report received from the county of Smyth.
	16	7	Jas. E. Brown,	311	279	299	26	59	318	61	73	2	114	97	67	12	-	33	31	-	64	-	309	309	
9	17	7	Ed. Johnston,	251	310	324	12	97	453	54	71	2	84	101	24	1	-	32	34	-	66	-	240	240	
	18	9	E. S. Duncan, (resigned.)	602	1008	900	21	146	911	145	117	4	128	206	74	26	1	77	64	-	141	-	363	363	
10	19	10	Geo. H. Lee, Dav. M'Comas,	301	465	256	11	110	307	63	57	2	274	343	84	24	-	49	44	-	93	-	425	425	
	20	11	Joseph L. Fry,	435	458	464	3	170	630	158	162	4	119	146	79	21	-	63	62	11	136	-	364	364	No report from the new county of Hancock.
			Total,	8432	10423	9009	178	2063	12219	3309	2038	82	1515	1936	871	254	4	950	906	79	1935				The mileage of the judges is taken from the last year's report, and is not entirely accurate, some of the judges not having settled their accounts.
			Average of circuits,	401	496	429	8	98	581	157	97	3	72	92	41	12	-	43	41	3	87				

Judgments at law,	9,009
Interlocutory decrees,	3,309
Final decrees,	2,038
Total decisions from which appeals may be had,	14,356

Number of appeals allowed, 116—being about five-sixths of one per cent. of the total of decisions of the circuit courts.

Causes decided in court of appeals, 92

Excess of new appeals over decisions, 24

E. E.

GEORGE W. MUNFORD, *C. H. D.*

REMARKS OF CLERKS.

FIRST CIRCUIT.

SURRY.

Note 1. Of the number reported to have been received at law, one was a motion by a security against a co-security, and one was an appeal in a road case.

NANSEMOND.

2. All judgments on motions, judgments confessed in the office, all dismissions in court or otherwise, and office judgments confirmed, are embraced in number of suits decided.

PRINCESS ANNE.

3. All judgments in court and dismissions at rules are included under the head of suits decided.

NORFOLK CITY.

4. In the number of suits at law commenced, 6 cases of writs of habeas corpus, and 5 motions are included. In the number decided at law, 6 cases of writs of habeas corpus, 5 judgments on motions, 22 confessions of judgments in the office, and 33 dismissions at rules, are included. In the number of final decrees in chancery, 8 dismissions at rules are included.

SECOND CIRCUIT.

DINWIDDIE.

5. Judgments on motions, dismissions at rules and office judgments, are not embraced in this report.—One chancery suit removed to Greenesville circuit court.

BRUNSWICK.

6. In consequence of the illness of Judge Gholson, no court was held in the spring.

SUSSEX.

7. One appeal from county court decided, and executions awarded on two delivery bonds.

PRINCE GEORGE.

8. In this list is included all motions on delivery bonds, appeals, &c. In consequence of the illness of the late estimable Judge Gholson, he held no court at the spring term.

AMELIA.

9. No court held for spring of 1848, on account of the illness of the Judge.

FOURTH CIRCUIT.

KING WILLIAM.

10. Judgments on motions, &c., not included in this report.

ESSEX.

11. Number at law pending embraces all on court docket at rules, which includes all rules against witnesses, and all motions. Number decided includes all judgments on forthcoming bonds and office judgments, and all rules of court discharged. In chancery, interlocutory decrees include all orders except orders continuing suits. I would be pleased to see the law repealed, as I know of no practical good from it; and there is no compensation for the trouble, which is not a little.

KING AND QUEEN.

12. Three suits on law side removed to other courts.

MIDDLESEX.

13. I have stated the number pending on 30th August 1848, and not the number which were pending during the period intervening between 30th August 1847 and 30th August 1848, there being some doubt on my mind in interpreting the act on the subject, believing that the legislature intended the report to embrace only those pending on said 30th August 1848, as the phraseology of the act is, "the number pending at the time of making such report." In the number decided at common law, I have embraced those disposed

of at rules, as well as those disposed of by the court in term time. The final decrees in chancery also embrace those disposed of at rules, as well as those acted on by the court. I have not embraced judgments on forthcoming bonds in the superior court, as the original judgments were embraced in the number of decisions, and a subsequent judgment on a forthcoming bond, if reported, would have given more decisions than suits commenced and pending.

GLOUCESTER.

14. The number of suits and causes pending, are those on the court docket 30th August. The number decided includes dismissions.

FIFTH CIRCUIT.

WESTMORELAND.

15. Motions on forthcoming bonds not included in return.

SIXTH CIRCUIT.

FAUQUIER.

16. Sixty-six motions not included in this statement. All chancery orders which did not end suits and remove them from the docket, regarded as interlocutory decrees.

LOUDOUN.

17. The intermediate term was held in April 1848. Thirty-six judgments on forthcoming bonds, &c., and one decree on motion, not included in this report.

FAIRFAX.

18. Judgments on forthcoming bonds and motions not included.

ALEXANDRIA.

19. Judgments on forthcoming bonds not included, nor judgments confessed in the office.

STAFFORD.

20. Among the number of suits at law commenced are four motions on forthcoming bonds. In the prosecutions there is one indictment for felony.

SEVENTH CIRCUIT.

CHESTERFIELD.

21. The suits decided include 28 judgments on forthcoming bonds, 52 office judgments and dismissions at rules; and including also dismissions in court, whether by act of the parties or otherwise. The suits removed are all from Chesterfield county court. Among the interlocutory decrees, orders granting leave to defendants to file answers, and orders assigning guardians ad litem, are not included. In suits pending, those on the court docket only are included, and not those at rules. Among the prosecutions was one for felony, of which the accused was convicted and sentenced to the penitentiary.

POWHATAN.

22. Of the 12 days stated as the session of the court in the fall of 1847, nine days were at the regular term of the court in November 1847, and three days at a special term in the month of February 1848. And of the nine days stated as the session of the court in the spring of 1848, six days were at the regular term of the court in May 1848, and the three days at a special term in July 1848.

GOOCHLAND.

23. In making out the lists of suits pending at law and in chancery, such only are included as stand on the court dockets for trial or decision. All at the rules are consequently excluded. Twenty-eight office judgments have been confirmed within the year, which are not included in the number of suits at law decided.

TWENTY-FIRST CIRCUIT.—Law Side.

HENRICO AND CITY OF RICHMOND.

24. The number commenced includes seven writs of scire facias, five writs of supersedeas, and one appeal. The number decided includes judgments on forthcoming bonds and on motions in other cases; judgments confessed in the office, also nonsuits and dismissions in court, and exclusive of several decisions on writs of habeas corpus, (one of which cases occupied the court more than a week,) and of judgments entered pursuant to decisions of the court of appeals. The number of prosecutions pending, includes two cases in which new trials are awarded by general court. The prosecutions decided are all for felonies. The court was engaged on the civil docket 78 days, on the criminal 29 days.

TWENTY-SECOND CIRCUIT.—Chancery Court.

HENRICO AND CITY OF RICHMOND.

25. Of the total number of days in session, Judge P. N. Nicholas occupied the bench in the trial of chancery suits which Judge Robertson could not properly hear 26 days. Of the number of interlocutory decrees, fourteen were rendered by Judge Nicholas; and of the number of final decrees, five were rendered by him.

EIGHTH CIRCUIT.

BUCKINGHAM.

26. In consequence of the sickness of the Judge, no court was held in September 1847.

APPOMATTOX.

27. In consequence of the illness of the Judge, no term of his court was held for this county in October 1847.

CAMPBELL.

28. No court was held at the fall term of 1847, in consequence of the indisposition of the Judge.

NINTH CIRCUIT.

LUNENBURG.

29. In the number of law decisions are included seven judgments on forfeited forthcoming bonds, and one on motion of security against principal. In the number of chancery decisions, is included one judgment on a forfeited forthcoming bond. These motions are not included in the number of suits commenced.

TENTH CIRCUIT.

HENRY.

30. Among the final judgments and decrees are embraced judgments on forthcoming bonds, but no cause that was dismissed at rules or abated by the sheriff's return. Four days of the spring term were consumed in the trial of a will case, in consequence of which, many office judgments were set aside and not reached during the term.

FRANKLIN.

31. In the reported number of suits at law commenced and decided there were seventy-three motions upon which final judgments were rendered. There was one prisoner tried for felony, and acquitted at the fall term.

PITTSYLVANIA.

32. The number pending at law includes all cases on the issue docket, rule docket, confirmed in court, motions on forfeited forthcoming bonds, and other motions not relating to suits pending. The number decided includes all office judgments, dismissions at rules or in court, abatements, &c. Number pending in chancery includes all suits on the rule docket, issue docket or injunction docket. Number interlocutory decrees includes all orders for leave to file bills and answers, or any other intermediate order, except continuances. Number final decrees includes two motions on forfeited forthcoming bonds, dismissions, and any other order disposing of a cause; also, entries of affirmance by court of appeals. In addition to final decrees, there were two orders permiting guardians to remove the estate of their wards, and one appointing a guardian.

BEDFORD.

33. Of causes at common law there are on the court docket 121, at rules 80. In chancery, 110 on court docket ang 123 at rules. Judgments on delivery bonds, 68 in number, are not included; and all motions are excluded. A contest in relation to a will occupied five days of the fall term.

CARROLL.

34. Number of motions, notices, &c. 17 ; number of felonies 2.

ELEVENTH CIRCUIT.

LOUISA.

35. Of the number decided at law, 23 were office judgments and 10 motions There have been thirteen dismissions at law in court, and thirteen dismissions and abatements at rules, and one dismission in chancery in court.

FLUVANNA.

36. In the number of suits commenced and decided, I have embraced judgments on delivery bonds, of which there were 26 on the law side of the court and 3 on the chancery side.

CULPEPER.

37. Twenty judgments on forthcoming bonds included in number of suits decided.

RAPPAHANNOCK.

38. Rules against witnesses are not included in this report. No motions on forthcoming bonds.

TWELFTH CIRCUIT.

NELSON.

40. The number of suits commenced embraces only original suits, writs of scire facias are not included, and in the number decided at common law are included forty-three judgments on delivery bonds. In chancery causes, interlocutory decrees do not include eighty-three orders giving leave to file answers, awarding scire facias to revive suits, &c. Final decrees do not include eleven delivery bonds nor dismissions.

AUGUSTA.

41. On the common law side there are 44 judgments on forthcoming bonds, three writs of habeas corpus and two writs of supersedeas not included in the number commenced or in the number decided. On the chancery side there are judgments on four forthcoming bonds not included in the number commenced or decided.

THIRTEENTH CIRCUIT.

JEFFERSON

42 In the number of common law suits decided, are included forty-five judgments on forfeited forth coming bonds.

BERKELEY.

43. About 40 motions on delivery bonds and others not embraced in this report.

MORGAN.

44. Number of suits decided does not include motions on notices and forthcoming bonds, &c. Numbe of interlocutory decrees does not include orders in chancery.

HAMPSHIRE.

45. On the chancery docket 85 for trial, 74 on the deferred iussues, and 38 at rules.

FREDERICK.

46. The great difference between the number of chancery suits pending and the number decided, is owing to the fact that a large number of suits descending from the old chancery district court, and which are standing on the deferred docket, waiting for reports of marshals and commissioners to sell lands, &c. and cannot well go off the docket.

CLARKE.

47. Nine judgments on forthcoming bonds are not included.

FOURTEENTH CIRCUIT.

WARREN.

48. There were within the year three judgments on forfeited forthcoming bonds, which are not counted in this report. There was a summer term held on the 30th August 1848.

FIFTEENTH CIRCUIT.

LEE.

49. There was an intermediate term in June of one day. The court generally commences at an early hour and adjourned late in the evening.

SCOTT.

50. The suits commenced at law, include two motions on delivery bonds, one petition for a writ of mandamus and three writs of supersedeas; and in those determined are included two motions on delivery bonds, one petition for a mandamus, four writs of supersedeas, and 21 of which the judgments entered a the rules were made final.

RUSSELL.

51. Office judgments entered as of the last day of the term, dismissions in the office and motions on forthcoming bonds are included with the suits at law decided.

TAZEWELL.

52. No causes in chancery were removed from county court; twenty judgments on forthcoming bonds and four rules and motions included in number of suits at law decided; two forthcoming bonds in final decrees.

WASHINGTON.

53. The clerks throughout the state would no doubt unite in an appeal to the Legislature to strike the law under which this report is made, from the statute book.

SIXTEENTH CIRCUIT.

WYTHE.

54. I understand that it is the practice of some clerks in making their reports, to include in the number of suits commenced, all motions on delivery bonds; and in the suits decided, all judgments on those bonds. And to report as interlocutory decrees all orders, such as the revival of causes on the death of parties, the appointments of guardians ad litem, &c. My practice is different. I hope the Legislature or the attorney general will give some instructions to the clerks throughout the state on this point.

GRAYSON.

55. Notices on delivery bonds and other notices, rules, &c. not included in this report.

GILES.

56. The causes reported in chancery do not embrace the suits at rules, none of which were in a condition for final decrees.

MERCER.

57. Judgments on forthcoming bonds are not included in this return.

SEVENTEENTH CIRCUIT.

BOTETOURT.

58. Of the suits at law decided, 24 were judgments on delivery bonds. By a comparison of this report with the last one, it will be seen that the number of suits at law "commenced" still continues to get smaller and smaller, whilst the number of chancery suits "commenced" has increased a little. It will also be seen that the number of prosecutions "commenced" has greatly increased. The most of these are for gaming.

GREENBRIER.

59. The above report embraces no judgments on forfeited forthcoming bonds; no orders in chancery causes directing settlement of accounts made on the motion of parties; orders appointing guardians or reviving suits, &c.

EIGHTEENTH CIRCUIT.

FAYETTE.

60. No judgments on notices or delivery bonds included in this report.

KANAWHA.

61. The number pending at law and in chancery includes all suits at rules. The number decided on the law side includes judgments on forthcoming bonds and dismissions. Judge Lee sat at the spring term 1848, Judge Duncan in the fall of 1847.

PUTNAM.

62. There was one cause in chancery dismissed, not included in any column in this report.

RANDOLPH.

63. Two judgments on forthcoming bonds included in the number of causes decided at law. There was no court held in the spring in consequence of the resignation of Judge Duncan.

BRAXTON.

64. There are some judgments on forthcoming bonds included in the list of judgments.

TAYLOR.

65. I have included all suits and prosecutions commenced between the 30th day of August 1847, and the 30th day of August 1848, all suits, prosecutions and motions on forthcoming bonds decided during the time aforesaid, all suits and prosecutions pending on the day last aforesaid, all decrees which are interlocutory in their nature, and all decrees of the court ending chancery causes.

NICHOLAS.

66. Motions on forthcoming bonds not included in this report.

NINETEENTH CIRCUIT.

MASON.

67. The column of suits commenced, includes writs of supersedeas and prohibition; that of suits decided, includes dismissals and abatements, but excludes judgments on forthcoming bonds.

GILMER.

68. An onerous duty; heavy penalty for failure, without a corresponding compensation.

TWENTIETH CIRCUIT.

PRESTON.

69. Judgments on forthcoming bonds and notices not included.

MONONGALIA.

70. The number of suits and causes pending includes those at rules. The number decided at law includes motions on forthcoming bonds.

MARION.

71. Motions, rules, petitions, &c., not included. In the number decided at law, I have included one cause removed to the circuit superior court of law and chancery of Barbour county.

WETZEL.

72. The column marked decided, includes dismissals.

OHIO.

73. The number pending includes those (law and chancery) at rules. The number decided includes judgments on forthcoming bonds, dismissions in court and at rules, and judgments confessed in office. The Judge having Barbour added his circuit, the court of which was to be held after this county, the spring term here was necessarily short.

ABSTRACT

FROM THE

REPORTS OF THE CLERKS

OF THE

COURT OF APPEALS,

AND OF THE

CIRCUIT SUPERIOR COURTS

OF

LAW AND CHANCERY,

FOR THE

YEAR ENDING THE 30TH OF AUGUST, 1849,

EXHIBITING

THE STATE OF SUITS

IN THEIR

RESPECTIVE COURTS.

CLERK'S OFFICE, Dec 8, 1849.

SIR,

As required by law, I have the honor to present an abstract from the reports of the clerks of the court of appeals, and of the circuit superior courts of law and chancery, exhibiting the state of the suits instituted in their respective courts, and the number of days the courts were in session during the year ending the 30th of August, 1849.

No reports have been received from the clerks of the circuit courts of Warwick, Richmond County, Nicholas, Ritchie, Logan, Monongalia, Wetzel and Tazewell. A report has been received from one of the clerks, who has failed to state the court for which he is clerk, and it has not therefore been added to the circuit to which it should be attached.

I am, very respectfully,

Yours, &c.

GEORGE W. MUNFORD,

C. H. D.

To the Honorable the Speaker of the House of Delegates.

ABSTRACT FROM THE REPORTS OF THE CLERKS

OF THE

COURT OF APPEALS, AND OF THE CIRCUIT SUPERIOR COURTS OF LAW AND CHANCERY,

For the year ending 30th *August*, 1849, *exhibiting the state of Suits in their respective Courts.*

COURT OF APPEALS.

JUDGES.	CLERKS.	LOCATION OF COURTS.	Suits commenced.	Pending.	Decided.	No. of days in Session.	REMARKS OF CLERKS.
William H. Cabell, *President*, Francis T. Brooke, - John J. Allen, - - Briscoe G. Baldwin, - William Daniel, -	Joseph Allen,	Richmond,	79	514	59	132	The session of the court commenced on Monday, October 16th, 1848, and ended Saturday, 12th May, 1849, comprising 157 days, having had within that time two recesses, one of 25 days and the other of 26 days, and having actually sat 132 days, exclusive of Sundays.
	John A. North,	Lewisburg,	69	161	51	46	
		Total,	148	675	110	178	

SPECIAL COURT OF APPEALS.

JUDGES.	CLERKS.	LOCATION OF COURTS.	Suits commenced.	Pending.	Decided.	No. of days in Session.	REMARKS OF CLERKS.
	Joseph Allen,	Richmond,	-	-	61	64	
	Total of both regular and special courts, -	-	148	675	171	242	

CIRCUIT SUPERIOR COURTS OF LAW AND CHANCERY.

Districts.	Circuits.	JUDGES.	CLERKS.	COUNTIES.	Suits at Law.				Causes in Chancery.					Prosecutions.					Terms. Days in session.				Remarks of Clerks.
					No. commenced.	No. pending.	No. decided.	No. removed from courts	No. commenced.	No. pending	No. interlocutory decrees.	No. final decrees.	No. removed from county courts.	No. commenced.	No. pending.	No. decided.	No. nolle prosequis.	Changes of venue.	Fall.	Spring.	Intermediate or special.	Total.	
1st	1st	R. H. Baker.	L. R. Edwards,	Southampton,	135	7[illegible]	66	1	15	3[illegible]	26	13	-	9	1[illegible]	7	2	-	4	3	-	7	
			Joseph Turner,	Greenesville,	36	18	4[illegible]	-	5	1[illegible]	2	6	-	7	7	-	-	-	2	4	-	6	
			W. P. Underwood,	Surry,	24	17	17	-	2	[illegible]	3	3	-	4	5	1	-	-	2	1	-	3	Note 1.
			N. P. Young,	Isle of Wight,	52	16	47	-	6	1[illegible]	9	7	-	4	4	2	-	-	2	2	-	4	
			Joseph Prentiss,	Nansemond,	26	15	2[illegible]	-	4	1[illegible]	11	4	-	3	[illegible]	12	-	-	3	3	-	6	Note 2.
			J. J. Burroughs,	Princess Anne,	54	36	71	1	2	1[illegible]	4	4	-	8	6	1	1	-	3	3	-	6	Note 3.
			John Williams,	Norfolk City,	134	137	129	5	31	51	27	31	2	5	3	5	-	-	42	15	-	57	Note 4.
			Arthur Emmerson,	Norfolk County,	109	2[illegible]	8[illegible]	-	[illegible]	2[illegible]	15	15	-	42	24	57	4	-	12	12	-	24	
				Total in Circuit,	570	324	481	7	74	157	97	83	2	82	61	75	7	-	70	43	-	113	
	2d	John W. Nash,	John P. Crump,	Dinwiddie,	81	52	25	1	16	49	20	20	-	7	8	8	-	-	11	6	-	17	Note 5.
			F. Fitzgerald,	Nottoway,	101	5[illegible]	9[illegible]	4	16	49	30	14	[illegible]	14	16	7	1	-	5	5	-	10	Note 6.
			E. G. Leigh,	Amelia.	110	102	157	-	34	53	17	11	-	6	17	4	1	-	7	4	-	11	
			Wm. S. Dance,	Powhatan,	1[illegible]9	77	96	1	9	7[illegible]	2[illegible]	11	1	19	15	5	2	-	5	9	-	14	Note 7.
			E. R. Turnbull,	Brunswick,	4[illegible]	4[illegible]	51	5	1[illegible]	25	17	17	-	[illegible]	12	3	9	-	3	5	-	8	
			J. T. J. Mason,	Sussex,	3[illegible]	22	4[illegible]	-	1	15	26	8	-	2	3	3	-	-	2	2	-	4	Note 8.
			Ro. Gilliam,	Prince George,	17	3	14	-	4	1[illegible]	3	9	-	17	15	4	2	-	[illegible]	2	-	5	
			H. B. Gaines,	Petersburg,	146	105	209	1	41	124	37	55	-	15	16	11	4	-	24	20	-	44	Note 9.
				Total in circuit	636	45[illegible]	689	12	111	375	166	145		82	100	45	19	-	60	53	-	113	
2d	3d	G. P. Scarburg.	Thos. O. Cogbill,	James City and Williamsburg,	79	47	91	9	29	124	39	35	[illegible]	9	2	2	38	-	9	8	-	17	
			Bolivar Shield,	York.	28	2[illegible]	1[illegible]	3	4	17	4	-	-	3	18	3	-	-	6	3	-	120	Note 10.
				Warwick,																			
			S. S. Howard.	Elizabeth City,	47	18	77	1	6	2[illegible]	8	5	-	-	-	-	1	-	5	4	-	9	Note 11.
			Louis P. Rogers,	Northampton,	25	13	3[illegible]	-	18	24	15	12	-	5	1	2	2	-	[illegible]	4	-	10	
			J. Poulson,	Accomack,	68	5[illegible]	97	1	19	4[illegible]	62	11	1	[illegible]	4	13	11	-	42	19	-	61	
				Total in circuit.	247	150	317	14	76	240	128	63	[illegible]	23	25	18	52	-	68	38	-	217	

2d	4th	J. B. Christian,	Ro. Pollard,	King William,	42	23	45	1	9	31	27	9	1	5	4	1	-	-	3	4	-	7	Note 12.
			Robert Pollard,	King & Queen,	48	38	39	1	8	33	10	8	-	3	3	5	-	-	8	7	-	15	
			Jas. Roy Micou,	Essex,	58	50	87	1	5	29	15	12	-	6	6	-	1	-	4	4	-	8	
			Robert N. Trice,	Middlesex,	21	18	8	1	13	43	7	9	-	4	2	2	-	-	2	3	-	5	Note 13.
			John R. Cary,	Gloucester,	62	65	77	3	12	74	26	10	-	5	3	8	1	-	7	7	-	14	Note 14.
			Shepard G. Miller,	Mathews,	57	51	25	-	11	91	11	14	1	2	1	1	-	-	4	2	-	6	
				Total in circuit,	268	245	281	7	58	301	96	62	2	25	19	17	2	-	28	27	-	55	
3d	5th	John T. Lomax,	Rob't. T. Dunaway,	Lancaster,	20	13	20	-	2	4	2	3		1	1	1	-	-	1	3	-	4	
			J. R. Stith,	Northumberland,	57	61	38	-	4	11	3	3	1		-	-	-	-	2	1	-	3	
				Richmond co.,																	-		
			William Hutt,	Westmoreland,	66	113	72	-	7	53	21	8	-	4	2	3	-	-	3	3	-	6	Note 15.
			Wm. S. Brown,	King George,	24	18	23	-	2	12	2	5	-	6	9	3	-	-	2	2	-	4	Note 16.
			Robert Hudgin,	Caroline,	57	65	60	9	6	57	45	40	-	6	4	3	-	-	5	4	-	9	
			J. J. Chew,	Spotsylvania,	61	57	20	-	8	426	33	17	-	5	3	10	-	-	23	14	-	37	
				Total in circuit,	285	327	273	9	29	563	106	76	1	22	19	20	-	-	36	27	-	63	
	6th	John Scott,	Wm. F. Phillips,	Fauquier,	157	242	183	2	43	373	225	56	-	3	4	1	1	-	11	12	-	22	Note 17.
			Th. P. Knox,	Loudoun,	136	244	84	3	17	166	45	12	2	4	4	1	-	-	5	-	-	5	Note 18.
			P. D. Lipscomb,	Prince William,	36	76	87	5	10	120	18	23	-	5	6	1	-	-	5	4	-	9	
			F. D. Richardson,	Fairfax,	79	54	30	1	21	156	39	22	-	1	-	1	1	-	4	-	-	4	Note 19.
			Cassius F. Lee,	Alexandria,	59	134	28	1	22	105	10	4	-	6	5	1	-	-	2	-	-	2	Note 20.
			J. M. Conway,	Stafford,	22	21	10	-	3	25	4	8	-	1	2	-	-	-	2	-	-	2	Note 21.
				Total in circuit,	499	773	427	12	119	945	341	125	2	20	21	5	2		29	16	-	45	
4th	7th	Jno. B. Clopton,	R. W. Flournoy,	Chesterfield,	83	120	76	4	25	107	23	26	1	14	26	24	10	-	9	7	2	18	Note 22.
			Ed. T. Christian,	Charles City,	24	19	20	3	4	24	3	1	-	2	2	-	-	-	3	2	1	6	
			J. D. Christian,	New Kent,	7	16	16	-	11	23	20	3	-	1	-	1	1	-	5	3	-	8	
			Nar. W. Miller,	Goochland,	99	182	80	-	9	73	19	13	3	3	5	1	1	-	7	4	-	11	Note 23.
			Philip B. Winston,	Hanover,	32	131	63	1	26	150	48	27		3	5		2	-	15	8	-	23	
				Total in circuit,	245	468	255	8	75	377	113	70	4	23	38	26	14	-	39	24	3	66	
	21st	P. N. Nicholas, (dead,)	John Robinson,	Henrico and city of Richmond,	235	378	282	9	-	-	-	-	-	31	18	19	12		53	53		106	Note 24.

Districts.	Circuits.	JUDGES.	CLERKS.	COUNTIES.	Suits at Law.				Causes in Chancery.					Prosecutions.					Terms. Days in Session				Remarks of Clerks.
					No. commenced.	No. pending.	No. decided.	No removed from other courts.	No. commenced.	No. pending.	No. interlocutory decrees.	No. final decrees.	No. removed from county courts.	No. commenced.	No. pending.	No. decided.	No. nolle prosequis.	Changes of venue.	Fall.	Spring.	Intermediate or special.	Total.	
4th	2d	Jno. Robertson,	Powhatan Roberts,	Henrico and city of Richmond,	-	-	-	-	88	1591	239	74	3	-	-	-	-	-	72	14	21	107	Note 25.
	8th	Dan. A. Wilson,	John Daniel	Cumberland, -	76	56	82	7	8	70	18	14	-	2	12	-	-	-	7	8	-	15	
			Rolfe Eldridge,	Buckingham, -	142	156	153	1	31	154	33	44	1	4	4	2	1	-	13	16	-	29	
			H. F. Bocock,	Appomattox, -	62	68	57	-	10	37	7	10	-	-	3	2	1	-	5	10	-	15	Note 26.
			John D. Alexander,	Campbell, -	193	208	143	9	20	91	55	5	2	2	6	6	-	-	11	11	-	22	
			David Rodes,	Lynchburg, -	89	147	159	4	44	288	96	33	1	4	5	3	4	1	35	22	-	57	Note 27.
				Total in circuit,	562	635	594	21	93	640	209	106	4	16	30	13	6	1	71	67	-	138	
5th	9th	William Leigh	William Holt,	Halifax, -	110	45	115	-	27	93	40	25	1	44	41	22	7	-	10	10	-	20	
			Winslow Robinson.	Charlotte, -	74	74	57	-	9	32	23	23	-	9	6	7	-	-	5	5	-	10	
			B. J. Worsham,	Prince Edward,	91	87	115	2	17	103	25	24	1	2	8	2	1	-	8	4	-	12	
			Thomas W. Winn,	Lunenburg, -	58	83	20	-	12	40	6	6	-	3	9	4	3	-	3	-	-	3	Note 28.
			Richard B. Baptist,	Mecklenburg.	100	59	80	-	24	54	15	16	1	6	21	7	2	-	8	8	-	16	
				Total in circuit	433	348	387	2	89	322	109	94	3	64	85	42	13	-	4	27	-	61	
	10th	N. M. Taliaferro,	J. N. Zentmeyer,	Floyd, -	28	28	33	3	10	34	24	14	-	9	14	22	12	-	5	5	-	10	
			Samuel G. Staples.	Patrick, -	70	96	46	3	20	31	17	10	1	17	22	12	2	-	9	8	-	17	
			Anthony M. Dupuy,	Henry, -	63	69	107	-	4	26	21	26	1	26	22	18	6	-	6	5	-	11	Note 29.
			M. G. Carper,	Franklin, -	315	121	276	2	28	102	78	31	2	9	16	10	5	-	7	11	-	18	Note 30.
			Wm. H. Tunstall,	Pittsylvania, -	203	388	202	2	41	179	113	50	1	21	39	18	1	-	13	17	-	30	Note 31.
			Joseph Wilson,	Bedford, -	211	208	203	6	33	226	29	37	3	3	11	15	2	-	7	9	-	16	Note 32.
				Total in circuit,	890	910	867	16	136	598	282	168	8	85	124	95	28	-	47	55	-	102	
6th	11th	Rich'd H. Field,	John Hunter,	Louisa, -	7	103	48	1	10	67	35	8	3	2	3	3	1	-	6	7	-	13	Note 33.
			A. Shepherd, Jr.,	Fluvanna, -	61	73	83	1	18	45	21	20	1	3	6	3	1	-	7	5	-	12	Note 34.

6th	11th	Rich'd H. Field,	P. S. Fry,	Orange,	74	127	47	-	10	57	24	6	-	9	11	6	2	-	6	7	-	13	
			Robert Pritchett,	Greene,	47	28	34	-	10	12	5	8	-	2	2	-	-	-	4	5	-	9	Note 35.
			Belfield Cave,	Madison,	23	37	53	-	5	46	16	4	-	2	3	1	2	-	4	7	-	11	
			R. G. Ward,	Culpeper,	46	66	89	1	21	117	51	24	-	5	10	6	4	-	17	12	-	29	
			W. J. Menifee,	Rappahannock,	33	35	21	4	10	44	27	7	-	1	7	6	1	-	6	6	-	12	Note 36.
				Total in circuit,	341	469	375	7	84	388	179	77	4	24	42	25	11	–	50	49	–	99	
	12th	L. P. Thompson,	Robert Tinsley,	Amherst,	163	209	170	8	31	314	95	24	-	8	13	4	-	1	11	14	-	25	
			Sam'l McD. Reid,	Rockbridge,	109	105	108	-	35	183	72	8	-	18	28	40	-	-	9	11	-	20	
			Howell L. Brown,	Nelson,	155	269	106	-	34	309	43	34	-	6	8	4	5	-	16	13	-	29	Note 37.
			Alex'r Garrett,	Albemarle,	207	377	275	2	18	161	14	8	2	25	42	31	6	-	11	20	-	31	
			Nich. C. Kinney,	Augusta,	126	275	158	3	56	438	146	46	2	21	11	13	-	-	19	41	5	65	Note 38.
				Total in circuit,	760	1235	817	13	174	1405	370	120	4	78	102	92	11	1	66	99	5	170	
7th	13th	J. R. Douglass,	Robert T. Brown,	Jefferson,	146	154	184	-	34	276	68	32	-	1	3	-	2	1	15	12	-	27	Note 39.
			John Strother,	Berkeley,	74	119	95	-	16	164	37	34	-	1	7	2	-	-	6	6	-	12	Note 40.
			Isaiah Buck,	Morgan,	26	36	23	-	3	28	10	5	-	4	8	6	-	-	3	3	-	6	Note 41.
			John B. White,	Hampshire,	151	124	148	-	17	161	72	38	-	8	10	5	3	-	7	6	-	13	Note 42.
			J. Kean,	Frederick,	95	79	111	-	30	342	38	12	1	6	13	6	4	-	3	5	-	8	Note 43.
			H. H. Lee,	Clarke,	75	40	77	-	-	12	47	13	8	7	13	-	1	1	3	4	-	7	Note 44.
				Total in circuit,	567	552	638	-	100	983	272	134	9	27	54	19	10	2	37	36	-	73	
	14th	Daniel Smith,	Gibson T. Jones,	Page,	7	5	10	-	8	18	10	-	-	1	1	3	2	-	3	1	-	4	Note 45.
			Samuel C. Williams,	Shenandoah,	55	11	38	-	6	41	13	5	1	1	1	1	-	-	2	2	-	4	Note 46.
			Robt. Turner,	Warren,	16	13	15	-	10	24	8	7	-	-	2	2	-	-	3	2	-	5	Note 47.
			C. Lobb,	Hardy,	61	46	54	1	19	140	42	16	-	1	2	-	2	-	3	4	-	7	
			Z. Dyer,	Pendleton,	12	11	3	-	5	16	1	-	-	6	14	6	3	-	3	2	-	5	
			L. W. Gambill,	Rockingham,	110	69	56	1	13	82	10	9	-	23	23	6	1	-	7	6	-	13	
				Total in circuit.	261	155	176	2	61	321	84	37	1	42	43	18	8	-	21	17	-	38	
8th	15th	Benj. Estill,	J. W. S. Morison,	Lee,	20	48	25	-	5	42	6	7	-	11	48	8	1	-	4	6	-	10	Note 48.
			S. H. Morison,	Scott,	54	43	42	1	8	33	3	9	1	46	42	19	5	-	5	5	-	10	Note 49.
			James P. Carroll,	Russell,	38	73	38	-	5	20	3	5	-	14	32	7	3	1	6	3	-	9	Note 50.
				Tazewell,																			
			Connally F. Trigg,	Washington,	56	63	48	-	14	107	17	20	-	35	40	33	7	1	8	16	-	24	Note 51.
			Ja's F. Pendleton,	Smyth,	35	32	65	-	25	78	40	16	-	17	23	19	6	-	4	4	-	8	
				Total in circuit,	203	259	218	1	57	280	69	57	1	123	185	86	22	2	27	34	-	61	

Districts.	Circuits.	JUDGES.	CLERKS.	COUNTIES.	SUITS AT LAW.				CAUSES IN CHANCERY.					PROSECUTIONS.					TERMS. Days in Session.				REMARKS OF CLERKS.
					No. commenced.	No. pending.	No. decided.	No. removed from other courts.	No. commenced.	No. pending.	No. interlocutory decrees.	No. final decrees.	No. removed from county courts.	No. commenced.	No. pending.	No. decided.	No. nolle prosequis	Changes of venue.	Fall.	Spring.	Intermediate or special.	Total.	
8th	16th	Jas. E. Brown,	W. Alexander Stuart,	Wythe,	71	72	54	-	19	102	24	24	-	52	63	23	-	-	10	9	9	28	
			Orville Anderson,	Grayson,	28	31	22	5	3	20	2	7	1	13	38	8	2	-	3	3	-	6	Note 52.
			Madison D. Carter,	Carroll,	67	35	51	-	12	24	17	10	-	18	28	25	6	-	6	5	-	11	Note 53.
			R. D. Montague,	Montgomery,	49	43	48	-	9	47	12	9	-	9	20	24	3	-	12	5	-	17	
			J. B. Baskerville,	Pulaski,	36	26	30	-	8	17	5	6	-	4	8	3	-	-	4	5	-	9	
			R. A. French,	Giles,	58	44	71	-	9	16	13	8	-	37	30	10	12	-	6	3	-	9	Note 54.
			Alexander Mohood,	Mercer,	31	30	28	-	4	13	12	8	-	13	9	6	-	-	4	2	-	6	Note 55.
			John Hutchinson,	Monroe,	85	58	51		11	64	15	10	-	7	10	12	2	-	5	5	-	10	
				Total in circuit,	427	339	355	5	75	303	100	82	1	153	206	111	25	-	50	37	9	96	
9th	17th	E. Johnston,	Henry W. Bowyer,	Botetourt,	78	92	88	-	20	199	9	23	-	4	40	5	1	-	10	9	-	19	Note 56.
			Andrew Fudge,	Alleghany,	35	44	26	-	7	39	8	6	-	4	3	1	-	-	2	3	-	5	
			F. Johnston,	Roanoke,	21	15	9	3	6	14	7	9	1	4	4	3	-	-	3	5	-	8	Note 57.
			Charles L. Francisco,	Bath,	20	23	45	-	10	51	20	22	-	4	4	4	-	-	5	5	-	10	
			A. Stephenson, jr.,	Highland,	21	18	16	1	4	5	-	-	-	4	3	1	-	-	1	4	-	5	Note 58.
			Wm. Skeen,	Pocahontas,	55	45	47	-	10	34	4	6	-	10	6	5	3	-	3	2	-	5	
			John A. North,	Greenbrier	89	105	73	-	14	95	23	12	1	18	22	14	5	-	6	6	-	12	Note 59.
				Total in circuit,	319	342	304	4	61	437	71	78	2	48	82	33	9	-	30	34	-	64	
	18th	George H. Lee,	H. M. Dickinson,	Fayette,	40	51	28	1	18	51	6	17	-	20	25	11	5	-	5	5	-	10	Note 60.
			A. W. Quarrier,	Kanawha,	275	491	219	-	55	178	34	10	-	8	56	13	4	-	30	-	-	30	Note 61.
			H. H. Forbes,	Putnam,	75	78	18	-	8	17	-	-	-	-	-	-	-	-	2	-	-	2	Note 62.
			B. L. Brown,	Randolph,	19	34	40	-	6	33	10	22	-	9	11	4	-	-	6	6	-	12	
			John Talbott,	Lewis,	96	220	155	4	48	260	20	31	-	37	36	27	9	-	16	11	-	27	
			W. Newlon,	Braxton,	38	55	38	1	13	56	15	9	-	5	14	6	2	-	4	3	-	7	Note 63.

			G. G. Davisson,	Harrison,	77	132	106	8	32	268	35	81	-	80	74	12	15	-	20	13	-	33	
			Adolphus Armstrong,	Taylor.	19	27	15	3	14	29	8	9	-	7	7	3	-	-	5	5	-	10	
				Nicholas,																			
				Total in circuit,	389	638	619	17	194	892	128	179	-	164	223	76	35	-	88	43	-	131	
10th	19th	D. McComas,	J. H. Neal,	Wood,	92	208	85	2	21	135	16	22	-	25	48	31	9	-	10	11	16	37	Note 64.
			A. G. Stringer,	Wirt,	41	38	12	2	10	15	2	-	2	6	9	-	-	-	-	3	-	3	Note 65.
				Ritchie,																			
			D. G. Morrill,	Jackson,	71	156	42	-	17	73	9	5	-	102	122	26	1	-	8	8	9	25	Note 66.
			G. W. Stribling,	Mason,	27	37	31	2	-	19	1	6	-	7	17	16	7	-	8	4	-	12	Note 67.
			John Samuels,	Cabell,	12	14	13	1	14	14	13	4	-	110	122	26	14	-	7	7	-	14	Note 68.
			E. Bloss,	Wayne,	15	6	8	-	21	9	12	3	-	34	16	18	-	-	4	4	-	8	
				Logan,																			
			B. E. Barrett,	Boone,	10	5	9	-	4	9	-	2	-	7	14	5	2	-	1	3	-	4	
			Will. Hatcher,	Gilmer,	68	101	38	5	27	63	6	9	1	3	6	3	1	-	-	5	-	5	Note 69.
				Total in circuit,	336	565	238	12	114	337	59	51	3	294	354	105	34	-	38	45	25	108	
	20th	Joseph L. Fry,	John P. Byrne,	Preston,	43	43	42	-	38	70	22	30	-	4	11	4	-	-	6	6	-	12	Note 70.
				Monongalia,																			
			James O Watson,	Marion,	63	74	43	18	23	48	36	29	-	15	11	11	7	-	8	9	-	17	Note 71.
			D. Hickman,	Tyler,	17	39	29	-	6	51	6	7	-	6	4	6	-	-	5	5	5	15	
				Wetzel,																			
			F. D. Hickman,	Doddridge,	26	32	17	2	19	25	3	3	-	21	22	4	1	-	3	3	4	10	
			Adam Kuhn,	Brooke,	35	56	27	-	6	65	12	9	-	10	7	8	1	-	5	6	-	11	
			J. H. Atkinson,	Hancock,	10	14	9	-	11	13	5	-	-	2	2	-	-	-	1	2	-	3	
			Alex. T. Laidley,	Ohio,	176	264	70	-	48	173	9	41	-	10	39	13	-	-	7	-	23	30	Note 72.
			James D. Morris,	Marshall,	48	52	21	-	16	53	8	18	-	2	2	5	8	-	5	5	-	10	
			E. D. Wilson,	Barbour,	35	80	25	1	30	121	-	4	3	8	15	8	6	-	8	-	-	8	Note 73.
				Total in circuit,	453	654	283	11	97	619	101	141	3	78	113	59	23	-	48	36	32	116	

E. E.

GEORGE W. MUNFORD, *C. H. D.*

RECAPITULATION.

CIRCUIT SUPERIOR COURTS OF LAW AND CHANCERY.

Number of suits, &c., in each Circuit, August 30, 1849.

Districts.	Circuits.	No. of counties, towns and cities in each circuit.	JUDGES.	Suits at Law. No. commenced.	No. pending.	No. decided.	No. removed from other courts.	Causes in Chancery. No. commenced.	No. pending,	No. interlocutory decrees.	No. final decrees.	No. removed from county courts.	Prosecutions. No. commenced.	No. pending.	No. decided.	No. nolle prosequis.	Changes of venue.	Terms. Days in session. Fall.	Spring.	Intermediate.	Total.	Miles Travelling. To general court.	In circuit.	Total.	REMARKS.
1	1	8	Richard H. Baker,	570	324	481	7	74	157	97	83	2	82	61	75	7	-	70	43	-	113	-	519	519	The mileage of the judges who sat in the case of Martin *vs.* Tucker, in the special court of appeals, is included in the amount of mileage in their respective circuits.
	2	8	John W. Nash,	636	455	689	12	111	375	166	145	1	82	100	45	19	-	60	53	-	113	-	839	839	
3	3	6	Geo. P. Scarburg,	247	150	317	14	76	240	128	63	3	23	25	18	52	-	68	38	-	217	-	1046	1046	
	4	6	John B. Christian,	268	245	281	7	58	301	96	62	2	25	19	17	2	-	28	27	-	55	-	500	500	
3	5	7	John T. Lomax,	285	327	273	9	29	563	106	76	-	22	19	20	.	-	36	27	-	63	420	509	929	
	6	6	John Scott,	499	773	427	12	119	945	341	125	2	20	21	5	2	-	29	16	-	45	448	579	1027	
4	7	5	John B. Clopton,	245	468	255	8	75	377	113	70	4	23	38	26	14	-	39	24	3	66	-	762	762	
	21	2	Phil. N. Nicholas, (dead,)	235	378	282	9	-	-	-	-	-	31	18	19	12	-	53	53	-	106				
	22	2	John Robertson,	-	-	-	-	88	1591	239	74	3	-	-	-	-	-	72	14	21	107	-	330	330	
	8	5	Daniel A. Wilson,	562	635	594	21	93	640	209	106	4	16	30	13	6	1	71	67	-	138	520	319	839	
5	9	5	William Leigh,	433	348	387	2	89	322	109	94	3	64	85	42	13	-	31	27	-	61	-	1079	1079	
	10	6	N. M. Taliaferro,	890	910	867	16	136	598	282	168	8	85	124	95	28	-	47	55	-	102	652	654	1306	
6	11	7	Richard H. Field,	341	469	375	7	84	388	179	77	4	24	42	25	11	-	50	49	-	99				

	12	5	L. P. Thompson,	760	1235	817	13	174	1405	370	120	4	78	102	92	11	1	66	99	5	170	-	1730	1730
7	13	6	J. R. Douglass,	567	552	638	-	100	983	272	134	9	27	54	19	10	2	37	36	-	73	-	840	840
	14	6	Daniel Smith,	261	155	176	2	61	321	84	37	1	42	43	18	8	-	21	17	-	38	516	500	1016
8	15	6	Benj. Estill,	103	259	218	1	57	280	69	57	1	123	185	86	22	2	27	34	-	61	-	592	592
	16	8	Ja's E. Brown,	427	339	355	5	75	303	100	82	1	153	206	111	25	-	50	37	9	96	-	668	668
9	17	7	Edw. Johnston,	319	342	304	4	61	437	71	78	2	48	82	33	9	-	30	34	-	64	-	460	460
	18	9	George H. Lee,	389	638	619	17	194	892	128	179	-	164	223	76	35	-	88	43	-	131	-	975	975
10	19	10	Dav. McComas,	336	565	238	12	114	337	59	51	3	294	354	105	34	-	38	45	25	108	-	1872	1872
	20	11	Joseph L. Fry,	453	654	283	21	197	619	101	141	3	78	113	59	23	-	48	36	32	116	-	1662	1662
			Total,	9026	9821	8876	199	2065	12074	3319	2022	60	154	1944	999	343	6	1062	874	95	2142	2556	16435	19091
			Average of circuits,	429	467	422	9	98	574	158	96	2	71	92	47	16	-	50	41	4	102	121	821	954

Judgments at law, - - -	8,876
Interlocutory decrees, - - -	3,319
Final decrees, - - -	2,022
Total decisions from which appeals may be had,	14,217

Number of appeals allowed,	148—being rather more than one per cent. of the total decisions of the circuit courts.
Causes decided in court of appeals, regular and special,	171
Excess of decisions over appeals,	23

E. E.

GEO. W. MUNFORD, *C. H. D.*

REMARKS OF CLERKS.

FIRST CIRCUIT.

(*Note* 1.)—SURRY.—Of the number of suits stated to have been decided at law, three were dismissions in court, and two were motions on forthcoming bonds.

(*Note* 2.)—NANSEMOND.—All judgments on motions, judgments confessed in the office, all dismissions in court or otherwise, and office judgments confirmed, are embraced in number of suits decided.

(*Note* 3.)—PRINCESS ANNE.—All judgments in court and dismissions at rules are included under the head of suits decided: also judgments on appeals; and under the head of suits commenced is included a case of ejectment.

(*Note* 4.)—NORFOLK CITY.—In the number of suits commenced, two writs of *habeas corpus* and one motion are included. In the number decided, two writs of *habeas corpus*, one motion and twenty-two dismissions at rules are included. In the number of final decrees, fourteen dismissions at rules are included.

SECOND CIRCUIT

(*Note* 5.)—DINWIDDIE.—Judgments on motions, dismissions at rules, and office judgments are not embraced in this report. Two chancery causes removed to Petersburg circuit court. The regular intermediate terms held in the fall were almost exclusively consumed in the trial of criminals. The number of suits reported as pending, is the number of suits which were on the court docket at the spring term 1849, exclusive of office judgments.

(*Note* 6.)—NOTTOWAY.—Motions on delivery bonds and notices in other cases, contests about wills, roads, &c., not embraced, nor writs of error and *supersedeas*.

(*Note* 7.—)—POWHATAN.—The prosecutions reported were all for misdemeanors except one, and that was for murder. The two prosecutions in which *nolle prosequis* were entered, are included in the five prosecutions reported as decided; of the nine days stated as the session of the court in the spring of 1849, seven days were at the regular term of the court in May 1849 and two days at a special term in June 1849.

(*Note* 8.)—SUSSEX.—Executions awarded on 4 forfeited forthcoming or delivery bonds.

(*Note* 9.)—PETERSBURG.—A continuance of the law imposing this duty accomplishes no good, either real or imaginary, except what may perhaps accrue to the public printer by the annual publication of the various and numerous reports made upon the subject, unless he too, like the poor clerks, is forced to perform the service at his own cost. Presuming it to be the intention of the legislature in the passage of all laws, either to create some good or to avert some impending evil, I made enquiry of several legal friends for the purpose of finding out, if I could, the reason for the enactment of this very useless statute, and was informed by them that they understood the reason to be based upon an application from some of the judges of the circuit courts to have their salaries increased, and that the legislature thought it best before proceeding to consider of the matter to require such reports from the clerks in order the more clearly to ascertain whether the judges rendered to the commonwealth a sufficient amount of services to justify such increase.—No action to my knowledge has been taken by the legislature upon the subject since the first reports were made, and I now respectfully ask how long the law is to continue upon the statute book. Without concert with any of my brother clerks, I beg to file this as my petition for its repeal, otherwise that such reasonable allowance be provided for by law for the service hereafter to be performed, as equity and good conscience may seem to dictate, and your petitioner, as in duty bound, will ever pray, &c.

H. B. GAINES, *Clerk.*

THIRD CIRCUIT.

(*Note* 10.)—YORK COUNTY.—The three suits at law removed from the county court of York.

(*Note* 11.)—ELIZABETH CITY.—The number of suits and causes pending includes those at rules—the number decided at law includes judgments on forthcoming bonds, on motions, appeals and dismissions at rules.

FOURTH CIRCUIT.

(*Note* 12.)—KING WILLIAM.—Thirteen judgments on forthcoming bonds, and three on motions for money paid as security, not included in the number of suits reported.

(*Note* 13.)—MIDDLESEX.—The prosecutions were presentments by the grand jury. In the number of suits pending I have included forthcoming bonds.

(*Note* 14.)—GLOUCESTER.—In the suits, causes and prosecutions commenced, these instituted by original process only are included, not motions and orders of court. The number pending includes those on the court docket on the 3 th August. The number decided includes dismissions, but not motions on forthcoming bonds,

This is a duty required of the clerks without any compensation whatever, and the law ought to be repealed.

FIFTH CIRCUIT.

(*Note* 15.)—WESTMORELAND.—Motions not included in this return. One chancery cause removed from the circuit superior court of Alexandria.

(*Note* 16.)—KING GEORGE.—Motions on forthcoming bonds not included. The number of suits in our county is becoming "small by degrees and beautifully less."

SIXTH CIRCUIT.

(*Note* 17.)—FAUQUIER.—Fifty-four motions made and decided within the year, not included in this statement.

(*Note* 18.)—LOUDOUN.—Ten judgments on motions at common law are not included in this report. No court was held at the spring term 1849, in consequence of the illness of the judge.

(*Note* 19.)—FAIRFAX.—No court held in the spring, in consequence of the sickness of Judge Scott.

(*Note* 20.)—ALEXANDRIA.—The judge was taken sick the second day of the fall term, and unable to continue the court; and his sickness prevented his holding the spring term.

(*Note* 21.)—STAFFORD.—Six motions on forthcoming bonds not included.

SEVENTH CIRCUIT.

(*Note* 22.)—CHESTERFIELD.—In suits commenced and decided, judgments on forthcoming bonds are not included, of which there were 30 at law and 2 in chancery. In suits pending, those at rules are not included, nor are motions on delivery bonds included either amongst those commenced or decided. In final decrees are included some which are in part final and in part interlocutory. Interlocutory decrees do not include orders of publication, leave to file answers, &c. Of prosecutions 7 were for felony, 5 against one person for forgery. He was acquitted of one, and *nolle prosequis* as to the other four.

(*Note* 23.)—GOOCHLAND.—In making out the lists of suits pending at law and in chancery, such only are included as stand on the court dockets for trial or decision—all at rules are consequently excluded. Forty-four office judgments have been confirmed within the year, which are not included in the number of suits at law decided.

EIGHTH CIRCUIT.

(*Note* 26.)—Appomattox.—This report does not include judgments on forfeited forthcoming bonds.

(*Note* 27.)—Lynchburg.—The number of suits at law decided includes judgments on delivery bonds, dismissions at rules and confessions of judgment. Interlocutory decrees include all orders made in a cause excepting the final decision.

NINTH CIRCUIT.

(*Note* 28.)—Lunenburg.—In the number of decisions at law are included nine judgments on forfeited forthcoming bonds which are not included in the number commenced.

TENTH CIRCUIT.

(*Note* 29.)—Henry.—Twenty judgments on forfeited forthcoming bonds are included in the list of cases decided at law. In addition to the interlocutory and final decrees embraced in this report, there were 15 orders made during the year, making new parties, appointing guardians *ad litem*, and leave to file bills, answers, &c., 7 of the commonwealth's cases reported as decided were rules against grand jurors and witnesses. Abatements and dismissions at rules are not embraced in this report.

(*Note* 30.)—Franklin.—In the number of suits at law reported as commenced and decided, are 90 motions, upon 85 of which final judgments were rendered. In the number of interlocutory decrees in the chancery causes, all orders not final, (except continuances,) are embraced.

(*Note* 31.)—Pittsylvania.—The number pending at law includes all cases on the issue docket, ru le docket, judgments confessed in court, motions on forfeited forthcoming bonds and other motions not relating to suits pending. The number decided includes all office judgments, dismissions at rules, or in court, abatements, &c. Number pending in chancery includes all suits on the rule docket, issue docket or injunction docket. Number of interlocutory decrees includes all orders for leave to file bills and answers, or any other intermediate order except continuances. Number of final decrees includes seven motions on forfeited forthcoming bonds, dismissions and any other order disposing of a cause. In addition to final decrees there was one order permitting a guardian to remove the estate of his wards. At the spring term the court was engaged six days in getting a jury and trying a pauper case of long standing.

(*Note* 32.)—Bedford.—Of the causes depending at law, 84 are at rules and 124 on the court docket. In chancery, 127 at rules and 99 on court docket. Judgments on delivery bonds, 61 in number, are not included.

ELEVENTH CIRCUIT.

(*Note* 33.)—Louisa.—Of the number decided at law, 18 were office judgments, and 11 motions. There have been ten dismissions at law in court, and 13 dismissions and abatements at rules. There were also 3 dismissions in chancery at rules, and 2 in court. There were also a number of motions in chancery in court, such as for leave to file answers, &c., which I have considered do not fall under any head of this report.

(*Note* 34.)—Fluvanna.—In the number of suits commenced and decided, I have not embraced judgments on delivery bonds, of which there are 24 on the law-side of said court, and one on the chancery side.

(*Note* 35.)—Greene.—No judgments on motions or delivery bonds included in this report.

(*Note* 36.)—Rappahannock.—Judgments on forthcoming bonds are not included. Two of the chancery causes reported as commenced, have been reinstated upon the docket for re-hearing.

TWELFTH CIRCUIT.

(*Note* 37.)—Nelson.—In the number of suits decided at common law, 42 judgments on delivery bonds and other motions are not included. In chancery, judgments on delivery bonds and all orders granting leave to file answers and reviving suits, are not included among the interlocutory decrees. By reference to my last report, it would seem that there is an error as to the number of chancery suits now pending; that error occurred in the report of my predecessor.

(*Note* 38.)—AUGUSTA.—In the number of suits instituted, decided, &c., at common law, are not included 26 judgments on delivery bonds and 4 motions and judgments on constable's bond. In those decided on the chancery side are not included 3 judgments on delivery bonds.

THIRTEENTH CIRCUIT.

(*Note* 39.)—JEFFERSON.—Of the number of common law cases decided, forty were judgments on forfeited forthcoming bonds.

(*Note* 40.)—BERKELEY.—Judgments on forthcoming bonds not included in this report.

(*Note* 41.)—MORGAN.—There were 14 judgments on forthcoming bonds in addition to the suits decided; also two judgments confessed in the clerk's office.

(*Note* 42.)—HAMPSHIRE.—Among the common law causes decided are nine motions. In chancery there are sixty causes in the trial docket; 79 on the deferred issue docket and 22 at rules.

(*Note* 43.)—FREDERICK.—Forthcoming bonds not included. Of these were ten upon which execution was awarded. The great disparity between the number of chancery causes pending and the number decided, is accounted for by the fact that they are the remains of the docket of the old chancery district court, which have been permitted to sleep by the inattention of the parties and their counsel. These, however, are being disposed of gradually.

(*Note* 44.)—CLARKE.—Of the 75 new actions at law, two were writs of *scire facias*. Twelve judgments on forthcoming bonds are included in the number of law causes decided.

FOURTEENTH CIRCUIT.

(*Note* 45.)—PAGE.—I think the clerk ought to be entitled to a copy of the report for his trouble.

(*Note* 46.)—SHENANDOAH.—Number pending does not include (in suits at law) cases standing on the office-judgment docket on the 31st August. Number decided include office-judgments and dismissions, but not judgments on forthcoming bonds. In chancery, interlocutory decrees include all orders but continuances. Final decrees include dismissions.

(*Note* 47.)—WARREN.—Judgments on forfeited forthcoming bonds are not noticed in this report.

FIFTEENTH CIRCUIT.

(*Note* 48.)—LEE.—Judgments on forthcoming bonds not included.

(*Note* 49.)—SCOTT.—Suits commenced at law, include seven motions on delivery bonds, and one writ of *supersedeas*.

(*Note* 50.)—RUSSELL.—Amongst causes decided, are embraced all final dismissions, office judgments and judgments on forthcoming bonds. The judge, at the fall term, sat till required to leave for his court in Tazewell: at the spring term all the causes ready for trial were disposed of at the end of the third day.

(*Note* 51.)—WASHINGTON.—At the spring term of the court, about eight days of the term were consumed in the trial of a tedious civil cause, and a criminal prosecution for murder, sent to this court from the county of Russell.

SIXTEENTH CIRCUIT.

(*Note* 52.)—GRAYSON.—This report does not comprehend motions on forfeited delivery bonds, notices or other summary proceedings, nor does it comprehend rules for contempts, &c.

(*Note* 53.)—CARROLL.—The number of motions, notices, &c., were twenty-two.

(*Note* 54.)—GILES.—The causes in chancery do not embrace the suits at rules—none of which were in a condition for final decrees.

(*Note* 55.)—MERCER.—There were seven judgments on forthcoming bonds, during the year ending 31st August 1849, which are not embraced in this return.

SEVENTEENTH CIRCUIT.

(*Note* 56.)—Botetourt.—Of the suits at law decided, fourteen were judgments upon delivery bonds. Of the final decrees in chancery, four were dismissions at rules in the office. A comparison of this report with the last, will shew a falling off in the number of chancery suits commenced of about one half. In addition to the suits embraced in this report, there were 31 reports of the assessors to the James River and Kanawha Company of the damages sustained by the proprietors of lands along the line of said improvement in Botetourt county, which are returned to this court, 8th January 1849, to be acted upon. Seventeen of these reports were confirmed at the April term 1849, and ordered to be recorded ; three others have since been confirmed ; nine have been remanded back to a new board of assessors, which last mentioned, together with two others which have not been acted upon, are still pending upon the docket of this court.

(*Note* 57.)—Roanoke.—This list does not embrace judgments on delivery bonds, or on notices of any kind.

(*Note* 58.)—Highland.—Motions on forthcoming bonds, or rules against witnesses or absent grand jurors, are not included in this report.

(*Note* 59.)—Greenbrier.—Judgments on forthcoming bonds not included in causes decided.

EIGHTEENTH CIRCUIT.

(*Note* 60.)—Fayette.—Sunday intervening both terms.

(*Note* 61.)—Kanawha.—The number pending include all the suits at rules.

(*Note* 62.)—Putnam.—The column marked decided at law, includes dismissions at rules and office confessions.

(*Note* 63.)—Braxton.—Twenty-six forthcoming bonds and one notice, which judgments have been entered up, are not included in the list of judgments. Also six rules pending, not included in the list of causes pending.

NINETEENTH CIRCUIT.

(*Note* 64.)—Wood.—Judgment on forthcoming bond not included.

(*Note* 65.)—Wirt.—The act of last winter changing the time of holding our courts, the fall term was not held until September 1849.

(*Note* 66.)—Jackson.—Under the recent change of the law our fall term comes in August, consequently three regular terms were held within the year ending August 31st, 1849, but I have reported only two regular terms and a special, leaving the August term to be embraced in my next report.

(*Note* 67.)—Mason.—No business of any consequence was done at the spring term, owing to the unexpected and uncalled for change in the terms of all the courts of the circuit, (made by act of last winter,) of which even the officers of the court were not apprised till within two or three days before the beginning of the term, and nineteen-tweentieths of the people of the county were wholly uninformed.

(*Note* 68.)—Cabell.—In a number of prosecutions depending in this court from two to six persons are included in the same presentment, &c., and if decided against one and continued as to the rest, no notice is taken of it.

(*Note* 69.)—Gilmer.—Fall term sits after 30th August.

TWENTIETH CIRCUIT.

(*Note* 70.)—Preston.—Twenty-one causes pending at law are at rules, and twenty-three causes in chancery are at rules. Judgments on forthcoming bonds and notices not included.

(*Note* 71.)—Marion.—Judgments on delivery bonds and rules against witnesses, &c., not included. In the causes commenced in chancery, I have included one cause transferred from Harrison county circuit court to this court. Of the causes at law removed from other courts, 17 were from Harrison county circuit court and one from the superior court of the county of Henrico and city of Richmond.

(*Note* 72.)—Ohio.—Causes at rules are included in those pending. Causes decided include dismissions at rules and judgments confirmed in the office. Apprehension in regard to the prevalence of cholera in Wheeling, no court was held in the spring or summer of 1849. Up to the present we have mercifully escaped the pestilence, and Wheeling may be considered as one of the healthy cities of the land.

(*Note* 73.)—Barbour.—There was no court held here last fall, and most of the spring term was taken up in criminal prosecutions.

TWENTY-FIRST CIRCUIT.

(*Note* 25.)—Henrico and City of Richmond—Law side.—The number of suits commenced, includes five writs of *supersedeas* and five writs of *scire facias*. The number decided, includes judgments on forthcoming bonds and on motions in other cases: judgments confessed in the office; also non-suits and dismissions in court, and exclusive of several decisions on writs of *habeas corpus ad subjiciendum*, and of judgments entered pursuant to decisions of court of appeals. The number of prosecutions decided, embrace offences by convicts. Each term the court was engaged on criminal docket 14 days, and on civil docket 39 days.

TWENTY-SECOND CIRCUIT.

(*Note* 24.)—Richmond and Henrico—Chancery side.—Two of the suits commenced were writs of *scire facias* to revive decrees. Besides the number of final decrees in court, there were eleven dismissions at the rules. Besides the three suits stated to have been removed from county courts, there were four removed to this court from other circuit courts. At the January term, Judge Robertson occupied the bench 69 days; the other three days Judge Nicholas held the court for the decision of causes for the trial of which Judge Robertson declined to sit. The June term was held exclusively by Judge Robertson. Six days of the July term were occupied by Judge Clopton for the trial of two suits, for the trial of which neither Judge Robertson nor Judge Nicholas could sit. The balance of that term Judge Nicholas occupied the bench. Of the number of final decrees, Judge Nicholas rendered four, and Judge Clopton two.

APPENDIX.

CLERK'S OFFICE, January 18th, 1850.

SIR,

In preparing the abstract from the reports of the clerks of the circuit superior courts of the commonwealth, I find that I have been unintentionally led into error, which I feel it my duty to make known to the house.

The statement of the mileage of several of the judges of the circuit courts, I have been informed by them, is incorrect. The statement was obtained from the third clerk in the auditor's office, and copied by me as furnished, and the error into which that officer has fallen, was no doubt accidental.

I have since procured from the auditor, a correct statement, which is herewith submitted.

In addition to the reports received at the time the abstract was prepared, I have received reports from the clerks of the circuit courts of Logan, Ritchie, Tazewell and Wetzel, which are also submitted.

I have the honor to be,

Most respectfully, yours, &c.

GEORGE W. MUNFORD, *C. H. D.*

To the Hon. Speaker of the House of Delegates.

A CORRECTED STATEMENT

Of Mileage paid to the Judges of the Circuit Superior Courts of Law and Chancery for the year ending 30th August, 1849.

Districts.	Circuits.	No. of counties, towns and cities in each Circuit.	JUDGES.	Miles Travelling. To Special Court of Appeals and General Court.	In Circuit.	Special and intermediate terms.	Total.
1	1	8	Richard H. Baker,	-	519	-	519
	2	8	John W. Nash,	-	771	68	839
2	3	6	George P. Scarburg,	-	740	306	1046
	4	6	John B. Christian,	-	500	-	500
3	5	7	John T. Lomax,	420	441	*68	929
	6	6	John Scott,	448	†204	-	652
4	7	5	John B. Clopton,	-	493	238	731
	21	2	Philip N. Nicholas, (dead).				
	22	2	John Robertson.				
	8	5	Daniel A. Wilson,	-	330	-	330
5	9	5	William Leigh,	520	319	-	839
	10	6	N. M. Taliaferro,	-	705	‡374	1079
6	11	7	Richard H. Field,	618	622	16	1256
	12	5	Lucas P. Thompson,	-	480	-	480
7	13	6	J. R. Douglass,	-	529	-	529
	14	6	Daniel Smith,	796	506	-	1302
8	15	6	Benjamin Estill,	-	592	-	592
	16	8	James E. Brown,	-	612	56	668
9	17	7	Edward Johnston,	-	650	§330	980
	18	9	George H. Lee,	-	975	-	975
10	19	10	David McComas,	-	1132	740	1872
	20	11	Joseph L. Fry,	-	948	‖714	1662
				2802	12059	2910	17771

Given under my hand, at the auditor's office, this 17th of January, 1850.

JA'S E. HEATH, *Auditor.*

*Includes 24 miles, distance travelled to hold special court in Judge Scott's circuit.
†Judge Scott was prevented by sickness from attending all of his courts.
‡Special court of appeals in the case of Martin *vs.* Tucker.
§ " " " " " "
‖ " " " " " "

CIRCUIT SUPERIOR COURTS OF LAW AND CHANCERY.

					Suits at Law.				Causes in Chancery.					Prosecutions.					TERMS. Days in session.				
Districts.	Circuits.	Judges.	Clerks.	Counties.	Commenced.	Pending.	Decided.	Removed from other courts.	Commenced.	Pending.	Interlocutory decrees.	Final decrees.	Removed from county courts.	Commenced.	Pending.	Decided.	Nolle prosequis.	Changes of venue.	Fall.	Spring.	Intermediate or special.	Total.	REMARKS OF CLERKS.
8	15	Benj. Estill,	G. W. G. Brown,	Tazewell,	27	44	63	-	15	55	34	11	-	10	10	19	9	-	5	4	-	9	Motions on forth coming bonds are included in the suits at law decided.
		Total in circuit	as modified by pre-	ceding return,	230	303	281	1	72	335	103	68	1	133	195	105	31	2	32	38	-	70	
10	19	D. McComas,	F. Hinchcomb,	Ritchie,	33	35	13	-	12	25	8	5	1	16	31	6	18	-	3	5	-	8	
			Wm. Straton,	Logan,	2	17	1	-	2	10	-	2	-	22	72	10	3	-	6	5	-	11	
		Total in circuit	as modified by pre	ceding return,	371	617	252	12	128	372	67	58	4	332	457	121	55	-	47	55	25	127	
	20	Joseph L. Fry,	Friend Cox,	Wetzel,	27	20	10	-	12	17	-	-		13	32	7	-	-	2	2	-	4	The column 'decided' includes dismissions.
		Total in circuit	as modified by pre-	ceding return,	477	674	293	21	209	636	101	141	3	91	145	66	23	-	50	38	32	120	

E. E.

GEORGE W. MUNFORD, *C. H. D.*

January 18*th*, 1850.

ABSTRACT

FROM THE

REPORTS OF CLERKS

OF THE COURT OF APPEALS AND CIRCUIT COURTS, RELATIVE TO THE SUITS IN THEIR RESPECTIVE COURTS, FOR THE YEAR 1849–'50.

COURT OF APPEALS.

Judges.	*Clerks.*	*Location of Courts.*	Suits commenced.	Pending.	Decided.	Number of days in session.	REMARKS OF CLERKS.
William H. Cabell, Pres't Francis T. Brooke, John J. Allen, Briscoe G. Baldwin, William Daniel,	Joseph Allen,	Richmond, Lewisburg.	127	517	63	131 exclusive of Sundays.	—The term of the Court commenced on the 15th of October, 1849, and ended on the 14th of May, 1850, comprising 160 days,—having had within that time two recesses, one of 25 and the other of 26 days. Four days there were not a sufficient number of judges present to constitute a Court.

SPECIAL COURT OF APPEALS.

CIRCUIT COURTS.

Districts.	Circuits.	Judges.	Clerks.	Counties.	Suits at Law. No. commenced	Suits at Law. No. pending.	Suits at Law. No. decided.	Suits at Law. No. removed from other Courts.	Causes in Chancery. No. commenced	Causes in Chancery. No. pending.	Causes in Chancery. No. Interlocutory decrees.	Causes in Chancery. No final decrees	Causes in Chancery. No. remov. from County courts.	Prosecutions. No. commenced	Prosecutions. No. pending.	Prosecutions. No. decided.	Prosecutions. No. nolle prosequis.	Prosecutions. Changes of Venue.	Terms. Days in session. Fall.	Terms. Days in session. Spring.	Terms. Days in session. Intermediate or special.	Terms. Days in session. Total.	Remarks of Clerks.
1	1	R. H. Baker.	L. R. Edwards,	Southampton,	72	51	91		12	33	33	12		7	9	8			4	3		7	Of the number of actions at law stated to have been decided, 4 were dismissions in court, and 3 were confessions of judgment in the clerk's office.
			Joseph Turner,	Greenesville,	52	45	28			9		3			1	6			2	2		4	
			Wm. P. Underwood,	Surry,	10	4	17		3	6	7	2		5	4	5			2	2		4	
			Jno. P. Young,	Isle of Wight,	26	18	30		9	12	11	13		7	7	4			2	2		4	
			Joseph Prentis,	Nansemond,	67	23	49		5	14	12	6		3	3	2			2	2		4	
			J. J. Burroughs,	Princess Anne,	52	43	45	1	4	6	5	10		5	3	9		1	4	3		7	The case in which the venire was changed, was one for the supposed violation of the revenue laws, and was not strictly a change of venire, but was renewed by consent from the county court of Princess Anne.
			John Williams,	Norfolk City,	175	155	96	1	30	68	21	13		14	18	24	66		57	24		82	21 suits at law were dismissed at Rules and 10 of the same judgments were confessed in the office. There were 90 judgments on verdicts and by default, and 19 cases were dismissed in court during the year. Of the chancery suits seven were dismissed at Rules.
			Arthur Emmerson,	Norfolk County,	153	114	77	6	16	39	8	12	1	13	17	22			12	13	1	25	
					607	453	423	8	79	187	97	71	1	54	62	80	66	1	85	51	1	137	
	2	John W. Nash.	John P. Crump,	Dinwiddie,	47	80	46		10	47	10	9		4	10	5			6			6	
			F. Fitzgerald,	Nottoway,	37	35	46		6	41	19	14	1	3	8	13	6		3	5		8	
				Amelia,																			
			Wm. S. Dance,	Powhatan,	37	48	68	2	16	75	24	12			4	1			8	6		14	
			E. R. Turnbull,	Brunswick,	31	27	45		9	25	10	7	2	7	13	3	3		5	4		9	
			J. T. J. Mason,	Sussex,	22	13	31		2	10	10	7				3			1	1		2	
				Prince George,																			
			H. B. Gaines,	Petersburg,	104	131	41		22	138	33	28	5	10	20	5	4		29		14	43	
2	3	Geo. P. Scarburg,	Thos. O. Cogbill,	James City and Williamsburg,	41	44	52	1	16	137	37	4	3	2	3				8	10		18	
			Bolivar Sheild,	York,	17	17	9	3	3	22			1	1		13	10		4	5		9	

				Warwick,																			
			S. S. Howard,	Elizabeth City,	31	20	27		9	33	11	1							3	4		7	Two of the suits decided were dismissed at Rules.
			Lewis P. Rogers,	Northampton,	13	3	23		5	17	12	12		1	2				4	3		7	
				Accomack,																			
				King William,																			
	4	J. B. Christian,	Robert Pollard,	King & Queen,	66	43	49	2	6	33	18	8	1	2	2	2	1		4	5	9	18	
				Essex,																			
				Middlesex,																			
				Gloucester,																			
				Mathews,																			
3	5	John T. Lomax,		Lancaster,																			
				Northumberland,																			
				Richmond county,																			
			Wm. Hutt,	Westmoreland,	79	107	91		7	42	18	12		1	1	2			4	3		7	
			Wm. S. Brown,	King George,	34	23	27		6	12	4	2		1	4	4	3		1	2		3	
				Caroline,																			
			J. J. Chew,	Spottsylvania,	43	37	42		11	407	36	19		12	12	3	1		16	19		35	The great disparity in the number of suits pending and those decided, requires explanation. It is accounted for from the fact, that nearly all of these causes were transferred from the late Superior Court of Chancery for the Fredericksburg District, and have been generally abandoned by the parties and their counsel.

Districts.	Circuits.	Judges.	Clerks.	Counties.	Suits at Law. No. commenced.	No. pending.	No. decided.	Number removed from other circuits.	Causes in Chancery. No. commenced.	No. pending.	No. interlocutory decrees.	No. final decrees.	No. removed from County Courts.	Prosecutions. No. commenced.	No. pending.	No. decided.	No. nolle prosequis.	Changes of Venue.	TERMS. Days in session. Fall.	Spring.	Intermediate or special.	Total.	
	6	John W. Tyler,	Wm. F. Philips,	Fauquier, Loudoun, Prince William,	107	213	167	7	72	414	238	30		4	2	5	1		9	12	6	27	
			F. D. Richardson,	Fairfax, Alexandria,	81	122	115	1	31	137	80	42		17	13	8	1		6	5		11	
			J. M. Conway,	Stafford,	19	22	26		13	33	6	10	2	3	4	1			3	4		7	In the suits at law, there was a judgment for one defendant and against the other in the same suit. In the prosecutions, two for felony sent from County Courts.
4	7	John B. Clopton.																					
			N. W. Miller,	Chesterfield, Charles City, New Kent, Goochland,	94	216	103	1	17	68	22	20	2	2	3	2			10	10		20	All suits at Rules are omitted. 49 office judgments have been confirmed, not included in the number of suits at law decided.
			Wm. O. Winston,	Hanover,	38	113	46		14	132	56	28	1	1	7				9	10	3	22	
	21	John S. Caskie,		Henrico & City of Richmond.																			
	22	John Robertson,		Henrico & City of Richmond,					85	1598	311	78	4						35	14	108	157	Besides the number of final decrees in Court, there were five dismissions at the Rules. Of the number of days in session seventeen were occupied by Judge Caskie, and eight by Judge Clopton. Of the final decrees, Judge Caskie rendered one.

																							Remarks
	8	Daniel A. Wilson.	B. B. Woodson,	Cumberland,	69	62	78	1	15	79	15	15	1	19	28	3			5	8		13	
				Buckingham,																			
				Appomattox,																			
				Campbell,																			
			David Rodes,	Lynchburg,	90	194	131	9	24	280	95	28	6	4	3	5			50	34		84	
5	9	William Leigh.	Wm. Holt,	Halifax,	92	82	149	15	54	161	57	44	1	56	62	47	5		13	13	10	36	Besides the suits commenced, there were a great many motions upon which judgments were rendered, and not included in suits decided. There were four prisoners tried for felony at the Spring term, all of whom were acquitted.
				Charlotte,																			
			B. J. Worsham,	Prince Edward,	67	59	96	2	18	94	35	27	1	77	75	3	4		8	9		17	
			Ths. W. Winn,	Lunenburg,	48	44	87	1	11	32	20	20	2	75	54	24	3		6	5		11	
				Mecklenburg.																			
	10	N. M. Taliaferro,	J. N. Zentmeyer,	Floyd,	12	15	25	4	14	38	35	7		8	16	6			6	3		9	
				Patrick,																			
				Henry,																			
			M. G. Carper,	Franklin,	160	98	168	2	27	97	72	34		17	18	13	1		9	10		19	
			Wm. H. Tunstall,	Pittsylvania,	142	173	145		28	112	30	32	2	8	15	14	1		19	13		32	Of the 173 suits at law pending, 90 are upon the issue docket, 7 on the office judgment docket, and 76 on the rule docket; most of the latter, however, by steps which will be taken, and September and October Rules following, will be put upon the office judgment docket at October Term next. Of the law cases decided, 75 were office judgments. At the Fall Term, (October 1849,) three days were consumed in examining witnesses upon an appeal from the County Court in a will case. Six days in one case of an issue *devisavit vel non*, 3 in another, and a day in each of the two last by arguments of counsel, in neither of which did the jury agree in a verdict.
				Bedford																			

DISTRICTS.	CIRCUITS.	*Judges.*	*Clerks.*	*Counties.*	*Suits at Law.* No. commenced.	No. pending.	No. decided.	Number removed from Circuit Courts.	*Causes in Chancery.* No. commenced.	No. pending.	No. interlocutory decrees.	No. final decrees.	No. removed from County Courts.	*Prosecutions.* No. commenced.	No. pending.	No. decided.	No. nolle prosequis.	Changes of Venue.	TERMS. *Days in session.* Fall.	Spring.	Intermediate or special.	Total.	
6	11	Richard H. Field.	John Hunter,	Louisa,	80	140	47	6	13	66	15	12	1	5	4	2	1		5	8	7	20	Of the number of actions at law pending 7 original suits count twice, being in court as to some parties and at Rules as to others. 1 prosecution was dismissed in court. There were 8 actions at law dismissed in court, and two suits in Chancery dismissed in court.
			A. Shepherd, jr.,	Fluvanna,	41	57	73		19	51	20	24	1	4	5	3	1		6	5		11	Judgments on delivery bonds not included.—Of these, there are 18 on the law side of the Court.
				Orange,																			
			Rob't Pritchett,	Greene,	27	26	19		4	17	7	9	1	5	5		1	3	3	5		8	
				Madison,																			
			R. G. Ward,	Culpeper,	50	91	32	4	18	119	39	19		4	10	2	2		16	12	1	29	
			W. J. Menifee,	Rappahannock,	18	21	32	2	9	42	18	13	1	5	7	2	1		4	4		8	Motions on forthcoming bonds, other motions, and proceedings against witnesses, &c. not included.
	12	L. P. Thompson.	Robert Tinsley,	Amherst,	122	205	133	7	31	335	76	10	1	11	22	2			2	14		16	
			S. McD. Reid,	Rockbridge,	93	103	95		31	107	79	28	1	23	18	34			9	11		20	
				Nelson,																			
				Albemarle,																			
				Augusta,																			
7	13	J. R. Douglass.		Jefferson,																			
				Berkeley,																			
			Isaiah Buck,	Morgan,	40	43	27	2	6	32	16	5			2	5	1		2	2		4	Judgments on forthcoming bonds and motions not included.
			John B. White,	Hampshire,	182	169	149	1	27	161	40	29		2	7	5	2		6	4		10	
				Frederick,																			
				Clarke,																			
	14	Daniel Smith.	G. T. Jones,	Page,	13	1	14		4	7	6	5	1	4	4				2	1		3	
				Shenandoah,																			
			Robert Turner,	Warren,	29	16	26		6	25	12	5	1	2	1	2	1		2	2		4	
			Charles Lobb,	Hardy,	75	61	35	1	19	143	35	9		1		1			2	2		4	
			Z. Dyer,	Pendleton,	13	9			2	21	1	2		8	18	2				2		2	
				Rockingham,																			

8	15	Benj'n Estill.	S. H. Morison,	Lee, Scott,	44	71	33		3	38	5	2	1	53	38	23	1	6	5	11	The suits commenced at law include one caveat.
			James P. Carroll,	Russell,	48	58	39		15	31	7	6		24	35	17	2	4	4	8	
			Connally F. Trigg,	Tazewell, Washington, Smyth,	54	51	57		25	125	12	10		26	31	30	8	6	8	14	
	16	James E. Brown.	Rice D. Montague,	Wythe, Grayson, Carroll, Montgomery,	41	39	44		9	45	10	12		11	16	10	2	5	4	9	
			Rufus A. French,	Pulaski, Giles,	80	49	72		14	55	32	10		8	11	9	12	4	4	8	
			John Hutchison,	Mercer, Monroe,	71	40	70		11	62	24	8		21	22	8		6	5	11	
9	17	E. Johnston.	Andrew Fudge,	Botetourt, Alleghany,	19	20	26		5	33	7	7		5	5	3		2	3	5	
			Chs. L. Francisco,	Roanoke, Bath,	24	30	27	3	8	60	15	5		4		4		4	4	8	
			A. Stephenson, jr.	Highland, Pocahontas, Greenbrier,	34	25	22	1	6	10		3		12	12	2	1	3	3	6	Motions on forthcoming bonds or rules against witnesses, absent grand jurors, &c., not included.
	18	Mathew Dunbar.	H. M. Dickinson,	Logan, Boone, Fayette, Nicholas,	41	63	25		13	47	6	13		6	10	7	12	5	5	10	Sunday intervening both terms.
			H. H. Forbes,	Wyoming, Raleigh, Putnam,	37	46	82		9	22	1	4	1	13	11		2	3	6	9	Suits at law decided include dismissions at Rules and in court.
			A. W. Quarrier,	Kanawha,	415	434	448	1	39	191	64	13	1	21	51	10	12	30	31	61	
0	19	David McComas.	Jas. J. Neal,	Gilmer, Ritchie, Wood,	159	270	71		33	157	22	26		8	40	18	12	13	17	30	Judgments on forthcoming bonds not included.
			George W. Stribbling,	Wirt, Jackson, Mason,	35	50	14		6	20		2		19	25	17	1	2	6	8	
			E. Bloss,	Cabell, Wayne,	22	6	21		8	9		17		48	32	18		5	4	9	

CIRCUITS.	Judges.	Clerks.	Counties.	Suits at Law.				Causes in Chancery.					Prosecutions.					TERMS. Days in session.			
				No. commenced.	No. pending.	No. decided.	Number removed from Circuit Courts.	No. commenced.	No. pending.	No. interlocutory decrees.	No. final decrees.	No. removed from County Courts.	No. commenced.	No. pending.	No. decided.	No. nolle prosequis.	Changes of Venue.	Fall.	Spring.	Intermediate or special.	Total.
20	Joseph L. Fry,		Hancock,																		
			Brooke,																		
		Alex. T. Laidley,	Ohio,	204	191	206		48	152	42	58		8	8	34	6		22	17	28	67
		James D. Morris,	Marshall,	46	44	42		22	55	13	20		1	1		2		5	7		12
			Wetzel,																		
			Tyler,																		
		Francis D. Hickman,	Doddridge,	29	32	25	2	11	30	7	2	2	8	15	12	3		4	5		9
		W. J. Willey,	Monongalia,	48	40	42		60	94	27	19		3	8	9	3		8	8		16
22	George H. Lee,		Marion,																		
			Preston,																		
		Adolphus Armstrong,	Taylor,	17	28	21	1	3	23	5	9	2	1	5	3			5	6		11
		E. D. Wilson,	Barbour,	37	93	33	13	29	122	15	11	25	5	6	10	3		8	8		16
		B. L. Brown,	Randolph,	28	47	16		6	34	6	7		32	31	14			7	4		11
			Braxton,																		
		J. Talbot,	Lewis,	121	210	63	2	69	273	25	22	1	37	37	21	8		8	15		23
			Harrison,																		

STATEMENT

OF THE

WHOLE NUMBER

OF

JUSTICES OF THE PEACE

IN THE

STATE OF VIRGINIA,

FROM 1830 TO THE PRESENT TIME.

EXECUTIVE DEPARTMENT,
November 6, 1850.

SIR—I transmit herewith "a statement of the whole number of Justices of the Peace in the state, so arranged as to show the number in each county and corporation thereof; and the number commissioned in the several counties and corporations in each year, from and including the year 1830 to the present time"—called for by resolution of the Convention of 29th ult.

Very respectfully, yours, &c.,

WM. H. RICHARDSON,

Sec. Commonwealth.

S. D. WHITTLE, Esq., Sec. of the Convention.

STATEMENT

Of the whole number of Justices of the Peace in the State, so arranged as to show the number in each county and corporation thereof; and the number commissioned in the several counties and corporations in each year, from and including the year 1830 *to the present time. October* 31, 1850.

Counties and Corporations.	Justices in commission.	Justices commissioned from, and includ'g the year 1830.	
ACCOMACK	21	In 1832	3
		35	8
		39	12
		49	10
ALBEMARLE . . .	55	1830	8
		32	2
		35	12
		38	19
		41	10
		43	8
		46	7
ALLEGHANY . . .	18	1831	8
		38	6
		39	7
		46	4
AMELIA	29	1830	4
		33	5
		34	4
		36	6
		40	8
		42	5
		43	4
		49	5
AMHERST	26	1832	18
		36	8
		42	16
		43	4
APPOMATTOX . . .	30	1845	20
		46	13
AUGUSTA	51	1830	6
		32	9
		34	7
		36	12
		37	3
		39	2
		40	3
		42	7
		44	5
		45	5
		47	2
ALEXANDRIA . . .	17	1847	20
		48	3
BARBOUR	32	1843	33
		44	1
BATH	15	1836	11
		47	7
BEDFORD	33	1832	14
		37	10
		41	8
BERKELEY	42	1832	9
		34	7

Counties and Corporations.	Justices in commission.	Justices commissioned from, and includ'g the year 1830.	
BERKELEY		In 1836	7
		38	7
		41	4
		43	1
		47	6
		50	4
BOTETOURT . . .	35	1832	2
		34	6
		35	9
		36	5
		37	5
		38	6
		40	6
		49	6
BRAXTON	23	1836	18
		37	6
		38	6
		40	5
		41	5
		42	6
		44	3
		47	8
		49	5
BROOKE	19	1835	7
		38	5
		39	3
		40	6
		44	7
		46	5
		49	6
BRUNSWICK . . .	35	1832	5
		36	10
		48	12
BUCKINGHAM . . .	31	1831	13
		36	10
		43	12
		45	5
		49	6
BOONE	18	1847	24
CABELL	22	1832	6
		34	2
		38	4
		41	8
		44	3
		47	2
		50	3
CAMPBELL	41	1832	3
		34	5
		36	5
		41	5
		46	17

Counties and Corporations.	Justices in commission.	Justices commissioned from, and includ'g the year 1830.	
CAMPBELL		In 1849	4
CAROLINE	34	1832	10
		37	7
		38	1
		42	10
		45	4
		47	8
CARROLL	30	1842	14
		43	6
		48	2
		49	9
CHARLES CITY . . .	15	1831	4
		34	6
		39	4
		43	4
		48	5
CHARLOTTE	35	1836	12
		39	8
		45	4
CHESTERFIELD . . .	36	1831	7
		33	6
		34	4
		37	10
		38	4
		40	8
		44	8
		47	7
		48	6
CLARKE	23	1836	20
		39	5
		50	4
CULPEPER	47	1831	12
		33	9
		34	4
		36	6
		39	2
		41	5
		42	4
		45	9
		49	8
CUMBERLAND . . .	31	1832	9
		36	5
		38	5
		41	3
		44	3
		47	1
		49	6
DANVILLE	elected annually		
DINWIDDIE	23	1830	12
		34	12
		38	12
		43	12
DODDRIDGE	17	1845	17
		46	7
ELIZABETH CITY . .	14	1831	7
		33	1
		36	5
		37	3
		39	3
		42	1
		45	7
ESSEX	20	1832	8
		35	8
		38	4
		43	6
FAIRFAX	33	1831	7
		35	10
		37	11
FAIRFAX		In 1841	8
		44	4
		47	12
FAUQUIER	64	1830	17
		32	13
		35	18
		36	3
		38	21
		48	4
		50	10
FAYETTE	22	1831	10
		32	8
		33	12
		37	4
		41	2
		45	10
		49	3
FLOYD	22	1831	12
		33	7
		34	2
		41	5
		42	1
		47	7
FLUVANNA	42	1832	11
		34	12
		37	9
		38	3
		42	6
		46	15
FRANKLIN	43	1831	4
		36	8
		39	14
		49	17
FREDERICK	37	1831	14
		36	13
		38	1
		40	3
		43	6
		47	12
FREDERICKSBURG . .	10	1830	1
		31	2
		32	1
		33	1
		34	1
		35	1
		36	1
		38	1
		39	1
		41	1
		43	2
		44	1
		46	1
		48	1
		49	2
		50	1
GILES	30	1834	6
		37	12
		42	3
		44	4
		46	6
GILMER	29	1845	24
		47	5
		48	6
		49	7
GLOUCESTER	20	1830	8
		31	10
		33	6
		41	7

Counties and Corporations.	Justices in commission.	Justices commissioned from, and includ'g the year 1830.	
GLOUCESTER		In 1848	7
GOOCHLAND	31	1831	5
		33	6
		35	9
		39	17
		44	6
		50	6
GRAYSON	23	1831	6
		33	2
		34	13
		38	12
		45	12
GREENBRIER	43	1832	6
		35	9
		40	3
		44	6
		45	8
		47	8
		49	1
		50	8
GREENE	16	1833	16
		44	7
GREENSVILLE . . .	21	1831	7
		33	6
		34	9
		37	7
		41	9
		44	5
		47	11
		49	3
HALIFAX	47	1830	8
		34	6
		36	11
		38	5
		39	3
		40	2
		41	3
		43	2
		45	1
		47	4
		49	6
HAMPSHIRE	35	1833	12
		36	3
		41	5
		42	9
		44	5
		45	2
		49	10
HANOVER	39	1831	8
		34	6
		37	9
		40	8
		41	5
		45	9
		48	7
HARDY	28	1834	8
		38	10
		39	5
		41	3
		42	8
		47	8
		49	3
HARRISON	28	1832	9
		33	3
		35	6
		36	2
		37	4
		38	3
HARRISON		In 1841	9
		43	10
		47	2
		48	5
		50	1
HENRICO	25	1830	5
		33	6
		35	1
		36	9
		38	2
		40	9
		44	4
		49	4
HENRY	34	1832	3
		36	6
		39	7
		42	12
		49	12
HIGHLAND	21	1847	19
		48	5
HANCOCK	18	1848	11
		49	6
		50	1
ISLE OF WIGHT . . .	29	1832	8
		38	10
		40	3
		42	5
		44	6
		50	1
JACKSON	22	1831	15
		32	5
		36	8
		38	7
		39	1
		43	2
		48	6
JAMES CITY	12	1831	4
		32	2
		33	4
		35	3
		38	3
		41	3
		45	4
		48	3
JEFFERSON	31	1831	2
		34	4
		36	10
		38	6
		39	5
		41	7
KANAWHA	37	1831	3
		33	3
		35	3
		36	3
		39	8
		40	2
		41	1
		43	8
		45	2
		46	2
		47	5
		48	2
		50	7
KING & QUEEN . . .	30	1834	3
		38	7
		42	8
		49	14
KING GEORGE . . .	16	1831	8

Counties and Corporations.	Justices in commission.	Justices commissioned from, and includ'g the year 1830.	
KING GEORGE . . .		In 1837	9
		47	2
KING WILLIAM . . .	21	1833	6
		35	6
		41	9
		47	8
LANCASTER	21	1830	6
		31	6
		37	2
		39	2
		40	6
		43	4
		46	6
LEE	29	1834	4
		37	6
		40	7
		42	2
		43	3
		46	5
		48	6
LEWIS	32	1833	14
		34	4
		36	3
		37	3
		38	3
		40	9
		41	4
		43	6
		44	8
		46	10
		49	11
LOGAN	26	1832	5
		33	1
		34	1
		35	5
		37	3
		39	3
		41	5
		43	3
		46	3
		47	9
		49	1
LOUDOUN	61	1833	20
		37	11
		40	5
		41	11
		45	5
		46	9
		49	18
LOUISA	48	1832	8
		34	7
		37	13
		42	6
		43	9
		46	14
LUNENBURG	32	1831	4
		37	10
		40	5
		43	3
		47	9
LYNCHBURG	elected annually		
MADISON	30	1831	6
		34	4
		36	4
		38	8
		42	4
		45	9
		48	1
MARION	33	In 1842	27
		45	7
		46	4
MARSHALL	30	1835	16
		37	6
		39	1
		41	6
		42	1
		50	12
MASON	22	1832	5
		33	1
		38	7
		41	5
		42	2
		45	2
		46	6
		49	3
MATHEWS	13	1833	5
		40	5
		47	4
MECKLENBURG . . .	47	1830	1
		32	9
		33	2
		38	17
		41	3
		42	7
		44	9
		45	6
MERCER	25	1837	18
		38	8
		40	6
		44	4
		46	6
		47	1
MIDDLESEX	14	1830	3
		33	5
		34	4
		37	6
		40	5
		46	6
MONONGALIA	38	1831	6
		33	6
		34	7
		37	14
		40	5
		42	8
		43	3
		44	2
		45	8
		46	1
		47	7
MONROE	31	1832	4
		36	3
		41	7
		45	7
		47	7
		49	5
MONTGOMERY . . .	25	1833	4
		37	9
		40	7
		45	6
		47	1
		49	5
MORGAN	14	1830	1
		35	4
		38	7
		39	2
		42	2

Counties and Corporations.	Justices in commission.	Justices commissioned from, and includ'g the year 1830.	
MORGAN		In 1845	2
		47	2
NANSEMOND	25	1830	8
		41	9
		48	8
NELSON	28	1836	18
		40	3
		47	5
NEW KENT	18	1831	5
		33	3
		34	5
		38	4
		42	4
		43	5
		49	7
NICHOLAS	18	1831	6
		33	6
		35	6
		39	9
		41	10
		45	6
		47	4
NORFOLK COUNTY	29	1832	8
		36	22
		41	1
		44	7
		45	6
		47	2
NORFOLK CITY . . . Under the act of Feb. 13, 1845, are elective.	10	1831	2
		33	1
		35	3
		36	1
		37	1
		38	2
NORTHAMPTON . . .	16	1830	5
		33	2
		35	4
		37	3
		40	3
		41	2
		42	2
		47	3
		48	5
NORTHUMBERLAND .	25	1833	9
		35	8
		37	4
		40	4
		47	6
NOTTOWAY	19	1831	8
		35	6
		37	6
		43	7
OHIO	26	1835	11
		38	1
		39	3
		40	5
		44	8
		47	1
ORANGE	23	1831	13
		34	6
		35	4
		41	7
PAGE	19	1831	22
		32	3
		33	6
		35	1
		36	3
		38	2
PAGE		In 1845	3
		47	2
		50	2
PATRICK	29	1832	11
		35	3
		49	12
PENDLETON	21	1831	3
		32	1
		37	5
		40	1
		43	5
		45	1
		46	2
		47	1
		49	4
PETERSBURG . . .	elec	ted annually	
PITTSYLVANIA . . .	57	1832	18
		33	6
		38	16
		44	25
POCAHONTAS	26	1832	6
		33	4
		36	1
		38	1
		43	3
		44	10
		45	3
		48	6
POWHATAN	25	1830	9
		33	4
		37	5
		41	5
		42	7
		45	8
		47	7
PRESTON	39	1832	9
		34	4
		36	6
		37	3
		38	4
		39	6
		41	3
		43	3
		44	2
		45	7
		46	1
		47	2
		48	2
		49	2
PRINCE EDWARD . .	31	1830	4
		32	1
		33	6
		36	6
		40	9
		43	10
		45	9
PRINCE GEORGE . .	20	1832	6
		35	6
		40	6
		42	10
		45	6
PRINCE WILLIAM . .	23	1830	4
		31	3
		33	2
		34	4
		35	3
		36	5
		39	8

Counties and Corporations.	Justices in commission.	Justices commissioned from, and includ'g the year 1830.	
PRINCE WILLIAM . .		In 1840	3
		44	4
		46	2
PRINCESS ANNE . .	14	1831	8
		34	4
		42	8
PULASKI	17	1839	23
		43	2
		45	4
		48	2
PUTNAM	14	1848	16
RANDOLPH	36	1830	12
		32	13
		38	16
		42	14
		44	12
		48	15
RAPPAHANNOCK . .	39	1833	38
		34	1
		36	1
		37	3
		38	3
		40	6
		42	8
		44	5
		45	3
		49	4
RICHMOND CITY . .	elec	ted annually	
RICHMOND COUNTY .	17	1831	6
		35	5
		37	6
		42	7
		46	6
RITCHIE	20	1843	7
		44	4
		45	10
		46	10
		48	2
		49	2
ROANOKE	30	1838	22
		40	1
		41	2
		46	10
		49	5
ROCKBRIDGE	39	1830	3
		34	7
		35	2
		36	6
		38	4
		39	3
		41	6
		42	3
		44	6
ROCKINGHAM	36	1830	4
		31	2
		37	7
		41	1
		45	9
		48	5
RUSSELL	40	1831	5
		33	6
		36	3
		37	4
		39	1
		42	3
		43	1
		44	6
		45	1
RUSSELL		In 1846	2
		49	7
RALEIGH	14	1850	15
SCOTT	40	1831	6
		34	6
		35	3
		36	2
		37	3
		42	6
		43	11
		45	2
SHENANDOAH	39	1832	1
		33	8
		35	4
		36	3
		37	8
		42	7
		46	5
		47	7
		50	6
SMYTH	38	1832	25
		33	4
		35	7
		38	2
		46	15
		47	2
SOUTHAMPTON . . .	35	1832	11
		37	10
		42	12
		47	17
SPOTTSYLVANIA . .	23	1831	4
		33	6
		37	5
		41	6
		46	6
STAFFORD	24	1830	7
		32	6
		35	2
		38	6
		41	3
		43	5
		46	8
SURRY	15	1831	6
		34	2
		37	4
		39	1
		42	2
		47	6
SUSSEX	36	1830	1
		32	7
		37	8
		41	6
		43	2
		46	10
		50	14
STAUNTON	elec	ted annually	
TAYLOR	21	1844	17
		46	3
		47	1
TAZEWELL	43	1832	8
		34	3
		35	2
		37	8
		39	2
		41	8
		47	21
TYLER	31	1832	8
		36	8

Counties and Corporations.	Justices in commission.	Justices commissioned from, and includ'g the year 1830.	
TYLER		In 1838	7
		41	8
		45	8
		47	8
WARREN	23	1836	16
		37	11
		41	2
		43	4
WARWICK	13	1831	6
		34	4
		40	6
WASHINGTON . . .	46	1831	3
		33	5
		34	2
		36	7
		37	7
		39	11
		40	4
		42	6
		44	7
		49	6
WAYNE	20	1842	13
		44	3
		49	4
WESTMORELAND . .	29	1832	10
		36	8
		39	10
		44	4
		47	9
WILLIAMSBURG . . .	9	1834	2
		35	2
		36	1
		42	1
WILLIAMSBURG . . .		In 1846	1
		48	1
		49	2
		50	1
WOOD	23	1832	4
		33	2
		34	3
		35	6
		39	5
		41	2
		42	3
		46	8
		47	2
		50	2
WYTHE	43	1833	8
		36	5
		37	2
		38	11
		39	8
		41	8
WETZEL	21	1846	26
WIRT	18	1848	16
		49	3
WYOMING	15	1850	15
WHEELING	elec	ted annually	
YORK	15	1833	7
		39	10
		43	6
		44	8
		48	8
TOTAL	3911		5306

SUMMARY.

Justices now in commission, ...3911

Justices elected annually in the following towns and corporations, viz:

City of Richmond..	13
" Wheeling..	6
Town of Petersburg..	12
" Lynchburg..	12
" Winchester..	6
" Staunton..	6
" Danville..	6
TOTAL....	3972

Justices commissioned from, and including the year 1830..............5306

WM. H. RICHARDSON, *Sec'y Commonwealth.*

November 5, 1850.

www.ingramcontent.com/pod-product-compliance
Lightning Source LLC
LaVergne TN
LVHW022039110826
845151LV00007B/51

9781425544911